TEACH YOURSELF W9-AJZ-542

nepali

nepali

Michael Hutt

and

Abhi Subedi

TEACH YOURSELF BOOKS

For UK order queries: please contact Bookpoint Ltd, 39 Milton Park, Abingdon, Oxon OX14 4TD. Telephone: (44) 01235 400414, Fax: (44) 01235 400454. Lines are open from 9.00–6.00, Monday to Saturday, with a 24 hour message answering service. Email address: orders@bookpoint.co.uk

For U.S.A. & Canada order queries: please contact NTC/Contemporary Publishing, 4255 West Touhy Avenue, Lincolnwood, Illinois 60646–1975, U.S.A. Telephone: (847) 679 5500, Fax: (847) 679 2494.

Long renowned as the authoritative source for self-guided learning – with more than 30 million copies sold worldwide – the *Teach Yourself* series includes over 200 titles in the fields of languages, crafts, hobbies, and other leisure activities.

British Library Cataloguing in Publication Data
A catalogue entry for this title is available from The British Library.

Library of Congress Catalog Card Number: On file

First published in UK 1999 by Hodder Headline Plc, 338 Euston Road, London, NW1 3BH.

First published in US 1999 by NTC/Contemporary Publishing, 4255 West Touhy Avenue, Lincolnwood (Chicago), Illinois 60646–1975, U.S.A.

The 'Teach Yourself' name and logo are registered trade marks of Hodder & Stoughton Ltd.

Copyright © 1999 Michael Hutt and Abhi Subedi

Typeset by Transet Limited, Coventry, England.
Printed in Great Britain for Hodder & Stoughton Educational, a division of Hodder Headline Plc, 338 Euston Road, London NW1 3BH by Cox & Wyman Ltd, Reading, Berkshire.

Impression number   10 9 8 7 6 5 4 3 2
Year   2004 2003 2002 2001 2000 1999

CONTENTS

INTRODUCTION

Welcome to Teach Yourself Nepali

Nepali is a member of the Indo-Aryan group of languages that includes most of the languages of the northern half of the Indian sub-continent. These languages are derived from Sanskrit in much the same way that the European Romance languages are derived from Latin, and each has developed its own distinctive character over the course of many centuries. Nepali is the lingua franca of the central and eastern Himalaya, and the national language of Nepal. It is also recognised by the Indian Constitution as a major language of India because of its dominance in Sikkim and the Darjeeling district of West Bengal. Bhutan promotes the use of its own national language, Dzongkha, but there too Nepali is widely spoken and understood.

Nepal is one of the world's most linguistically variegated countries; more than 40 different languages have been recorded. Just over half the population has Nepali as its mother tongue: the mother-tongue Nepali-speakers are primarily the higher caste and politically dominant Bahuns (Brahmins) and Chetris. Most of the rest of the population speaks either Indo-Aryan languages such as Maithili, Bhojpuri, Awadhi and Hindi, or Tibeto-Burman languages such as Tibetan, Tamang, Newari, Gurung, Magar, Rai and Limbu. The use of these languages was discouraged until 1990, when a democracy movement succeeded in granting some rights to Nepal's linguistic minorities. However, the level of bilingualism with Nepali is now very high in most parts of the kingdom.

This book is designed to enable those with no previous knowledge of Nepali to progress to a point where they can communicate effectively in Nepali on a range of everyday topics, and can also read and write the language. Like every language, Nepali has a range of different styles and levels of sophistication. A hillfarmer who has a Tibeto-Burman language as his mother tongue may use the same verb ending for all genders, numbers and levels of politeness, because for him Nepali is a workaday link-language that enables him to communicate with people who have other languages as their mother tongue. In contrast, an educated urbanite will use various verb endings which depend not only upon the number and gender of the subjects performing the actions of the verbs, but also on how polite s/he chooses to be about them. Meanwhile, inside the royal palace a completely new set of verbs and honorific vocabulary (not covered here!) comes into play.

By and large, the Nepali in this book is that which Nepali speakers use unselfconsciously in the various situations that are introduced. Where choices arise, however, we err towards the more grammatically correct. While accepting that some Nepali speakers would not make the same choices in everyday conversation, we take the view that it is better to learn rules before learning the exceptions to those rules. Similarly, the language of this book admits only a handful of English words, although many Nepali-speakers (particularly in the capital) do make free use of English vocabulary in their conversation.

How to use the book

The book is divided into 24 units. Each unit contains from one to three Nepali dialogues (in **Unit 13**, instead of a dialogue, there is an exchange of letters, in **Unit 20** a prose passage). In the first four units all of the Nepali appears in both Devanagari (the script in which Nepali is written) and Roman transliteration. Each dialogue is followed by a box containing the new vocabulary it contains, and a literal English translation. Each dialogue or passage is followed by a section of more detailed grammatical explanation including further examples and exercises. The key to each exercise is given at the end of the book, followed by a complete end vocabulary.

You should begin by learning the characters of the Devanagari script and their pronunciation. Although the book can be used on its own, the descriptions of the sound of each character can only be approximate and the cassette that is available to accompany the book will be of great help to you in developing accurate pronunciation at an early stage.

You may choose how to approach each unit: you might wish to learn the dialogue and its meaning first by hearing and repeating it, and then work through the translation and the grammar section to understand why it means what it does; alternatively, you might prefer to work through the grammar section first and then turn back to the dialogue to see the grammar in action, as it were. Whichever way you approach each unit, it is important not to move on until you have:

■ mastered the dialogue;
■ fully digested the grammar section and the examples it contains;
■ learned all new vocabulary;
■ completed the exercises and checked them against the key;
■ repeated the exercises if they were not correct the first time.

The grammatical explanations are intended to be as clear and jargon-free as possible, although it is not possible to explain the structures of a language without using some grammatical terminology. The book cannot claim to cover every feature of Nepali, but it does contain all of the most common verb constructions and a basic vocabulary of some 1600 words. It will equip you with what you need to speak and read, and if you continue with Nepali after you have mastered this book your vocabulary and your familiarity with more complex constructions will grow very quickly. As well as helping you to master the Nepali language, the dialogues are also intended to provide you with an insight into Nepali culture and daily life.

The authors of this book wish you all the very best in your efforts to learn the Nepali language.

Further reading

Other beginners' courses in Nepali include Tika B. Karki and Chij K. Shrestha's *Basic Course in Spoken Nepali* (Kathmandu, various editions) and David Matthews's *A Course in Nepali* (London, School of Oriental and African Studies, 1984). The first of these has been used for many years to teach Nepali to Peace Corps volunteers without introducing the Devanagari script. The second adopts a more academic approach and also introduces more complex grammatical structures.

Once you have completed *Teach Yourself Nepali*, you might wish to move on to the later units of the Matthews course to supplement your understanding of Nepali grammar. You will also find the following textbooks useful: M.K. Verma and T.N. Sharma's *Intermediate Nepali Structure* and *Intermediate Nepali Reader*, both published by Manohar

Publishers in New Delhi in 1979; and Michael Hutt's *Modern Literary Nepali: an Introductory Reader*, published by Oxford University Press in New Delhi in 1997.

The best Nepali-English dictionary currently on the market is *A Practical Dictionary of Modern Nepali*, produced by an editorial board headed by Ruth Laila-Schmidt and published by Ratna Sagar Publishers in New Delhi in 1993. Ralph Turner's celebrated Nepali dictionary, first published in 1930, was reprinted in India in 1981; this is a work of immense interest, but is perhaps a little forbidding for a beginner in the language.

Pradyumna P. Karan and Hiroshi Ishii's *Nepal: a Himalayan Kingdom in Transition* (United Nations University Press, 1996) is a good introduction to all aspects of the country, while Jan Salter and Harka Gurung's beautifully illustrated book *Faces of Nepal* (Himal Books, Kathmandu, 1996) describes the cultures of Nepal's many ethnic groups.

For English translations from modern Nepali literature, see Michael Hutt's *Himalayan Voices: an Introduction to Modern Nepali Literature* (University of California Press, 1991); for a descriptive account of the history of Nepali literature, see Abhi Subedi's *Nepali Literature: Background and History* (Sajha Publishers, Kathmandu, 1978).

Acknowledgements

The authors wish to thank Govinda Giri Prerana, Bindu Subedi and John Whelpton for their invaluable comments and suggestions on various sections and drafts of the book, and the Research and Publications Committee of the School of Oriental and African Studies for facilitating this collaboration. We are also grateful to Subhas Rai for providing us with the drawings that illustrate a number of the dialogues.

Abbreviations & symbols

M	middle (case)	Dr	doctor
L	low (case)	Er.	elder
H	high (case)	Yr.	younger
Q	question	Mat.	maternal
A	answer	Pat.	paternal
S	statement	bro	brother
m.	masculine	sis	sister
f.	feminine	D	daughter
cj.ptc.	conjunctive participle	S	son

All dialogues are marked 🎧, and you will see 📼 beside those passages that you can listen to on the cassette that accompanies this book.

The key vocabulary boxes, marked 🔑, follow each dialogue. Use these to make sure you've understood the dialogue.

The exercises, throughout the book, giving you plenty of opportunity to practice the Nepali language points as you learn them, are marked ✅.

📱 indicates the grammar items that provide the 'nuts and bolts' of the Nepali language.

THE NEPALI SCRIPT AND SOUND SYSTEM

Nepali is written in the **Devanāgarī** (or 'Nagari') script, which is also used for Hindi, Sanskrit and Marathi, with only minor modifications being made to accommodate the special features of the Nepali sound system. Devanagari is a phonetic script, which means that almost every word is pronounced exactly as it is written: learning a character means also learning a sound. The system is comprised of three kinds of characters: vowels, consonants, and conjunct characters. There are no capital letters.

Vowels

The Devanagari script has 11 vowels. Every vowel except अ **a** has two symbols. The first symbol is the full form of the vowel, called the *vowel character*. This is used when the vowel is the first letter of a word or syllable, and when it follows another vowel. The second symbol is the *vowel sign*, which is used after a consonant, i.e. when the vowel is the second letter of a syllable. The alphabet begins with the vowels, and the vowel characters are as follows:

अ		**a** like the 'a' in *ago*, but like the 'o' in *pot* when it follows a labial consonant (a consonant pronounced on the lips)
आ	ā	like the 'a' in *father*
इ	i	like the 'ee' in *feet*; rarely like the 'i' in *hit*
ई	ī	like the 'ee' in *feet*
उ	u	like the 'oo' in *food*; rarely like the 'u' in *put*
ऊ	ū	like the 'oo' in *food*
ऋ	ṛ	like the 'ri' in *trip*, *ripple* (only occurs in words borrowed from Sanskrit)
ए	e	like the first part of the vowel sound in *made*
ऐ	ai	like the 'oy' sound in *boy* or the 'i' sound in *quite*
ओ	o	like the first part of the vowel sound in *hole*
औ	au	like the 'ow' sound in *cow*

Consonants

The Devanagari script has 33 consonants. The traditional Indian system very helpfully orders consonants according to the way they are pronounced, and they are listed here in alphabetical order. Each of the first five groups of consonants has as its final member a nasal consonant (a consonant pronounced through the nose).

Each Devanagari character is followed by a Roman transliteration which consists of the consonant followed by the letter **a**. This is because, in the absence of any other vowel sign, each consonant is held to contain the inherent अ **a** vowel. Because each Devanagari consonant therefore comes to represent a syllable, some scholars call the Devanagari system a 'syllabary' rather than an 'alphabet'. In words that end in a consonant, the inherent **a** of the final letter is sometimes pronounced, but is more often silent. This final **a** will appear in transliteration only when it is to be pronounced.

Two important contrasts that exist in Nepali, but not in English, should be pointed out. The first is between *aspirated* and *non-aspirated* consonants, the second between *dental* and *retroflex* consonants.

■ Aspirated consonants are pronounced with a strong expulsion of breath, while non-aspirated consonants are pronounced with only minimal breath being expelled. The amount of breath expelled during the pronunciation of an English consonant is usually somewhere between these two extremes, so discipline is required to learn the Nepali way: less breath than normal while uttering a non-aspirated consonant, much more breath than normal while uttering an aspirated one. Hold a mirror in front of your face as you practise, and compare the extent to which it clouds up in each instance! Or put a hand in front of your mouth to feel the difference. Take care also to utter each aspirate consonant as a single sound: although the second letter of the Roman transliteration of Devanagari aspirates is 'h', this is there to indicate the expulsion of breath, not to suggest that there are two separate sounds.

■ To pronounce Nepali words correctly, it is also important to differentiate between dental consonants and retroflex consonants, and most particularly between dental **ta** and **da** and retroflex ṭa and ḍa. For dental consonants the tongue should touch the back of the upper front teeth, for retroflex consonants it should be curled back up against the roof of the mouth. For the English 't' and 'd' the tongue is held somewhere between these two positions, which sounds like a retroflex to a Nepali-speaker's ear. Learners therefore need to work harder to pronounce dental consonants than they do to pronounce retroflex ones, though they often imagine the opposite.

Velar or guttural consonants (pronounced in the throat)

क	**ka**	as the 'k' in *skit*
ख	**kha**	as **ka** but with a strong release of breath
ग	**ga**	as the 'g' in *go*
घ	**gha**	as **ga** but with a strong release of breath
ङ्	**ṅ**	as the 'n' in *sing*

Palatal consonants (pronounced at the palate or the upper gum-line)

च	**ca**	like the 'ch' in *cheese*, but with less release of breath and pronounced with the tip of the tongue touching the lower front teeth
छ	**cha**	somewhere between the 'ch' in *cheese* and the 'ts' in *tsar*, pronounced with a strong release of breath
ज	**ja**	as the 'j' in *jug*
झ	**jha**	as **ja** but with a strong release of breath
ञ	**ña**	as the 'n' in *injury*

Retroflex consonants (pronounced with the tongue curled back to touch the palate)

ट	ṭa	like the 't' in *stop*, but with the tongue curled up to touch the roof of the mouth
ठ	ṭha	as ṭa but with a strong release of breath
ड	ḍa	*when the first letter of a syllable:* as the 'd' in *dug*, but with the tongue curled up to touch the roof of the mouth
		in the middle or at the end of a word: as the 'r' in *rug*, but with the tongue curled up to touch the roof of the mouth
ढ	ḍha	as ḍa but with a strong release of breath
ण	ṇa	like the 'n' in *and* , but with the tongue curled up to touch the roof of the mouth

Dental consonants (pronounced with the tongue touching or close to the upper front teeth)

त	ta	like the 't' in *tip*, with the tip of the tongue against the back of the upper front teeth
थ	tha	as ta but with a strong release of breath
द	da	as the 'd' in *dip*
ध	dha	as da but with a strong release of breath
न	na	as the 'n' in *nip*

Labial consonants (pronounced on the lips)

प	pa	as the 'p' in *pot*
फ	pha	as pa but with a strong release of breath; often like the 'f' in *father*
ब	ba	as the 'b' in *bud*
भ	bha	as ba but with a strong release of breath; sometimes like a breathy 'v' as in *driver*
म	ma	as the 'm' in *mud*

Semi-vowels

य	**ya**	as the 'y' in *yes*
र	**ra**	like the 'r' in *run*, but pronounced with a trill of the tongue, not on the lips
ल	**la**	like the 'l' in *lot*, but pronounced with the tongue further forward
व	**va**	pronounced either as the 'b' in *bud* or as the 'w' in *worse*

Sibilant ('hissing') consonants

श	**śa**	as the 'sh' in *shun*, but also frequently pronounced 's'
ष	**ṣa**	as the 'sh' in *shun*, but also frequently pronounced 's'
स	**sa**	as the 's' in *sun*

Aspirate consonant

ह	**ha**	as the 'h' in *hug*

 Script exercise 1

Make a flash card for each character, with the Devanagari letter on the front and the Roman transliteration on the back. Use these to help you memorise each character.

 Script exercise 2

Write out the following Nepali words in Devanagari:

jhan	saral	thap	bhavan	kamal	had
chad	bakhat	jarah	yas	ṭhag	ḍar
tara	gaṇa	śahar	daśak	nabh	vaś
calan	ṭaṭh	ma	ghar	phaṭ	rath
dhaval	ḍhab	lay	paḍha	ṣaṭh	khatam

Constructing syllables

Every vowel except अ **a** has a vowel sign which is added to a consonant to form a syllable. The अ **a** vowel is inherent in the consonant itself. When a vowel other than अ **a** is added to a consonant, it automatically replaces the अ **a** vowel. Vowel signs are attached to the consonant क् **k** in the following ways:

क् **k**	+	अ **a**	=	क	**ka**
क **ka**	+	आ **ā**	=	का	**kā**
क **ka**	+	इ **i**	=	कि	**ki**
क **ka**	+	ई **ī**	=	की	**kī**
क **ka**	+	उ **u**	=	कु	**ku**
क **ka**	+	ऊ **ū**	=	कू	**kū**
क **ka**	+	ऋ **ṛ**	=	कृ	**kṛ**
क **ka**	+	ए **e**	=	के	**ke**
क **ka**	+	ऐ **ai**	=	कै	**kai**
क **ka**	+	ओ **o**	=	को	**ko**
क **ka**	+	औ **au**	=	कौ	**kau**

A vowel sign is generally attached to the stem or downstroke of a consonant – to the foot of the downstroke in the case of उ **u**, ऊ **ū**, and ऋ **ṛ**, to the head of the downstroke in the case of ए **e** and ऐ **ai**, as an additional downstroke attached by a loop to the head of the stem in the cases of इ **i** and ई **ī**, and as an additional downstroke with or without extra elements in the cases of आ **ā**, ओ **o**, and औ **au**. क **ka** is a single-stemmed consonant, but some consonants have two downstrokes, and in such cases the vowel sign must be attached to the right-hand member of the pair. The consonant ग **ga** is an example:

ग	गा	गि	गी	गु	गू	गृ	गे	गै	गो	गौ
ga	**gā**	**gi**	**gī**	**gu**	**gū**	**gṛ**	**ge**	**gai**	**go**	**gau**

The consonant र **ra** is an exception to these general rules when it takes the vowel signs ु **-u** and ू **-ū**. Instead of attaching these to the foot of the downstroke, you should allow them to nestle higher up in the crook of the character:

र	+	उ	=	रु **ru**
र	+	ऊ	=	रू **rū**

A consonant can only support one vowel at a time. In words in which one vowel follows directly after another, the second vowel must always appear as a full vowel character. Thus, to write the word **duī** *(two)* you must write दु **du** followed by ई **ī** in its full form: दुई. Similarly, note the spellings खाउ **khāu**, गाई **gāī**, and लिए **lie.**

Script exercise 3

Write out the following Nepali words in Devanagari:

luṭapīt	bemausam	aghāunu	ghṛṇā	anauṭho
auṣadhi	bhautik	risāunu	ainā	deū
khicaḍī	dobāto	gūdh	hariyo	ukusamukus
itarinu	janatā	yahī	nakhāū	choṭakarī
oḍār	bṛhat	phūladānī	guruko	śarīr
sāikal	jhilimili	taipani	bhailo	vīṇā
śiśī	yātāyāt	āmā	thego	īśān
ḍaul	eghāra	ūṣār		

Nasalisation

Every vowel can be nasalised. To pronounce a nasalised vowel, direct as much as you can of the breath that is involved in its pronunciation towards the nasal cavity. In Nepali, nasalisation is indicated by a sign called चन्द्रबिन्दु **candrabindu** (literally, *moon dot),* whose name describes its appearance well: ˘. In Roman transliteration, nasalisation is represented by a *tilde* over the vowel (e.g. **ã**).

The चन्द्रबिन्दु **candrabindu** is written either over the nasalised vowel itself, e.g. कहाँ **kahã**, or above the consonant to which the vowel is attached, e.g. गरूँ **garũ**, हूँ **hũ**. If any part of the vowel is written above the headstroke, the चन्द्रबिन्दु **candrabindu** is reduced to its बिन्दु **bindu** or 'dot', e.g. छिंडी **chĩḍī**, गरें **garẽ.**

In some Nepali words it is customary to represent nasalisation not with the चन्द्रबिन्दु **candrabindu** but with a conjunct of which the first member is one of the nasal consonants. The two most common combinations are:

ङ्	ṅ	+	क	ka	=	ङ्क	ṅka
ङ्	ṅ	+	ग	ga	=	ङ्ग	ṅga

Thus, certain words can be spelled in two different ways: हाँगो **hãgo** or हाङ्गो **hāṅgo**; गुरुं **gurũg** or गुरुङ्ग **guruṅg**. The conjuncts tend to be used in words that are felt to be unique to the language, while चन्द्रबिन्दु **candrabindu** is used in words that Nepali shares with Hindi, Sanskrit, etc.

☑ Script exercise 4

Write out the following Nepali words in Devanagari:

hã	chāyã	nayã	gāũ	sãga
gāũchu	āinā	diinã	tapāĩ	jãdaina
pãc	aũlo	garẽ	sãsār	ãkhā
guruṅg	chāṅgā	mānāṅ	aṅg	

Conjunct characters

The spellings of many Nepali words involve the combination or clustering of two or more consonants; these combinations are known as *conjuncts*. By joining two consonants in this way, you cancel out the inherent अ **a** between them.

Certain combinations produce what are in effect new characters rather than recognisable combinations of their constituent consonants. These *special* conjuncts are listed below:

Special conjunct characters				
क **ka**	+	ष **ṣa**	=	क्ष **kṣa** (often pronounced 'che')
ज **ja**	+	ञ **ña**	=	ज्ञ **jña** [pronounced 'gya']
श **śa**	+	र **ra**	=	श्र **śra**
त **ta**	+	त **ta**	=	त्त **tta**
त **ta**	+	र **ra**	=	त्र **tra**
द **da**	+	य **ya**	=	द्य **dya**

Half characters

More than half of all the conjuncts are formed simply by dropping a downstroke from the first member and then joining what remains to the full form of the second member. For instance, to produce the conjunct **gya**, consisting of the consonants ग **ga** and य **ya**, remove the second downstroke of ग **ga** to produce ग and add this to the full form of य **ya** to produce the conjunct ग्य.

The following table shows all the half characters, followed by examples of ways in which they are combined with full characters to form conjuncts.

Full character		Half character	Examples
क्	k	क	क्क **kka**, क्ख **kkha**, क्ट **kṭa**
क्ष	kṣa	क्ष	क्ष्म **kṣma**, क्ष्य **kṣya**
ख	kha	ख	ख्य **khya**, ख्न **khna**, ख्छ **khcha**
ग	ga	ग	ग्य **gya**, ग्ल **gla**, ग्व **gva**
घ	gha	घ	घ्छ **ghcha**, घ्न **ghna**, घ्य **ghya**
च	ca	च	च्च **cca**, च्छ **ccha**, च्य **cya**
ज	ja	ज	ज्ज **jja**, ज्य **jya**, ज्व **jva**
झ	jha	झ	झ्य **jhya**, झ्द **jhda**, झ्न **jhna**
ञ	ñ	ञ	ञ्च **ñca**, ञ्ज **ñja**
ण	ṇ	ण	ण्ट **ṇṭa**, ण्ठ **ṇṭha**, ण्य **ṇya**
त	ta	त	त्म **tma**, त्य **tya**, त्स **tsa**
त्त	tta	त्त	त्त्व **ttva**
थ	tha	थ	थ्य **thya**
ध	dha	ध	ध्छ **dhcha**, ध्य **dhya**, ध्व **dhva**
न	na	न	न्त **nta**, न्द्र **ndra**, न्ह **nha**
प	pa	प	प्ठ **pṭha**, प्प **ppa**, प्स **psa**
फ	pha	फ	फ्न **phna**
ब	ba	ब	ब्ज **bja**, ब्द **bda**, ब्ब **bba**
भ	bha	भ	भ्य **bhya**
म	ma	म	म्न **mna**, म्प **mpa**, म्ह **mha**
य	ya	य	य्य **yya**
ल	la	ल	ल्क **lka**, ल्द **lda**, ल्ल **lla**
व	va	व	व्य **vya**
श	śa	श	श्य **śya**, श्ल **śla**, श्व **śva**
ष	ṣa	ष	ष्ठ **ṣṭha**, ष्ण **ṣṇa**, ष्य **ṣya**
स	sa	स	स्क **ska**, स्ट **sṭa**, स्त **sta**

The halant

If the diagonal stroke called हलन्त **halant** is placed at the foot of a consonant, it removes its inherent अ **a**. हलन्त **halant** is used regularly in verbs, but very rarely in other words. It is also used to show that a conjunct exists between two consonants whose joining cannot be represented in any other way. The round or oval characters ट, ठ, ड, ढ, द cannot drop a downstroke and remain recognisable. For this reason, if they are the first member of a conjunct they will keep their full form and the junction will be effected by the हलन्त **halant**, e.g.

ड	ḍa	+	ड	ḍa	=	ड्ड	ḍḍa
ट	ṭa	+	द	da	=	ट्द	ṭda
ठ	ṭha	+	म	ma	=	ठ्म	ṭhma
ट	ṭa	+	न	na	=	ट्न	ṭna

Conjuncts containing the consonant र ra

When र **ra** is the first member of a conjunct combination, it takes a form known as रेफ **reph**, which is a hook (ˆ) written above the headstroke of the second member of the conjunct combination, e.g. गर्छ **garcha**, गर्न **garna**. If a vowel sign follows the consonant to which र **ra** is being joined, the रेफ **reph** sign must move to the right, i.e. to the end of the syllable it precedes: गर्दा **gardā**, भर्ती **bhartī**, गर्ने **garne**.

When र **ra** is the first member of a conjunct of which the second member is य **ya**, it is written instead as a curved dash: गर्यो **garyo**, पर्यो **paryo**.

When र **ra** is the second member of a conjunct it is written as a diagonal slash down from the left of the lower part of the downstroke of the first member of the conjunct: राम्रो **rāmro**, उग्र **ugra**. If the first member of the conjunct has two stems, the diagonal slash will be added to the right-hand stem. If the first member of the conjunct is an oval or round consonant, a slightly different form is used: ड्र **ḍra**, ट्र **ṭra**. Note also the forms स्र **sra**, ह्र **hra**, श्र **śra**.

Other special cases

If the second member of a conjunct is य **ya** and the first member is a retroflex consonant, the य **ya** takes a special form (य):

| ट | ṭa | + | य | ya | = | ट्य | ṭya |
| ड | ḍ | + | य | ya | = | ड्य | ḍya |

Conjuncts that consist of two identical retroflex consonants may be represented with the characters arranged vertically, e.g.

| ट | ṭa | + | ट | ṭa | = | ट्ट | ṭṭa |

The consonants द **da** and ह **ha** form the following special conjuncts:

द **da**	+	ग **ga**	=	द्ग **dga**	ह **ha**	+	र **ra**	=	ह्र **hra**
द **da**	+	द **da**	=	द्द **dda**	ह **ha**	+	व **va**	=	ह्व **hva**
द **da**	+	ध **dha**	=	द्ध **ddha**	ह **ha**	+	ल **la**	=	ह्ल **hla**
द **da**	+	भ **bha**	=	द्भ **dbha**	ह **ha**	+	म **ma**	=	ह्म **hma**
द **da**	+	व **va**	=	द्व **dva**	ह **ha**	+	न **na**	=	ह्न **hna**

 Script exercise 5

Write out the following Nepali words in Devanagari:

kakṣā	jñān	natra	śrīmān	hlāsā	vidyā
divya	mahattā	lakṣya	hāttī	garchin	śānti
subbā	sakdaina	śabda	bhāgya	haptā	ṭhaṭṭā
pakkā	aḍḍā	jhyāl	āphno	phyā̃knu	rāmro
kṛṣṇa	dṛśya	pradhān	paddhati	bharyaṅ	viśva
bhañjyāṅg	pañcāyat	garthyo	khelcha	kāṭyo	garyo
kāṭhmāḍaũ	paḍhyo	vīrendra	bujhnu	mvāī	kyā
dhvani	āgrejī	kvāppa	prakhyāt	icchā	acyūt
ujjval	ṭrak	aṇḍā	utkṛṣṭa	tattva	ātmā
drava	dvārā	ārambh	rāṣṭra	svāsthya	hissī

Visarga

Visarga is a sign like a colon (but with its dots further apart) that occurs at the end or in the middle of certain words. It is pronounced as **ha** and is transliterated as **ḥ**. The only word in this book that requires **visarga** is दुःख **duḥkha**.

Numerals

The Nepali numerals are as follows:

१	२	३	४	५	६	७	८	९	०
1	2	3	4	5	6	7	8	9	0

Dictionary order

अ	a	क	ka	ठ	ṭha	ब	ba
आ	ā	ख	kha	ड	ḍa	भ	bha
इ	i	ग	ga	ढ	ḍha	म	ma
ई	ī	घ	gha	ण	ṇa	य	ya
उ	u	ङ	ṅa	त	ta	र	ra
ऊ	ū	च	ca	थ	tha	ल	la
ऋ	ṛ	छ	cha	द	da	व	va
ए	e	ज	ja	ध	dha	श	śa
ऐ	ai	झ	jha	न	na	ष	ṣa
ओ	o	ञ	ña	प	pa	स	sa
औ	au	ट	ṭa	फ	pha	ह	ha

The nasalised form of a vowel always precedes its unnasalised form in the dictionary order: thus, words beginning with अँ will come before words beginning with अ, words beginning with कुँ before words beginning with कु, etc.

Stress and accent

In Sanskrit, the language from which Nepali originally developed, consonants are always pronounced with their inherent अ **a** unless हलन्त **halant** is there to cancel it out. In Nepali, however, this is no longer the rule. The हलन्त **halant** is used only to mark the absence of a final अ **a** at the end of certain verb endings where without it some ambiguity of meaning could arise, or to mark the absence of the inherent अ **a** between two consonants that cannot be conjoined to form a conjunct in any other way. Otherwise, some words that end in a consonant but no vowel sign are pronounced with a final अ **-a**, whereas others are not. Although the best way to learn pronunciation is by hearing Nepali words spoken, certain rules can be discerned here:

The following categories of words should usually be pronounced as they are written (i.e. with the inherent अ **a** unless this is cancelled out with the हलन्त **halant**):

1 verb forms, where the हलन्त **halant** is used whenever necessary to cancel the inherent अ **a**: दिएर **diera**, गर **gara**, गर्छन् **garchan**, पढ्छन् **paḍhchan**;
2 most adverbs and postpositions: तर **tara**, बाहिर **bāhira**, आज **āja**, तिर **-tira**;
3 repetitive onomatopoeic words: सललल **salalala**;

4 words of one syllable: म **ma**, त **ta**;

5 words whose final syllable is a conjunct: कर्म **karma**, भक्त **bhakta**;

6 most words ending in a semi-vowel: मह **maha**, शिव **śiva**.

An inherent -a is usually not pronounced:[*]

1 at the end of postpositions of two or more syllables that are written as separate words (i.e. that are not joined to the noun or pronoun they follow): समेत **samet**, बाहेक **bāhek**;

2 in words (other than verbs) consisting of Cv-Ca: दिन **din**, or V-Ca: औल **aul**;

3 in words (other than verbs) consisting of Cv-Cv-Ca: नेपाल **nepāl**, विकास **bikās,** किताब **kitāb**;

4 in words consisting of Cv-Ca-Cv-Ca, where both medial and final अ **a** are dropped: किनमेल **kinmel**, खलबल **khalbal**, तरवार **tarvār**, लतपत **latpat**.

[*] Cv = syllable consisting of consonant + any vowel (including अ **a**). Ca = syllable consisting of consonant + अ **a**.

Punctuation

Devanagari now employs all of the punctuation symbols used in English, with the exception of the full stop. This consists instead of a single downstroke: ।

Samples of Nepali handwriting

सर्वप्रथम छोरी जन्मेकी उपलक्ष्यमा धेरै धेरै बधाइ।
अहिले त छोरी छोरी भइसकी होली।

तपाईं नेपाल आएर गएपछि यहाँका नदीमा धेरै पानी बगिरहेकी छ।

मेरो एउटा मित्र त्यहां छन् हुन् सक्छन् हुँदा मेरो मनमा कति हर्ष भएको छ।

तपाईं काठमाडौं आएपछि भएपछि हाम्रो भेट हुने नै छ।

Keys to script exercises

Script exercise 2

झन	सरल	थप	भवन	कमल	हृद
छद	बखत	जरह	यस	ठग	डर
तर	गण	शहर	दशक	नभ	वश
चलन	ठठ	म	घर	फट	रथ
धवल	ढब	लय	पढ	षठ	खतम

Script exercise 3

लुटपीट	बेमौसम	अघाउनु	घृणा	अनौठो
औषधि	भौतिक	रिसाउनु	ऐना	देऊ
खिचडी	दोबाटो	गूढ	हरियो	उकुसमुकुस
इतरिनु	जनता	यही	नखाऊ	छोटकरी
ओडार	बृहत	फूलदानी	गुरुको	शरीर
साइकल	झिलिमिलि	तैपनि	भैलो	वीणा
शिशी	यातायात	आमा	थेगो	ईशान
डौल	एघार	ऊषार		

Script exercise 4

हाँ	छायाँ	नयाँ	गाउँ	सँग
गाउँछु	आइनँ	दिइनँ	तपाई	जाँदैन
पाँच	औंलो	गरें	सँसार	आँखा
गुरुङ	छाङ्गा	मानाङ्	अङ्ग	

Script exercise 5

कक्षा	ज्ञान	नत्र	श्रीमान	ह्लासा	विद्या
दिव्य	महत्ता	लक्ष्य	हात्ती	गर्छिन्	शान्ति
सुब्बा	सर्वदैन	शब्द	भाग्य	हप्ता	ठट्टा
पक्का	अड्डा	झ्याल	आफ्नो	फ्याँक्नु	राम्रो
कृष्ण	दृश्य	प्रधान	पद्धति	भ्च्याङ्	विश्व
भ्ज्ज्याङ्ग	पञ्चायत	गर्थ्यो	खेल्छ	काट्चो	गन्यो
काठ्माडौं	पढ्चो	वीरेन्द्र	बुझ्नु	म्वाई	क्या
ध्वनि	अँग्रेजी	क्वाप्प	प्रख्यात	इच्छा	अच्यूत
उज्ज्वल	ट्रक	अण्डा	उत्कृष्ट	तत्त्व	आत्मा
द्रव	द्वारा	आरम्भ	राष्ट्र	स्वास्थ्य	हिस्सी

1 | ARE YOU BINDU?
तिमी बिन्दु हौ ?

In this unit you will learn how to:

■ identify yourself and others
■ ask and answer simple questions
■ exchange greetings
■ address people politely
■ apply adjectives to nouns

1 Meeting the bus

Gita and Bindu, two young women from Hetauda, have just arrived in Kathmandu to take up their college courses. Bimal Kumar, a senior male student, has been sent to meet them.

बिमल कुमार	नमस्ते !
Bimal Kumār	**namaste!**
	Hello!
गीता	हजुर ?
Gītā	**hajur?**
	Pardon?
बिमल कुमार	नमस्ते ! तिमी गीता हौ ?
Bimal Kumār	**namaste! timī Gītā hau?**
	Hello! Are you Gita?
गीता	हो, म गीता हुँ ।नमस्ते ।
Gītā	**ho, ma Gītā hū̃. namaste.**
	Yes, I am Gita. Hello.
बिमल कुमार	अनि तिमी बिन्दु हौ ?
Bimal Kumār	**ani timī Bindu hau?**
	And are you Bindu?
बिन्दु	हजुर, म बिन्दु हुँ ।
Bindu	**hajur, ma Bindu hū̃.**
	Yes, I am Bindu.
बिमल कुमार	ल, राम्रो । म बिमल कुमार हुँ ।
Bimal Kumār	**la, rāmro. ma Bimal Kumār hū̃.**
	Right, good. I am Bimal Kumar.
बिन्दु	नमस्ते बिमल कुमारजी! तपाई सन्चै हुनुहुन्छ ?
Bindu	**namaste Bimal Kumārjī! tapāī̃ sancai hunuhuncha?**
	Hello Bimal Kumarji! Are you well?
बिमल कुमार	सन्चै । तिमीहरू नि ?
Bimal Kumār	**sancai. timīharū ni?**
	I am well. How about you?
गीता	सन्चै ! तपाई शिक्षक हुनुहुन्छ ?
Gītā	**sancai! tapāī̃ śikṣak hunuhuncha?**
	We are well. Are you a teacher?
बिमल कुमार	होइन, म विद्यार्थी हुँ । तिमीहरू पनि विद्यार्थी हौ, होइन ?
Bimal Kumār	**hoina, ma vidyārthī hū̃. timīharū pani vidyārthī hau, hoina?**
	No, I am a student. You are students too, aren't you?
बिन्दु	हजुर, हामीहरू पनि विद्यार्थी हौँ ।
Bindu	**hajur, hāmīharū pani vidyārthī haũ.**
	Yes, we are students too.

नमस्ते ! **namaste!** *hello!* (Hindu greeting; also used for *goodbye*)

हजुर? **hajur?** *yes? pardon?*

तिमी... हौ **hau?** *you are...* or *are you...?*

हो **ho** *yes* (literally, *is*)

म... हुँ **ma... hũ** *I am...*

अनि **ani** *and*

हजुर **hajur** *yes*

ल **la** *there!* or *that's it!*

राम्रो **rāmro** *good*

बिमल कुमारजी **Bimal Kumārjī** -jī is added to his name for politeness *

सन्चै **sancai** *well, in good health*

तपाई... हुनुहुन्छ ? **tapāĩ hunuhuncha** *you are...* or *are you...?*

नि ? **ni ?** *what about...?*

तिमीहरू **timīharū** *you* (plural)

शिक्षक **śikṣak** *teacher*

होइन **hoina** *no* (literally, *is not*)

पनि **pani** *too, also*

विद्यार्थी **vidyārthī** *student, students*

होइन ? **hoina?** *is that not so?*

हामीहरू... हौं **hāmīharū... haũ** *we... are*

* Some Nepali-speakers add the suffix -ज्यू **-jyū** to names instead. The
suffix -जी **-jī** is common to both Hindi and Nepali.

Grammar

1 *Is* and *are* in Nepali

In English you say that something or someone *is* large, or *is* a policeman,
or *is* in Kathmandu. But in Nepali a distinction is made between two
different kinds of *is*, and in the plural between two kinds of *are*. These two
forms are:

a) The हो **ho** form which normally defines the thing or person you are
talking about with a noun:

| ऊ प्रहरी हो । | **ū praharī ho.** | *He is a policeman.* |
| यो काठ्माडौँ हो । | **yo kāṭhmāḍaũ ho.** | *This is Kathmandu.* |

b) The छ **cha** form which describes with an adjective, or locates a thing
or person:

त्यो ठूलो छ ।	**tyo ṭhūlo cha.**	*That is big* (describing).
ऊ काठ्माडौंमा छ ।	**ū kāṭhmāḍaūmā cha.**	*He is in* (**-mā**) *Kathmandu* (locating).

If you wish to say that something is large you must use छ **cha** for *is*, because you are describing it; if you wish to say that someone is in Kathmandu, you must again use छ **cha** for *is*, because you are locating them; but if you wish to state that someone is a policeman you must use हो **ho** for *is*, because you are defining him. छ **cha** and हो **ho** have different forms, depending on which of the Nepali pronouns (the words for *I*, *we*, *you*, *he*, *she*, *it* and *they*) is their subject. These forms are introduced in the pages that follow.

2 First person pronouns (*I*, *we*)

The first person pronouns are म **ma** *I* and हामी **hāmī** *we*. हामी **hāmī** *we* is sometimes used to mean *I* in place of म **ma**, though not with the pomposity of the English 'royal we'. When it is necessary to make it absolutely clear that हामी **hāmī** is intended to mean *we* in the plural, the pronoun is pluralised to become हामीहरू **hāmīharū**.

3 Second person pronoun (*you*)

When speaking to a person, you must address that person using a pronoun (a word for *you*) that reflects whether you are senior to him/her, or vice versa, and to what degree. This kind of seniority can depend, among other things, on age difference, family relationships, gender or social class.

The three levels of politeness, working upward, are:

LOW	(intimate or contemptuous)
MIDDLE	(familiar)
HIGH	(polite and super-polite)

LOW: the intimate or contemptuous तँ **tā** (*you* or *thou*) is used to address a social inferior (a junior servant, one's own small child, an animal, etc.), to express contempt or anger (one driver to another after a collision between their cars, perhaps!), or to address someone with whom one's relationship is intimate. Foreign speakers of Nepali will never use this pronoun. It can only be used to address an individual, and therefore has no plural form.

MIDDLE: the familiar तिमी **timī** (roughly equivalent to the French *tu*) is used to address persons significantly younger or of lower social standing

elf (servants, children, etc.) or to address friends with whom an
d informal relationship exists. To form the plural, you add the
g suffix -हरू **-harū**.

HIGH: the polite तपाई **tapāī** (roughly equivalent to the French *vous*) is
used to address most equals and all superiors except those to whom
especial deference is due. (Foreign speakers of Nepali inevitably find
themselves using this word for *you* more commonly than any other. In
fact, they will probably feel more comfortable using it to address people,
such as servants or porters, whom Nepalis would tend to address as तिमी
timī). To form the plural, you add the pluralising suffix -हरू **-harū**.

The super-polite हजुर **hajur** is sometimes used to express especial
deference when addressing someone. It takes the same verb-forms as the
other High pronouns. It might be used by a lower grade employee to
address his employer, for example, or by a new bride to address her
husband. It is also used as a polite word of assent (हजुर ! **hajur!** *Yes!*) or
to indicate that one has not heard or understood (हजुर ? **hajur?** *Pardon
me?*).

4 *I am, you are, we are* with हो *ho*

Singular		
म हुँ	**ma hū**	*I am*
तँ होस्	**tã hos**	*you* (Low) *are*
तिमी हौ	**timī hau**	*you* (Middle) *are*
तपाई हुनुहुन्छ	**tapāī hunuhuncha**	*you* (High) *are*
Plural		
हामी हौं	**hāmī haũ**	*we are* (occasionally *I am*)
हामीहरू हौं	**hāmīharū haũ**	*we are*
तिमीहरू हौ	**timīharū hau**	*you* (Middle) *are*
तपाईंहरू हुनुहुन्छ	**tapāīharū hunuhuncha**	*you* (High) *are*

Negatives

Each affirmative form of हो **ho** has a negative form:

affirmative			*negative*		
हुँ	**hũ**	*I am*	होइन	**hoina**	*I am not*
हौँ	**haũ**	*we are*	होइनौँ	**hoinaũ**	*we are not*
होस्	**hos**	*you* (Low) *are*	होइनस्	**hoinas**	*you* (Low) *are not*
हौ	**hau**	*you* (Middle) *are*	होइनौ	**hoinau**	*you* (Middle) *are not*
हुनुहुन्छ	**hunuhuncha**	*you* (High) *are*	हुनुहुन्न	**hunuhunna**	*you* (High) *are not*

5 Nouns

Nearly all Nepali nouns have masculine gender. The only feminine nouns are those that are female and human. Many feminine nouns end in **-ī**. Here are some examples of feminine nouns:

केटी	**keṭī**	*girl*	आइमाई	**āimāī**	*woman*
आमा	**āmā**	*mother*	छोरी	**chorī**	*daughter*
दिदी	**didī**	*elder sister*	बहिनी	**bahinī**	*younger sister*
श्रीमती	**śrīmatī**	*wife*	साली	**sālī**	*wife's younger sister*

There is no definite article *the* in Nepali, nor is there an indefinite article *a.* Therefore a sentence such as ऊ विद्यार्थी हो **ū vidyārthī ho** can be translated as *s/he is a student* or as *s/he is the student*, depending on the context.

All nouns, and most pronouns, are pluralised simply by adding the suffix -हरू **-harū**:

Singular			**Plural**		
मान्छे	**mānche**	*person*	मान्छेहरू	**māncheharū**	*people*
नेपाली	**nepālī**	*Nepali*	नेपालीहरू	**nepālīharū**	*Nepalis*
तपाई	**tapāī**	*you* (High)	तपाईहरू	**tapāīharū**	*you people* (High)
तिमी	**timī**	*you* (Middle)	तिमीहरू	**timīharū**	*you people* (Middle)

However, it is not necessary to attach -हरू **-harū** to a noun when some other word in the sentence makes it clear that the noun is plural. In the following sentences, the word that takes the plural suffix is the one that the speaker wishes to emphasise:

हामीहरू शिक्षक हौं ।   **hāmīharū śikṣak haũ.** *We are teachers.*

There is no need to add -हरू **-harū** to शिक्षक **śikṣak** as well as to हामी **hāmī**. हामी **hāmī** is emphasised.

तिमीहरू विद्यार्थी हौ ।   **timīharū vidyārthī hau.** *You are students.*

There is no need to add -हरू **-harū** to विद्यार्थी **vidyārthī** as well as to तिमी **timī**. तिमी **timī** is emphasised.

हामी शिक्षकहरू हौं ।   **hāmī śikṣakharū haũ.** *We are <u>teachers</u>.*

शिक्षक **śikṣak** is emphasised.

तिमी विद्यार्थीहरू हौ ।   **timī vidyārthīharū hau.** *You are <u>students</u>.*

विद्यार्थी **vidyārthī** is emphasised.

6 Asking and answering questions

In everyday spoken Nepali, the only difference between a statement and a question is the intonation. To put it simply: the tone of your voice goes up at the end of a question, while at the end of a statement it goes down:

यो काठ्माडौं हो ।   **yo kāṭhmāḍaũ ho.** *This is Kathmandu.*

                  (हो **ho** pronounced in a low tone.)

यो काठ्माडौं हो ?   **yo kāṭhmāḍaũ ho?** *Is this Kathmandu?*

                  (हो **ho** pronounced in a rising tone.)

Nepali does possess words for *yes* and *no*: these are अँ **ã** and अहँ **ahã** respectively.

Q यो काठ्माडौं हो ?   **yo kāṭhmāḍaũ ho?** *Is this Kathmandu?*
A अँ, काठ्माडौं हो ।   **ã, kāṭhmāḍaũ ho.** *Yes, this is Kathmandu.*

or

A अहँ, पोखरा हो ।   **ahã, pokharā ho.** *No, this is Pokhara.*

However, when answering a question it is more common to respond with the affirmative or negative form of the verb with which the question ended:

Q यो काठ्माडौं हो ?	**yo kāṭhmāḍaũ ho?**	*Is this Kathmandu?*
A हो, काठ्माडौं हो ।	**ho, kāṭhmāḍaũ ho.**	*Yes, this is Kathmandu.*

or

A होइन, यो पोखरा हो ।	**hoina, yo pokharā ho.**	*No, this is Pokhara.*

हजुर **hajur** is often used for *yes*:

Q त्यो रमेश हो ?	**tyo Rameś ho?**	*Is that Ramesh?*
A हजुर, रमेश हो ।	**hajur, Rameś ho.**	*Yes, that's Ramesh.*

Often, हो **ho** *is* and होइन **hoina** *is not* are also used to mean *yes* and *no* regardless of the verb in the question:

Q तपाई रमेशजी हुनुहुन्छ ?	**tapāī̃ Rameśjī hunuhuncha?**	*Are you Rameshji?*
A हो, म रमेश हुँ ।	**ho, ma Rameś hũ.**	*Yes, I am Ramesh.*

or

A होइन, म ओम हुँ ।	**hoina, ma Om hũ.**	*No, I am Om.*

2 Arriving at the college

Gita and Bindu reach the college with Bimal Kumar.

गीता
Gītā
यो महेन्द्र महाविद्यालय हो ?
yo Mahendra mahāvidyālay ho?
Is this Mahendra College?

बिमल कुमार
Bimal Kumār
हो । यो महेन्द्र महाविद्यालय हो ।
ho. yo Mahendra mahāvidyālay ho.
Yes. This is Mahendra College.

बिन्दु
Bindu
ती मान्छेहरू को हुन् ?
tī māncheharū ko hun?
Who are those people?

बिमल कुमार
तिनीहरू विद्यार्थी हुन् । यो सलील हो, त्यो गणेश हो, र तिनीहरू माया र अम्बिका हुन् ।

Bimal Kumār
tinīharū vidyarthī hun. yo Salīl ho, tyo Ganeś ho, ra tinīharū Māyā ra Ambikā hun.
They are students. This is Salil, that is Ganesh, and those are Maya and Ambika.

गीता
Gītā अनि त्यो मान्छे शिक्षक हो ?
ani tyo mānche śikṣak ho?
And is that person a teacher?

बिमल कुमार हजुर । वहाँ डाक्टर रमेश थापा हुनुहुन्छ । नमस्कार डाक्टर थापा !
Bimal Kumār **hajur. vahā̃ ḍākṭar Rameś Thāpā hunuhuncha. namaskār ḍākṭar Thāpā !**
Yes. He is Dr Ramesh Thapa. Hello, Dr Thapa!

रमेश थापा नमस्कार बिमल कुमारजी । वहाँहरू को हुनुहुन्छ ?
Ramesh Thāpā **namaskār Bimal Kumārjī. vahā̃harū ko hunuhuncha?**
Hello, Bimal Kumarji. Who are they?

बिमल कुमार वहाँहरू गीता खड्का र बिन्दु शर्मा हुनुहुन्छ । नयाँ विद्यार्थीहरू ।
Bimal Kumār **vahā̃harū Gītā Khaḍkā ra Bindu Śarmā hunuhuncha. nayā̃ vidyārthīharū.**
They are Gita Khadka and Bindu Sharma. New students.

रमेश थापा नमस्ते, नमस्ते ।
Ramesh Thāpā **namaste, namaste.**
Hello, hello.

गीता र बिन्दु नमस्ते हजुर ।
Gītā ra Bindu **namaste hajur.**
Hello, sir.

महेन्द्र महाविद्यालय **Mahendra mahāvidyālay** *Mahendra College*
ती **tī** *those*
मान्छेहरू **māncheharū** *people*
को *who?*
हुन् **hun** *are*
र **ra** *and*
डाक्टर **ḍākṭar** *doctor*
नमस्कार **namaskār** *hello or goodbye* (more formal than नमस्ते **namaste**)
नयाँ **nayā̃** *new*

EXERCISE 1 Answer the following questions about yourself:

१ तपाई बिमल कुमार हुनुहुन्छ ?   **tapāī̃ Bimal Kumār hunuhuncha?**
२ तपाई विद्यार्थी हुनुहुन्छ ?   **tapāī̃ vidyārthī hunuhuncha?**
३ तपाई नेपाली हुनुहुन्छ ?   **tapāī̃ nepālī hunuhuncha?**

⚙️ Grammar

7 Third person pronouns (*he, she, they*)

If you are speaking about a person, the pronoun you choose must reflect whether that person is senior or junior to you in age, social class, etc., and must also indicate whether s/he is in the proximity or not when you speak. The same three levels of politeness exist here that apply to the second person pronouns, although they are not exact equivalents in terms of their usage:

LOW   (simple reference)
MIDDLE   (polite reference)
HIGH   (honorific reference)

LOW third person pronouns are:

ऊ **ū** *he/she*
यो **yo** *it, this*
त्यो **tyo** *it, that*

ऊ **ū** *he/she* is used to refer to a person in his/her absence when there is no need to talk about that person with deference or politeness. ऊ **ū** cannot be used as a pronoun to refer to things or objects, and is used only to refer to human beings.

While यो **yo** and त्यो **tyo** both mean *it*, the difference between them is that यो **yo** refers to something near to the speaker ('this') while त्यो **tyo** refers to something away from the speaker ('that'). यो **yo** and त्यो **tyo** have the plural forms यी **yī** and ती **tī** respectively: the first of these is often pronounced without its initial *y*, i.e. *ī.*

यो **yo** and त्यो **tyo** can also sometimes be used to mean *he* or *she,* but this can sound impolite and it is better to use only ऊ **ū** to refer to people at this level of politeness.

MIDDLE pronouns उनी **unī**, यिनी **yinī** and तिनी **tinī** are in their singular forms generally a feature of cultured or literary Nepali rather than of colloquial speech. When they are used in speech, they refer most commonly to women. They are used to refer to persons who are felt to deserve a modicum of honorific reference, but not the full-blown honorific grade (one example might be a man speaking about his wife).

उनी **unī** and तिनी **tinī** have distant reference, while यिनी **yinī** refers to a person who is physically close to the speaker. The plural forms उनीहरू **unīharū**, यिनीहरू **yinīharū** and तिनीहरू **tinīharū** are used much more commonly in speech than the singular forms, and here they are simply pronouns that refer, politely but not exceptionally politely, to persons in the plural. उनीहरू **unīharū** is in most contexts the word you should use to refer to people as *they*.

HIGH pronouns यहाँ **yahā̃** and वहाँ **vahā̃** and their plural forms यहाँहरू **yahā̃harū** and वहाँहरू **vahā̃harū** are used to refer to persons very politely in their presence and absence respectively. Inevitably, you will be more polite about a person who can hear what you are saying, so वहाँ **vahā̃** is generally used only for persons deserving especial deference and respect: one's parents, teacher, etc. वहाँ **vahā̃** is often pronounced and sometimes written as उहाँ **uhā̃**.

8 *He is, she is, it is, they are* with हो *ho*

Singular		
LOW		
ऊ हो	**ū ho**	*s/he* (distant, Low) *is*
यो हो	**yo ho**	*it/ this* (nearby, Low) *is*
त्यो हो	**tyo ho**	*it/that* (distant, Low) *is*
MIDDLE		
उनी हुन्	**unī hun**	*s/he* (distant, Middle) *is*
यिनी हुन्	**yinī hun**	*s/he* (nearby, Middle) *is*
तिनी हुन्	**tinī hun**	*s/he* (distant, Middle) *is*
HIGH		
यहाँ हुनुहुन्छ	**yahā̃ hunuhuncha**	*s/he* (nearby, High) *is*
वहाँ हुनुहुन्छ	**vahā̃ hunuhuncha**	*s/he* (distant, High) *is*
Plural		
LOW		
यी हुन्	**yī hun**	*they* (nearby, Low) *are*
ती हुन्	**tī hun**	*they* (distant, Low) *are*
MIDDLE		
उनीहरू हुन्	**unīharū hun**	*they* (distant, Middle) *are*
यिनीहरू हुन्	**yinīharū hun**	*they* (nearby, Middle) *are*
तिनीहरू हुन्	**tinīharū hun**	*they* (distant, Middle) *are*
HIGH		
यहाँहरू हुनुहुन्छ	**yahā̃harū hunuhuncha**	*they* (nearby, High) *are*
वहाँहरू हुनुहुन्छ	**vahā̃harū hunuhuncha**	*they* (distant, High) *are*

Negatives

Each affirmative form of हो **ho** has a negative form:

affirmative	negative	
LOW SINGULAR		
हो **ho** *is*	होइन **hoina**	*is not*
LOW PLURAL & MIDDLE SINGULAR		
हुन् **hun** *are/is*	होइनन् **hoinan**	*are not/is not*
HIGH SINGULAR & PLURAL		
हुनुहुन्छ **hunuhuncha** *is/are*	हुनुहुन्न **hunuhunna**	*are not/is not*

To be (using हो **ho** to define people's nationalities). Here are some examples:

affirmative

म अँग्रेज हुँ।	**ma ãgrej hū.**	*I am English.*
हामी जर्मन हौँ।	**hāmī jarman haũ.**	*We are German.*
तिमी भारतीय हौ।	**timī bhāratīya hau.**	*You (M) are Indian.*
तपाई नेपाली हुनुहुन्छ।	**tapāī nepālī hunuhuncha.**	*You (H) are Nepali.*
ऊ अमेरिकन हो।	**ū amerikan ho.**	*S/he (L) is American.*
उनी पाकिस्तानी हुन्।	**unī pākistānī hun.**	*S/he (M) is Pakistani.*
वहाँ चिनियाँ हुनुहुन्छ।	**vahã ciniyã hunuhuncha.**	*S/he (H) is Chinese.*

negative

म जर्मन होइन।	**ma jarman hoina.**	*I am not German.*
हामी अँग्रेज होइनौँ।	**hāmī ãgrej hoinaũ.**	*We are not English.**
तिमी अमेरिकन होइनौ।	**timī amerikan hoinau.**	*You (M) are not American.*
तपाई चिनियाँ हुनुहुन्न।	**tapāī ciniyã hunuhunna.**	*You (H) are not Chinese.*
ऊ हिन्दुस्तानी होइन।	**ū hindustānī hoina.**	*S/he (L) is not Indian.*
उनी नेपाली होइनन्।	**unī nepālī hoinan.**	*S/he (M) is not Nepali.*
वहाँ पाकिस्तानी हुनुहुन्न।	**vahã pākistānī hunuhunna.**	*S/he (H) is not Pakistani.*

* The terms अमेरिकन **amerikan** *American* and अँग्रेज **ãgrej** *English* are often used to refer generally to foreigners or white people.

तैँ **tã**, the Low word for *you*, would not be used in sentences such as the above. An example of its use would be:

तैँ मूर्ख होस्।	**tã mūrkh hos.**	*You (L) are an idiot.*

9 *This, that, these* and *those*

यो **yo** and त्यो **tyo** and their plural forms यी **yī** and ती **tī** are most commonly used as adjectives to mean *this, that, these* and *those:*

त्यो मान्छे नेपाली हो ।	**tyo mānche nepālī ho.**	*That person is Nepali.*
यो केटा विद्यार्थी हो ।	**yo keṭā vidyārthī ho.**	*This boy is a student.*
ती मान्छेहरू अँग्रेज होइनन् ।	**tī māncheharū ãgrej hoinan.**	*Those people are not English.*
यी बहिनीहरू गीता र बिन्दु हुन् ।	**yī bahinīharū Gītā ra Bindu hun.**	*These young girls are Gita and Bindu.*

10 Adjectives

Adjectives are of two types:

    (a) inflecting adjectives which end in the vowel -ओ **-o,**
    (b) invariable adjectives ending in some other vowel, or in a consonant.

The endings of adjectives of type (a) must change ('inflect') according to the number and gender of the noun they describe. The endings are:

    -ओ **-o** in the masculine singular,
    -ई **-ī** in the feminine singular,
    -आ **-ā** in the masculine and feminine plural.

(a) Inflecting adjectives

ठूलो राजा	**ṭhūlo rājā**	*great king*
ठूला राजाहरू	**ṭhūlā rājāharū**	*great kings*
राम्रो केटा	**rāmro keṭā**	*good boy*
राम्रा केटाहरू	**rāmrā keṭāharū**	*good boys*
सेतो किताब	**seto kitāb**	*white book*
सेता किताबहरू	**setā kitābharū**	*white books*
सानी केटी	**sānī keṭī**	*small girl*
साना केटीहरू	**sānā keṭīharū**	*small girls*

(b) Invariable adjectives

गरीब किसान	**garīb kisān**	*poor farmer*
गरीब किसानहरू	**garīb kisānharū**	*poor farmers*
सफा कोठा	**saphā koṭhā**	*clean room*
सफा कोठाहरू	**saphā koṭhāharū**	*clean rooms*
धनी मान्छे	**dhanī mānche**	*rich man / person*

धनी मान्छेहरू	**dhanī māncheharū**	*rich men / people*
नयाँ कलम	**nayā̃ kalam**	*new pen*
नयाँ कलमहरू	**nayā̃ kalamharū**	*new pens*

EXERCISE 2 Complete the following sentences with the appropriate form of हो **ho** to form an affirmative statement. Work in transliteration first, then write the sentences out in Devanagari:

1	म अँग्रेज...	**ma ãgrej...**
2	हामी विद्यार्थी...	**hāmī vidyārthī...**
3	तिमी हिन्दुस्तानी...	**timī hindustānī...**
4	तिमीहरू किसान ...	**timīharū kisān...**
5	तपाई शिक्षक...	**tapāī̃ śikṣak...**
6	ऊ शिक्षक...	**ū śikṣak...**
7	उनी धनी मान्छे...	**unī dhanī mānche...**
8	ती मान्छेहरू प्रहरी...	**tī māncheharū praharī...**
9	वहाँ नेपाली...	**vahā̃ nepālī...**
10	यहाँहरू भारतीय...	**yahā̃harū bhāratīya...**

EXERCISE 3 Convert the affirmative statements into negative statements by changing the forms of the verbs.

EXERCISE 4 Translate into Nepali, giving both the script and the transliteration forms, taking care to give the adjectives the correct endings:

1	*good farmer*	*6*	*rich farmers*
2	*big book*	*7*	*good books*
3	*rich girl*	*8*	*small girls*
4	*new boy*	*9*	*poor boys*
5	*good king*	*10*	*rich kings*

2 | HOW FAR IS IT TO KATHMANDU, BROTHER?

काठ्माडौं कति टाढा छ दाइ ?

In this unit you will learn how to:

■ describe and ask about things and people
■ discuss distances and locations
■ use relationship terms to address people

3 A view of Kathmandu

Two villagers have reached a hilltop overlooking the Kathmandu Valley. From there they can see Kathmandu and the villages that surround it. They discuss the view.

रामे त्यो शहर काठ्माडौं हो, होइन ?
Rāme **tyo śahar kāṭhmāḍaũ ho, hoina?**
That town is Kathmandu, isn't it?

घने हो, त्यो शहर काठ्माडौं हो ।
Dhane **ho, tyo śahar kāṭhmāḍaũ ho.**
Yes, that town is Kathmandu.

रामे काठ्माडौं ठूलो छ, होइन ?
Rāme **kāṭhmāḍaũ ṭhūlo cha, hoina?**
Kathmandu is big, isn't it?

घने हो, धेरै ठूलो छ ।
Dhane **ho, dherai ṭhūlo cha.**
Yes, it's very big.

रामे काठ्माडौं कस्तो छ ? राम्रो छ ?
Rāme **kāṭhmāḍaũ kasto cha? rāmro cha?**
What is Kathmandu like? Is it nice?

घने राम्रै छ ।
Dhane **rāmrai cha.**
It's quite nice.

रामे अनि त्यो कुन गाउँ हो ?
Rāme **ani tyo kun gāũ ho?**
And which village is that?

घने त्यो गाउँ होइन, भक्तपुर शहर हो ।
Dhane **tyo gāũ hoina, bhaktapur śahar ho.**
That is not a village, that is Bhaktapur town.

रामे ए । त्यो शहर सानो छ, होइन ?
Rāme **e. tyo śahar sāno cha, hoina?**
Oh. That town is small, isn't it?

घने हो, अलि सानो छ । धेरै ठूलो छैन । तर भक्तपुर धेरै पुरानो शहर हो ।
Dhane **ho, ali sāno cha. dherai ṭhūlo chaina. tara bhaktapur dherai purāno śahar ho.**
Yes, it is quite small. It is not very big. But Bhaktapur is a very old town.

शहर	**śahar** *town*	गाउँ	**gāū** *village*
घेरै	**dherai** *very*	भक्तपुर	**bhaktapur** *Bhaktapur*
छ	**cha** *is*	ए	**e** *Oh*
कस्तो	**kasto** *like what? how?*	अलि	**ali** *quite*
राम्रै	**rāmrai** *quite nice*	तर	**tara** *but*
कुन	**kun** *which?*	पुरानो	**purāno** *old*

EXERCISE 5 Answer the following questions in Nepali about **Dialogue 3**. If your answer to 1 is in the affirmative, write the Nepali for *Yes, Kathmandu is big*; if your answer is negative, write the Nepali for *No, Kathmandu is not big, it is small*, and so on.

१. काठ्माडौं ठूलो छ ?   **kāṭhmāḍaū ṭhūlo cha?**
२. भक्तपुर गाउँ हो?   **bhaktapur gaū ho?**
३. काठ्माडौं राम्रो छ?   **kāṭhmāḍaū rāmro cha?**
४. काठ्माडौं ठूलो शहर हो ?   **kāṭhmāḍaū ṭhūlo śahar ho?**
५. भक्तपुर पुरानो छ?   **bhaktapur purāno cha?**
६. भक्तपुर नयाँ शहर हो?   **bhaktapur nayā̃ śahar ho?**

Grammar

11 Pronouns with छ *cha*

You must use the हो **ho** form of the verb *to be* if you are defining something or someone with a noun, but if you are locating the thing or person you are talking about or describing it with an adjective you must use the छ **cha** form. The High forms हुनुहुन्छ **hunuhuncha** (affirmative) and हुनुहुन्न **hunuhunna** (negative), which were introduced in **Unit 1**, are the same regardless of whether they are defining, describing or locating. The other forms are as follows:

Verb form		Pronoun(s)
छु	**chu**	म **ma**
छौं	**chaũ**	हामी **hāmī** and हामीहरू **hāmīharū**
छस्	**chas**	तैं **tā̃**
छौ	**chau**	तिमी **timī** and तिमीहरू **timīharū**
छ	**cha**	ऊ **ū** यो **yo** त्यो **tyo**
छन्	**chan**	उनी **unī** यिनी **yinī** and तिनी **tinī**
		यी **yī** and ती **tī**
		उनीहरू **unīharū**, यिनीहरू **yinīharū** and
		तिनीहरू **tinīharū**

Negatives

Each affirmative form of छ has a negative form:

Affirmative		Negative				
छु	**chu**	*(I) am*	छैन	**chaina**	*am not*
छौं	**chaũ**	*(we) are*	छैनौं	**chainaũ**	*are not*
छस्	**chas**	*(you) are* (L)	छैनस्	**chainas**	*are not*
छौ	**chau**	*(you) are* (M)	छैनौ	**chainau**	*are not*
छ	**cha**	*is* (L)	छैन	**chaina**	*is not*
छन्	**chan**	*is* (M)/ *are* (L)	छैनन्	**chainan**	*is/are not*

Feminine forms of छ **cha**

If you are talking *to* a particular woman or girl and addressing her as तँ **tã** or तिमी **timī** you can choose to use the following feminine forms of छ **cha**:

तँ छेस्	**tã ches**	*you* (Low) *are*
तिमी छ्यौ	**timī chyau**	*you* (Middle) *are*

If you are talking *about* a particular woman or girl and intend to use the Low pronoun for *she* (ऊ **ū**), you can choose to use the feminine form of छ **cha**, which is छे **che**:

ऊ छे	**ū che**	*she* (Low) *is*

If you are talking *about* a particular woman or girl and are using one of the Middle words for *he* or *she* (उनी **unī**, यिनी **yinī**, or तिनी **tinī**), you can choose to use the feminine form of छन् **chan**, which is छिन् **chin**:

उनी छिन्	**unī chin**	*she* (distant, Middle) *is*
यिनी छिन्	**yinī chin**	*she* (nearby, Middle) *is*
तिनी छिन्	**tinī chin**	*she* (distant, Middle) *is*

These feminine forms are not used very consistently in everyday spoken Nepali, but they are often used by men to refer politely to their wives and other female relatives, and they should always be used in the written language. There are no feminine negative forms of छ **cha**.

12   अलि **ali** *quite* and धेरै **dherai** *very, many*

Nepali adjectives can be qualified or emphasised by putting the words अलि **ali** *quite* or धेरै **dherai** *very* in front of them.

ऊ अलि दुब्लो छ।	**ū ali dublo cha.**	*He is quite thin.*

राम धेरै मोटो छैन ।	**Rām dherai moṭo chaina.**	*Ram is not very fat.*
उनी अलि होची छिन् ।	**unī ali hocī chin.**	*She is rather short.*
म धेरै अग्लो छु ।	**ma dherai aglo chu.**	*I am very tall.*

A second way to qualify or emphasise an adjective is to change its ending to -ऐ **-ai** if it ends in a vowel or to add -ऐ **-ai** to the end of the word if it ends in a consonant:

दुब्लो	dublo	*thin*	दुब्लै	dublai	*quite thin*
मोटो	moṭo	*fat*	मोटै	moṭai	*quite fat*
होचो	hoco	*short in stature*	होचै	hocai	*rather short in stature*
अग्लो	aglo	*tall*	अग्लै	aglai	*fairly tall*
राम्रो	rāmro	*good, nice*	राम्रै	rāmrai	*nice enough*
सानो	sāno	*small*	सानै	sānai	*rather small*
सफा	saphā	*clean*	सफै	saphai	*clean enough*

धेरै **dherai** *very* has a second meaning, which is *many*. It means *very* when it comes before an adjective, but if it comes before a noun, or on its own, it means *many*:

| Q नेपालमा धेरै शहरहरू छन् ? | **nepālmā dherai śaharharū chan?** | *Are there many towns in Nepal?* |
| A अहँ, धेरै छैनन् । | **ahã, dherai chainan.** | *No, there are not many.* |

But if you want to ask *are there many big towns in Nepal?* you have the problem that धेरै ठूला शहरहरू **dherai ṭhūlā śaharharū** could be taken to mean <u>very</u> *big cities* instead of <u>many</u> *big cities*. You get over this problem by moving the position of धेरै **dherai** in the sentence:

| Q नेपालमा ठूला शहरहरू धेरै छन् ? | **nepālmā ṭhūlā śaharharū dherai chan?** | *Are there many big towns in Nepal?* ('are big towns many in Nepal?') |
| A अहँ, धेरै छैनन् । | **ahã, dherai chainan.** | *No, there are not many.* |

One other commonly used word is अलिकति **alikati** *a small quantity of*, which should only be used to qualify nouns:

अलिकति दूध	**alikati dūdh**	*a little milk*
अलिकति चिनी	**alikati cinī**	*a little sugar*
अलिकति पानी	**alikati pānī**	*a little water*

...gatives) begin with a क
...s a set pattern. Those
...ng with त्य **ty-** or उ **u-** are
...rds that ask a question.

'this-word'		'that-word'		interrogatives	
	ऊ	**ū** *he/she*		को	**ko** *who?*
यो **yo** *it/this*	त्यो	**tyo** *it/that*		के	**ke** *what?*
यो **yo** *it/this*	त्यो	**tyo** *it/that*		कुन	**kun** *which?*
यति **yati** *this much*	त्यति	**tyati** *that much*		कति	**kati** *how much?*
यस्तो **yasto** *like this*	त्यस्तो	**tyasto** *like that*		कस्तो	**kasto** *like what?*
यहाँ **yahā̃** *here*	त्यहाँ	**tyahā̃** *there*		कहाँ	**kahā̃** *where?*

उति **uti** and उस्तो **usto** are alternative forms for *that much* and *like that* respectively.

Because कुन **kun** means *which?*, an enquiry that involves the use of कुन **kun** may use either the verb हो **ho** or the verb छ **cha**:

यो कुन देश हो ?	**yo kun deś ho?**	*Which country is this?*
यो देश नेपाल हो ।	**yo deś nepāl ho.**	*This country is Nepal.*
पसलमा कुन साबुन सस्तो छ ?	**pasalmā kun sābun sasto cha?**	*In the shop which soap is cheap?*
काठ्माडौंमा कुन होटेल राम्रो छ ?	**kāṭhmāḍaūmā kun hoṭel rāmro cha?**	*In Kathmandu, which hotel is good?*

Because कस्तो **kasto** means *like what?*, a question in which it is used usually asks for a 'describing' reply. So, an enquiry that involves the use of कस्तो **kasto** usually uses the verb छ **cha**:

यो देश कस्तो छ ?	**yo deś kasto cha?**	*What is this country like?*
यो देश राम्रो छ ।	**yo deś rāmro cha.**	*This country is good.*
यो पानी कस्तो छ?	**yo pānī kasto cha?**	*What is this water like?*
यो पानी सफा छ ।	**yo pānī saphā cha.**	*This water is clean.*

However, it is also possible to ask *what kind of country is this?*, in which case you are asking for a 'defining' statement and calling for the use of हो **ho**:

यो कस्तो देश हो?	**yo kasto deś ho?**	*What kind of country is this?*
यो धेरै धनी देश हो ।	**yo dherai dhanī deś ho.**	*This is a very rich country.*
यो कस्तो पानी हो?	**yo kasto pānī ho?**	*What kind of water is this?*
यो मैलो पानी हो ।	**yo mailo pānī ho.**	*This is dirty water.*

14 The simple sentence

You have no doubt realised by now that Nepali has a different word order from English. In Nepali, the natural place for the verb is at the end of a sentence. Simply, an English speaker says *I am English,* while a Nepali speaker says:

| म नेपाली हूँ । | **ma nepālī hū̃.** | *'I Nepali am'.* |
| तपाई विद्यार्थी हुनुहुन्छ । | **tapāī vidyārthī hunuhuncha.** | *'You student are'.* |

Unless there is some good reason for it not to, a Nepali sentence will always begin with a subject and end with a verb: everything else will come in between. If a change is made to this word order it has an effect on the meaning of a sentence: it may emphasise something, or express hesitation or doubt:

| नेपाली हूँ म । | **nepālī hū̃ ma.** | *I'm a <u>Nepali</u>, I am!* |
| विद्यार्थी हुनुहुन्छ तपाई ? | **vidyārthī hunuhuncha tapāī̃?** | *Are you a <u>student,</u> then?* |

4 Near and far

Salil has just arrived in town and he needs to visit the bank and the post office. He asks a passer-by for directions.

सलील ए भाइ, नमस्ते ! यहाँ हुलाक घर छ ?
Salīl **e bhāi, namaste! yahā̃ hulāk ghar cha?**
Oh (younger) brother, hello! Is there a post office here?

रने छ दाइ ।
Rane **cha dāi.**
    Yes, (elder) brother.

सलील यहाँबाट हुलाक घर कति टाढा छ ?
Salīl **yahā̃bāṭa hulāk ghar kati ṭāḍhā cha?**
    How far is the post office from here?

रने धेरै टाढा छैन, नजिकै छ दाइ ।
Rane **dherai ṭāḍhā chaina, najikai cha dāi.**
    It's not very far, it's quite near, (elder)
    brother.

सलील त्यहाँ बैंक पनि छ ?
Salīl **tyahā̃ baĩk pani cha?**
    Is there a bank there too?

रने छ, बैंक पनि छ । ठूलै छ ।
Rane **cha, baĩk pani cha. ṭhūlai cha.**
    Yes, there's a bank too. It's quite big.

सलील हुलाक घरदेखि बैंक धेरै टाढा छ ?
Salīl **hulāk ghardekhi baĩk dherai ṭāḍhā cha?**
    Is the bank very far from the post office?

रने अहँ, त्यो पनि नजिकै छ । बैंक र हुलाक घर यहाँबाट
    टाढा छैन ।
Rane **ahã, tyo pani najikai cha. baĩk ra hulāk**
    ghar yahā̃bāṭa ṭāḍhā chaina.
    No, that's quite near too. The bank and the
    post office are not far from here.

सलील आज बैंक र हुलाक घरमा भीड छ ?
Salīl **āja baĩk ra hulāk gharmā bhīḍ cha?**
    Are the bank and the post office crowded today?

रने छैन दाइ । आज बैंक र हुलाक घर बन्द छन् । आज सरकारी बिदा छ ।
Rane **chaina dāi. āja baĩk ra hulāk ghar banda chan. āja**
    sarkārī bidā cha.
    No, (elder) brother. Today the bank and the post office
    are closed. There's a government holiday today.

भाइ **bhāi** *(younger) brother*
यहाँ **yahā̃** *here*
हुलाक घर **hulāk ghar** *post office*
दाइ **dāi** *(elder) brother*
यहाँबाट **yahā̃bāṭa** *from here*
कति **kati** *how much?*
टाढा **ṭāḍhā** *far, distant*
नजिकै **najikai** *quite near*
त्यहाँ **tyahā̃** *there*

बैंक **baĩk** *bank*
हुलाक घरदेखि **hulāk ghardekhi** *from the post office*
आज **āja** *today*
भीड **bhīḍ** *crowd*
घर **ghar** *house, home, building*
बन्द **banda** *shut, closed*
सरकारी **sarkārī** *governmental*
बिदा **bidā** *holiday*

Grammar

15 Postpositions: -मा -mā, -बाट -bāṭa, -देखि -dekhi

In English there is a category of words called prepositions: *to, at, in, from, for,* etc. These are called prepositions because they come *in front of* the noun or pronoun they are acting upon: *to the man, at the house, from London,* etc. The Nepali equivalents of these words are called postpositions because they come *after* the noun they are acting upon: *the man to, the house at, London from.* In writing they must always be joined to the end of the noun or pronoun.

The postposition -मा **mā** means *in, at* or *on:*

नेपालमा	**nepālmā**	*in Nepal*
टेबुलमा	**ṭebulmā**	*on the table*
बैंकमा	**baĩkmā**	*at the bank*

Two other postpositions that are used in **Dialogue 4** are -बाट -**bāṭa** *from* and -देखि -**dekhi** *from, since.* Both of these mean *from,* but only -देखि -**dekhi** can also be used with expressions of time:

काठ्माडौंबाट	**kāṭhmāḍaũbāṭa**	*from Kathmandu*
लण्डनदेखि	**laṇḍandekhi**	*from London*
आजदेखि	**ājadekhi**	*from today*
हिजोदेखि	**hijodekhi**	*since yesterday*

If you need to ask how far away something is, you will use the adjective टाढा **ṭāḍhā** *distant* with one or other of these two postpositions. When stating or discussing distances, the word टाढा **ṭāḍhā** must usually be retained, even when you also mention some units or measures of distance.

भक्तपुरबाट काठ्मार्डौं कति	**bhaktapurbāṭa**	*How distant is*
टाढा छ ?	**kāṭhmāḍaũ kati**	*Kathmandu from*
	ṭāḍhā cha?	*Bhaktapur?*
भक्तपुरबाट काठ्मार्डौं आठ	**bhaktapurbāṭa**	*Kathmandu is eight*
माइल टाढा छ ।	**kāṭhmāḍaũ āṭh māil**	*miles distant from*
	ṭāḍhā cha.	*Bhaktapur.*

If you wish to say that something has been the case for a certain period of time, and still is the case, you should use -देखि -**dekhi** with the present tense of the verb:

म हिजोदेखि नेपालमा छु।	**ma hijodekhi**	*I am in Nepal since*
	nepālmā chu.	*yesterday.*
अबदेखि म नेपालमा छु।	**abadekhi ma**	*From now on I am*
	nepālmā chu.	*in Nepal.*

Units of distance

Nepalis think in terms of both miles and kilometres, though the metric system is gradually becoming prevalent:

आठ माइल	**āṭh māil**	*eight miles*
नौ किलोमिटर	**nau kilomiṭar**	*nine kilometres*

In the hills of Nepal, a traditional measure of distance is the कोस **kos**, which is usually interpreted to mean *two miles*, or sometimes *half an hour's walk*. Foreigners walking in Nepal often find the कोस **kos** an elusive concept, perhaps because it measures distance partly in terms of the time taken to travel it, and because Nepalis are naturally much more adept at negotiating the steep ups and downs of their landscape than foreign visitors.

16 Using relationship terms to address people

It is common practice in Nepali for people to address others, whether they are strangers, friends, or acquaintances, by using a relationship term. Obviously, you need to judge which term is appropriate for the person you are addressing, but it is perfectly acceptable to address a male younger than yourself as भाइ **bhāi** *younger brother,* or a female who is older than you as दिदी **didī** *elder sister.* Elderly people may be addressed as बा **bā** *father* or आमा **āmā** *mother;* no stigma is attached to age in Nepal. These terms are often also added to people's personal names in conversation: अमिता दिदी **Amitā didī,** सलील भाइ **Salīl bhāi.** A chart of kinship terminology is given in the Appendices at the back of this book.

नेपाली परिवार **nepālī parivār** *A Nepali family*

1 To be addressed and referred to with High pronouns

बुवा, बा	**buvā** or **bā**	*father*
आमा, मा	**āmā** or **mā**	*mother*
बुवा-आमा, बा-आमा	**buvā-āmā** or **bā-āmā**	*mother and father*
हजुरबा, बाजे	**hajurbā** or **bāje**	*grandfather*
हजुरआमा, बज्यै	**hajurāmā** or **bajyai**	*grandmother*

2 To be addressed with High pronouns and usually referred to with High (male) or Middle (female) pronouns

स्वास्नी, श्रीमती	**svāsnī** or **śrīmatī** *	*wife*
लोग्ने, श्रीमान्	**logne** or **śrīmān** *	*husband*
दिदी	**didī**	*elder sister*
दाइ, दाज्यू, दाजु	**dāi** or **dājyū** or **dāju**	*elder brother*

3 To be addressed with Middle pronouns and usually referred to with Low (male) and Middle (female) pronouns

भाइ	**bhāi**	*younger brother*
बहिनी	**bahinī**	*younger sister*
छोरा	**chorā**	*son*
छोरी	**chorī**	*daughter*
छोराछोरी	**chorāchorī**	*sons and daughters*
नाति	**nāti**	*grandson*
नातिनी	**nātinī**	*granddaughter*
नाति-नातिनी	**nāti-nātinī**	*grandchildren*

*When referring to a known individual, the foreign speaker should use the honorific terms श्रीमान् **śrīmān** and श्रीमती **śrīmatī**. लोग्ने **logne** and स्वास्नी **svāsnī** are used to refer to husbands and wives more generally. In rural areas, some people use the words जोई **joī** or बूढी **būḍhī** ('old woman') for *wife* and पोई **poī** or बूढा **būḍhā** ('old man') for *husband*.

✔ **EXERCISE 6** Translate the following sentences into Nepali, referring to the box above for the correct levels of politeness when choosing which form of the verb to use.

1 Younger brother is at school.
2 Elder brother is in Darjeeling.
3 Elder sister is at Mahendra Mahāvidyālay.
4 Tomorrow mother and father are at home.
5 There are many brothers and sisters in the family.

☑ **EXERCISE 7** Convert the affirmative Nepali sentences you have completed for Exercise 6 into negative statements, by changing the forms of the verbs.

☑ **EXERCISE 8** Here is a simple map of the part of Nepal in which you are staying, showing:

1	सरस्वती मन्दिर	**sarasvatī mandir**	Saraswati temple
2	बजार	**bajār**	marketplace
3	पसलहरू	**pasalharū**	shops
4	बैंक	**baĩk**	bank
5	हुलाक घर	**hulāk ghar**	post office
6	प्रहरी थाना	**praharī thānā**	police station
7	होटेल	**hoṭel**	hotel
8	डाँफे लज	**ḍãphe laj**	Danphe Lodge
9	सेती खोला	**setī kholā**	Seti Khola (a river)
10	सडक	**saḍak**	road

Referring to the map, and assuming that you are staying in the lodge, answer the following questions in Nepali:

१ प्रहरी थाना नजिक छ ?	**praharī thānā najik cha?**
२ हुलाक घर टाढा छ ?	**hulāk ghar ṭāḍhā cha?**
३ लजबाट बजार कति टाढा छ ?	**lajbāṭa bajār kati ṭāḍhā cha?**
४ बजारमा के के छ ?	**bajārmā ke ke cha?**
५ प्रहरी थाना कहाँ छ ?	**praharī thānā kahã cha?**
६ सरस्वती मन्दिर बजारबाट कति टाढा छ ?	**sarasvatī mandir bajārbāṭa kati ṭāḍhā cha?**

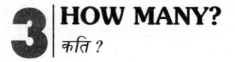

3 HOW MANY?

कति ?

In this unit you will learn how to:

■ count and enumerate people, things and units
■ talk about portable possessions

5 Students at the language school

The Minister for Education is visiting a school and is asking the teacher
how many students are studying each language.

मन्त्री नेपाली कक्षामा कतिजना विद्यार्थीहरू छन् ?
mantrī **nepālī kakṣāmā katijanā vidyārthīharū chan?**
How many students are there in the Nepali class?

शिक्षक दसजना विद्यार्थी छन् । पाँचजना केटा र पाँचजना केटी ।
śikṣak **dasjanā vidyārthī chan. pā̃cjanā keṭā ra pā̃cjanā keṭī.**
There are ten students. Five boys and five girls.

मन्त्री ए । अनि अँग्रेजी कक्षामा कतिजना विद्यार्थीहरू छन् ?
mantrī **e. ani ā̃grejī kakṣāmā katijanā vidyārthīharū chan?**
Oh. And how many students are there in the English class?

शिक्षक त्यो कक्षा अलि ठूलो छ । नौजना केटा र दसजना केटी छन् । जम्मा उन्नाइसजना
विद्यार्थीहरू छन् ।
śikṣak **tyo kakṣā ali ṭhūlo cha. naujanā keṭā ra dasjanā keṭī chan.
jammā unnāisjanā vidyārthīharū chan.**
*That class is quite big. There are nine boys and ten girls. All
together there are 19 students.*

मन्त्री नेपाली कक्षामा विदेशीहरू मात्रै छन् ?
mantrī **nepālī kakṣāmā videśīharū matrai chan?**
Are there only foreigners in the Nepali class?

शिक्षक विदेशीहरू मात्रै छन् मन्त्रीज्यू । तीनजना चिनियाँ, पाँचजना अँग्रेज, र दुईजना
जर्मन छन् ।
śikṣak **videśīharū mātrai chan mantrījyū. tīnjanā ciniyā̃, pā̃cjanā
ā̃grej, ra duījanā jarmaṇ chan.**
*There are only foreigners, Minister. Three Chinese, five
English and two Germans.*

मन्त्री **mantrī** *minister*
कक्षा **kakṣā** *class*
मा **mā** *in*
कतिजना **katijanā** *how many?*
दसजना **dasjanā** *ten*
पाँचजना केटा **pā̃cjanā keṭā** *five boys*
पाँचजना केटी **pā̃cjanā keṭī** *five girls*

नौजना केटा **naujanā keṭā** *nine boys*
दसजना केटी **dasjanā keṭī** *ten girls*
जम्मा **jammā** *all together, in total*
उन्नाइसजना **unnāisjanā** *19*
विदेशीहरू **videśīharū** *foreigners*
मात्रै **mātrai** *only*
मन्त्रीज्यू **mantrījyū** *form of address for a minister*

Grammar

17 The Nepali numerals

The Nepali numerals are very similar to the Hindi numerals, with only a few exceptions. The system is complex, and it is necessary to learn each number from one to 100 as a separate item of vocabulary, though each group of ten has its own internal logic and it is occasionally possible to guess! The first ten numbers are given here, both on their own and with the classifier suffixes they often need to take (as explained below). You are advised to learn the numbers in sets of ten (see the appendices).

Numbers and numeral classifiers: summary

	number		+ human classifier	+ non-human classifier
1	१	एक **ek**	एकजना **ekjanā**	एउटा **euṭā**
2	२	दुई **duī**	दुईजना **duījanā**	दुइटा **duiṭā**
3	३	तीन **tīn**	तीनजना **tīnjanā**	तीनवटा **tīnvaṭā**
4	४	चार **cār**	चारजना **cārjanā**	चारवटा **cārvaṭā**
5	५	पाँच **pā̃c**	पाँचजना **pā̃cjanā**	पाँचवटा **pā̃cvaṭā**
6	६	छ **cha**	छजना **chajanā**	छवटा **chavaṭā**
7	७	सात **sāt**	सातजना **sātjanā**	सातवटा **sātvaṭā**
8	८	आठ **āṭh**	आठजना **āṭhjanā**	आठवटा **āṭhvaṭā**
9	९	नौ **nau**	नौजना **naujanā**	नौवटा **nauvaṭā**
10	१०	दस **das**	दसजना **dasjanā**	दसवटा **dasvaṭā**

18 Numbers of people

When you are using numbers to enumerate human nouns – i.e. words that represent people – you should add the classifier -जना **janā** to the end of the number. It is incorrect to say एक मान्छे **ek mānche** *one person:* the correct form is एकजना मान्छे **ekjanā manche.** If the number is plural, there is no need to add the plural suffix -हरू **-harū** to the noun, because the number already tells you that there is more than one person and therefore -हरू **-harū** is superfluous:

एकजना मान्छे	**ekjanā manche**	*one person*
दुईजना लोग्ने-मान्छे	**duïjanā logne-mānche**	*two men* (literally, husband-person)
तीनजना स्वास्नी-मानिस	**tīnjanā svāsnī-mānis**	*three women* (literally, wife-person)

The words मान्छे **mānche** and मानिस **mānis** are interchangeable, though the first is used more commonly. Both mean *person,* but unless qualified by the addition of स्वास्नी **svāsnī** (*woman/wife*) they can usually be taken to represent a male.

EXERCISE 9   Answer the following questions in Nepali on **Dialogue 5**:

नेपाली कक्षामा:   **nepālī kakṣāmā:**
१. कतिजना विद्यार्थीहरू छन् ?   **katijanā vidyārthīharū chan?**
२. कतिजना अँग्रेजहरू छन् ?   **katijanā ãgrejharū chan?**
३. कतिजना जर्मनहरू छन् ?   **katijanā jarmanharū chan?**
अँग्रेजी कक्षामा:   **ãgrejī kakṣāmā:**
४. कतिजना विद्यार्थीहरू छन् ?   **katijanā vidyārthīharū chan?**
५. कतिजना केटाहरू छन् ?   **katijanā keṭāharū chan?**
६. कतिजना केटीहरू छन् ?   **katijanā keṭīharū chan?**

6 Setting up the exam room

Poshan, a junior teacher, is setting up a room for an examination. Ramesh, the principal, comes to check that all is well.

रमेश   यो कोठामा कतिवटा टेबुल छन् ?
Ramesh   **yo koṭhāmā kativaṭā ṭebul chan?**
            How many tables are there in this room?

पोषण   दसवटा छन् हजुर ।
Poshan   **dasvaṭā chan hajur.**
            There are ten, sir.

रमेश   अनि कतिवटा मेच छन् ?
Ramesh   **ani kativaṭā mec chan?**
            And how many chairs are there?

पोषण	आठवटा मात्रै छन् ।
Poshan	āṭhvaṭā mātrai chan.
	There are only eight.

रमेश	ए। कक्षामा दसजना विद्यार्थी छन् , होइन ?
Ramesh	e. kakṣāmā dasjanā vidyārthī chan, hoina?
	Oh. There are ten students in the class, aren't there?

पोषण	हजुर, दसजना छन् । अर्को कोठामा दुई-चारवटा मेच छन् ।
Poshan	hajur, dasjanā chan. arko koṭhāmā duī-cārvaṭā mec chan.
	Yes, there are ten. There are a few chairs in the next room.

रमेश	ठीक छ । कलम र कागतहरू पनि ठीक छन् ?
Ramesh	ṭhīk cha. kalam ra kāgatharū pani ṭhīk chan?
	OK. Are the pens and papers OK too?

पोषण	हरेक टेबुलमा एउटा कलम र कागत छ हजुर ।
Poshan	harek ṭebulmā euṭā kalam ra kāgat cha hajur.
	On each table there is a pen and paper, sir.

कोठा **koṭhā** *room*	अर्को **arko** *other, next*
कतिवटा **kativaṭā** *how many?*	दुई-चारवटा **duī-cārvaṭā** *two or four* (= 'a few')
टेबुल **ṭebul** *table*	ठीक **ṭhīk** *fine, correct*
दसवटा **dasvaṭā** *ten*	कलम **kalam** *pen*
मेच **mec** *chair*	कागत **kāgat** *paper*
आठवटा **āṭhvaṭā** *eight*	हरेक **harek** *each, every*
मात्रै **mātrai** *only*	एउटा **euṭā** *one* or *a*

Grammar

19 Numbers of things

When you are using numbers to enumerate non-human nouns – i.e. animals and inanimate objects – you must always add the classifier -वटा **vaṭā** to the end of the number. It is incorrect to say चार किताब **cār kitāb** *four books*: the correct form is चारवटा **cārvaṭā kitāb**. Again, -हरू **-harū** is superfluous when the number is plural.

The classifier -वटा **vaṭā** is not pronounced as it is spelled: the correct pronunciation is 'auṭā'. It is added to the numbers in a rather less regular way than the classifier -जना **janā.** When it is added to एक **ek** *one*, the combination produces एउटा **euṭā**, pronounced and often spelled यौटा **yauṭā**, and when it is added to दुई **duī** *two* the combination produces दुइटा **duiṭā**, pronounced 'dwīṭā'. For obvious practical reasons, these two are used very commonly in everyday spoken Nepali.

एउटा किताब	**euṭā** ('yauṭā') **kitāb**	*one book*
दुइटा मेच	**duiṭā** ('dwīṭā') **mec**	*two chairs*

Perhaps because Nepali does not have an indefinite article *a*, एउटा **euṭā** is often used with human nouns, e.g. एउटा मान्छे **euṭā mānche** *one man* or *a man* to refer to a person about whom the speaker feels no need to be especially polite.

20 How many?

When you are asking the question *how many?* you must add one of the classifiers to the interrogative कति **kati**, the choice of classifier depending upon whether you are asking about people or other things. Because -जना **janā** can only be used to enumerate people and -वटा **vaṭā** can only be used to enumerate things and animals, the combination of a number plus a classifier can also be used on its own:

घरमा कतिजना मान्छे छन् ?	**gharmā katijanā** **mānche chan?**	*How many people are* *in the house?*
दसजना छन् ।	**dasjanā chan.**	*There are ten.*
घरमा कतिवटा कोठा छन् ?	**gharmā kativaṭā** **koṭhā chan?**	*How many rooms are* *there in the house?*
तीनवटा छन् ।	**tīnvaṭā chan.**	*There are three.*

However, when the question concerns units of measurement, कति **kati** can be used without a classifier suffix (see **Grammar 22**).

7 Kamal and Amrit

Kamal bumps into Amrit on the street. Kamal, an office worker, always has money to spare, while Amrit, a young student, is always penniless.

कमल	अहो अमृत भाइ !
Kamal	**aho Amṛt bhāi!**
	Oh, it's Amrit!
अमृत	नमस्कार कमल दाइ !
Amrit	**namaskār Kamal dāi!**
	Hello, Kamal!

कमल	नमस्कार ! अहिले कतातिर ?
Kamal	**namaskār! ahile katātira?**
	Hello! Where are you off to now?
अमृत	घरतिर ।
Amrit	**ghartira.**
	Home.
कमल	अनि हालखबर कस्तो छ ?
Kamal	**ani hālkhabar kasto cha?**
	And how are things?
अमृत	राम्रै छ ।
Amrit	**rāmrai cha.**
	Fine.
कमल	आज तिमीसँग पैसा छ ?
Kamal	**āja timīsãga paisā cha?**
	Do you have any money on you today?
अमृत	मसँग? अलिकति छ । एक मोहर मात्रै छ ।
Amrit	**masãga? alikati cha. ek mohar mātrai cha.**
	On me? I have a little. I have just one half-rupee.
कमल	केही छैन । आज मसित दस रुपियाँ छ ।
Kamal	**kehī chaina. āja masita das rupiyā̃ cha.**
	It doesn't matter. I've got ten rupees today.
अमृत	मसँग न पैसा छ न चुरोट छ । तपाईंसँग चुरोट छ ?
Amrit	**masãga na paisā cha na curoṭ cha. tapāĩsãga curoṭ cha?**
	I have neither money nor cigarettes. Do you have a cigarette?
कमल	छ, मसँग एक बट्टा याक चुरोट छ ।
Kamal	**cha, masãga ek baṭṭā yāk curoṭ cha.**
	Yes, I have a packet of Yak cigarettes.
अमृत	आहा, याक चुरोट राम्रो छ !
Amrit	**āhā, yāk curoṭ rāmro cha!**
	Oh, Yak cigarettes are good!
कमल	होइन, तिमी सानो केटा हौ । धूम्रपान खराब छ ।
Kamal	**hoina, timī sāno keṭā hau. dhūmrapān kharāb cha.**
	No, you are a small boy. Smoking is bad.

अहो **aho** (an exclamation of pleasure or surprise)
अहिले **ahile** *now*
कता **katā** *where, in which direction*
तिर **tira** *towards*
घरतिर **ghartira** *towards home*
हालखबर **hālkhabar** *news*
तिमीसँग **timīsāga** *with you*
पैसा **paisā** *money*
मसँग? **masāga?** *with me?*
एक मोहर **ek mohar** *one **mohar** (a half-rupee)*
केही छैन **kehī chaina** *it doesn't matter*
आज **āja** *today*
मसित **masita** *with me*
दस रुपियाँ **das rupiyā̃** *ten rupees*
चुरोट **curoṭ** *cigarette*
न... न... **na... na** *neither... nor...*
एक बट्टा **ek baṭṭā** *one packet*
आहा **āhā** (another exclamation of pleasure or surprise)
धूम्रपान **dhūmrapān** *smoking* (a rather highflown Sanskrit term)
खराब **kharāb** *bad*

Grammar

21 Possession of portable items

Nepali does not have a verb that is the equivalent of the English *to have* or *to own*, but establishes ownership and possession in different ways. The first way is used in relation to things that someone can carry around on his/her person. Often, these are things that are disposable or acquired temporarily: money, for instance, comes and goes, and items such as pens generally run out of ink and have to be discarded.

Possession is indicated by using either one of two postpositions that both have exactly the same meaning: *with.* The two words are -सँग **sāga** (sometimes spelt सङ्ग **saṅga**) and -सित **sita**. These are added directly on to nouns, names and pronouns:

केटासँग	**keṭāsāga**	or	केटासित	**keṭāsita** *with the boy*
कुमारसँग	**Kumārsāga**	or	कुमारसित	**Kumārsita** *with Kumar*
मसँग	**masāga**	or	मसित	**masita** *with me*

Having added one or other of these words to the possesser, all that is left to create a simple statement of possession is to state the thing possessed and end with the verb, which is always छ **cha** (because you are *locating* the possession on the person of the possessor):

त्यो मान्छेसँग दुई रुपियाँ छ ।	**tyo mānchesãga**	*That man has two*
	duī rupiyā̃ cha.	*rupees (on his person).*
ऊसँग एउटा कलम छ ।	**ūsãga euṭā kalam cha.**	*He has a pen*
		(on his person).

If the statement or question is about someone *not* possessing something, use the negative form of छ **cha**.

मसित पैसा छैन ।	**masita paisā chaina.**	*I don't have any money*
		(on my person).
गीतासँग साबुन छैन ।	**Gītāsãga sābun chaina.**	*Gita does not have any*
		soap (with her).

22 Using numbers without classifiers

When you are talking about sums of money, weights and measures, units of time, distances, or any other kind of measure or unit, there is no need to add a classifier to the numerals involved, or to use the plural suffix -हरू -**harū**. Nor is it correct to use the plural form of a verb when its subject is a plural numerical quantity.

Currency

The Nepali रुपियाँ **rupiyā̃** *rupee* consists of 100 पैसा **paisā**. There are also special words for a quarter-rupee (सुका **sukā**) and a half-rupee (मोहर **mohar** or मोहोर **mohor**), though these terms are gradually falling into disuse, partly as a result of inflation. The abbreviation for *rupee* is Rs. in Roman script, and रु॰ **ru.** in Devanāgarī. The Nepali rupee is sometimes referred to as the ने॰ रु॰ **ne. ru.** (short for नेपाली रुपियाँ **nepālī rupiyā̃**), to distinguish it from the भा॰ रु॰ **bhā. ru.** (भारतीय रुपियाँ **bhāratīya rupiyā̃**) or Indian rupee.

Prices and sums of money can be expressed in three different ways:

- by using numbers with the terms साढे **sāḍhe** *plus one half*, सवा **savā** *plus one quarter* and पौने **paune** *minus one quarter*. There are special words for *one and a half* and *two and a half*:

एक रुपियाँ	ek rupiyā̃	रु॰ १	Rs.1
सवा एक रुपियाँ	savā ek rupiyā̃	रु॰ १.२५	Rs.1.25
डेढ रुपियाँ	ḍeḍh rupiyā̃	रु॰ १.५०	Rs.1.50
पौने दुई रुपियाँ	paune duī rupiyā̃	रु॰ १.७५	Rs.1.75
दुई रुपियाँ	duī rupiyā̃	रु॰ २	Rs.2
सवा दुई रुपियाँ	savā duī rupiyā̃	रु॰ २.२५	Rs.2.25
अढाई रुपियाँ	aḍhāī rupiyā̃	रु॰ २.५०	Rs.2.50

- by expressing small sums in terms of मोहर **mohar** and सुका **sukā**:

एक रुपियाँ सुका	ek rupiyā̃ sukā	रु॰ १.२५	Rs.1.25
तीन मोहर	tīn mohar	रु॰ १.५०	Rs.1.50
तीन मोहर सुका	tīn mohar sukā	रु॰ १.७५	Rs.1.75
पाँच मोहर	pā̃c mohar	रु॰ २.५०	Rs.2.50
पाँच मोहर सुका	pā̃c mohar sukā	रु॰ २.७५	Rs.2.75

- by expressing sums in terms of रुपियाँ **rupiyā̃** and पैसा **paisā**:

एक रुपियाँ पच्चीस पैसा	ek rupiyā̃ paccīs paisā	रु॰ १.२५	Rs.1.25
एक रुपियाँ पचास पैसा	ek rupiyā̃ pacās paisā	रु॰ १.५०	Rs.1.50
दुई रुपियाँ पच्चीस पैसा	duī rupiyā̃ paccīs paisā	रु॰ २.२५	Rs.2.25
दुई रुपियाँ पचास पैसा	duī rupiyā̃ pacās paisā	रु॰ २.५०	Rs.2.50

Weights and capacities

There are two systems of measuring weights and quantities current in Nepal. One is the metric European system of kilogrammes (किलो **kilo**), the other is a more complicated traditional system based on capacity, which is particularly suited to measuring quantities of grain:

चौथाई	cauthāī	one quarter of a **mānā**
आधा माना	ādhā mānā	half a **mānā**
एक माना	ek mānā	one **mānā** (= 0.7 litres or 20 ounces)
एक कुरुवा	ek kuruvā	(= two **mānā**s)
एक पाथी	ek pāthī	(= eight **mānā**s)
एक मुरी	ek murī	(= 20 **pāthī**s)

Neither kind of unit requires the use of classifiers or plural suffixes:

एक किलो आलु	**ek kilo ālu**	*one kilo of potatoes*
पाँच किलो स्याउ	**pā̃c kilo syāu**	*five kilos of apples*
दुई माना चामल	**duī mānā cāmal**	*two mānās of rice*
एक पाथी दाल	**ek pāthī dāl**	*one pāthī of lentils*

Note that words such as *cup* and *pot* are also treated as measures of quantity in phrases such as the following, and therefore the numbers do not take a classifier:

| दुई कप चिया | **duī kap ciyā** | *two cups of tea* |
| एक पाट चिया | **ek pāṭ ciyā** | *one pot of tea* |

Units of time

एक सेकण्ड	**ek sekaṇḍ**	*one second*
एक छिन	**ek chin**	*one moment*
दुई मिनेट	**duī mineṭ**	*two minutes*
तीन घण्टा	**tīn ghaṇṭā**	*three hours*
चार दिन	**cār din**	*four days*
पाँच हप्ता	**pā̃c haptā**	*five weeks*
छ महिना	**cha mahinā**	*six months*
सात वर्ष	**sāt varṣa**	*seven years*

EXERCISE 10 Translate the following sentences into Nepali:

1 I have ten rupees and a packet of cigarettes.
2 We have been in Nepal for three weeks.
3 There are ten men, three women and five boys in the post office.
4 How much money do you have with you?
5 That Indian man has no money, but the Nepali boy has ten rupees.
6 The rich farmer has ten **pāthī**s of rice and ten kilogrammes of potatoes.
7 There are two cups of tea on each table.
8 The teacher has no books and the students have no pens.

EXERCISE 11 Write six Nepali sentences that define each of the people in the left-hand column as teachers, using an appropriate form of the verb *to be* from the right-hand column. Then do the same thing for each once again, but this time locating them at home.

भाइ	bhāi			हुनुहुन्छ	hunuhuncha
दिदी	didī			हो	ho
भाइहरू	bhāiharū	शिक्षक	śikṣak	छन्	chan
दाज्यू	dājyū	घरमा	gharmā	हुन्	hun
आमा	āmā			छ	cha
म	ma			छिन्	chin
				हुँ	hū̃
				छु	chu

EXERCISE 12   Translate into Nepali:

1 one week
2 two men
3 three books
4 four boys
5 five rupees
6 six chairs
7 seven women
8 eight classes
9 nine kilos
10 ten foreigners
11 two kilos
12 seven and a half kilos
13 three **pāthīs**
14 two and a half **mānās**
15 three rupees and seventy-five **paisā**
16 nine and a half rupees.

WHOSE IS IT?

कसको हो ?

In this unit you will learn how to:

■ talk about ownership
■ express and ask about knowledge
■ ask further questions

8 Jyoti's houses

Anil and Bijay are comparing notes on Jyoti, a new acquaintance.

अनिल	ज्योतिका कतिवटा घरहरू छन् ? तपाईलाई थाहा छ ?
Anil	**Jyotīkā kativaṭā gharharū chan? tapāīlāī thāhā cha?**
	How many houses does Jyoti have? Do you know?
बिजय	थाहा छ । ज्योतिका दुइटा घर छन् : एउटा सानो र एउटा ठूलो ।
Bijay	**thāhā cha. Jyotikā duiṭā ghar chan: euṭā sāno ra euṭā ṭhūlo.**
	I know. Jyoti has two houses: one big and one small.
अनिल	ए । ज्योतिको सानो घर कहाँ छ ?
Anil	**e. Jyotiko sāno ghar kahā̃ cha?**
	I see. Where is Jyoti's small house?
बिजय	ज्योतिको सानो घर बजारमा छ । त्यहाँ ज्योतिको बुवाको एउटा पसल पनि छ ।
Bijay	**Jyotiko sāno ghar bajārmā cha. tyahā̃ Jyotiko buvāko euṭā pasal pani cha.**
	Jyoti's small house is in the marketplace. Jyoti's father has a shop there too.
अनिल	अनि ज्योतिको ठूलो घर नि ?
Anil	**ani Jyotiko ṭhūlo ghar ni?**
	And what about Jyoti's big house?
बिजय	ज्योतिको ठूलो घर पोखराबाट दुई कोस टाढा छ ।
Bijay	**Jyotiko ṭhūlo ghar Pokharābāṭa duī kos ṭāḍhā cha.**
	*Jyoti's big house is two **kos** away from Pokhara.*

अनिल त्यो घर निक्कै ठूलो छ ?

Anil **tyo ghar nikkai ṭhūlo cha?**

Is that house very large?

बिजय हो, निक्कै ठूलो छ । त्यो घरमा दसवटा कोठा छन् ।

Bijay **ho, nikkai ṭhūlo cha. tyo gharmā dasvaṭā koṭhā chan.**

Yes, it's very large. There are ten rooms in that house.

अनिल ज्योतिको परिवार पनि ठूलो छ ?

Anil **Jyotiko parivār pani ṭhūlo cha?**

Is Jyoti's family large too?

बिजय ठूलो छैन, तर उनीहरू धनी छन् । हरेक शहरमा ज्योतिको बुवाका दुई-चारवटा पसल छन् ।

Bijay **ṭhūlo chaina, tara unīharū dhanī chan. harek śaharmā Jyotiko buvākā duī-cārvaṭā pasal chan.**

It's not large, but they are rich. Jyoti's father has several shops in every town.

अनिल अनि ज्योतिको दाजु-भाइ छैनन् ?

Anil **ani Jyotiko dāju-bhāi chainan?**

And does Jyoti not have any brothers?

बिजय छैनन् । ज्योतिकी एउटी बहिनी छ, कान्ती । हिजोआज उनी दार्जीलिङ्को एउटा स्कूलमा छिन् ।

Bijay **chainan. Jyotikī euṭī bahinī cha, Kāntī. hijoāja unī Darjeelingko euṭā skūlmā chin.**

No. He has one sister, Kanti. Nowadays she is at a school in Darjeeling.

ज्योतिका **Jyotīkā** *Jyoti's, belonging to Jyoti (plural possessions)*
थाहा **thāhā** *knowledge, information*
ज्योतिको **Jyotīko** *Jyoti's, belonging to Jyoti (single possession)*
निक्कै **nikkai** *very (used only with adjectives)*
दाजु-भाइ **dāju-bhāi** *brothers*
ज्योतिकी **Jyotikī** *Jyoti's, belonging to Jyoti (female possession)*
एउटी **euṭī** *one (feminine ending)*
हिजोआज **hijoāja** *nowadays*
दार्जीलिङ्ग **Dārjīliṅg** *Darjeeling*
स्कूल **skūl** *school*

🗝 Grammar

23   Ownership: -को -ko, -की -kī, -का -kā with nouns and names

Unless you are using -सँग -**sāga** or -सित -**sita** to talk about possessions that are 'with' an owner at the time, the particle -को -**ko** must be used to link an owner to a thing that is owned. The particle performs the same function, and occurs in the same place in a sentence or phrase, as the 'apostrophe s' ('s) in English, and can be attached to nouns and names in the same way:

| रामको किताब | **Rāmko kitāb** | *Ram's book* |
| सेतीको बुवा | **Setīko buvā** | *Seti's father* |

However, -को -**ko** behaves like an inflected adjective in that the vowel must change according to the number and gender of whatever is owned – to -**ī** when a female human noun is owned, and to -**ā** when the owned nouns are plural:

| रमेशकी आमा | **Rameśkī āmā** | *Ramesh's mother* |
| नेपालका गाउँहरू | **Nepālkā gaūharū** | *Nepal's villages* |

As in statements of possession using -सँग -**sāga** or -सित -**sita**, statements of ownership involve the use of the verb छ **cha**:

| रमेशका दुईजना दाजु छन् । | **Rameśkā duījanā dāju chan.** | *Ramesh has two elder brothers.* |
| बिन्दूको दाजु छैन । | **Bindūko dāju chaina.** | *Bindu does not have an elder brother.* |

However, if something is being identified as a belonging then it becomes necessary to use हो **ho** instead of छ **cha**:

| यो सानो घर ज्योतिको हो । | **yo sāno ghar Jyotiko ho.** | *This small house is Jyoti's.* |
| ऊ बिन्दूको दाजु होइन । | **ū Bindūko dāju hoina.** | *He is not Bindu's elder brother.* |

It is possible to use -को -**ko** in a string of ownerships:

ज्योतिको साथी	**Jyotiko sāthī**	*Jyoti's friend*
ज्योतिको साथीको बुवा	**Jyotiko sāthīko buvā**	*Jyoti's friend's father*
ज्योतिको साथीको बुवाको घर	**Jyotiko sāthīko buvāko ghar**	*Jyoti's friend's father's house*

| ज्योतिको साथीको बुवाको घरका झ्यालहरू | **Jyotiko sāthīko buvāko gharkā jhyālharū.** | *Jyoti's friend's father's house's windows* |

24 Words for and: र ra, अनि ani

So far you have met two different Nepali words that are both translated as *and*. र **ra** is used to link pairs or the members of a group of nouns, pronouns, or names:

| ज्योति, अम्बिका र राम | **Jyoti, Ambikā ra Rām** | *Jyoti, Ambika and Ram* |
| बैंक र हुलाक घर | **baĩk ra hulāk ghar** | *the bank and the post office* |

अनि **ani**, on the other hand, is used to mean *and* when we wish to introduce another topic or to ask an additional question: it can often mean *and then*. In spoken Nepali, a sentence can never begin with र **ra**, but it is possible to begin a sentence with अनि **ani**.

अनि बैंक कहाँ छ ?	**ani baĩk kahã cha?**	*And where is the bank?*
अनि ?	**ani?**	*And then? anything else?*
अनि तिमी को हौ ?	**ani timī ko hau?**	*And who are <u>you</u>?*

A third word for *and* that is used only in scholarly, formal or official contexts as a substitute for र **ra** is the Sanskrit loan तथा **tathā**.

25 *I know, you know*, etc. using थाहा **thāhā**

थाहा **thāhā**, often pronounced **thā**, means *knowledge* or *information*. The most common way to state that you know something is to say that the knowledge exists *for you* or *to you*, using the postposition -लाई **-lāī**, which means *to* or *for* :

मलाई थाहा छ ।	**malāī thāhā cha.**	*I know* ('to me there is knowledge').
तपाईलाई थाहा छैन ।	**tapāĩlāī thāhā chaina.**	*You do not know* ('to you there is not knowledge').
बिन्दूलाई पक्का थाहा छ ?	**Bindūlāī thāhā cha?**	*Does Bindu know for sure?* ('to Bindu is there certain knowledge?')

These questions and statements are frequently abbreviated:

थाहा छ ।	**thāhā cha.**	*I know.*
थाहा छ ?	**thāhā cha?**	*Do you know?*
थाहा छैन ।	**thāhā chaina.**	*I don't know.*

9 Ratan's motorcar

Subir and Anand have just spotted their friend Ratan driving past in a red car.

सुबीर रातो मोटरमा त्यो को हो ?
Subīr **rāto moṭarmā tyo ko ho?**
Who is that in the red car?

आनन्द रतन, होइन ?
Ānand **Ratan, hoina?**
It's Ratan, isn't it?

सुबीर हो, त्यो रतन हो ।
Subīr **ho, tyo Ratan ho.**
Yes, that's Ratan.

आनन्द त्यो रातो मोटर रतनजीको आफ्नो मोटर हो ?
Ānand **tyo rāto moṭar Ratanjīko āphno moṭar ho?**
Is that red car Ratanji's own car?

सुबीर होइन, रतनको साथीको मोटर हो ।
Subīr **hoina, Ratanko sāthīko moṭar ho.**
No, it's Ratan's friend's car.

आनन्द तपाईंको पनि मोटर छ ?
Ānand **tapāīko pani moṭar cha?**
Do you too have a car ?

सुबीर अहँ, मेरो मोटर छैन । तर मेरो दाज्यूको एउटा मोटर छ ।
Subīr **ahã, mero moṭar chaina. tara mero dājyūko euṭā moṭar cha.**
No, I don't have a car. But my elder brother has a car.

आनन्द तपाईंको दाज्यूको मोटर कस्तो छ ?
Ānand **tapāīko dājyūko moṭar kasto cha?**
What's your elder brother's car like?

सुबीर   दाज्यूको मोटर अलि पुरानो छ, तर राम्रो छ, एकदम राम्रो । तपाईंको मोटर छ कि छैन नि ?

Subīr   dājyūko moṭar ali purāno cha, tara rāmro cha, ekdam rāmro. tapaĩko moṭar cha ki chaina ni?

Elder brother's car is rather old, but it's nice, really nice. So do you have a car or not?

आनन्द   छैन! मेरो एउटा साइकल मात्रै छ ।

Ānand   chaina! mero euṭā sāikal mātrai cha.

No! I have only a bicycle.

रातो **rāto** *red*	साथी **sāthī** *friend*
मोटर **moṭar** *car*	एकदम **ekdam** *really, very*
आफ्नो **āphno** *own*	साइकल **sāikal** *bicycle*

EXERCISE 13   Answer the following questions about **Dialogue 9**:

१   रतनजीको आफ्नो मोटर छ ?   **Ratanjīko āphno moṭar cha?**
२   रातो मोटर रतनको हो ?   **rāto moṭar ratanko ho?**
३   सुबीरको आफ्नो मोटर छ ?   **Subīrko āphno moṭar cha?**
५   सुबीरको दाज्यूको मोटर छ कि छैन ?   **Subīrko dājyūko moṭar cha ki chaina?**

Grammar

26   Ownership using -को -ko, -की -kī, -का -kā with unchanged ('direct case') pronouns

The postposition -को -**ko** can be added to two kinds of pronouns in exactly the same way that it is added to nouns and names, i.e. without requiring any change to be made to these pronouns. The two categories are:

(i)   The most polite pronouns (तपाई **tapāĩ**, यहाँ **yahā̃**, वहाँ **vahā̃**, हजुर **hajur**),
(ii)   Plural pronouns that end in -हरू.

यहाँको शुभनाम के हो ?	**yahā̃ko śubhanām ke ho?**	*What is this person's name?* [*]
वहाँको काम के हो ?	**vahā̃ko kām ke ho?**	*What is his job?*
उनीहरूको लुगा अनौठो छ !	**unīharūko lugā anauṭho cha!**	*Their clothing is strange!*

*Using शुभनाम **śubhanām** *auspicious name* to ask a personal name is more polite than using नाम **nām**.

27 *My, your, our*

-को **-ko** cannot be added to the pronouns म **ma** *I*, तैँ **tã** *you*, तिमी **timī** *you* and हामी **hāmī** *we*. Instead, these four pronouns have special ownership ('genitive') forms:

म	**ma**	*I*	becomes	मेरो	**mero**	*my, mine*
तैँ	**tã**	*you*	becomes	तेरो	**tero**	*your, yours*
तिमी	**timī**	*you*	becomes	तिम्रो	**timro**	*your, yours*
हामी	**hāmī**	*we*	becomes	हाम्रो	**hāmro**	*our, ours*

मेरो नाम जेनी हो ।	**mero nām Jenī ho.**	*My name is Jenny.*
तिम्रो नाम सोनाम होइन, छिरिङ्ग हो ।	**timro nām Sonām hoina, Chiring ho.**	*Your name is not Sonam, it is Tsering.**
हाम्रो थर अधिकारी हो ।	**hāmro thar Adhikārī ho.**	*Our family name is Adhikari.*

* These are both Tibetan names, current among people who live along Nepal's northern border, and also among Tibetan refugees in Nepal. Nepali does not have a letter to represent the Tibetan sound **ts**, so it uses छ **ch** instead.

EXERCISE 14 Create sentences that state ownership, using the elements provided:

Owner	Quantity	Possession
E.g. I	2	houses
= मेरा दुइटा घर छन्	**merā duiṭā ghar chan**	*I have two houses*
1. Dhan Bahādur's wife	2	elder sisters
2. I	0	mother and father
3. My mother	4	grandchildren
4. They	0	sons and daughters
5. He (High)	9	cows (गाई **gāī**)
6. We	5	fat buffaloes (भैँसी **bhaĩsī**)

28 One's own: emphasising ownership using आफ्नो **āphno**

The word आफ्नो **āphno** means *own* and can be used with any of the possessive pronouns. It does not matter whether it is being used to mean *my own* or *your own* or anyone else's *own*; the word remains the same. It is an adjective, however, so its ending must change according to the number and gender of the thing or things owned:

मेरो आफ्नो साथी	**mero āphno sāthī**	*my own friend*
तपाईंका आफ्ना छोराछोरी	**tapāīkā āphnā chorāchorī**	*your own children*
अमिताकी आफ्नी बहिनी	**Amitākī āphnī bahinī**	*Amita's own younger sister*

To emphasise that the thing that is owned is the owner's very own possession and does not belong to anyone else, the ending of आफ्नो **āphno** is changed to **-ai**:

रमेशको आफ्नै साइकल ।	**Rameśko āphnai sāikal.**	*Ramesh's very own bicycle.*
अमिताकी आफ्नै बहिनी ।	**Amitākī āphnai bahinī.**	*Amita's very own younger sister.*
यिनीहरू मेरा आफ्नै छोराछोरी हुन्।	**yinīharū merā āphnai chorāchorī hun.**	*These are my own children.*

29 Asking questions: the use of कि ki

The word order of a question in Nepali is exactly the same as the word order of a statement: when spoken, the difference lies in the intonation; when written, the only difference between a statement and a question is the absence or presence of a question-mark. However, Nepali-speakers frequently end a question with the questioning word कि ? **ki?** which literally means *or...?* हो कि ? **ho ki ?** and छ कि ? **cha ki ?** mean *is it or...?* and *is there or...?*

| यो तपाईंको आफ्नो साइकल हो कि ? | **yo tapāīko āphno sāikal ho ki?** | *Is this your own bicycle, or...?* |
| तपाईंको घरमा साइकल छ कि ? | **tapāīko gharmā sāikal cha ki?** | *Is there a bicycle in your house, or...?* |

The question might also include the negative form of the verb, to mean *is it or isn't it?* or *is there or isn't there?*

चिया हो ?	**ciyā ho?**	*is it tea?*
चिया हो कि ?	**ciyā ho ki?**	*is it tea or...?*
चिया हो कि होइन ?	**ciyā ho ki hoina?**	*is it tea or not?*
चिया छ ?	**ciyā cha?**	*is there any tea?*
चिया छ कि ?	**ciyā cha ki?**	*is there any tea or...?*
चिया छ कि छैन ?	**ciyā cha ki chaina?**	*is there any tea or not?*

These last three questions carry the implication that if there is any tea the speaker would like to drink it. Similarly, a sentence such as:

तपाईंको घरमा नून छ कि ?**tapāīko gharmā**   *Is there salt in your*
                     nūn cha ki?   *house?*

suggests that the person asking the question is in need of salt.

EXERCISE 15   Translate into Nepali:

1 You (Middle) are my son's friend, aren't you? Is your name Gautam
   (**gautam**)?
2 Is your (Middle) friend's father's name Ganesh Man (**gaṇeś mān**)? Do
   you know or don't you?
3 His (High) name is Laksmi Nath (**lakṣmī nāth**). I know that.
4 My home is not far from here. Where is your (Middle) home?
5 Your (High) father is at the bank. Does your mother know?
6 Their (Middle) cows are in our field. Don't they know?
7 Our family name is Pokharel (**pokharel**). We are Brahmins.
8 This is not your (Middle) watch. It is my mother's.

EXERCISE 16   Write a simple account of the members of your
family, along the following lines:

  My name is... My home is in...
  In my family we are... people: (list the members of your family, using
  relationship terms).
  Next, give the following information about each member of your
  family:
  My elder sister's name is...
  She is in... (give the name of the town where she lives).
  Repeat this information for each member of your family.
  If any of your siblings is married, state the name of their husband
  or wife.

10 Whose book is this?

रश्मि   यो कसको किताब हो ?
Raśmi   **yo kasko kitāb ho?**
             Whose book is this?

प्रीति   मेरो विचारमा त्यो सूर्यकी छोरीको किताब हो ।
Prīti   **mero vicārmā tyo Sūryakī chorīko kitāb ho.**
             I think that is Surya's daughter's book.

रश्मि **Raśmi**	सूर्यकी छोरी छ र ? मलाई थाहा छैन । **Sūryakī chorī cha ra? malāī thāhā chaina.** *Does Surya have a daughter then? I don't know.*
प्रीति **Prīti**	मेरो विचारमा उनका एकजना छोरा र एकजना छोरी छन् । **mero vicārmā unkā ekjanā chorā ra ekjanā chorī chan.** *I think he has one son and one daughter.*
रश्मि **Raśmi**	छोरीको नाम के हो त ? **chorīko nām ke ho ta?** *What's the daughter's name then?*
प्रीति **Prīti**	थाहा छैन । **thāhā chaina.** *I don't know.*
रश्मि **Raśmi**	छोराको नाम के हो ? **chorāko nām ke ho?** *What's the son's name?*
प्रीति **Prīti**	उसको नाम गिरीश हो । **usko nām Girīś ho.** *His name is Girish.*
रश्मि **Raśmi**	अनि उसको उमेर कति हो ? थाहा छ ? **ani usko umer kati ho? thāhā cha?** *And how old is he? Do you know?*
प्रीति **Prīti**	उसको उमेर कति हो थाहा छैन । **usko umer kati ho thāhā chaina.** *I don't know how old he is.*
रश्मि **Raśmi**	ए ठीकै छ नि ! किताबमा गिरीशको नाम छ । यो किताब उसैको हो । **e ṭhīkai cha ni! kitābmā Girīśko nām cha. yo kitāb usaiko ho.** *Oh, it's OK. Girish's name is on the book. This book is his.*

कसको **kasko** *whose?*	उमेर **umer** *age*
विचार **vicār** *thought, opinion*	उसैको **usaiko** *his (and no-one else's)*
र ? **ra?** *indeed? then?*	

EXERCISE 17   Answer the following questions about **Dialogue 10**:

१	सूर्यका कतिजना छोरा-छोरी छन् ?	**Sūryakā katijanā chorā-chorī chan?**
२	प्रीतिको विचारमा सूर्यकी छोरी छ कि छैन ?	**Prītiko vicārmā Sūryako chorī cha ki chaina?**
३	सूर्यको छोराको नाम के हो ?	**Sūryako chorāko nām ke ho?**
४	अनि किताबमा कसको नाम छ ?	**ani kitābmā kasko nām cha?**

Grammar

30 Ownership using -को -ko, -की -kī, -का -kā with changed ('oblique case') pronouns

Nepali grammar has only two cases. A noun or pronoun is always in either the 'direct' case, which means that it remains as it appears in a dictionary, or the 'oblique' case, which means that its ending might need to change.

A word will always take the 'oblique case' when a postposition has been added to it; whether this means that its ending actually has to change depends on what the word is. Generally, nouns do not change in the oblique case, but certain pronouns do. When -को -ko is added to pronouns (except (i) the most polite forms, (ii) plurals ending in -हरू -harū and (iii) म ma, तैं tā, तिमी timī, and हामी hāmī – see **Grammar 26 and 27**), the pronouns have to be modified slightly, and are said then to have changed into the oblique case, from their original, unchanged direct case:

direct case		*oblique case*		+ को -ko		
ऊ	**ū**	उस	**us**	उसको	**usko**	*his/her*
यो	**yo**	यस	**yas**	यसको	**yasko**	*his/her/its*
त्यो	**tyo**	त्यस	**tyas**	त्यसको	**tyasko**	*his/her/its*
उनी	**unī**	उन	**un**	उनको	**unko**	*his/her* (polite)
यिनी	**yinī**	यिन	**yin**	यिनको	**yinko**	*his/her* (polite)
तिनी	**tinī**	तिन	**tin**	तिनको	**tinko**	*his/her* (polite)

The oblique forms of the pronouns यो **yo** *this* and त्यो **tyo** *that* are not pronounced exactly as they are spelled:

direct form		oblique form		pronunciation
यो	**yo**	यस	**yas**	'es'
त्यो	**tyo**	त्यस	**tyas**	'tes'

When the postposition -लाई **-lāī** is added to the oblique forms of यो **yo**, त्यो **tyo**, and ऊ **ū** the word is often pronounced as if the 's' has been lost and the 'l' has been doubled:

	spelling	pronunciation
यसलाई	**yaslāī**	'ellāī'
त्यसलाई	**tyaslāī**	'tellāī'
उसलाई	**uslāī**	'ullāī'

All of the pronouns in the box on page 67 must change to their oblique forms whenever a postposition is added to them. The examples given in the box show what happens when the postposition is -को **-ko**, but exactly the same changes are necessary when other postpositions are involved:

| उनलाई थाहा छैन । | **unlāī thāhā chaina.** | *S/he does not know.* |
| यसमा चिनी छ? | **yasmā cinī cha?** | *Is there (any) sugar in this?* |

An exception to this rule is the postposition -सँग **-sāga** *with*, which is always added to the unchanged ('direct case') form of a pronoun:

| ऊसँग पैसा छैन । | **ūsāga paisā chaina.** | *He has no money (on his person).* |

When यो **yo** and त्यो **tyo** are being used before a noun to mean *this* and *that*, they should take their oblique form if a postposition is added to the noun.

यो शहर	**yo śahar**	*this town*
becomes		
यस शहरमा	**yas śaharmā**	*in this town*
त्यो दिन	**tyo din**	*that day*
becomes		
त्यस दिनदेखि	**tyas dindekhi**	*since that day*

However, this is a rule that is often ignored in everyday spoken Nepali. It is particularly likely to be ignored if यो **yo** and त्यो **tyo** are separated from the noun they describe by another adjective or adjectives. The longer the following phrase becomes, the more permissible it is to use the direct form यो **yo** *this* instead of its oblique form यस **yas**:

In this town:	यस शहरमा	**yas śaharmā**
or	यो शहरमा	**yo śaharmā**
In this big town:	यस ठूलो शहरमा	**yas ṭhūlo śaharmā**
or	यो ठूलो शहरमा	**yo ṭhūlo śaharmā**
In this big old town:	यस ठूलो पुरानो शहरमा	**yas ṭhūlo purāno śaharmā**
or	यो ठूलो पुरानो शहरमा	**yo ṭhūlo purāno śaharmā**

यी **yī** *these* and ती **tī** *those* do not take oblique forms:

यी शहरहरू	**yī śaharharū**	*these towns*
यी शहरहरूमा	**yī śaharharūmā**	*in these towns*
ती घरहरू	**tī gharharū**	*those houses*
ती घरहरूबाट	**tī gharharūbāṭa**	*from those houses*

31 Interrogatives: कसको **kasko** *whose,* केको **keko** *of what,* कहाँको **kahā̃ko,** *of / from where?*

The Nepali word for *who?* is को ? **ko?**. When the -को **-ko** that links owner to owned is added to the को **ko** that means *who?*, the latter must change to its oblique form, which is कस **kas**:

को **ko** *who?*	+	-को **-ko** *'s*	=	कसको **kasko** *whose?*

कसको किताब	**kasko kitāb**	*whose book?*
कसका छोराहरू	**kaskā chorāharū**	*whose sons?*
कसकी बहिनी	**kaskī bahinī**	*whose sister?*

Most other interrogatives (e.g. के **ke** *what?*, कहाँ **kahā̃** *where?*) do not have an oblique form, so they do not change when -को **-ko** is added to them:

यो केको मासु हो ?	**yo keko māsu ho?**	*What kind of meat is this?*
त्यो कुखुराको मासु हो ।	**tyo kukhurāko māsu ho.**	*That is chicken's meat.*

In English it is said that a person is 'from' a particular place, if that is where that person resides or has his/her origin. In Nepali, the same expression uses the genitive -को **-ko**, instead of any word meaning *from:*

ऊ कहाँको मान्छे हो ?	**ū kahā̃ko mānche ho?**	*Where is he from?* (literally, 'he is a person of where?')
ऊ गोरखाको मान्छे हो ।	**ū Gorkhāko mānche ho.**	*He is from Gorkha.* (literally, 'he is a person of Gorkha').

| यो कहाँको चामल हो ? | yo kahāko cāmal ho? | *Where is this rice from?* |
| त्यो पोखराको चामल हो । | tyo Pokharāko cāmal ho. | *It is rice from Pokhara.* |

✔ EXERCISE 18 Create sentences that state ownership, observing grammatical rules to the letter and using the elements provided:

	Owner	Quantity	Possession
E.g.	he	2	house
	= उसका दुइटा घर छन्	**uskā duiṭā ghar chan**	*he has two houses*
1	That boy	2	houses
2	This big village	only 1	teashop
3	He (Low)	8	daughters
4	She (Middle)	4	sons
5	This man	many	friends
6	Who	0	friend?

5 | **WHAT DO YOU DO?**
तपाई के गर्नुहुन्छ ?

In this unit you will learn how to:

■ talk about what you and others do normally, habitually or in the near future

■ use simple adverbs

■ discuss times, days, and frequency

11 The cook and the pilot

Ravi is soon to marry Shailendra's younger sister, and the two men are meeting for the first time. Ravi's job takes him all over South Asia, while Shailendra is tied down to his work in a Kathmandu hotel. Ravi, who is very much Shailendra's elder, feels he knows more about the world than Shailendra, but Shailendra has the last word.

रवि तिमी शैलेन्द्र, होइनौ ?

शैलेन्द्र हजुर, म शैलेन्द्र । तपाई रविज्यू हुनुहुन्छ, होइन ?

रवि हो, म रवि ।

शैलेन्द्र तपाई कहाँ काम गर्नुहुन्छ, रविज्यू ?

रवि म आर॰ एन॰ ए॰ सी॰मा काम गर्छु । अनि तिमी नि ?

शैलेन्द्र म साँग्रिला होटेलमा काम गर्छु ।

रवि तिमी कहिलें काहीं नेपालबाहिर पनि जान्छौ ?

शैलेन्द्र अहँ । म कहिल्यै पनि बाहिर जाँदिन । म सधैं यहीं हुन्छु । तर तपाई सधैं बाहिर जानुहुन्छ, होइन ?

रवि अँ, अलि अलि घुम्छु । दिल्ली जान्छु, कलकत्ता जान्छु, ढाका जान्छु, कराँची जान्छु । कहिले काहीं दुवई पनि जान्छु ।

शैलेन्द्र तपाई के काममा बाहिर जानुहुन्छ ?

रवि म हवाई जहाजको पाइलट हुँ नि !

शैलेन्द्र लण्डन जानुहुन्न ?

रवि जाँदिन । धेरै जसो म भारत मात्रै जान्छु । धेरै विदेशी पर्यटकहरू हाम्रो विमानबाट नेपाल आउँछन् ।

शैलेन्द्र म पनि हाम्रो होटेलमा विदेशी पाहुनाहरूको लागि खाना पकाउँछु नि ।

रवि ए, तिमी भान्से हौ ?

शैलेन्द्र हो, म पाँच वर्षदेखि त्यस होटेलको भान्से हुँ ।

रवि ल, कस्तो राम्रो ! अबदेखि म हरेक शनिवार तिम्रो होटेलमा आउँछु र मीठो खाना खान्छु ।

शैलेन्द्र तर म यहाँ हुँदिन ! एक हप्तापछि म लण्डन जान्छु । त्यहाँ म एउटा नयाँ रेष्टुराँ खोल्छु ।

काम गर्नु *to work*	लण्डन *London*
आर॰ एन॰ ए॰ सी॰ *Royal Nepal Air Corporation*	धेरै जसो *usually*
होटेल *hotel*	भारत *India*
जानु *to go*	पर्यटक *tourist*
कहिले काहीं *sometimes*	विमान *flight*
बाहिर *outside*	आउनु *to come*
कहिल्यै पनि *never*	पाहुना *guest*
यहीं *right here*	-को लागि *for*
सधैं *always*	खाना *food*
हुनु *to be*	पकाउनु *to cook*
अलि अलि *a little*	भान्से *cook*
घुम्नु *to travel*	शनिवार *Saturday*
दिल्ली *Delhi*	मीठो *tasty*
कल्कत्ता *Calcutta*	खानु *to eat*
ढाका *Dhaka*	हप्ता *week*
कराँची *Karachi*	पछि *after*
दुबई *Dubai*	रेष्टुराँ *restaurant*
हवाई जहाज *aeroplane*	खोल्नु *to open*
पाइलट *pilot*	

Ravi	You're Shailendra, aren't you?
Shailendra	Yes, I'm Shailendra. You are Ravijyu, aren't you?
Ravi	Yes, I'm Ravi.
Shailendra	Where do you work, Ravijyu?
Ravi	I work at RNAC (the Royal Nepal Air Corporation). And you?
Shailendra	I work at the Shangri-la Hotel.
Ravi	Do you go outside Nepal sometimes too?
Shailendra	No. I never go outside. I am always here. But you always go outside, don't you?

Ravi	Yes, I travel a little. I go to Delhi, I go to Calcutta, I go to Dhaka, I go to Karachi. Sometimes I go to Dubai as well.
Shailendra	On what work do you go outside?
Ravi	I am an aeroplane pilot, you know!
Shailendra	Don't you go to London?
Ravi	No I don't. Usually I go only to India. Many foreign tourists come to Nepal by our flight.
Shailendra	I too cook food for the foreign guests in our hotel, you know.
Ravi	Oh, you're a cook?
Shailendra	Yes, I've been that hotel's cook for five years.
Ravi	There, how splendid! From now on I will come to your hotel every Saturday and eat good food.
Shailendra	But I shan't be here! After a week I go to London. There I will open a new restaurant.

Grammar

32 The dictionary form of verbs

A verb is a word that indicates the performance or occurrence of an action, or the existence of a state or condition. English verbs are words like *see, run, do, eat* and *hear*. So far, you have encountered the various forms of छ and हो that mean *am, is,* and *are*. These are all forms of the Nepali verb हुनु **hunu** *to be*.

The dictionary form of a Nepali verb always ends in -नु **-nu**. This -नु ending is attached to the 'verb base' – the part of the verb that distinguishes it from all other verbs.

For instance,

गर्नु **garnu** *to do* consists of verb base गर्- **gar-** + the dictionary form ending -नु **-nu**;

बस्नु **basnu** *to sit, to reside* consists of verb base बस्- **bas-** + the dictionary form ending -नु **-nu**;

बोल्नु **bolnu** *to speak* consists of verb base बोल्- **bol-** + the dictionary form ending -नु **-nu**,

and so on.

33 The habitual present tense

A tense is a set of forms of a verb which indicates what the relationship is between the time the verb is spoken or written and the time when its action takes place. That is: are you speaking or writing the verb after it has taken place, while it is taking place, or before it takes place? Most Nepali verbs have a full set of past, present and future tenses. The *habitual present* tense is used to make statements about habits or regular occurrences such as *I do, he lives, they eat, she takes*, etc. It can also be used to refer to the future: *I go tomorrow, they come next year, she arrives on Thursday*, etc.

The *habitual present* tense of all Nepali verbs consists of the verb base + a verb ending. (The verb bases introduced here are the present tense verb bases. As will be explained later on, there are also past tense bases.) Nasalisation is added between the base and ending of certain verbs. If the verb is affirmative (*I do, I go, I come*), its ending is one of the छ forms of हुनु *to be* as set out in **Grammar 11**. If the verb is negative (*I do not, I don't go, I don't come*), its ending will be -दैन् **dain** + the same ending taken by छ in the affirmative form of the verb. The only exception to this rule is the form of the verb taken by म, where -छु in the affirmative becomes -दिन **dina** in the negative:

Affirmative		Negative		
-छ	**-cha**	-दैन	**-daina**	(with ऊ, यो, त्यो)
-छु	**-chu**	-दिन	**-dina**	(with म)
-छस्	**-chas**	-दैनस्	**-dainas**	(with तँ)
-छौ	**-chau**	-दैनौ	**-dainau**	(with तिमी)
-छौं	**-chaũ**	-दैनौं	**-dainaũ**	(with हामी, हामीहरू)
-छन्	**-chan**	-दैनन्	**-dainan**	(with यी, ती, उनी, यिनी, तिनी, and the plural forms of उनी, यिनी and तिनी)

There are three categories of verb: C-verbs, V-verbs and VV-verbs. If the base of a verb ends in a consonant, it is a C-verb; if it ends in a vowel it is a V-verb and if it ends in two vowels it is a VV-verb:

Dictionary form			Base		Category
गर्नु	**garnu**	*to do*	गर्-	**gar-**	C-verb
बस्नु	**basnu**	*to sit, reside*	बस्-	**bas-**	C-verb
हुनु	**hunu**	*to be*	हु-	**hu-**	V-verb
खानु	**khānu**	*to eat*	खा-	**khā-**	V-verb
लिनु	**linu**	*to take*	लि-	**li-**	V-verb
आउनु	**āunu**	*to come*	आउ-	**āu-**	VV-verb
पिउनु	**piunu**	*to drink*	पिउ-	**piu-**	VV-verb

The way in which the verb base and the ending are joined together depends on which category the verb belongs to. All C-verbs behave in the same way as the verb गर्नु *to do,* in which the final consonant of the base forms a conjunct with the ending:

गर्नु garnu *to do*

		Affirmative			Negative	
singular						
म	गर् + -छु	=	गर्छु	गर्	+ -दिन =	गर्दिन
हामी, हामीहरू	गर् + -छौं	=	गर्छौं	गर्	+ -दैनौं =	गर्दैनौं
तँ	गर् + -छस्	=	गर्छस्	गर्	+ -दैनस्=	गर्दैनस्
तिमी, तिमीहरू	गर् + -छौ	=	गर्छौ	गर्	+ -दैनौ =	गर्दैनौ
ऊ, यो, त्यो (m.)	गर् + -छ	=	गर्छ	गर्	+ -दैन =	गर्दैन
उनी, यिनी, तिनी	गर् + -छन्	=	गर्छन्	गर्	+ -दैनन्=	गर्दैनन्
यी, ती						
उनीहरू, यिनीहरू, तिनीहरू						

In V-verbs, a 'half n' (ं) is infixed between the base and the ending in the affirmative form, and the vowel is nasalised in the negative form. This is an important spelling convention, though both affirmative and negative forms are pronounced as if there is an 'n' in the middle of the word:

जानु **jānu** *to go*

		Affirmative		Negative	
singular					
म	जा + ँ + -छु	= जान्छु	जा ँ + दिन	=	जाँदिन
हामी, हामीहरू	जा + ँ + -छौं	= जान्छौं	जा ँ + -दैनौं	=	जाँदैनौं
तैँ	जा + ँ + -छस्	= जान्छस्	जा ँ + दैनस्	=	जाँदैनस्
तिमी, तिमीहरू	जा + ँ + -छौ	= जान्छौ	जा ँ + दैनौ	=	जाँदैनौ
ऊ, यो, त्यो	जा + ँ + -छ	= जान्छ	जा ँ + दैन	=	जाँदैन
उनी, यिनी, तिनी यी, ती उनीहरू, यिनीहरू, तिनीहरू	जा + ँ + -छन्	= जान्छन्	जा ँ + दैनन्	=	जाँदैनन्

In VV-verbs, the second of the two vowels is nasalised before the ending is added:

आउनु **āunu** *to come*

		Affirmative		Negative	
singular					
म	आउ ँ + -छु	= आउँछु	आउ ँ + -दिन	=	आउँदिन
हामी, हामीहरू	आउ ँ + -छौं	= आउँछौं	आउ ँ + -दैनौं	=	आउँदैनौं
तैँ	आउ ँ + -छस्	= आउँछस्	आउ ँ + -दैनस्	=	आउँदैनस्
तिमी, तिमीहरू	आउ ँ + -छौ	= आउँछौ	आउ ँ + -दैनौ	=	आउँदैनौ
ऊ, यो, त्यो	आउ ँ + -छ	= आउँछ	आउ ँ + -दैन	=	आउँदैन
उनी, यिनी, तिनी यी, ती उनीहरू, यिनीहरू, तिनीहरू	आउ ँ + -छन्	= आउँछन्	आउ ँ + -दैनन्	=	आउँदैनन्

With the High pronouns (तपाई, वहाँ, यहाँ, हजुर) the verbs behave differently. The base is simply the dictionary form ending in -नु, and the affirmative and negative endings are -हुन्छ **huncha** and -हुन्न **hunna** respectively. The verbs remain exactly the same in the singular and the plural.

High forms

गर्नु **garnu** *to do*

Affirmative			Negative		
गर्नु + -हुन्छ	=	गर्नुहुन्छ	गर्नु + -हुन्न	=	गर्नुहुन्न

आउनु **āunu** *to come*

Affirmative			Negative		
आउनु + -हुन्छ	=	आउनुहुन्छ	आउनु + -हुन्न	=	आउनुहुन्न

34 Using the habitual present tense

The habitual present tense is used

■ for habitual actions in the present:

| म पोखरामा काम गर्छु । | *I work in Pokhara.* |
| उनीहरू नेपालमा बस्छन् । | *They live in Nepal.* |

■ to describe facts or situations that are regularly or generally true:

| दार्जीलिङ्गको चिया मीठो हुन्छ । | *Darjeeling tea is good-tasting.* |
| नेपालका धेरै किसानहरू गरीब हुन्छन् । | *Many of Nepal's farmers are poor.* |

■ for actions that are going to occur at a specific time, usually in the near future:

| भोलि म लण्डन जान्छु । | *Tomorrow I (shall) go to London.* |
| म एक घण्टापछि तपाईंलाई भन्छु । | *After an hour I shall tell you.* |

The habitual present tense of हुनु can be used in place of the हो and छ forms, in order to create an important difference of meaning. Compare the following four sentences:

म यहाँ छु ।   *I am here.*
This is a simple statement of fact and therefore it needs nothing more than the simple present tense छ.

म यहाँ हुन्छु ।   *I am here.*
This means *I am here (on a regular basis)* or *I shall be here.*

आज म यहाँ छु ।   *I am here today.*
Again, this is a simple statement of fact and therefore it needs nothing more than the simple present tense छ.

आज म यहाँ हुन्छु ।   *I am here today.*
This implies that I am regularly here on this particular day: *this is where I am on this day of the week* or that this is a statement about the future: *I shall be here today.*

Any sentence that is in the present tense and uses an adverb such as *usually, always, every day, monthly, often*, etc. must use this tense:

| म हरेक दिन अफिसमा हुन्छु । | *I am in the office every day.* |
| ऊ सधैं त्यहाँ हुन्छ । | *He is always there.* |

35 धेरै जसो *usually*

धेरै जसो is a combination of धेरै *much, many* with जसो *similarly.* Therefore the phrase means, literally, *like much* or *like many,* and is used to mean *mostly* or *usually:*

ऊ धेरै जसो कुन रेष्टुराँमा भात खान्छ ?	*In which restaurant does he usually eat?**
नेपालीहरू धेरै जसो हिन्दू हुन्छन् ।	*Nepalis are mostly Hindus.*

* भात *rice* is virtually a synonym for *food* in Nepali.

36 मात्रै *only,* पनि *also, too, even*

मात्रै (and occasionally its non-emphasised form मात्र) is used to mean much the same thing as the English word *only,* but it comes after the noun or pronoun it qualifies in a sentence:

म मात्रै भारत जान्छु ।	*Only I go to India* (I am the only one who goes to India).
म भारत मात्रै जान्छु ।	*I go only to India* (India is the only place I go to).
ऊ मात्रै भात खान्छ ।	*Only he eats rice* (he is the only one who eats rice).
ऊ भात मात्रै खान्छ ।	*He eats only rice* (rice is the only thing he eats).

The first meaning of पनि is *too* or *also:*

म पनि भारत जान्छु ।	*I too go to India* (as well as other people).
म भारत पनि जान्छु ।	*I go to India too* (as well as to other countries).
ऊ पनि भात खान्छ ।	*He too eats rice* (as well as other people).
ऊ भात पनि खान्छ ।	*He eats rice too* (as well as other foods).

The second meaning of पनि is *even,* especially when it is used in negative statements:

घरमा भात पनि छैन ।	*There isn't even any rice in the house.*
मसँग एक रुपियाँ पनि छैन ।	*I don't have even one rupee.*
तिम्रो घरमा मूसा पनि भोको हुन्छ ।	*In your house even a mouse is hungry.*

37 कहिले ? *when?,* कहिले काहीं *sometimes,* कहिल्यै पनि *never*

कहिले is primarily an interrogative word meaning *when?*

तपाई भारत कहिले जानुहुन्छ ?	*When do you/will you go to India?*
उनीहरू बजार कहिले जान्छन् ?	*When do they/will they go to the market?*

Two very useful two-word phrases that include कहिले and its emphasised form कहिल्यै are: कहिले काहीं *sometimes,* and कहिल्यै पनि *never.* The first is usually only used in affirmative statements, the second can be used only in negative statements; both can form part of a question:

Q तिमी कहिले काहीं नेपाल जान्छौ?   *Do you go to Nepal sometimes?*
A अहँ, म कहिल्यै पनि जाँदिन ।   *No, I never go.*

Q वहाँ कहिल्यै पनि त्यहाँ जानुहुन्न ?   *Does he never go there?*
A कहिल्यै पनि जानुहुन्न तर कहिले   *He never goes, but sometimes I go.*
 काहीं म जान्छु ।

38   Modes of transport

The postposition -बाट, despite its primary meaning of *from,* is also used to mean *by* in connection with modes of transport:

वहाँ साइकलबाट आउनुहुन्न ।   *He does not come by bicycle.*
सुरेश ट्याक्सीबाट घर जाँदैन, बसबाट   *Suresh doesn't go home by taxi,*
 जान्छ ।   *he goes by bus.*

39   New postpositions: -पछि *after,* -सम्म *up to,* -को लागि *for*

The single-word postpositions -पछि *after* and -सम्म *up to, until* (pronounced **samma**) are used in exactly the same way as other simple postpositions:

त्यसपछि   *after that*
दुई बजेपछि   *after 2 o'clock*
भोलिसम्म   *until tomorrow*
पोखरासम्म   *as far as Pokhara*

-सम्म is often used in phrases that also contain either -बाट *from* or -देखि *from, since* (do not forget that only -देखि can be used with expressions of time to mean *since*):

उनी दिल्लीदेखि काठमाडौंसम्म हवाई   *She goes from Delhi to*
 जहाजबाट जान्छिन् ।   *Kathmandu by plane.*
वहाँ दुई बजेदेखि छ बजेसम्म घरमा हुनुहुन्छ । *From two o'clock until*
          six o'clock he is at home.
तिनीहरू मेरो घरसम्म मात्रै आउँछन् ।   *They only come as far as my house.*

-को लागि is one of a small number of two-word postpositions that begin with the ownership suffix -को. It means *for,* in the sense of *for the sake of* or *intended for:*

ऊ मेरो बुवाको लागि खाना पकाउँछ ।   *He cooks food for my father.*
यो किताब उसको लागि हो ।   *This book is for him.*
तिमी मेरो लागि के गर्छौ ?   *What do you do for me?*

EXERCISE 19   Translate into Nepali:

1 We won't go to the market today. There isn't even one rupee in the
   house.
2 What work does Rāju do? He works in the Nepal Rāṣṭra Bank. His
   elder brother works there too.
3 Where do you (High) live? Nowadays I live in Kathmandu.
4 Does your (High) younger brother go to the office by taxi? No, he goes
   by bus.
5 People from Darjeeling usually speak good Nepali.

EXERCISE 20   Construct sentences along the following lines:

Subject	Time	Place	Verb
1 म	every day	Kathmandu	go.
2 उनीहरू	usually	in Pokhara	live.
3 तिमी	always	in father's shop	speak(बोल्नु) Nepali.
4 हामीहरू	nowadays	in Ram's office	work.
5 ऊ	never	in school	speak English.
6 त्यो मान्छे	after one week	London	goes.

12 Women in the villages

Anne, a Nepali-speaking British woman who works in Kathmandu, is
making her first visit to rural Nepal. She is now on familiar terms with
Shanti, who lives in the village where she is staying. Unusually for a
Nepali woman of her age, Shanti is unmarried.

एन   तिमी धेरै जसो कति बजे उठ्छ्यौ ?

शान्ती   म धेरै जसो छ बजे उठ्छु । तर मेरी भाउज्यू चार बजेतिर उठ्छिन् ।

एन   किन त्यति बिहानै उठ्छिन् ? चार बजेतिर अँध्यारो नै हुन्छ, होइन ?

शान्ती   अँध्यारै हुन्छ, जाडो पनि हुन्छ ! भाउज्यू उठ्छिन् र धारातिर जान्छिन् । त्यसपछि उनी
            घरका सबै मानिसको लागि चिया पकाउँछिन् ।

एन   तर तिमीलाई सजिलो छ । बिहान काम छैन, होइन ?

शान्ती   म यहाँ बा-आमाको घरमा बस्छु नि, मेरो भागमा घरको काम धेरै हुँदैन ।

एन अनि तिम्रो दाज्यू कति बजेतिर उठ्नुहुन्छ नि ?

शान्ती वहाँ सात बजेसम्म सुत्नुहुन्छ । त्यसपछि उठ्नुहुन्छ, हातमुख धुनुहुन्छ, चिया खानुहुन्छ
र खेततिर जानुहुन्छ ।

एन खेतमा तिम्रो दाज्यू एक्लै जानुहुन्छ ?

शान्ती होइन, वहाँ बुवा र भाइसँग जानुहुन्छ ।

एन उनीहरू बेलुका मात्रै फर्कन्छन् कि ?

शान्ती होइन, एघार बजेपछि गाउँका सबै लोग्नेमान्छेहरू खेतबाट फर्कन्छन् । अनि साढे एघार
बजेतिर भात खान्छन् ।

एन सधैं स्वास्नी-मानिसहरू भात पकाउँछन् कि ?

शान्ती भात पकाउनु सधैं स्वास्नी-मानिसहरूको काम हुन्छ ।

एन लोग्नेमान्छेहरू कहिल्यै पनि भात पकाउँदैनन् ?

शान्ती कहाँ लोग्नेमान्छेहरू भात पकाउँछन् ? पकाउँदैनन्, हाम्रो घरमा त्यो पनि भाउज्यूको
काम हुन्छ !

एन तिमीहरू बेलुका पनि भात खान्छौ ?

शान्ती हो । हामीहरू बिहान बेलुका दिनको दुई पटक भात खान्छौं ।

एन तिम्रो भाउज्यूको जिन्दगी कति गाह्रो छ !

शान्ती बिहापछि स्वास्नी-मानिसहरूको जिन्दगी गाह्रो हुन्छ ।

एन अनि तिमी बिहा गर्दिनौ त ?

शान्ती अहँ, म कहिल्यै पनि बिहा गर्दिन ।

कति बजे *at what time?*	सजिलो *easy*
उठ्नु *to get up*	बस्नु *to live, reside*
छ बजे *at six o'clock*	भाग *share*
भाउज्यू *elder brother's wife*	सुत्नु *to sleep*
-तिर *about*	हातमुख *hands and face*
त्यति *so, that much*	धुनु *to wash*
बिहानै *early morning*	खेत *wet or irrigated field*
अँध्यारो *dark*	एक्लै *alone, on one's own*
नै emphasising word	फर्कनु *to return*
जाडो *cold*	साढे एघार बजे *at half past eleven*
धारा *spring, watersource*	पटक *time, turn*
त्यसपछि *after that, then*	जिन्दगी *life*
सबै *all* (emphasised)	गाह्रो *hard*
चिया *tea*	बिहा *marriage*

Anne	At what time do you usually get up?
Shanti	I usually get up at 6 o'clock. But my sister-in-law gets up at about 4 o'clock.
Anne	Why does she get up so early in the morning? At about 4 o'clock it is very dark, isn't it?
Shanti	It certainly is dark, and it's cold too. Sister-in-law gets up and goes to the spring. Then she makes tea for everyone in the house.
Anne	But it's easy for you. In the morning you've no work, is that so?
Shanti	I live here in my parents' home you see, I don't have much housework to do.
Anne	And when does your (elder) brother get up then?
Shanti	He sleeps until 7 o'clock. Then he gets up, washes his face and hands, drinks tea and goes to the fields.
Anne	Does your brother go to the fields on his own?
Shanti	No, he goes with Father and younger brother.
Anne	Do they only return in the evening?
Shanti	No, after 11 o'clock all the men of the village return from the fields. And at about half past 11 they eat rice.
Anne	Is it always the women who cook the rice?
Shanti	Cooking the rice is always the women's job.
Anne	Do the men never cook the rice?
Shanti	Where do men ever cook rice?[*] They do not, in our house that is always sister-in-law's job.

Anne	Do you eat in the evening too?
Shanti	Yes. We eat in the morning and the evening, twice a day.
Anne	How hard your sister-in-law's life is!
Shanti	After marriage women's life is hard.
Anne	And will you not marry then?
Shanti	No, I will never marry.

*This is sarcastic, and should not be taken literally.

🔊 Grammar

40 The habitual present tense: feminine forms

The छ forms of हुनु have special feminine forms (see **Grammar 11**). These may be used as feminine endings in the habitual present tense:

तँ आउँछेस् ।	*You* (Low) *come.*
तिमी गर्छ्यौ ।	*You* (Middle) *do.*
ऊ जान्छे ।	*She* (Low) *goes.*
उनी सुत्छिन् ।	*She* (Middle) *sleeps.*

Each of the four affirmative endings has a negative counterpart. The difference between these and the masculine negative endings is that the -दै- **-dai-** of the masculine becomes -दि- **-di-** in the feminine:

तँ आउँदिनस् ।	*You* (Low) *do not come.*
तिमी गर्दिनौ ।	*You* (Middle) *do not do.*
ऊ पकाउँदिन ।	*She* (Low) *does not cook.*
तिनी रुँदिनन् ।	*She* (Middle) *does not weep.*

It is fairly uncommon for speakers of Nepali to use these forms in conversation, and in many contexts they would sound almost pedantically over-correct. They are encountered much more commonly in literary, official, and journalistic language.

41 Times of day

The word बजे is derived from the verb बज्नु which means *to ring, strike.* It translates as *at... o'clock:*

एक बजे	*at 1 o'clock*
दुई बजे	*at 2 o'clock*
तीन बजे	*at 3 o'clock*

Three further words are of use here: साढे *plus a half;* सवा *plus a quarter;* पौने *minus a quarter:*

सवा तीन बजे	*at a quarter past 3*
साढे पाँच बजे	*at half past 5*
पौने चार बजे	*at a quarter to 4*

This is the general pattern, but there are two exceptions to it:

■ Instead of साढे एक बजे, it is customary to express *half past 1* as डेढ बजे;
■ Instead of साढे दुई बजे, it is customary to express *half past 2* as अढाई बजे.

To make it clear whether one is talking about a.m. or p.m. (because most Nepalis do not use the 24-hour clock), it is sometimes necessary to specify the time of day when using बजे, by using one of the following terms:

बिहान	*morning* (from dawn to late morning)
दिउँसो	*daytime* (from late morning to dusk); also used to mean *afternoon*
बेलुका	*evening* (after sunset, before night begins)
राति	*night*

बिहान आठ बजे	*at 8 o'clock in the morning*
दिउँसो दुई बजे	*at 2 o'clock in the afternoon*
बेलुका छ बजे	*at 6 o'clock in the evening*
राति दस बजे	*at 10 o'clock at night*

Two further times of day are साँझ *dusk* and मध्यान्न *midday.*

42 Days of the week

The word for *day* that is used to denote a day-long period of time is दिन, but when it is necessary to specify one particular day of the week, the word used for *day* is वार (pronounced **bār**):

आज के वार हो?   *What day (of the week) is it today?*

Accordingly, each day of the week has a Nepali name that ends in वार, just as the names of English weekdays end in '-day':

Sunday	आइतवार	*Thursday*	बिहिवार
Monday	सोमवार	*Friday*	शुक्रवार
Tuesday	मङ्लवार	*Saturday*	शनिवार
Wednesday	बुधवार		

In Nepal, Sunday is the first working day of the week, and offices are closed on Saturdays. In India, both Saturday and Sunday are holidays.

In everyday spoken Nepali, the word अस्ति *the day before yesterday* is used to denote a day of the previous week, while अर्को *other* is used to denote a day of the week to come:

अस्ति शुक्रवार	*last Friday*
अर्को शनिवार	*next Saturday*

43 Frequency: पटक

The word पटक can be used in combination with a number to communicate the frequency of an occurrence:

एक पटक	*one time, once*
दुई पटक	*two times, twice*
तीन पटक	*three times*

These phrases can then be joined to a period of time (a week, a day, etc.), using either -को or -मा , to express how often something happens or is done within that period:

मेरी आमा एक हप्तामा एक पटक बजार जानुहुन्छ ।	*My mother goes to the market once a week.*
मेरी बहिनी हप्ताको पाँच पटक स्कूल जान्छे ।	*My younger sister goes to school five times a week.*

Nepali has several words that are near synonyms of पटक . These are चोटि, बाजि and पल्ट. For the time being, use पटक in preference to these others.

EXERCISE 21   Construct sentences along the following lines:

	Subject	*Time*	*Place*	*Verb*
1	तपाई	at 7 o'clock	at home	eat rice.
2	त्यो मान्छे	in the evening	in the hotel	drinks tea.
3	वहाँहरू	on Thursday	to my house	come.
4	यिनीहरू	twice a week	to the temple	go.
5	यो केटी	on Saturday	at a friend's house	sleeps.

✓ EXERCISE 22   Construct sentences along the following lines:

Subject	from	to	verb, etc.
1 म	2 p.m.	6 p.m.	am not at home.
2 तपाई	Wednesday	Friday	are not in Birāṭanagar.
3 उनीहरू	Tuesday	Thursday	do not work.
4 तिमी	8 a.m.	10.30 a.m.	do not go out.
5 यिनीहरू	1 p.m.	2 p.m.	do not study.

6 | GIVE ME 25 RUPEES
पच्चीस रुपियाँ दिनुहोस्

In this unit you will learn how to:

■ ask or tell people to do or not to do things
■ use the postposition -लाई with the indirect objects of verbs
■ use the alternative negative forms of the habitual present tense
■ use the postposition -तिर
■ use the words for *but, why* and *because;* express agreement and assent

13 Hiring a rickshaw

It is a late evening in winter. Ashok, a government official, needs to get to
his home in Maharajganj, a northern suburb of Kathmandu. Ran Bahadur,
a rickshaw driver, is not keen to travel out so far at this time of night, but
he is prepared to take Ashok part of the way if the price is right.

अशोक	ए रिक्शा ! खाली हो ?
रण बहादुर	खाली छ हजुर । बस्नुहोस् । कहाँ जानुहुन्छ ?
अशोक	महाराजगंज । कति पैसा लिन्छौ ?
रण बहादुर	हेर्नुहोस्, राति म महाराजगंज जान्नँ । टाढा छ, जाडो पनि छ । म तपाईलाई लाजिम्पाटसम्म मात्रै लान्छु । त्यहाँबाट ट्याक्सी लिनुहोस् न ।
अशोक	हुन्छ, हुन्छ । तर कति लिन्छौ नि? अनि हेर । मलाई अलि हतार छ । छिटो गर है ।
रण बहादुर	हतार छ हजुर ? ल, पचास रुपियाँ दिनुहोस् ।
अशोक	पचास रुपियाँ ? म त ट्याक्सीलाई पनि पचास रुपियाँ दिन्नँ !
रण बहादुर	ट्याक्सीलाई कति दिनुहुन्छ त ?
अशोक	यो ट्याक्सी होइन, रिक्शा हो । ल, बीस रुपियाँ लेऊ अनि हिंड !
रण बहादुर	तीस रुपियाँ दिनुहोस् साहेब । बीस रुपियाँमा म राति यस्तो जाडोमा कतै जान्नँ ।
अशोक	ठीकै छ । कतै नजाऊ ! म अर्को रिक्शा लिन्छु ।
रण बहादुर	यो जाडोमा तपाई अर्को रिक्शा पाउनुहुन्न । म मात्रै छु अहिले ।
अशोक	ठीकै छ । म ट्याक्सीबाट जान्छु । फरक पर्दैन ।

रण बहादुर टयाक्सी त झन् महंगो पर्छ हजुर ।अनि यतातिर राति टयाक्सी पाउनुहुन्न । हुन्छ, मलाई पच्चीस रुपियाँ दिनुहोस् । म छिटै लान्छु ।

अशोक ल, ल ।अब ढिलो नगर है , छिटो चलाऊ ।

रिक्शा *rickshaw*	है *hey! / do you hear?*
खाली *empty*	दिनु *to give*
बस्नु *to sit down*	त *though, but, then*
महाराजगंज *Maharajganj,* a suburb of Kathmandu	हिंड्नु *to set out, get going* *
लिनु *to take*	कतै *anywhere*
हेर्नु *to look*	पाउनु *to get, find*
लानु *to transport, take somewhere*	फरक पर्नु *to make a difference*
लाजिम्पाट *Lazimpat,* a part of Kathmandu	झन् *even more*
टयाक्सी *taxi*	महंगो पर्नु *to be expensive*
न *won't you?*	छिटै *quickly*
हुन्छ *all right*	अब *now*
हतार *hurry*	ढिलो गर्नु *to act slowly, be late*
छिटो गर्नु *to act quickly, hurry*	चलाउनु *to drive, operate*

* हिंड्नु means both *to walk* and *to begin a journey* or *to set out.*

Ashok	Hey rickshaw! Is it empty?
Ran Bahadur	It's empty, sir. Sit down. Where will you go?
Ashok	Maharajganj. How much money will you take?
Ran Bahadur	Look, I won't go to Maharajganj at night. It's a long way, and it's cold too. I will take you only as far as Lazimpat. Please take a taxi from there, won't you?
Ashok	All right, all right. But how much will you take? And look. I'm in a bit of a hurry. Go quickly.
Ran Bahadur	In a hurry sir? Right, give me 50 rupees.
Ashok	50 rupees? But I wouldn't even pay a taxi 50 rupees!
Ran Bahadur	How much would you pay a taxi then?
Ashok	This isn't a taxi, it's a rickshaw. Right, take 20 rupees and get going.
Ran Bahadur	Give me 30 rupees, Saheb. I won't go anywhere at night in this cold for 20 rupees.
Ashok	That's fine. Don't go anywhere! I'll take another rickshaw.
Ran Bahadur	You won't find another rickshaw in this cold. There's only me now.
Ashok	OK then. I'll go by taxi. It makes no difference.
Ran Bahadur	A taxi will be even more expensive, sir. And you won't get a taxi around here at night. All right, give me 25 rupees. I'll take you quickly.
Ashok	Right, right. Now don't be slow, drive quickly.

🔊 Grammar

44 The imperatives

An imperative is a form of a verb that is used to give orders or make requests. Imperatives range from peremptory commands to polite requests. In English, the different levels of politeness are usually distinguished by the use or omission of a word such as *please,* or a phrase such as *would you... ?* but in Nepali levels of politeness are implicit in the grammatical forms of the various imperatives. There are four levels of politeness, corresponding with the Low, Middle and High second-person pronouns plus an extra Super-Polite level.

The Low and Super-Polite are not forms that a foreign speaker is likely to use. The four levels are given below, using the verb गर्नु *to do.* The English translations are not meant to be literal, but to give a sense of the level of politeness.

LOW	गर्	**gar**	*do!* (used to give commands or advice to a person you would normally address as तैं)
MIDDLE	गर	**gara**	*do!* (used to instruct a person of lower status than yourself, or a familiar, whom you would address as तिमी)
HIGH	गर्नुहोस्	**garnuhos**	*please do!* (used to ask a request of someone you would address politely as तपाई)
SUPER-POLITE	गर्नुहोला	**garnuholā**	*please would you do!* (used to ask a request of someone you might address deferentially)

You are advised to use the High imperatives in all contexts, at least until you are sure of your reasons for using another level.

Negative imperatives are exactly the same as positive imperatives, except that they take a negative prefix, न- **na-**.

LOW	नगर्	**nagar**	*don't!*
MIDDLE	नगर	**nagara**	*don't!*
HIGH	नगर्नुहोस्	**nagarnuhos**	*please don't!*
SUPER-POLITE	नगर्नुहोला	**nagarnuholā**	*please would you not do!*

Clearly, the more polite the imperative is, the longer the word becomes: in its positive form the most polite is a word of four syllables, while the least polite has only one syllable. The High and Super-Polite forms consist of the dictionary form + a suffix (the suffixes are -होस् and -होला respectively). For C-verbs, the Low and Middle forms are simply the verb base without and with a final **-a** vowel respectively.

Summary of imperative forms

C-verbs

affirmative

	गर्नु *to do*	बस्नु *to sit*
Low	गर्	बस्
Middle	गर	बस
High	गर्नुहोस्	बस्नुहोस्
Super-Polite	गर्नुहोला	बस्नुहोला

negative

Low	नगर्	नबस्
Middle	नगर	नबस
High	नगर्नुहोस्	नबस्नुहोस्
Super-Polite	नगर्नुहोला	नबस्नुहोला

The Middle imperatives of all V- and VV-verbs take the suffix -ऊ **-ū**, which is added to the verb base. At Low and Middle levels, five commonly used V-verbs behave irregularly by adopting special imperative bases. These verbs are:

	Dictionary form	*Imperative base*
to take	लिनु	ले-
to give	दिनु	दे-
to wash	धुनु	धो-
to weep	रुनु	रो-
to be	हुनु	हो-

The second vowel is dropped from the bases of VV-verbs:

to come	आउनु	आ-
to send	पठाउनु	पठा-

Summary of imperative forms

V-verbs and VV-verbs

affirmative

	जानु *to go*	लिनु *to take*	धुनु *to wash*	आउनु *to come*	पठाउनु *to send*
Low	जा	ले	धो	आ	पठा
Middle	जाऊ	लेऊ	धोऊ	आऊ	पठाऊ
High	जानुहोस्	लिनुहोस्	धुनुहोस्	आउनुहोस्	पठाउनुहोस्
S-P	जानुहोला	लिनुहोला	धुनुहोला	आउनुहोला	पठाउनुहोला

negative

Low	नजा	नले	नधो	नआ	नपठा
Middle	नजाऊ	नलेऊ	नधोऊ	नआऊ	नपठाऊ
High	नजानुहोस्	नलिनुहोस्	नधुनुहोस्	नआउनुहोस्	नपठाउनुहोस्
S-P	नजानुहोला	नलिनुहोला	नधुनुहोला	नआउनुहोला	नपठाउनुहोला

One additional form of the imperative is simply the dictionary form of a verb with its final vowel lengthened from उ **u** to ऊ **ū**. This you use to give specific instructions to a person of lower status than yourself, or to a familiar. Again, the negative form has the prefix न-:

अब यो किताब पढ्नू ।   *Now read this book.*
रातो लुगा तातो पानीमा नधुनू ।   *Don't wash the red clothes in hot*
रँग जान्छ नि ।   *water. They'll fade, you know.*

EXERCISE 23   Translate the following commands into Nepali:

(a) addressing the person concerned as तिमी:
1 Hey, don't sit on that chair, sit on this chair.
2 Speak Nepali in Kathmandu, don't speak English.
3 Read the big red book, don't read the newspaper.
4 Give the boy an apple, don't give him an orange.

(b) addressing the person concerned as तपाईं:
5 Please don't come at 6 o'clock, come at about 8 o'clock.
6 Please tell me but don't tell him.
7 Please take this cup and give that cup to him.
8 Please go to Nepal. Please speak Nepali there.

45 The postposition -लाई -lāī as object marker

All verbs must have a subject: the subject of a verb is the thing or person that is performing the action of the verb. In the sentence *the man eats rice,* the verb is *eats* and its subject is *the man.* Many verbs (those verbs that are called 'transitive verbs', as explained in **Grammar 58**) can also have an object. In the sentence above, the object is *rice,* because that is what is eaten: the rice receives the action of the verb.

Objects can be of two kinds: *direct* or *indirect.* In Nepali, an indirect object must always carry the postposition -लाई, which will often be translatable as *to* or *at:*

म तिमीलाई भन्छु ।   *I say to you.*
ऊ मलाई दिन्छ ।   *He gives to me.*
तपाईं उसलाई दिनुहोस् ।   *Please give to him.*

In sentences that contain only one object, the general rule is that personal names, human nouns and human pronouns (*he, she, we,* etc.) should carry -लाई when they are the object of a verb, while inanimate nouns need not:

म भात खान्छु ।   *I eat rice.*
हामी टी॰ भी॰ हेर्छौं ।   *We watch television.*
उनीहरू गीत गाउँछन् ।   *They sing a song.*
ऊ चिठी लेख्छ ।   *He writes a letter.*

म वहाँलाई सोध्छु ।	*I'll ask him.*
उनीहरू मलाई हेर्छन् ।	*They watch me.*

However, there are certain situations in which this rule is broken:

■ in contexts in which a human being is being treated as a commodity that can be bought or given away (giving a daughter in marriage, for example), in which case it will be treated as an inanimate noun and will not take -लाई;

■ when an inanimate noun is being treated like an animate being (a devout person might bow to a book, or offer worship to a sacred rock, for instance), in which case it will be treated as an animate noun and take -लाई;

■ if the subject carries the subject-marking suffix -ले (introduced in **Grammar 59**) and it is obvious what its object is, it is sometimes unnecessary to mark the object with -लाई.

More complex sentences may include both a direct and an indirect object. In these the indirect object carries -लाई but the direct object does not, and the rules about animate and inanimate nouns become irrelevant:

म तिमीलाई यो कुरा भन्छु ।	*I say this thing to you.*
ऊ मलाई पैसा दिन्छ ।	*He gives money to me.*
तपाई उसलाई त्यो किताब दिनुहोस् ।	*Please give that book to him.*

This is a complex area of Nepali grammar, and the foreign learner must develop an intuitive sense of when to use and when not to use -लाई.

46 The habitual present tense: alternative negative forms

All V- and VV-verbs have a second series of negative endings, which sound more abrupt than the standard -दैन **-daina** range. In this, the दै **dai** or दि **di** syllable is replaced by a half **n** (न्) while the vowel of the verb base is no longer nasalised.

standard ending		*alternative ending*		
-दैन	**-daina**	-न्न	**-nna**	(with ऊ, यो, त्यो)
-दिन	**-dina**	-न्नँ	**-nnã**	(with म)
-दैनस्	**-dainas**	-न्नस्	**-nnas**	(with तैँ)
-दैनौ	**-dainau**	-न्नौ	**-nnau**	(with तिमी)
-दैनौँ	**-dainaũ**	-न्नौँ	**-nnaũ**	(with हामी, हामीहरू)
-दैनन्	**-dainan**	-न्नन्	**-nnan**	(with यी, ती, उनी, यिनी, तिनी, and the plural forms of उनी, यिनी and तिनी)

These endings are commonly used with the verbs जानु and खानु:

ऊ जान्न	*S/he does not / will not go*	ऊ खान्न	*S/he does not/will not eat*
म जान्नँ	*I do not / will not go*	म खान्नँ	*I do not / will not eat*
तैँ जान्नस्	*You do not / will not go*	तैँ खान्नस्	*You do not / will not eat*
तिमी जान्नौ	*You do not / will not go*	तिमी खान्नौ	*You do not / will not eat*
हामी जान्नौँ	*We do not / will not go*	हामीहरू खान्नौँ	*We do not / will not eat*
यिनी जान्नन्	*S/he does not/will not go*	उनीहरू खान्नन्	*They do not/will not eat*

The use of the alternative negative ending is obligatory in the phrases *I do not/will not give* and *I do not/will not take:*

म तपाईलाई मेरो साइकल दिन्नँ ।	*I shall not give you my bicycle.*
म तपाईको हातबाट पैसा लिन्नँ ।	*I will not take money from your hand.*

Otherwise, these alternative negative endings are generally interchangeable with the standard forms, but they are most often used with the first person pronoun (म *I*) to convey the sense of *I shall not* or *I will not* rather than *I do not*. That is, they are often used to express refusal to do something:

म भात खाँदिन ।	*I do not eat rice.*
म भात खान्नँ ।	*I will not eat rice.*
म स्कूल जाँदिन ।	*I do not go to school.*
म स्कूल जान्नँ ।	*I will not go to school.*

47 The postposition -तिर *towards*

-तिर **-tira** is a postposition used with words that denote a place or location. It means either (i) *in the direction of* that place or location, or (ii) *in the vicinity of* that place or location. It is also used (iii) with times of day to mean *about* or *approximately*.

(i) When the phrase or sentence involves a verb of movement -तिर means literally *in the direction of* (though often it can be translated as *to*):

दिदी दार्जीलिङ्गतिर जान्छिन् ।	*Elder sister goes to Darjeeling.*
पर्यटकहरू पहाडतिर जान्छन् ।	*Tourists go to the hills.*

(ii) If no verb of movement is involved in the phrase or sentence, -तिर means *in the vicinity of* the place or location to which it is added:

दार्जीलिङ्गतिर मान्छेहरू नेपाली बोल्छन् ।   *Around Darjeeling, people speak*
                                            Nepali.
पहाडतिर मौसम अलि चिसो हुन्छ ।   *In the hill areas the weather is*
                                            rather cold.

(iii) -तिर can be added to the word बजे *at... o'clock* to introduce a measure of vagueness to statements of time:

म एक बजेतिर आउँछु ।   *I'll come at about 1 o'clock.*
हामी दस बजेतिर भात खान्छौँ ।   *We eat at about 10 o'clock.*

48 The negative particle न

न **na** means *do not* before an imperative, but *won't you?* after an imperative:

भात नखानुहोस् ।   *Please don't eat the rice.*
यहाँ नआउनुहोस् ।   *Please don't come here*
भात खानुहोस् न ।   *Please eat the rice, won't you?*
यहाँ आउनुहोस् न ।   *Please come here, won't you?*

It also means both *neither* and *nor:*

यहाँ न पसल छ न स्कूल ।   *Here there is neither a shop*
                                            nor a school.
मसँग न पैसा छ न चुरोट ।   *I have neither any money nor*
                                            any cigarettes.

49 तर *but,* त *though*

There are two ways of saying *but* in Nepali. तर is pretty well an exact translation of *but* and can be used in much the same way as *but* at the beginning of or in the middle of a sentence:

किताब राम्रो छ, तर अलि छोटो छ ।   *The book is good, but it's*
                                            rather short.

भोलि म बिराटनगर जान्छु तर राति बस्दिन ।   *Tomorrow I shall go to Biratnagar*
                                            but I shall not stay the night.

त can never be the first word in a sentence. It can follow a time, or a subject, or something else, which it qualifies. When used in statements, it means *as for, though, but* or *however.*

म त शाकाहारी हुँ । म मासु खाँदिन ।	<u>I</u> am a vegetarian. I do not eat meat.
काठ्माडौँ त नेपालको राजधानी हो, भारतको राजधानी होइन ।	But Kathmandu is the capital of Nepal, not the capital of India.
नेपाली भाषा त सजिलै छ, किन बुझ्नुहुन्न ?	But the Nepali language is quite easy, why don't you understand?

त may also end a question or a command, in which case it translates as *then* or *in that case*:

तपाईंकी आमा नेपालमा हुनुहुन्छ ?	Is your mother in Nepal?
हुनुहुन्न ।	No.
कहाँ हुनुहुन्छ त ?	Where is she then?
भारतमा हुनुहुन्छ ।	She's in India.
तपाईं तीन बजेतिर मेरो घर आउनुहुन्छ ?	Will you come to my house at about three o'clock?
होइन, त्यो बेला फुर्सद हुँदैन ।	No, I don't have the time then.
कति बजे आउनुहुन्छ त ?	At what time will you come, then?
यो तिम्रो झोला हो ?	Is that your bag?
होइन ।	No.
कसको हो त ?	Whose is it then?
मेरो साथीको ।	My friend's.

50 हवस् and हुन्छ: *OK, all right*

If a Nepali-speaker is asked or told to do something, and s/he agrees to do it, the response given is commonly either हवस् **havas** or हुन्छ **huncha**. These words are both derived from the verb हुनु *to be*. हवस् translates as *may it be so*, and is a polite word that indicates assent. The middle व of हवस् is pronounced as if it were a vowel, and the word is pronounced **'haus'**:

ए धने, तिमी पाहुनाहरूको लागि चिया पकाऊ है ।	Hey Dhane, make tea for the guests!
हवस् हजुर ।	Certainly, sir.

हुन्छ means something like *it is good* or *OK;* it has much the same meaning as हवस् , but is rather less deferential.

EXERCISE 24   Translate into Nepali:

1 Those women never come to the bazaar on Thursday. When do they come, then? They usually come on Tuesday.

2 Foreigners go from Kathmandu to Lukla by plane. Nepalis usually go by bus up to Jiri. From Jiri they walk to Lukla.

3 At what time do those men go to the fields? They go at about 8 o'clock and they come home after three hours.

4 I will stay in Nepal only until tomorrow. At 10.30 tomorrow morning I go to Delhi. After that I go to London.

5 After 8 o'clock at night all the shops are shut. I won't go to the market for you now. I will go tomorrow morning.

6 What work will you (Middle) do for me? I'll go to the market for you (High), OK?

7 My younger sister never cooks food for the family. Sometimes elder sister cooks, sometimes mother cooks.

8 She (Low) goes to school every day, and so does he (Low). But their little brother doesn't go.

7 | THE BEST
सबभन्दा राम्रो

In this unit you will learn how to:

■ make comparisons
■ express likes and dislikes

14 Towns and villages

Bimla is doing her homework. She has to write an essay about the differences between life in a city and life in a village. Her younger brother and her parents are helping her out.

बिमला आज अलिकति स्कूलको काम छ । मलाई सहयोग गर्नुहोस् है बुवा ।

बुवा हुन्छ, म सहयोग गर्छु ।

बिमला सँसारको सबैभन्दा ठूलो शहर कुन हो, थाहा छ ?

सुरेश थाहा छ । काठ्माडौँ हो ।

बिमला सँसारको सबैभन्दा ठूलो शहर काठ्माडौँ हो ? कहाँको काठ्माडौँ हुनु ? काठ्माडौँभन्दा त दिल्ली ठूलो छ, होइन आमा ?

आमा हो, दिल्ली, लण्डन, टोक्यो सँसारका ठूला शहरहरू हुन् ।

बुवा तर टोक्योभन्दा ठूलो शहर छैन यो सँसारमा । टोक्यो सँसारको सबैभन्दा ठूलो शहर हो ।

बिमला ठीक छ । तपाईलाई ठूलो शहर मन पर्छ ? मलाई त मन पर्दैन ।

सुरेश किन मन पर्दैन ?

बिमला किनभने शहरको जीवन जटिल हुन्छ । गाउँको जीवन सजिलो हुन्छ ।

सुरेश कहाँको सजिलो हुनु ? शहरको जीवनभन्दा गाउँको जीवन बढी गाह्रो हुन्छ नि । गाउँमा न ठूला पसलहरू हुन्छन् न सिनेमा-घरहरू हुन्छन् न त राम्रा स्कूलहरू हुन्छन् । मलाई त शहर नै मन पर्छ ।

बिमला कुरा त ठीकै हो । तर गाउँमा हावा सफा हुन्छ, पानी पनि मीठो हुन्छ । गाउँमा दालभात स्वादिलो हुन्छ । होइन त आमा ?

आमा हो, तिम्रो कुरा साँचो हो । तर शहरमा यातायात, अस्पताल, स्कूल, बजारहरूका सुविधा हुन्छन् । धेरै मान्छेहरू शहरको जीवन मन पराउँछन् ।

बुवा बिमला, अब तिमीलाई गाउँ र शहरको जीवनमा फरक त थाहा छ । अब भन,
तिमीलाई शहर र गाउँमा कुन मन पर्छ ?

बिमला शहरको जिन्दगी मलाई मन पर्दैन । मलाई गाउँको जीवन देऊ !

सहयोग गर्नु *to assist, help*	जटिल *complicated, difficult*
सँसार *the world*	हावा *air*
सबैभन्दा ठूलो *biggest*	सफा *clean*
-भन्दा *than*	स्वादिलो *tasty, flavoursome*
टोक्यो *Tokyo*	कुरा *thing, matter*
मन पर्नु *to be liked*	साँचो *true*
किन *why?*	यातायात *transport*
किनभने *because*	अस्पताल *hospital*
जीवन *life*	सुविधा *facility, convenience*
	मन पराउनु *to like*

Bimala Today I have some school work. Please help me, Father.

Father All right, I'll help.

Bimala Which is the world's biggest city, do you know?

Suresh I know. It's Kathmandu.

Bimala The world's biggest city is Kathmandu? How can it be Kathmandu? Delhi is bigger than Kathmandu, isn't it Mother?

Mother Yes, Delhi, London, Tokyo are the world's big cities.

Father But there is no city bigger than Tokyo in this world. Tokyo is the world's biggest city.

Bimala OK. Do you like big towns? I don't like them.

Suresh Why don't you like them?

Bimala Because town life is complicated. Village life is easy.

Suresh How can it be easy? Village life is much harder than town life. In a village there are neither big shops nor cinemas, nor are there good schools. The town is what I like.

Bimala What you say is true enough. But in a village the air is clean, and the water tastes good too. In a village the food is flavoursome. Isn't that so, Mother?

Mother Yes, what you say is true. But in a town there are the facilities of transport, hospitals, schools and marketplaces. Many people like town life.

Father Bimala, now you know the difference between village and town life. Tell me now, out of the town and the village, which do you prefer?

Bimala I don't like town life. Give me village life!

▣ Grammar

51 Comparatives and superlatives

When you compare things in English, you say that something is *bigger than* or *better than* something else. Much the same convention exists in Nepali, where the equivalent of the English preposition *than* is a postposition, -भन्दा. But in Nepali the adjective remains the same as it would if you were simply describing what you are talking about – for example, राम्रो *good* remains as राम्रो *good,* and there is no single Nepali word that means *better.* Comparative sentences can be cast either way:

मेरो घर तिम्रो घरभन्दा ठूलो छ ।	*My house is bigger than your house.*
तिम्रो घरभन्दा मेरो घर ठूलो छ ।	*Than your house my house is bigger.*
त्यो दाल यो दालभन्दा मीठो हुन्छ ।	*That **dāl** is tastier than this **dāl**.*
यो दालभन्दा त्यो दाल मीठो हुन्छ ।	*Than this **dāl** that **dāl** is tastier.*

The words बढी or ज्यादा *more,* or the emphatic ज्यादै *much more,* are often put in front of the adjective to make it absolutely clear that a comparison is being made:

मेरो गाउँ तिम्रो गाउँभन्दा बढी ठूलो छ ।	*My village is bigger than yours.*
जुम्लाका स्याउ ज्यादै मीठो हुन्छन् ।	*Apples from Jumla are much tastier.*

To express a superlative – that is, to say that something is the *best* or the *cheapest* – the same construction is used, except that instead of comparing something to one or a number of other things you simply compare it to सब, *all,* or to सबै, *absolutely all:*

मेरो गाउँ सबभन्दा ठूलो छ ।	*My village is the biggest (of all).*
तातोपानीका सुन्तला सबैभन्दा मीठो हुन्छन् ।	*Oranges from Tatopani are the tastiest (of all).*

Since all of these examples have been descriptive, they have used either छ or हुन्छ. However, it is possible to define something as *the biggest village* or *the cheapest rice:* in these cases the noun may be mentioned twice (though it need not be), and the हो form of the verb can be used:

मेरो घर सबभन्दा ठूलो (घर) हो ।	*My house is the biggest (house).*
त्यो आँप सबभन्दा मीठो (आँप) हो ।	*That mango is the tastiest (mango).*
अमेरिकनहरू सँसारका सबैभन्दा धनी मानिसहरू हुन् ।	*Americans are the world's richest people.*

✔ **EXERCISE 25**   Translate into Nepali:

1 London is bigger than Kathmandu.
2 American people are usually richer than English people.
3 Kathmandu is further from England than Delhi.
4 Kathmandu is Nepal's biggest town.
5 Which is the world's poorest country?
6 There is no language easier than Nepali.

52 Likes and dislikes using मन पर्नु man parnu

The simplest way of expressing a like or a dislike of something is to use the verb phrase मन पर्नु which literally means *mind* (मन) *to fall* (पर्नु) but translates as *to be liked*. The subject of this verb phrase is not the person who is doing the liking, but the thing that is being liked.

If no person is mentioned in a statement that uses मन पर्नु, then the person who is doing the liking is most probably the person who is making the statement:

त्यो गीत मन पर्छ ।	*That song is liked.* ('I like that song').
लण्डन मन पर्दैन ।	*London is not liked.* ('I do not like London').
यो पत्रिका मनै पर्दैन ।	*This magazine is not liked at all.* ('I do not like this magazine at all').

If no person is mentioned in a question that uses मन पर्नु, then the person who is doing the liking is most probably the person to whom the question is being addressed:

नीलो रँग मन पर्छ ?	*Is blue colour liked?* ('do you like blue?')
रातो रँग मन पर्छ कि मन पर्दैन ?	*Is red colour liked or not?* ('do you like red or don't you?')

If it is necessary to state *by whom* a thing is liked or disliked, then the person who likes, or the pronoun that stands for that person, must take the postposition -लाई :

मलाई पहेँलो रँग मन पर्छ ।	*I like the colour yellow.*
सुशीललाई हरियो रँग मन पर्छ ।	*Sushil likes the colour green.*
तपाईलाई कालो रँग मन पर्दैन ?	*Do you not like the colour black?*
उसलाई यो सेतो कपडा मन पर्दैन ।	*He does not like this white cloth.*

Less commonly, the liker of something can become the subject of this kind of sentence by using the verb मन पराउनु, in which case the postposition -लाई is sometimes added to the thing that is liked.

म खैरो रँग मन पराउँछु ।	*I like the colour brown.*
तपाई प्याजी रँगलाई मन पराउनुहुन्छ ?	*Do you like the colour purple?*

EXERCISE 26　　Construct sentences about likes and dislikes along the following lines:

Person	Colour	likes?
Example:		
my mother	red	✗ = मेरी आमालाई रातो रँग मन पर्दैन ।
		✓ = मेरी आमालाई रातो रँग मन पर्छ ।
1　grandfather	blue	✓
2　my elder sisters	black	✗
3　you (High)	green	✓
4　his younger brothers	yellow	✗
5　they	purple	✓

53　किन *why*, किनभने *because*

किन ? *why?* can be used on its own to ask a question:

A आज म अफिस जान्छु ।	*Today I shall go to the office.*
B किन ?	*Why?*
A उसलाई त्यो पसल मन पर्छ ।	*He likes that shop.*
B किन ?	*Why?*

More commonly, however, किन ? *why?* is part of a longer question:

आज तपाई किन छिटै अफिस जानुहुन्छ ?	*Why will you go to the office early today?*
उसलाई त्यो पसल किन मन पर्छ ?	*Why does he like that shop?*

In such questions, the position of किन ? depends on what the question asked actually focuses on. In these examples, it focuses on *going to the office* and on *liking,* so it is positioned immediately before them in the sentence. Nepali questions very rarely begin with किन ?. The replies to such questions generally, however, do begin with किनभने, *because*:

किनभने अफिसमा धेरै काम छ ।	*Because there is a lot of work at the office.*
किनभने त्यो पसल अलि सस्तो हुन्छ ।	*Because that shop is quite cheap.*

किनभने *because* can of course be used in a sentence to link a cause and its effect:

म गाईको मासु खाँदिन किनभने म हिन्दू हुँ । *I do not eat beef because I am a Hindu.*

ऊ नेपाली बोल्दैन किनभने ऊ हिन्दीभाषी हो ।*He does not speak Nepali because he is a Hindi-speaker.*

✔ EXERCISE 27   पढेर बुझ्नुहोस् (*Read and understand*)

The following is your first encounter with a passage of connected prose. Look up any unfamiliar words in the Nepali-English glossary at the back of the book, and then answer the questions that follow in Nepali.

हामी नेवार हौँ । हाम्रो घर एउटा सानो शहरमा छ । शहरको नाम साँखु हो । काठमाडौँदेखि हाम्रो घर अलि टाढा छ । तर बा हरेक दिन काठमाडौँ जानुहुन्छ । वहाँको अफिस त्यहाँ छ । कहिले काहीं म बासँग जान्छु । म हरेक दिन जान्नँ । भोलि म बासँग जान्छु किनभने भोलि धेरै किनमेल छ । म बालाई मदत गर्छु। मा कहिल्यै पनि काठमाडौँ जानुहुन्न । वहाँ घरै बस्नुहुन्छ र घरको काम गर्नुहुन्छ । हामीहरूको लागि वहाँ भात पकाउनुहुन्छ । मालाई दुईजना बहिनी मदत गर्छन् । हाम्रो घरनजिक एउटा धारा छ । हरेक दिन बेलुकातिर कान्छी बहिनी गाग्री लिन्छे र धारा जान्छे । गाग्री भर्छे र घर ल्याउँछे । बारीमा इनार छ, तर हामीहरू कहिल्यै पनि इनारको पानी खान्नौँ । अर्को शहरका मान्छेहरू धेरैजसो बिरामी हुन्छन् किनभने उनीहरू इनारको पानी खान्छन् ।

प्रश्नहरू (*questions*)
१   हामी कहाँ बस्छौं ?
२   भोलि म बासँग किन शहर जान्छु ?
३   मा काठमाडौँ जानुहुन्छ ?
४   घरमा मा के गर्नुहुन्छ ?
५   बेलुका को धारा जान्छ ?
६   अर्को शहरका मान्छेहरू किन धेरैजसो बिरामी हुन्छन् ?

8 | I CAME YESTERDAY
म हिजो आएँ

In this unit you will learn how to:

■ use the simple past tense of verbs
■ use the agentive suffix **-le**
■ name the parts of the body

15 Sandhya drops by

Sandhya has come to call on her friend Asha. She had also called at the house the morning before, but had been surprised to find it deserted. Asha explains.

सन्ध्या हिजो तपाई कहाँ जानुभयो ?

आशा हिजो म कतै गइनँ । घरै बसें ।

सन्ध्या तर हिजो बिहान म तपाईंकहाँ आएँ । घरमा कोही पनि थिएन ।

आशा तपाई मकहाँ कति बजे आउनुभयो ?

सन्ध्या म सात, होइन, साढे सात बजेतिर आएँ । म अलि ढिलो भएँ ।

आशा अब सम्झें ! अस्ति बुवा, आमा र भाइहरू केही दिनको लागि नेपालगंज गए । हिजो शनिवार थियो, होइन ?

सन्ध्या हो, शनिवार थियो ।

आशा शनिवार बिहान म सधैं मन्दिर जान्छु । अनि हिजो बिहान हामीहरू साढे पाँच बजेतिर पशुपतिनाथको मन्दिर गयौं । घरमा कोही थिएन ।

सन्ध्या तपाई हरेक शनिवार पशुपतिनाथ जानुहुन्छ ?

आशा होइन । अस्ति शनिवार म वज्र जोगिनीको मन्दिर गएँ । कहिले काहीं म चाँगु नारायण पनि जान्छु ।

सन्ध्या हिजो कोसँग जानुभयो ?

आशा म धेरै जसो एक्लै जान्छु तर अस्ति मेरी दिदी बाग्लुङ्गबाट आइन् । अब केही दिनसम्म हाम्रो घरमा बस्छिन् । हामी सँग-सँगै मन्दिर गयौं । निक्कै रमाइलो भयो नि ।

सन्ध्या मन्दिरमा भीड थियो ?

आशा थिएन । शनिवार सात बजेपछि मात्र त्यहाँ भीड हुन्छ । हामीहरू त बिहानै गयौं अनि भीड थिएन ।

सन्ध्या तर तपाईहरू पशुपतिबाट सीधै फर्कनुभएन, होइन ? म तपाईको ढोकामा आधा घण्टासम्म पर्खें तर पनि तपाईहरू आउनुभएन । आखिर म निराश भएँ अनि घर फर्कें ।

आशा बीचबाटोमा ठूलो पानी पर्‍यो । हामीहरूसँग छाता थिएन । हामी केही बेरसम्म एउटा रूखको ओतमा बस्यौँ । तपाई भिज्नुभयो ? माफ गर्नुहोला कि ?

सन्ध्या होइन, केही छैन । मसँग छाता थियो । यतातिर आकाश अँध्यारो भयो र सिमसिमे पानी मात्रै पर्‍यो ।।

आशा हवस् त दिदी । आज त भेट भयो नि । बस्नुहोस्, चिया लिनुहोस्, सबै खबर सुनाउनुहोस् ।

हिजो	*yesterday*	तर पनि	*but even so*
कतै	*anywhere*	आखिर	*in the end*
घरै	*at home*	निराश	*without hope*
मकहाँ	*my place, my home*	बीचबाटोमा	*on the way*
तपाईकहाँ	*your place, your home*	ठूलो पानी	*heavy rain*
कोही	*someone*	बेर	*time (a quantity of)*
सम्झनु	*to remember*	रूख	*tree*
अस्ति	*day before yesterday*	ओत	*shelter* *
केही	*a few, some*	भिज्नु	*to get wet*
पशुपतिनाथको मन्दिर	*Pashupatinath temple*	माफ गर्नु	*to forgive*
वज्र जोगिनीको मन्दिर	*Bajra Jogini temple*	छाता	*umbrella*
चाँगु नारायण	*Changu Narayan (a temple)*	आकाश	*sky*
सँग-सँगै	*together, each with the other*	सिमसिमे पानी	*light rain*
रमाइलो	*enjoyable*	भेट हुनु	*to meet up*
सीधै	*directly, straight*	खबर	*news*
आधा	*half*	सुनाउनु	*to tell, relate*
पर्खनु	*to wait*		

* Nepali has two words for *shelter*: ओत means *shelter from the rain*, while छायाँ means *shelter from the sun*.

Sandhya	Where did you go yesterday?
Asha	I didn't go anywhere yesterday. I stayed at home.
Sandhya	But I came to your place yesterday morning. There was no one in the house.
Asha	What time did you come to my place?
Sandhya	I came at seven, no, at about half past 7. I was a bit late.
Asha	Now I've remembered! The day before yesterday Father, Mother and my younger brothers went to Nepalganj for a few days. Yesterday was Saturday, wasn't it?
Sandhya	Yes, it was Saturday.

Asha	On Saturday morning I always go to the temple. And yesterday morning we went to Pashupatinath temple at about half past 5. There was no-one at home.
Sandhya	Do you go to Pashupatinath every Saturday?
Asha	No. Last Saturday I went to Bajra Jogini temple. Sometimes I go to Changu Narayan temple too.
Sandhya	Who did you go with yesterday?
Asha	I usually go alone but the day before yesterday my elder sister came from Baglung. Now she will stay a few days in our house. We went to the temple together. It was very enjoyable, you know.
Sandhya	Was there a crowd at the temple?
Asha	No. There's a crowd there only after 7 o'clock on a Saturday. We went very early, so there wasn't a crowd.
Sandhya	But you didn't come straight back from Pashupati, did you? I waited at your door for half an hour but even so you did not come. In the end I lost hope and I went back home.
Asha	On the way back it rained heavily. We didn't have an umbrella. We sat in the shelter of a tree for a while. Did you get wet? Will you forgive me?
Sandhya	No, it doesn't matter. I had an umbrella. Over here the sky became dark and only light rain fell.
Asha	All right then sister. Today we have met up anyway. Please sit down, have some tea, tell me all the news.

Grammar

54 The simple past tense

The *simple past* tense refers to actions and events that happened in the past, or describes situations and conditions that were true in the past. It usually corresponds with the English *I went, you came, he said, they were, it was,* etc., but can also sometimes be similar to the English present perfect: *I've gone, the rain has come.*

Past tense verb bases

The past tense bases of all C-verbs and most V-verbs are the same as the present tense bases (that is, they are formed by taking the dictionary form and dropping the ending -नु – see **Grammar 33**). However, there are four particular V-verbs which form their past tense bases differently. These are:

Verb	Present tense base	Past tense base
धुनु *to wash*	धु-	धो-
रुनु *to weep*	रु-	रो-
जानु *to go*	जा-	ग-
हुनु *to be*	हु-	थि- or भ-

These four verbs take the same endings as all other verbs. It should also be noted that the final **-a** of the present tense base of the V-verb बिर्सनु *to forget* is dropped before the past tense ending is added:

Verb	Present tense base	Past tense base
बिर्सनु *to forget*	बिर्स- **birsa-**	बिर्स- **birs-**

The bases of VV-verbs in past tenses are shortened forms of the present tense verb bases (see **Grammar 33**). The second vowel of the present tense base is dropped to form the past tense base:

VV-verb	Present tense base	Past tense base
आउनु *to come*	आउ-	आ-
पकाउनु *to cook*	पकाउ-	पका-
पिउनु *to drink*	पिउ-	पि-

Past tense verb endings

The simple past tense is formed by taking the past tense base of a verb and adding an ending to it. As always, the choice of ending depends upon what or who the subject of the verb is, and the endings must be learned by heart. They are:

	Affirmative		Negative	
singular				
म	-एँ	**-ẽ**	-इनँ	**-inã**
हामी, हामीहरू	-यौँ	**-yaũ**	-एनौँ	**-enaũ**
तैँ	-इस्	**-is**	-इनस्	**-inas**
तिमी, तिमीहरू	-यौ	**-yau**	-एनौ	**-enau**
ऊ, यो, त्यो (m.)	-यो	**-yo**	-एन	**-ena**
ऊ, यो, त्यो (f.)	-ई	**-ī**	-इन	**-ina**
उनी, यिनी, तिनी (m.)	-ए	**-e**	-एनन्	**-enan**
उनी, यिनी, तिनी (f.)	-इन्	**-in**	-इनन्	**-inan**
यी, ती, उनीहरू etc.	-ए	**-e**	-एनन्	**-enan**

The boxes that follow contain the simple past tense forms of the VV-verb आउनु *to come* and the irregular V-verb जानु *to go*.

आउनु *to come*

	Affirmative			Negative		
	(I came, you came, etc.)			*(I did not come, you did not come, etc.)*		
म	आ + -एँ	=	आएँ	आ + -इनँ	=	आइनँ
हामी, हामीहरू	आ + -यौं	=	आयौं	आ + -एनौं	=	आएनौं
तैँ	आ + -इस्	=	आइस्	आ + -इनस्	=	आइनस्
तिमी, तिमीहरू	आ + -यौ	=	आयौ	आ + -एनौ	=	आएनौ
ऊ, यो, त्यो (m.)	आ + -यो	=	आयो	आ + -एन	=	आएन
ऊ, यो, त्यो (f.)	आ + -ई	=	आई	आ + -इन	=	आइन
उनी, यिनी, तिनी (m.)	आ + -ए	=	आए	आ + -एनन्	=	आएनन्
उनी, यिनी, तिनी (f.)	आ + -इन्	=	आइन्	आ + -इनन्	=	आइनन्
यी, ती, उनीहरू etc.	आ + -ए	=	आए	आ + -एनन्	=	आएनन्

जानु *to go*

	Affirmative			Negative		
	(I went, you went, etc.)			*(I did not go, you did not go, etc.)*		
म	ग + -एँ	=	गएँ	ग + -इनँ	=	गइनँ
हामी, हामीहरू	ग + -यौं	=	गयौं	ग + -एनौं	=	गएनौं
तैँ	ग + -इस्	=	गइस्	ग + -इनस्	=	गइनस्
तिमी, तिमीहरू	ग + -यौ	=	गयौ	ग + -एनौ	=	गएनौ
ऊ, यो, त्यो (m.)	ग + -यो	=	गयो	ग + -एन	=	गएन
ऊ, यो, त्यो (f.)	ग + -ई	=	गई	ग + -इन	=	गइन
उनी, यिनी, तिनी (m.)	ग + -ए	=	गए	ग + -एनन्	=	गएनन्
उनी, यिनी, तिनी (f.)	ग + -इन्	=	गइन्	ग + -इनन्	=	गइनन्
यी, ती, उनीहरू etc.	ग + -ए	=	गए	ग + -एनन्	=	गएनन्

The High forms of the simple past tense consist of the dictionary form of a verb (हुनु, आउनु, जानु etc.), combined with:

- the suffix -भयो in the affirmative
- the suffix -भएन in the negative.

These forms are always the same, regardless of the number and gender of their subject.

High forms

आउनु *to come*

   Affirmative   *Negative*

   आउनु + -भयो   =   आउनुभयो   आउनु + -भएन   =   आउनुभएन

जानु *to go*

   Affirmative   *Negative*

   जानु + -भयो   =   जानुभयो   जानु + -भएन   =   जानुभएन

Note the following examples in which the Nepali simple past tense must be translated with the English present perfect tense:

पानी आयो !	*It has begun to rain!*
गुरुजी आउनुभयो ?	*Has Guruji arrived?*
बत्ती गयो !	*Power cut!* [*]

* Power cuts are an unfortunate feature of daily life in Nepal. बत्ती means *lamp* but by extension it is also used to mean *electric light*. When power is restored after a power cut, the cry is बत्ती आयो !

55 The simple past forms of हुनु *to be:* थियो **and** भयो

	थि-		भ-	
	Affirmative	*Negative*	*Affirmative*	*Negative*
म	थिएँ	थिइनँ	भएँ	भइनँ
हामी, हामीहरू	थियौँ	थिएनौँ	भयौँ	भएनौँ
तैँ	थिइस्	थिइनस्	भइस्	भइनस्
तिमी, तिमीहरू	थियौ	थिएनौ	भयौ	भएनौ
ऊ, यो, त्यो (m.)	थियो	थिएन	भयो	भएन
ऊ, यो, त्यो (f.)	थिई	थिइन	भई	भइन
उनी, यिनी, तिनी (m.)	थिए	थिएनन्	भए	भएनन्
उनी, यिनी, तिनी (f.)	थिइन्	थिइनन्	भइन्	भइनन्
यी, ती, उनीहरू etc.	थिए	थिएनन्	भए	भएनन्

High forms

तपाईं, तपाईंहरू etc.	हुनुहुन्थ्यो	हुनुहुन्नथ्यो	हुनुभयो	हुनुभएन

The simple past tense of the verb हुनु *to be* has two forms. The थियो form translates as *was* or *were,* and this form of the verb is used to talk about situations and conditions in the past:

हिजो म नेपालमा थिइनँ, अमेरिकामा थिएँ ।	*Yesterday I was not in Nepal,* *I was in America.*
भात जूठो थिएन, चोखो थियो ।	*The food was not polluted,* *it was pure.**
हिजोको मौसम असाध्य नराम्रो थियो ।	*Yesterday's weather was very bad.*
धन बहादुरका दुइजना छोरा थिए ।	*Dhan Bahadur had two sons.*

---

* The word जूठो is loosely translated as *polluted*. Any food that has come into contact with someone's mouth – either directly, or indirectly via a hand or a utensil – is considered जूठो and therefore may not be eaten by any other person. This everyday concern about cleanliness and hygiene is given a deeper meaning by notions of caste and ritual purity. The observance of this rule is traditionally stricter among higher Hindu castes such as the Bahuns than among, for instance, the various Tibeto-Burman-speaking ethnic groups, and it also varies between families and social classes. While parents and elder siblings may share food with the younger children of a family, as an outsider you should observe these rules unless and until you know for sure that the people with whom you are eating do not observe them so strictly themselves. Food should be touched only with the right hand, because the left hand is used for toilet ablutions.

The भयो form refers to changes, events and transformations in the past and may often be translated as *happened* or *became*:

ऊ लाटो थियो, पछि त पण्डित भयो ।	*He was stupid, but later he* *became a Pandit.*
खाना तातो थियो, पछि त चिसो भयो ।	*The food was hot, but then it* *became cold.*
ऊ सुखी थियो, पछि त दुःखी भयो ।	*He was happy, but later he* *became sad.*
कोठा फोहोर थियो, पछि पनि सफा भएन ।	*The room was dirty, and later it* *didn't become clean either.*
ओहो गोविन्दजी, तपाईंलाई के भयो ? मलाई त केही भएन ।	*Oho Govindajī, what happened to* *you? Nothing has happened to me.*

The following pairs of statements illustrate the difference in the meaning of the two forms:

मेरी बहिनी बिरामी थिइन् ।	*My sister <u>was</u> ill.*
मेरी बहिनी बिरामी भइन् ।	*My sister <u>became</u> ill.*
कोठामा गर्मी थियो ।	*It <u>was</u> hot in the room.*
कोठामा गर्मी भयो ।	*It <u>became</u> hot in the room.*
पसलहरू बन्द थिए ।	*The shops <u>were</u> shut.*
पसलहरू बन्द भए ।	*The shops <u>became</u> shut.*

भयो and भएन are commonly used on their own to tell someone that something has or has not been done or completed, when both speakers know what it is that they are talking about. For instance, **A** and **B**, who are both staying in the same hotel, had previously been discussing **B**'s difficulty in getting an air ticket. **A** sees **B** coming back to the hotel, and he knows that he has been to the airline office. Instead of asking him *did you succeed in booking your ticket?* all he needs to say is:

A भयो ?   *Did it happen?/Any luck?*

to which **B** will give one of the following replies:

B भयो !   *Yes, it's done!*   or   **B** भएन !   *No, no luck!*

56 Location and movement

Nepali has two sets of words that mean *here, there,* and *where.* The first, ending in -हाँ, refers mainly to static locations, while the second, ending in -ता, is most commonly used with verbs of motion:

यहाँ	*here, in this place*	यता	*over here, in this direction, hither*
त्यहाँ	*there, in that place*	उता	*over there, in that direction, thither*
कहाँ	*where, in which place*	कता	*in which direction? whither?*
कहीं	*somewhere, in any place*	कतै	*to somewhere, in any direction*

57 *Someone* and *something*: the uses of केही and कोही

As an adjective, केही means *some* or *a few:*

केही दिन	*a few days*	केही पैसा	*some money*
केही मान्छेहरू	*some people*	केही न केही	*something or other*

As an adjective, कोही also means *some,* but can only be used with human nouns, and usually in the singular:

कोही मान्छे *some man (whom I do not know)*
कोही न कोही *someone or other*

Much more commonly, these two words are used as third-person pronouns, and they can be understood to have the following meanings, depending on the kind of sentence they occur in:

	Affirmative statement	Negative statement	Question
केही	*something*	*nothing*	*anything*
कोही	*someone*	*no-one*	*anyone*

घरमा कोही छ ? घरमा कोही छैन ।
उनीहरू बगैंचामा छन् ।

Is there anyone in the house?
There is no-one in the house.
They are in the garden.

तिम्रो हातमा के छ ? मेरो हातमा केही त छैन आमा ।

What do you have in your hand?
I don't have anything in my hand, mother.

In negative sentences पनि *even, also* can be added to both केही and कोही to heighten the negativity of the sentence: *nothing at all, nobody whatsoever:*

मेरो हातमा केही पनि छैन ।
I don't have anything at all in my hand.
घरमा कोही पनि छैन ।
There is no-one at all in the house.

EXERCISE 28 Translate into Nepali:

1 Please open the window, it has become very hot in this room.
2 Yesterday morning the children were all here. But today no-one came to school at all.
3 Last Wednesday it rained heavily. I didn't have an umbrella, and I got soaked.
4 Grandfather had two sons. One was called Sanju and one was called Niroj. Sanju became very rich but Niroj was very poor.
5 The people of that country were very poor and there was nothing at all in their houses.
6 Yesterday many people went to Paśupatināth temple, because yesterday was a full moon day (**pūrṇimā**).

६६ 16 A visit from Shankarprasad

Shankarprasad Acharya is a priest and teacher of high social status.
Motilal phoned Shankarprasad Acharya a little earlier, to invite him to his
house. He is anxious to cultivate good relations with such a man.
Shankarprasad Acharya has just arrived, but the domestic arrangements
are not running smoothly.

मोतीलाल आचार्यजी, नमस्कार।आरामै
हुनुहुन्छ ?

शंकरप्रसाद आराम । तपाईं नि ?

मोतीलाल मलाई राम्रो छ । बस्नुहोस्, के
लिनुहुन्छ तपाई ?

शंकरप्रसाद तपाईं जे लिनुहुन्छ म त्यही नै
लिन्छु नि ।

मोतीलाल हवस् त । एकै छिन । म
श्रीमतीलाई खबर गर्छु । आज
उनले के के पकाइन् मलाई
थाहा भएन । म सोध्छु, है ? ...
ए, अंजु, अंजु, तिमी कता गयौ
हँ ? खाना तयार भएन ?

अंजु हजुर ? म भरखरै बजारबाट
आएँ । के गर्नु र, काम धेरै छ ।
म एक्लै छु । म पहिला
चिया तयार गर्छु नि ।
तपाईंहरू बस्नुहोला ।

मोतीलाल ओहो कस्तो ढिलो भयो आज ।
मैले वहाँलाई घरमा बोलाएँ ।
वहाँ टाढाबाट आउनुभयो, तर
तिमीले खाना पकाएनौ ।

अंजु सुन्नुहोस् । मलाई गाली नगर्नुहोस् । घरमा अरू पनि धेरै काम थियो ।

मोतीलाल ठीक छ, ठीक छ, अब चाँडै गर । ... आचार्यजी, माफ गर्नुहोला । पहिला चिया
लिनुहुन्छ कि ?

शंकरप्रसाद हुन्छ, हुन्छ । केही छैन ।

मोतीलाल ए ल चिया पनि आइपुग्यो । बिस्कुट पनि लिनुहुन्छ कि ?

शंकरप्रसाद हुन्छ । एउटा दिनुहोस् न ।

आचार्यजी *a respectful title for a religious teacher or a learned man*
आरामै *in good health* (polite)
जे *that which*
त्यही *that same* (emphasised form of त्यो *that*)
एकै *just one*
खबर गर्नु *to inform*
सोध्नु *to ask*
तयार *ready*

भरखरै *recently, just now*
बोलाउनु *to call, invite*
गाली गर्नु *to tell off, abuse*
अरू *other, additional*
चाँडै गर्नु *to do immediately*
माफ गर्नु *to forgive*
पहिला *firstly*
आइपुग्नु *to arrive*
बिस्कुट *biscuit*

Motilal	Acharyaji, greetings. Are you well?
Shankarprasad	I am well. And you?
Motilal	I am well. Please sit down, what would you like?*¹
Shankarprasad	I will have whatever you are going to have.
Motilal	That's fine then. Just one moment. I will tell my wife. I don't know what*² she has cooked today. I'll ask her, all right? ... Oh, Anju, Anju, where have you gone, huh?*³ Isn't the food ready?
Anju	What? I have only just come from the market. What to do, indeed, there's lots of work. I am all alone. I'll prepare tea first, for sure. You people please sit down.
Motilal	Oho, how late things are today! I invited him to our home. He came from far away, but you didn't cook any food.
Anju	Listen. Don't tell me off. There was a lot of other work in the house.
Motilal	OK, OK, now do it immediately ... Acharyaji, please forgive (me). Will you first take tea?
Shankarprasad	Yes, yes. It doesn't matter.
Motilal	There now, the tea has arrived too. Would you like a biscuit as well?
Shankarprasad	Yes. Please give me one, would you?

*¹ के लिनुहुन्छ ?*what will you take?* is a more polite way of asking someone what they would like to eat or drink than के खानुहुन्छ *what will you eat?*
*² के is repeated because Motilal expects his wife to have cooked a number of different things.
*³ Motilal and his wife Anju are a traditional couple in that their use of pronouns is asymmetical: he addresses her as तिमी, while she calls him तपाई. Less traditional couples nowadays address one another as तिमी.

Grammar

58 Transitive and intransitive verbs

All Nepali verbs are either transitive or intransitive. When using the simple past tense of any verb it is important to know which category the verb belongs to.

A transitive verb is a verb that must have an object. For instance, we cannot *see* without seeing *something*, and that something is the object of our seeing: it receives the action of our seeing. We cannot *eat*, or *do*, or *make*, or *look*, without something being *eaten, done, made* or *looked at*: therefore, all of these verbs, plus many others, are said to be 'transitive' because they act upon something, which is their object.

An intransitive verb is a verb that cannot have an object. For instance, all verbs of motion are intransitive: we may go *to* a place, or come *from* a place, but these places are not receivers of the action of motion, they are simply destinations or sources.

59 Transitive verbs and the suffix -ले

The subject of a transitive verb in the simple past tense must take the agentive (or 'subject-marking') suffix -ले. Linguistically, -ले is a relic of an old passive construction, and it has the original meaning of *by*. Because -ले is a postposition, the subject word must change to the oblique case when -ले is added to it. म and तैं take special forms when -ले is added to them:

म	becomes	मै	producing	मैले
तैं	becomes	तै	producing	तैले

All of the other pronouns change in exactly the same way as they do with other postpositions:

ऊ	becomes	उस	producing	उसले	(often pronounced **ulle**)
यो	becomes	यस	producing	यसले	(often pronounced **elle**)
त्यो	becomes	त्यस	producing	त्यसले	(often pronounced **telle**)
को	becomes	कस	producing	कसले	(often pronounced **kalle**)
उनी	becomes	उन	producing	उनले	
यिनी	becomes	यिन	producing	यिनले	
तिनी	becomes	तिन	producing	तिनले	

मैले काम गरें ।	*I worked.*
हामीले फिलिम हेऱ्यौं ।	*We watched a film.*
उसले मलाई नमस्ते गरेन ।	*He did not greet me.*
उनीहरूले एउटा चिठी पनि लेखेनन् ।	*They did not write even one letter.*
तपाईंले उनलाई उपहार दिनुभयो ?	*Did you give her a present?*

Some commonly used verbs are a combination of a noun with either the
verb गर्नु *to do* or the verb हुनु *to be.* Such a verb is transitive with गर्नु but
intransitive with हुनु:

उनीहरूले सिनेमा-घर बन्द गरे ।	*They shut the cinema.*
सिनेमा-घर बन्द भयो ।	*The cinema closed.*
हामीहरूले काम शुरु गऱ्यौं ।	*We started work.*
काम शुरु भयो ।	*The work began.*
सरकारले हडताल खतम गऱ्यो ।	*The government stopped the strike.*
हडताल खतम भयो ।	*The strike ended.*

EXERCISE 29   Put the following sentences into the simple past tense,
beginning each new sentence with the word हिजो *yesterday* and removing
the word आज *today* :

१   आज तपाईं चिया खानुहुन्न ?
२   आज म एउटा किताब किन्छु ।
३   आज हामीहरू मासु खाँदैनौं ।
४   आज उनीहरू भात खाँदैनन् । उनीहरूको घरमा चामल छैन ।
५   आज तिमी रेडियो किन सुन्दैनौ ? आज अम्बर गुरुङ्ग गीत गाउनुहुन्छ ।
६   आज आमा उठ्नुहुन्न । वहाँ बिरामी हुनुहुन्छ ।

60   Further uses of -ले

a) With the subject of a transitive verb in tenses other than the past

-ले must always be affixed to the subject of a transitive verb in the simple
past tense, but it can also be used to emphasise the subject of a transitive
verb in the habitual present tense in the following circumstances:

■   if the sentence says that it is part of the natural order of things for the
subject to perform the verb, and therefore states that this is a role that is
specific to the subject:

कुखुराले फुल पार्छ ।	*A chicken lays eggs.*
बाघले बाख्रा खान्छ ।	*A tiger eats goats.*
घामले न्यानो दिन्छ ।	*Sunshine gives warmth.*
पक्का बाहुनले रक्सी खाँदैन ।	*A proper Brahmin does not*
	drink alcohol.

■ if the sentence is a question asking who or what is the subject of a transitive verb:

कसले त्यो कुरा भन्छ ?	*Who says that?*
आज कसले चिया बनाउँछ ?	*Who will make the tea today?*

■ if the sentence is a response to a question such as those above, or focuses in any way upon the subject of the verb:

आमाले भन्नुहुन्छ नि ।	*Mother says so, you know!*
आज भाइले चिया बनाउँछ ।	*Today younger brother will make the tea.*

b) To denote the use of faculties or instruments

हामी कानले सुन्छौँ ।	*We hear with (our) ears.*
हामी दाँतले टोक्छौँ ।	*We bite with (our) teeth.*
हामी आँखाले हेर्छौँ ।	*We look with (our) eyes.*
हामी मुखले बोल्छौँ ।	*We speak with (our) mouths.*
हामी नाकले सुँघ्छौँ ।	*We smell with (our) noses.*
नेपालीहरू दाहिने हातले भात खान्छन् ।	*Nepalis eat rice with (the) right hand.*
नेपालीहरू देब्रे हातले भात खाँदैनन् ।	*Nepalis do not eat rice with (the) left hand.*

c) With nouns to mark a causal function

यस कारणले	*because of this*
त्यस कारणले	*because of that*
के कारणले ?	*because of what?*

The phrases त्यस कारणले and यस कारणले mean *due to that cause* and *due to this cause* respectively, and they are commonly used to mean *so* or *thus*:

ऊ कलिलो उमेरको केटा हो । यस कारणले उसलाई चुरोट नदिनुहोला ।	*He is a boy of a tender age. So please do not give him a cigarette.*
पोहोर साल कम पानी पर्‍यो । त्यस कारणले बजारमा चामल साह्रै महंगो भयो ।	*Last year little rain fell. Therefore rice became very expensive in the market.*

The abbreviated forms of this phrase, त्यस कारण and त्यसैले, are very commonly used.

Other nouns can take -ले when they are the cause of an event or a condition, regardless of whether the main verb of the sentence is transitive or not:

| अनिकालको बेलामा धेरै मानिसहरू भोकले मर्छन् । | *In time of famine, many people die of hunger.* |
| मेरो लुगा पानीले भिज्यो । | *My clothes were made wet by rain.* |

EXERCISE 30 पढेर बुझ्नुहोस्

अस्ति शनिवार थियो । नेपालमा शनिवार बिदा हुन्छ र अस्ति सबै पसल र अफिसहरू बन्द थिए । त्यो दिन ठूलो पानी पनि पर्‍यो । रामसँग छाता थिएन, ऊ बाहिर गएन । उसले एउटा किताब पढ्यो । हिजो आइतवार थियो । नेपालमा आइतवार बिदाको दिन हुँदैन । हिजो पानी परेन र राम अफिस गयो । रामको बुवा पनि अफिस जानुभयो । रामकी आमा बिहानै मन्दिर जानुभयो । मन्दिरमा वहाँले पूजा गर्नुभयो र आठ बजेतिर घर फर्कनुभयो । राम र रामकी बहिनी माया साढे छ बजे उठे । उनीहरूले चिया र रोटी खाए । "अब म अफिस जान्छु र बाटोमा म एउटा छाता किन्छु" रामले भन्यो ।

प्रश्नहरू

१	अस्ति के वार थियो ?	५	हिजो राम कता गयो ?
२	अस्तिको मौसम कस्तो थियो ?	६	हिजो रामकी आमा कहाँ जानुभयो ?
३	अस्ति रामले के गर्‍यो ?	७	राम र माया कति बजेसम्म सुते ?
४	हिजो के वार थियो ?		

61 Parts of the body

HEAD		ARMS	
टाउको	head	पाखुरा	upper arm
मुख, अनुहार	face	हात	hand/forearm
आँखा	eye	औंला	finger
नाक	nose	कुहिनो	elbow
मुख	mouth	नङ	fingernail
कान	ear	बूढी औंला	thumb
कपाल	hair		
दाँत	tooth	**LEGS**	
जिब्रो	tongue	खुट्टा	leg
घाँटी	neck/throat	खुट्टा	foot
चिउँडो	chin	घुँडा	knee
दाढी	beard	कुर्कुच्चा	heel
		औंला	toe
BODY			
शरीर	body	**OTHER**	
पिठ्यूँ	back	रगत	blood
पेट	stomach	छाला	skin
छाती	breast/chest	हाड	bone
काँध	shoulder		
कम्मर	waist		
मुटु	heart		
फोक्सो	lung		

9 | I'LL GO WHEN I'VE EATEN

म भात खाएर जान्छु

In this unit you will learn how to:

■ use two verbs in one sentence
■ report information from other sources
■ use the continuous tenses of verbs
■ discuss people's ages

17 A day off work

Rajiv has just completed his first week at the office. He and Keshav discuss plans for their day off.

राजीव   भोलि हाम्रो छुट्टी होइन र ?

केशव   हो । भोलि त शनिवारै हो नि ! शनिवार हरेक अफिसको लागि छुट्टीको दिन हुन्छ । तपाईं छुट्टी लिनुहुन्न कि कसो ?

राजीव   लिन्छु नि ! तपाईं धेरै जसो छुट्टीको दिन कसरी बिताउनुहुन्छ ? दिनभरि सुत्नुहुन्छ ?

केशव   दिनभरि सुत्तिन । जिन्दगी त्यति लामो हुँदैन ! म छुट्टीका दिनहरू धेरै जसो केही-न-केही गरेर अथवा कता-न-कता गएर बिताउँछु । कहिले काहीं म अफिसका केही साथीहरूसँग भेटेर बाहिर जान्छु । आज बिहान मैले दौलतजीसँग कुरा गरें । भोलि पनि यस्तै कार्यक्रम छ रे ।

राजीव   भोलिको कार्यक्रम कहाँ छ नि ?

केशव   उनीहरू गोदावरी जान्छन् रे ।

राजीव   तपाईं पनि जानुहुन्छ कि ?

केशव   म कोशिश गर्छु । भोलि बिहान मेरी श्रीमती बजार जान्छिन् रे । त्यसैले भोलि बिहान म घरै बसेर नानीहरूलाई हेर्छु ।

राजीव   तपाईंका साथीहरू हिंडैरे जान्छन् ? अलि टाढा छ, होइन ?

केशव   हो, टाढै छ । उनीहरू बस चढेर जान्छन् रे । गोदावरीका बसहरू घण्टा-घण्टामा पाटन भएर जान्छन् रे ।

राजीव   गोदावरी पुगेर उनीहरू के गर्छन् ?

केशव   उनीहरू यहाँबाट केही खाने कुरा लिएर जान्छन् रे । केही हप्ता अघि हामीहरू पिकनिक लिएर सुन्दरीजल पनि गयौं । सुन्दरीजल पुगेर हामीहरूले खोलाको बगरमा बसेर खाना खायौं अनि रमाइलो गऱ्यौं । कोही साथीहरूले रूखको छायाँमा बसेर ताश खेले अथवा गफ गरे । कोही साथीहरू भुईंमा पल्टेर निदाए । त्यस्तै हुन्छ । भोलि तपाईं पनि गोदावरी जानुहुन्छ कि ?

राजीव   भोलि बिहान ससुरालीमा निम्तो छ । त्यस कारणले अप्ठ्यारो छ । उनीहरू कति बजेतिर हिंड्छन् ?

केशव   त्यो त अहिलेसम्म पक्का भएन । बेलुकातिर म दौलतजीलाई फोन गरेर पता लगाउँछु ।

राजीव   थाहा पाएर मलाई पनि फोन गर्नुहोस्, है त । भरे बेलुका म घरै हुन्छु ।

केशव   हवस् । भरे बेलुका म तपाईंलाई फोन गर्छु । अब त अबेर भयो । आज छुट्टीको दिन होइन, हाकिम रिसाएर हामीलाई गाली गर्नुहुन्छ ।

छुट्टी *day off, holiday*	पिकनिक *picnic*
कसो ? *how? in what manner?*	खोला *river*
बिताउनु *to spend time*	बगर *bank of a river*
दिनभरि *all day*	रमाइलो गर्नु *to enjoy oneself*
लामो *long*	छायाँ *shade*

केही-न-केही *something or other*	ताश *cards*
अथवा *or*	खेल्नु *to play*
कता-न-कता *somewhere or other*	गफ गर्नु *to chat*
भेट्नु *to meet*	भुई *ground*
कुरा गर्नु *to talk, converse*	पल्टनु *to lie down*
कार्यक्रम *programme*	निदाउनु *to fall sleep*
रे *a word marking information gathered elsewhere*	ससुराली *the home of a man's parents-in-law*
कोशिश गर्नु *to try*	निम्तो *invitation*
त्यसैले *therefore*	अठ्चारो *difficult, awkward*
नानी *small child*	फोन गर्नु *to phone*
हिंडेरै *on foot*	पक्का *decided*
बस चढ्नु *to board a bus*	पता लगाउनु *to find out*
पाट्न the second largest city of the Kathmandu valley	थाहा पाउनु *to find out*
भएर *via*	है त *OK then?*
पुग्नु *to reach, arrive*	भरे बेलुका *this evening*
खाने कुरा *things to eat; food*	हाकिम *boss*
अघि *ago*	रिसाउनु *to become angry*

Rajiv   Tomorrow's our day off, isn't it?

Keshav   Yes. Tomorrow *is* Saturday, you know! Saturday is a day off for every office. Won't you take the day off, or what?

Rajiv   I certainly will, you know! How do you usually spend a day off? Do you sleep all day?

Keshav   I do not sleep all day. Life isn't that long! I usually spend my days off doing something or other or going somewhere or other. Sometimes I meet up with some office friends and go out. This morning I talked to Daulatji. He says there is just such a programme tomorrow too.

Rajiv   Where is tomorrow's programme then?

Keshav   He says they will go to Godavari.*[1]

Rajiv   Will you go too?

Keshav   I shall try. My wife says she will go to the market tomorrow morning. So tomorrow morning I will stay at home and look after the children.

Rajiv   Will your friends go on foot? It's quite far, isn't it?

Keshav   Yes, it is rather far. They say they will go by bus. Apparently buses for Godavari go every hour, via Patan.

Rajiv	What will they do when they have reached Godavari?
Keshav	They say they will take some food from here. A few weeks ago we took a picnic to Sundarijal too.*² When we reached Sundarijal we sat on the riverbank and ate and enjoyed ourselves. Some friends sat in the shade of a tree and played cards or chatted. Some friends lay down on the ground and went to sleep. That's how it is. Will you go to Godavari tomorrow too?
Rajiv	Tomorrow morning we are invited to my in-laws' house. So it's difficult. At about what time will they leave?
Keshav	That has not been decided yet. This evening I'll phone Daulatji and find out.
Rajiv	When you find out please phone me too, OK? I'll be at home this evening.
Keshav	Sure. I'll phone you this evening. But now it's late. Today isn't a day off, the boss will get angry and tell us off.

*¹ A popular picnicking spot in the south of the Kathmandu Valley where there are botanical gardens.
*² A beauty spot to the northeast of Kathmandu.

Sājhā bus network map, Nepal.

🗝 Grammar

62   Two verbs with the same subject: the -एर participle

In English, if a sentence or a part of a sentence (a clause) contains two verbs performed by the same person, both of the verbs take the same tense and the word 'and' is used to link them, e.g. *I came and (I) sat down, I ate the rice and went out*. In Nepali, the first of the two verbs almost always takes a special form (called the 'conjunctive participle'), and the literal translation of the same sentences in Nepali becomes *having come in I sat down* and *having eaten the rice I went out*.

A participle is a form of a verb that may be used adjectivally (to describe nouns) or as one part of a verb phrase in certain tenses. Nepali has a variety of different participles, each with a different ending and its own technical name. In this book, each participle will be referred to by the ending that distinguishes it from all the others.

The conjunctive participle of a Nepali verb is most commonly formed by taking its past tense base and adding the ending -एर **-era** to it. Therefore, we will call it the '**-era** participle':

Verb	Past tense base	-era participle	
गर्नु	गर-	गरेर	*having done*
हिंड्नु	हिंड-	हिंडेर	*having walked*
लिनु	लि-	लिएर	*having taken*
जानु	ग-	गएर	*having gone*
आउनु	आ-	आएर	*having come*
हुनु	भ-	भएर	*having become, having been* *

*The base of हुनु is always भ- for a participle. थि- is never used as the base for a participle.

The **-era** participle refers to an action that takes place *before* the action of the main verb – that is, the final verb – of the sentence. But other than that it does not really have a tense of its own: the tense of the sentence is the tense that is given by the verb at the end. Therefore, the action described by the **-era** participle can be in any tense: past, present or future:

Nepali	**English**
म आएर बसें ।	*I came and sat down.*
म आएर बस्छु ।	*I come and sit down.*
म भोलि आएर बस्छु ।	*I shall come and sit down tomorrow.*

म भात खाएर बाहिर गएँ ।	I ate rice and went out.
म भात खाएर बाहिर जान्छु ।	I eat rice and go out.
भोलि म भात खाएर बाहिर जान्छु ।	Tomorrow I shall eat rice and go out.

In the English sentences, both verbs are in the same tense; in the Nepali versions only the main final verb has a tense. The subject of the Nepali sentence is usually stated at the very beginning of the sentence, as in these examples, but sometimes it is not mentioned until after the **-era** participle:

| भात खाएर म बाहिर जान्छु । | Having eaten rice I go out. |

The **-era** participle is formed in exactly the same way, no matter what or who the subject of the sentence is: the level of politeness is indicated by the main verb of the sentence. If the main verb is transitive and in a past tense, the subject must take -ले.

उसले झ्यालनेर बसेर एउटा केरा खायो ।	He sat near the window and ate a banana.
म उसको लुगा धोएर तपाईलाई दिन्छु ।	I shall wash his clothes and give them to you.
हिजो किशनजीले हाम्रो पसलमा आएर एक जोर जुत्ता किन्नुभयो ।	Yesterday Kishanji came into our shop and bought a pair of shoes.
उनीहरू खुम्बु गएर सगरमाथा चढे ।	They went to Khumbu and climbed Mount Everest.

भएर, the **-era** participle of हुनु *to be,* is also used to mean *via:*

| त्यो विमान दिल्ली भएर जान्छ । | That flight goes via Delhi. |
| उनीहरूको बस पोखरा भएर काठ्माडौं गयो । | Their bus went to Kathmandu via Pokhara. |

63 The reported speech-marker रे

रे can only be used as an appendage to a sentence, and never on its own. When it is added to the end of a statement, the word रे indicates that the person speaking has been told what s/he has just said by someone else. It is usually possible to ascertain who or what the source of the information is, but sometimes it is left quite vague, just as in English one reports a rumour by beginning 'I hear that... ' or 'they say that... '

If someone says:

| तपाईको छोरालाई भोक लाग्यो रे । | Your son is hungry (+ reported speech-marker) |

the presence of तपाईंको छोरा *your son* in the sentence means that the person speaking has probably been told by your son that he is hungry, in which case the sentence could be translated *your son says he's hungry*. However, it could also mean that someone else has informed the speaker of this fact: one can only be sure if one knows the context in which the statement is made.

Similarly, a sentence such as:

आज अफिस जाँदैन रे ।   *(He) won't go to the office today*
                                (+ reported speech-marker)

could mean *he says he won't go to the office today* or *she says he won't go to the office today* or *they say he won't go to the office today*. Without knowing the context in which the statement is made you really cannot choose between these translations.

This kind of confusion should not occur during a conversation, because the meaning is always clear in its context. Sometimes, however, a speaker will add रे to the end of a statement in order to disown responsibility for its truth or falsity. The following statements suggest that the speaker has heard the news s/he reports on the radio, or has read them in a newspaper:

आज पानी पर्दैन रे ।   *They say it will not rain today.*
भारतको राष्ट्रपति आज नेपाल आउँछ रे ।   *The Indian president comes to*
                                Nepal today, I hear.

If someone said something but you did not hear what they said, you might wish to ask someone else what was said. A quick way of doing this is simply to say:

के रे ?   *What was said?*

EXERCISE 31   Convert the following pairs of sentences into one sentence by changing the first verb into the **-era** participle.

Example

म घर जान्छु । त्यसपछि म खाना खान्छु ।   =   म घर गएर खाना खान्छु ।
I shall go home. After that I shall eat.   *I shall go home and eat.*

१   म नेपाल जान्छु । त्यसपछि म तपाईंलाई चिठी लेख्छु ।
२   म विचार गर्छु । म तपाईंलाई भन्छु ।
३   उनीहरू किताब किन्छन् । त्यसपछि तपाईंकहाँ आउँछन् ।
४   यो केटी स्कूल जान्छे । त्यहाँ अँग्रेजी सिक्छे ।
५   म अफिस जान्छु । म तपाईंलाई फोन गर्छु ।
६   वहाँ झापा जानुभयो । वहाँ मेरो दाइको घरमा बस्नुभयो ।

EXERCISE 32 Construct sentences that tell someone to do two things, one after the other, along the following lines:

तपाई / भात खानु / सुल्नु = तपाई भात खाएर सुल्नुहोस् ।
you / eat rice / sleep *You please eat the rice and go to sleep.*

१ तिमी / घर जानु / काम गर्नु
२ तपाई / रेडियो सुन्नु / घर जानु
३ तिमी / चुरोट लिनु / आउनु
४ तपाई / यो किताब पढ्नु / मलाई दिनु
५ तिमी / लण्डन पुग्नु / मकहाँ आउनु
६ तपाई / झापा जानु / मेरो दाइको घरमा बस्नु

18 A chance encounter in Darjeeling

Subir is a resident of Darjeeling, and Ashesh lives in Kathmandu. Some months ago the two men met while Subir was visiting Kathmandu. Now Subir is surprised to meet Ashesh unexpectedly in Darjeeling.

सुबीर अहो! तपाई यहाँ के गर्दै हुनुहुन्छ ? तपाईलाई देखेर म छक्क परें नि ! तपाईहरू दार्जीलिङ्गमा बसाइँ सर्नुभयो कि क्या हो ?

अशेष होइन, म एक हप्तादेखि यहाँको वन संरक्षण विभागमा काम गर्दै छु।पोहोर साल पनि म नेपालमा यस्तै काम गर्दै थिएँ नि ।

सुबीर अनि कति बस्नुहुन्छ दार्जीलिङ्गमा ? परिवार पनि सँगै छन् ?

अशेष श्रीमती र छोरीहरू मसँग छन् तर छोराहरूलाई छाडेर आयौं यसपालि । कान्छो छोराको उमेर अहिले तेह्र वर्ष भयो, जेठो छोरा चाहिं सोह्र वर्ष लाग्यो ।स्कूल नगई उनीहरूको प्रगति हुँदैन ।त्यस कारणले उनीहरू उतै पढ्दै छन् ।

सुबीर हो, तपाईका तीनजना छोरीहरू छन्, अब याद आयो ।कान्छी छोरीको नामचाहिं लक्ष्मी अनि जेठी छोरीकोचाहिं सरस्वती, होइन ? तर माहिंली छोरीको नाम के हो? मैले बिर्सें ।

अशेष माहिंली छोरीको नाम राधिका हो ।अहिले लक्ष्मी र राधिका एभरेष्ट होटेलमा पौडी खेल्दै छन् ।सरस्वती र मेरी श्रीमती बजारमा किनमेल गर्दै छन् ।स्कूलहरू भोलिदेखि खुल्छन् नि, आज छुट्टीको अन्तिम दिन हो ।

सुबीर उनीहरू भोलीदेखि कुनचाहिं स्कूल जान्छन् ? लोरेंटो कलेज ?

अशेष हो, लोरेंटो कलेज जान्छन् । स्कूल असाध्य राम्रो छ रे । त्यो कुरा थाहा पाएर उनीहरूलाई त्यही स्कूलमा राख्यौं हामीहरूले ।उनीहरू दुई महिनासम्म त्यहाँ पढ्छन् । दुई महिनापछि हामी काठ्माडौँ फर्कन्छौँ ।

सुबीर ठीक गर्नुभयो तपाईले ।अब तपाई एभरेष्ट होटेलसम्म हिंडेरै जानुहुन्छ ? निक्कै माथि छ नि, उकालो पनि छ ।

अशेष म बिर्सेर घरबाट पैसा नलिईकन निस्कें । त्यस कारणले हिंडेर जाँदै छु । तपाई कता जाँद हुनुहुन्छ ?

सुबीर मेरो अफिसको काम पाँच बजे सिद्धियो, अनि म ऊ त्यो चियापसलमा बसेर साथीहरूसँग गफ गर्दै थिएँ । अलिपछि घर जान्छु । मेरो घर पनि उतै छ नि । तर यो बाटोचाहिं अलि घुमाउरो छ । म तपाईसँग अलि माथिसम्म गएर तपाईलाई अर्को बाटो देखाउँछु, हुन्न ? त्यो बाटो नघुमीकन सीधै होटेलमा पुग्छ ।

अशेष बिस्तारै चिया खाएर आउनुहोस् न त । केही हतार छैन ।

सुबीर भैगो, चिया चिसो भयो । चिया नखाईकन आउँछु । अबेर भयो, श्रीमती रिसाउँछिन् । ल, साहूजी, म गएँ , नमस्कार ।

छक्क पर्नु *to be surprised*	खुल्नु *to open*
देख्नु *to see*	अन्तिम *last, final*
बसाइँ सर्नु *to move house*	कुनचाहिं *which?*
क्या *what?*	असाध्य *extremely*
वन *forest*	राख्नु *to put, place*
संरक्षण *conservation*	माथि *up, above*
विभाग *department*	उकालो *steep, uphill*
छाड्नु *to leave, quit*	निस्कनु *to come out*
यसपालि *this time*	सिद्धिनु *to end*
कान्छो *youngest*	ऊ त्यो *that one, over there*
जेठो *eldest*	-चाहिं *as for*
लाग्नु *to begin to be, tend towards*	घुमाउरो *indirect*
प्रगति *progress*	देखाउनु *to show*
उतै *there* (emphasised form of उता)	घुम्नु *to circle, wander*
पढ्नु *to study*	सीधै *directly*
याद *memory*	बिस्तारै *slowly, gently*
माहिंलो *second eldest*	भैगो *it's over*
बिर्सनु *to forget*	चिसो *cold*
पौडी खेल्नु *to swim*	अबेर *lateness*
किनमेल *shopping*	साहूजी *shopkeeper*

Subir Oho! What are you doing here? I was surprised to see you, you know! Have you moved to Darjeeling or what?

Ashesh No, I've been working in the Forest Conservation Department since one week ago. Last year too I was doing the same kind of work in Nepal, you know.

Subir And how long will you stay in Darjeeling? Are the family with you too?

Ashesh	My wife and daughters are with me but this time we came without our sons. The younger son is 13 years old now, the elder is just 14. If they don't go to school they won't make progress. So they are studying there.
Subir	Yes, you have three daughters, now I remember. The youngest is called Lakshmi and the eldest Sarasvati, is that not right? But what is the middle daughter's name? I have forgotten.
Ashesh	The middle daughter's name is Radhika. Now Lakshmi and Radhika are swimming at the Everest Hotel. Sarasvati and my wife are shopping in the market. The schools open from tomorrow, you know, today is the last day of the holiday.
Subir	Which school will they go to from tomorrow? Loretto College?
Ashesh	Yes, they will go to Loretto College. I hear the school is extremely good. When we got to know that we put them in that school. They will study there for two months. After two months we will return to Kathmandu.
Subir	You did the right thing. Are you going to walk to the Everest Hotel now? It's a long way up, you know, and it's steep too.
Ashesh	I forgot and I came out of the house without any money. That's why I'm walking. Where are you going?
Subir	My office work finished at 5 o'clock, and I was sitting in that teashop over there, chatting with my friends. I'll go home in a little while. My house is in the same direction, you know. But this path is rather indirect. I'll come a little way up with you and show you another path, no? That path goes straight to the hotel without any diversions.
Ashesh	But please drink your tea slowly and then come, won't you? There's no hurry.
Subir	Forget it,* the tea's gone cold. I'll come without drinking the tea. It's 6 o'clock now, it's late. My wife will be cross. Here, shopkeeper, I'm off, goodbye.

* भैगो is a colloquial expression meaning *that's over and done with*, or *that's not something that need detain us further*.

🔊 Grammar

64 The continuous tenses in -दै छ

The *continuous present* tense refers to actions that are occurring even as the verb is being stated, and is the exact equivalent of English verb phrases such as *I am going, they are watching, we are eating*. Just as in English, the tense can also be used to talk about the future, so long as something else in the sentence makes this clear: *I am going <u>tomorrow</u>, we are eating out <u>next Sunday</u>*. This tense of a verb consists of a word that is the Nepali equivalent of *going / watching / eating*, followed by the appropriate form of छ *is* or *are*. To form the first word, the ending -दै is added to the present tense base of the verb.

If the base ends in a vowel, this vowel must be nasalised. The ending is invariable: that is, it is always the same no matter what or who the subject of the verb may be. छ is the verb that must change according to number, gender and level of politeness.

गर्नु **garnu** *to do*

म	गर् + -दै छु	=	गर्दै छु	I am doing
हामी, हामीहरू	गर् + -दै छौं	=	गर्दै छौं	we are doing
तैं	गर् + -दै छस्	=	गर्दै छस्	you are doing
तिमी, तिमीहरू	गर् + -दै छौ	=	गर्दै छौ	you are doing
ऊ, यो, त्यो (m.)	गर् + -दै छ	=	गर्दै छ	he is doing
ऊ, यो, त्यो (f.)	गर् + -दै छे	=	गर्दै छे	she is doing
उनी, यिनी, तिनी (m.)	गर् + -दै छन्	=	गर्दै छन्	he is doing
उनी, यिनी, तिनी (f.)	गर् + -दै छिन्	=	गर्दै छिन्	she is doing
यी, ती, उनीहरू etc.	गर् + -दै छन्	=	गर्दै छन्	they are doing

जानु **jānu** *to go*

म	जा + ँ + -दै छु	=	जाँदै छु	I am going
हामी, हामीहरू	जा + ँ + -दै छौं	=	जाँदै छौं	we are going
तैं	जा + ँ + -दै छस्	=	जाँदै छस्	you are going
तिमी, तिमीहरू	जा + ँ + -दै छौ	=	जाँदै छौ	you are going
ऊ, यो, त्यो (m.)	जा + ँ + -दै छ	=	जाँदै छ	he is going
ऊ, यो, त्यो (f.)	जा + ँ + -दै छे	=	जाँदै छे	she is going
उनी, यिनी, तिनी (m.)	जा + ँ + -दै छन्	=	जाँदै छन्	he is going
उनी, यिनी, तिनी (f.)	जा + ँ + -दै छिन्	=	जाँदै छिन्	she is going
यी, ती, उनीहरू etc.	जा + ँ + -दै छन्	=	जाँदै छन्	they are going

---

The *continuous past* tense is used to describe what was actually going on at a particular time, and is the exact equivalent of English verb phrases such as *I was going, they were watching, we were eating*. It is formed by adding the invariable ending -दै to the present tense base of a verb to create the Nepali for *going / watching / eating,* just as in the continuous present tense. Instead of ending with छ, however, the verb phrase must end with the थि- form of the past tense of हुनु, meaning *was* or *were.* With High pronouns, these tenses end with हुनुहुन्छ in the present and हुनुहुन्थ्यो in the past.

Continuous present

हाम्रा साथीहरू गीत गाउँदै छन् ।
Our friends are singing a song.

बहिनी कविता पाठ गर्दै छे ।
Younger sister is reading out a poem.

आमा समाचार पत्र हेर्दै हुनुहुन्छ ।
Mother is looking at the newspaper.

Continuous past

हाम्रा साथीहरू ठट्टा गर्दै थिए ।
Our friends were joking.

बहिनी पूजा गर्दै थिई ।
Younger sister was performing puja.

आमा चिया पकाउँदै हुनुहुन्थ्यो ।
Mother was making tea.

Theoretically, the negative form of these tenses should be created by changing छ to छैन, थियो to थिएन, and so on. But in real life these forms are very rarely used. For instance, if someone asks: तपाईं काम गर्दै हुनुहुन्छ ? *are you working?,* and in fact you are simply reading a book, your answer should be along the lines of होइन, म किताब पढ्दै छु *No, I'm reading a book.*

There is a specialised continuous present form of छ *is.* This is used to say that something exists in a particular place, contrary to a listener's expectations, or to state or emphasise the fact of its existence plainly. It occurs only in the singular form छदै छ:

आखिर, पोखरामा हाम्रो घर छदै छ ।
After all, we do have a house Pokhara.

काठमाडौँमा विमानस्थल छदै छ नि !
There is an airport in Kathmandu, you know!

EXERCISE 33 Change the tense of the verb in the following sentences into the continuous present:

१   तपाईं अखबार पढ्नुहुन्छ ?
२   भाइ किताब पढ्छ ।
३   म बाहिर जान्छु ।

४ उनीहरू नेपाली भाषा बोल्छन् ।

५ अब ऊ त्यही कलमले चिठी लेख्छ ।

EXERCISE 34 Change the tense of the verb in the following sentences into the continuous past, and make any other changes to the sentences that thus become necessary:

१ बुवाले अखबार पढ्नुभयो ।

२ तिमीले त्यो किताब पढ्यौ ?

३ मैले जापानी भाषा सिकें ।

४ उनीहरूले टी॰ भी॰ हेरे ।

५ बुवाले बारीमा के गर्नुभयो ?

65 *Which one? This one!* The uses of -चाहिं

The word चाहिं is frequently added to adjectives, or to words such as यो, त्यो, कुन to replace a noun. In this context it can be understood to mean *one*:

अग्लोचाहिं	*the tall one*	त्योचाहिं	*that one*
रातोचाहिं	*the red one*	योचाहिं	*this one*
कुनचाहिं ?	*which one?*		

तपाईंको घर कुनचाहिं हो ? मेरो घर ऊ त्यो अग्लोचाहिं हो ।
Which one is your house? My house is that tall one over there.

तपाईंले कुनचाहिं किन्नुभयो ? सस्तोचाहिं किनें ।
Which one did you buy? I bought the cheap one.

The second usage of चाहिं is contrastive. Here it means *as for*:

म रातो बङ्गला स्कूल जान्छु । दाईचाहिं स्कूल जानुहुन्न, अफिस जानुहुन्छ ।
I go to Rato Bangala School. As for elder brother, (he) does not go to school, he goes to the office.

यो मान्छे बाहुन हो, त्योचाहिं नेवार हो ।
This man is a Brahmin, but that one is a Newar.

66 Other forms of the conjunctive participle

There are two other forms of conjunctive participle which mean much the same as, but are used less frequently than the -एर participle. These forms end in -ई -**ī** and -ईकन -**īkana**:

Verb		cj. ptc. 1	cj.ptc.2	cj.ptc. 3	
गर्नु	to do	गरेर	गरी	गरीकन	doing, having done
हिंड्नु	to walk	हिंडेर	हिंडी	हिंडीकन	walking, having walked
लिनु	to take	लिएर	लिई	लिईकन	taking, having taken
जानु	to go	गएर	गई	गईकन	going, having gone
हुनु	to be	भएर	भई	भईकन	being, having become

The negative forms of all participles are formed simply by adding the prefix न- **na-** to the affirmative form:

cj. ptc. 1	cj.ptc. 2	cj.ptc. 3	
नगरेर	नगरी	नगरीकन	not doing, not having done
नहिंडेर	नहिंडी	नहिंडीकन	not walking, not having walked
नलिएर	नलिई	नलिईकन	not taking, not having taken
नगएर	नगई	नगईकन	not going, not having gone
नभएर	नभई	नभईकन	not being, not having become

In practice, affirmative forms almost always take the -एर ending, while negative forms most usually take the -ईकन ending. Because -ईकन is the longest of the three possible endings, it is emphatic. Consider the differences between the following pairs of sentences:

म भात खाएर बाहिर गएँ ।	I ate and went out.
म भात नखाईकन बाहिर गएँ ।	I went out without having eaten.

The form ending in **-ī** is less commonly used, though it is obligatory in certain idiomatic expressions:

तपाईंसँग नभेटी हुँदैन ।	I simply have to meet you ('not meeting you will not be all right').
मेरी छोरीलाई सिनेमा नगई सुख छैन !	My daughter simply <u>has</u> to go to the cinema (literally, if my daughter does not go to the cinema there is no happiness).
आयो दसैं ढोल बजाई, गयो दसैं रिन बोकाई ।	Dasain came beating the drum, Dasain left, having given us debts to bear.*

* A proverb. ढोल बजाउनु *to play a drum;* बोकाई is from the verb बोकाउनु, which is the causative of बोक्नु *to carry.* Dasain is Nepal's most important annual Hindu festival.

Incidentally, Nepali poets are blessed by this wealth of choice, which makes it much easier for them to adjust the number of beats in a line of verse.

मेरा छोराछोरीहरू हात धोएर भात खान्छन् । *My children wash their hands*
हात नधोईकन भात खानु ठीक हुँदैन । *before they eat. It's not good to*
eat without washing your hands.

उनी नुहाएर सुत्छिन् । ननुहाईकन कहिल्यै पनि *She takes a shower before she*
सुत्दिनन् । *goes to bed. She never goes to*
bed without showering first.

EXERCISE 35 Construct sentences that state that each of the people in column 1 performed each of the verbs in column 3 *without* performing the verb in column 2, thus producing 12 different sentences:

1	2	3
उनका छोराहरू	भात खानु	चिठी लेख्नु
मेरी आमा		मन्दिर जानु
तिमी		
रामे		
रामेकी दिदी		
म		

67 Expressions of age

There are several ways in which a person's age is expressed in Nepali. The most straightforward is simply to define a person's age using हो :

मेरो छोराको उमेर बीस वर्ष हो । *My son's age is 20 years.*
संजयको बुवाको उमेर अस्सी वर्ष हो । *Sanjay's father's age is 80 years.*

More commonly, however, a person is described as being *of* a certain age, using the possessive -को :

मेरी जेठी छोरी बाइस वर्षकी हो । *My eldest daughter is 22 years old.*
म चालीस वर्षको हुँ र मेरी श्रीमती *I am 40 years old and my*
उनन्चालीस वर्षकी हुन् । *wife is 39.*

In all of the above examples, the verb at the end of the sentence is equally likely to be the past tense भयो, indicating that this is the age that has been attained or reached by the person concerned:

मेरो छोराको उमेर बीस वर्ष भयो ।
संजयको बुवाको उमेर अस्सी वर्ष भयो ।
मेरी जेठी छोरी बाइस वर्षकी भई ।
म चालीस वर्षको भएँ र मेरी श्रीमती उनन्चालीस वर्षकी भइन् ।

68 Further relationship terms

The various offspring of a family each has a title that indicates the relative status in terms of age. As average family size decreases, some of these titles are falling into disuse, but five are still quite common:

Brothers or sons	Sisters or daughters	
जेठो	जेठी	eldest
माहिंलो	माहिंली	second eldest
साहिंलो	साहिंली	third eldest
काहिंलो	काहिंली	fourth eldest
कान्छो	कान्छी	youngest

These terms are primarily adjectives:

मेरो जेठो छोरा केही वर्षसम्म बिराटनगरमा बस्यो ।	My eldest son stayed in Biratnagar for some years.
हिजो उसकी माहिंली छोरीको बिहा भयो ।	Yesterday his second daughter was married.
तपाई मभन्दा तीन वर्ष जेठो हुनुहुन्छ ।	You are three years older than me.

Although जेठो is used to mean *older* or *senior to*, both कान्छो and सानो *small* can be used to mean *younger* or *junior to*.

तिमी मभन्दा तीन वर्ष कान्छो छौ ।	
तिमी मभन्दा तीन वर्ष सानो छौ ।	You are three years younger than me.

कान्छा and जेठा are often used rather like nicknames for children. कान्छा and कान्छी *youngest* can also be used to address or refer to young children whose names one does not know:

ए कान्छी, एक छिन यता आऊ !	Hey girl, come here a minute!
ए कान्छा, चिया ल्याऊ !	Hey boy, bring the tea!

IN THE MARKET
बजारमा

In this unit you will learn how to:

■ discuss the prices and availability of various foods
■ declare needs and wants

19 Out shopping

Anjali and her younger sister have gone to the vegetable market to buy food for the evening meal. Dil Bahadur, who has a stall at the market, sells them some of the items they need.

ी, किन पाइँदैन ? यो तरकारी-पसल हो नि ! मकहाँ हरेक किसिमको
तरकारी सस्तोमा पाइन्छ ।

अञ्जली आलुको दाम कति हो ?

दिल बहादुर यो रातो आलु किलोको आठ रुपियाँ हो, त्यो सेतो आलु किलोको छ रुपियाँ हो ।
तपाईलाई कस्तो आलु चाहियो ?

अञ्जली कुनचाहिं मीठो हुन्छ नि ?

दिल बहादुर रातो आलु मीठो हुन्छ रे तर सेतोचाहिं पनि ठीकै छ । कुनचाहिं लिनुहुन्छ दिदी?

अञ्जली हामीलाई तीन किलो रातो आलु दिनुहोस् । प्याज छ ?

दिल बहादुर छ । किलोको दस रुपियाँ ।

अञ्जली एक किलो दिनुहोस् । रायोको साग मुठाको कति हो ?

दिल बहादुर मुठाको पाँच रुपियाँ । तपाईलाई कति चाहियो ?

अञ्जली एक मुठा मात्रै दिनुहोस् । अलि महंगो छ । चामल र दाल पनि छ ?

दिल बहादुर अहँ, छैन । यो तरकारी-पसल हो नि ! चामल र दालको लागि अर्को पसलमा
जानुहोस् ।

अञ्जली अनि मासु ?

दिल बहादुर मासु पनि यहाँ पाइँदैन । मासु खिचापोखरीमा पाइन्छ । त्यहाँ माछा पनि पाइन्छ ।

अञ्जली हुन्छ । अब हामी उतै जान्छौं । कति भयो ?

दिल बहादुर एक छिन, म हिसाब गर्छु । ल, उन्नचालीस रुपियाँ भयो ।

अञ्जली मसँग सयको नोट मात्रै छ । चानचुन छ ?

दिल बहादुर छ, त्यो समस्या होइन । तर तपाईहरूलाई खुर्सानी चाहिंदैन ?

अञ्जली अहँ, चाहिंदैन । आजलाई यति हो ।

दिल बहादुर कस्तो अनौठो कुरा ! सबै नेपालीहरूलाई खुर्सानी मन पर्छ, होइन ? तपाईहरूलाई
पिरो खाना मीठो लाग्दैन ?

अञ्जली मीठो त लाग्छ, तर हाम्रो घरमा आजकल अँग्रेज साथीहरू छन् । उनीहरूलाई
पिरो खाना मनै पर्दैन ।

चाहिनु	*to be wanted, needed*	मासु	*meat*
तरकारी	*vegetables*	खिचापोखरी	*Khichapokhari*
पाइनु	*to be available*		(an area of Kathmandu)
किसिम	*type, kind*	माछा	*fish*
सस्तो	*cheap*	हिसाब गर्नु	*to add up, calculate*
आलु	*potato(es)*	नोट	*note* (of currency)
दाम	*price*	चानचुन	*change*
प्याज	*onion(s)*	समस्या	*problem*
रायो	*mustard*	खुर्सानी	*chilli pepper(s)*
साग	*greens*	यति	*this much*
मुठा	*bunch*	अनौठो	*strange*
चामल	*uncooked rice*	पिरो	*spicy*
दाल	*lentils*	आजकल	*nowadays*

Anjali	Shopkeeper, hello!
Dil Bahadur	Hello sister. What do you want?
Anjali	Are vegetables available here?
Dil Bahadur	Yes they are, sister, why wouldn't they be? This is a vegetable shop, you know! In my shop every kind of vegetable is available cheaply.
Anjali	How much are the potatoes?
Dil Bahadur	These red potatoes are eight rupees a kilo, those white potatoes are six rupees a kilo. Which kind of potatoes would you like?
Anjali	Well, which one tastes good?
Dil Bahadur	They say the red potatoes are tasty, but the white ones are fine as well. Which will you take, sister?
Anjali	Give us three kilos of red potatoes. Do you have any onions?
Dil Bahadur	Yes. Ten rupees a kilo.
Anjali	Give me one kilo. How much are the mustard greens per bunch?
Dil Bahadur	Five rupees a bunch. How much do you want?
Anjali	Just give me one bunch. It's a bit expensive. Do you have rice and lentils too?
Dil Bahadur	No, I don't. This is a vegetable shop, you know! Please go to another shop for rice and lentils.
Anjali	And meat?
Dil Bahadur	You can't get meat here either. You can get meat in Khichapokhari. You can get fish there too.

Anjali	All right. We'll go there now. How much do I owe you?
Dil Bahadur	One moment, I'll add it up. Right, it comes to 39 rupees.
Anjali	I have only a 100 rupee note. Do you have change?
Dil Bahadur	Yes, that's not a problem. But don't you want any chilli peppers?
Anjali	No, we don't. This is enough for today.
Dil Bahadur	What a strange thing! All Nepalis like chilli, don't they? Don't you like spicy food?
Anjali	Yes we do, but nowadays we have some English friends at our house. They don't like spicy food at all.

Grammar

69 Needed and available: चाहिनु and पाइनु

The passive verbs पाइनु *to be obtained/be available* and चाहिनु *to be needed / be wanted* belong to a category of verbs called 'i-stem verbs' because a short **i** vowel (इ) is added to the verb base to create them. It is a feature of Nepali, and other related languages, that verbs such as *to want, need, get* are expressed in passive terms: rather than *I need,* Nepali-speakers say *is necessary to/for me;* instead of *I got,* they will often say *was obtained to/for me.* The thing that is wanted, needed or obtained is made the subject of the passive verb, while the wanter, needer or obtainer becomes its indirect object, marked by the postposition -लाई.

■ चाहिनु

चाहिनु *to be needed / wanted* is the passive form of the verb चाहनु *to wish.* चाहनु is used mostly with other verbs: *I wish to leave, I want to learn English* (see **Grammar 110**), whereas चाहिनु is used when some *thing* is needed or wanted.

The habitual present tense of चाहिनु is used to denote needs that are regular or habitual:

जिन्दगीमा मान्छेहरूलाई के चाहिन्छ ?	*What do people need in life?*
मान्छेहरूलाई पानी चाहिन्छ ।	*People need water.*
मान्छेहरूलाई अरू के चाहिन्छ ?	*What else do people need?*
मान्छेहरूलाई खाने कुरा पनि चाहिन्छ ।	*People also need food.*
बिरामीहरूलाई के चाहिन्छ ?	*What do sick people need?*
बिरामीहरूलाई औषधि चाहिन्छ ।	*Sick people need medicine.*

To express the sense *I want something,* Nepali uses the simple past tense चाहियो, e.g.:

मलाई चिनी चाहियो ।	*I want sugar.*
उसलाई पैसा चाहियो ।	*He wants money.*

Such sentences denote a need or desire that is very much in the *present*, despite the *past* tense of the verb. The person who is speaking considers that this need or desire arose immediately *before* s/he gave utterance to it.

The negative form चाहिंदैन is grammatically in the present tense, but it is used as the negative form of both चाहिन्छ and चाहियो to mean *is not wanted* or *is not needed:*

ए दिदी, तपाईलाई चिनी चाहियो ? अहँ, चाहिंदैन ।	*Hey elder sister, do you want some sugar? No I don't.*
स्वस्थ मानिसलाई औषधि पटक्कै चाहिंदैन ।	*A healthy person has absolutely no need of medicine.*

■ पाइनु

The passive verb पाइनु means *to be obtained/be available,* and it is the passive form of the verb पाउनु *to get/obtain.* Its most common use has the sense of *to be available:*

ए दिदी, यहाँ बास पाइन्छ ? यहाँ पाइँदैन हजुर, उता गएर सोध्नुहोस् ।	*Hey elder sister, is lodging available here? It is not available here sir, go and ask over there.*
नेपालमा गाईको मासु पाइँदैन तर राङ्गोको मासु पाइन्छ ।	*You cannot get beef in Nepal, but you can get buffalo meat.*

Sometimes the active and the passive form of the verb are equally appropriate. For instance, if you wish to inform someone that you received the letter they sent you, you can choose between the following:

अस्ति मैले तपाईको चिठी पाएँ ।	*I received your letter the other day.*
अस्ति तपाईको चिठी पाइयो ।	*Your letter was received the other day.*

If the passive form is used, it is normal to leave out a mention of who received the letter. This will be understood to be the person speaking unless it is stated otherwise.

EXERCISE 36   Answer the following questions about **Dialogue 19**:

१ दिल बहादुरको पसलमा तरकारी पाइन्छ ?

२ रातो आलुको दाम कति हो ?

३ अनि सेतो आलुको दाम नि ?

४ दिल बहादुरको पसलमा मासु पाइन्छ ?

५ मासु कहाँ पाइन्छ त ?

६ अञ्जलीलाई खुर्सानी चाहिन्छ कि चाहिँदैन ?

70   Food vocabulary

तरकारी	*Vegetables*	फलफूल	*Fruits*
आलु	*potato*	अम्बा	*guava*
काँक्रो	*cucumber*	आँप	*mango*
काउली, फूलकोपी	*cauliflower*	कागती	*lime*
बन्दा कोपी	*cabbage*	केरा	*banana*
गोलभेंडा	*tomato*	निबुवा	*lemon*
चना	*chickpea*	सुन्तला	*orange*
प्याज	*onion*	स्याउ	*apple*
फर्सी	*pumpkin*		
मूला	*radish*	**मासु**	**Meat**
रामतोरियाँ	*okra*	कुखुराको मासु	*chicken meat*
साग	*greens* (of several varieties)	खसीको मासु	*goat meat*
सिमी	*beans*	राङ्गोको मासु	*buffalo meat*
		सुँगुरको मासु	*pig meat*

Other foods			
अचार	*chutney*	अदुवा	*ginger*
कोदो	*millet*	खुर्सानी	*chilli*
घिउ	*ghee*	चामल	*rice* (uncooked)
दाल	*lentils*	दही	*yoghurt*
फुल	*egg*	भटमास	*soybean*
भात	*rice* (cooked)	मकै	*corn, maize*
माछा	*fish*	लसून	*garlic*
नौनी	*butter*		

71 Using -लाई **instead of** -को लागि

Although the principal use of -लाई is as an 'object-marker', it is often interchangeable with the postposition -को लागि *for:*

बुवाको लागि	or	बुवालाई	*for father*
एक महिनाको लागि	or	एक महिनालाई	*for a month*
मेरो लागि	or	मलाई	*for me*

यो कोसेली मेरी आमालाई हो ।	*This gift is for my mother.*
उषालाई ।	*For Usha* (dedication on the title page of a book of poems).
आजलाई तिमीलाई के के चाहियो ?	*What things do you need for today?*

EXERCISE 37 Create ten sentences using the elements below, first stating whether people need the nouns listed in the middle column, and then whether buffaloes (भैंसीहरू) need the same things:

मान्छेहरूलाई	पानी	चाहिन्छ or चाहिंदैन
भैंसीहरूलाई	हावा	
	घाँसपात (*fodder*)	
	शिक्षा (*education*)	
	बिजुली (*electricity*)	

11 | IT SEEMS FINE TO ME
मलाई ठीक जस्तो लाग्छ

In this unit you will learn how to:

■ describe feelings and impressions
■ discuss resemblances

 ## 20 A place to stay in Kathmandu

Dipak and Mahesh have both come to Kathmandu to study at Trichandra
College. Their first need was to find places to stay. They compare how
each has fared in the search for accommodation.

दीपक तपाईंले डेरा सजिलैसँग पाउनुभयो ?

महेश अहँ, पाइनँ । अलि गाह्रो भयो । बल्ल बल्ल ठमेलमा यो सानो कोठा पाइयो । तपाईंले नि ?

दीपक मलाई खूब राम्रो भयो । म बाग बजारमा एकजना साथीकहाँ बस्छु । उसको घरदेखि त्रिचन्द्र कलेज पाँच मिनेटमा पुगिन्छ । कलेज झ्यालबाट नै देखिन्छ !

महेश ओहो, मेरो डेरा त अलिक टाढा पर्‍यो । झ्यालबाट कुनै कलेज देखिँदैन । पसल, रेष्टुराँ र टूरिष्टहरू मात्रै देखिन्छन् र पप सँगीत मात्रै सुनिन्छ ।

दीपक डेरा तपाईंलाई राम्रो लागेन जस्तो छ ।

महेश कोठा ठीकै छ । तर घरपति काठ्माडौँ बाहिरको मान्छे हो । ऊ राम्रोसँग नेपाली बोल्दैन । कहिले काहीं ऊसँग कुरा मिल्दैन ।

दीपक कहाँको मान्छे हो ?

महेश ऊ मानाङ्को हो । तपाईं पनि एक पटक मानाङ्ग पुग्नुभयो, होइन ?

दीपक हो, म एक पटक गएँ । उतातिर नेपाली भाषा अलि कम बोलिन्छ किनभने त्यहाँका मानिसहरूको आफ्नै भाषा हुन्छ ।

महेश ठाउँ कस्तो लाग्यो त ?

दीपक मानाङ्ग त मलाई एकदम मन पर्‍यो । त्यहाँबाट हिमाल छर्लङ्ग देखिन्छ । हावाको सुईँ-सुईँ र खोला-नालाहरूको कलकल ध्वनी बाहेक अरू केही सुनिँदैन । ठमेल जस्तो होइन । एकदम सुन्दर र शान्त ठाउँ हो ।

डेरा *lodgings, rented accommodation*	घरपति *landlord*
सजिलैसँग *easily*	मिल्नु *to match, accord, come together*
बल्ल बल्ल *eventually, in the end*	मानाङ्ग *Manang (central Nepal)*
ठमेल a locality in north-central Kathmandu where many tourists stay	कम *little, less*
खूब *really, very*	बोलिनु *to be spoken*
बाग बजार *Bag Bazaar:* a locality in east-central Kathmandu	भाषा *language*
त्रिचन्द्र कलेज *Trichandra College*	ठाउँ *place*
पुगिनु *to be reached*	हिमाल *the Himalayas*
झ्याल *window*	छर्लङ्ग *clear, clearly*
देखिनु *to be seen, visible*	हावा *wind, air*
अलिक *slightly, a little*	सुईँ-सुईँ *sighing sound*
कुनै *any*	खोला-नालाहरू *rivers and streams*
टूरिष्ट *tourist*	कलकल *the sound of running water*
पप *pop*	ध्वनी *sound*
सँगीत *music*	बाहेक *except for*
सुनिनु *to be heard, audible*	सुन्दर *beautiful*
लाग्नु *to strike, affect, seem*	शान्त *peaceful*
जस्तो *like, similar to*	

Dipak	Did you find lodgings easily?
Mahesh	No, I didn't. It was rather difficult. In the end I found this little room in Thamel. What about you?
Dipak	It went very well for me. I will stay at a friend's place in Bag Bazaar. From his house you can reach Trichandra College in five minutes. You can even see the college from the window!
Mahesh	Oho, my lodgings are rather far away. You can't see any college from the window. You can see only shops, restaurants and tourists, and you can hear only pop music.
Dipak	It seems that you don't like the lodgings.
Mahesh	The room's OK. But the landlord comes from outside Kathmandu. He doesn't speak Nepali well. Sometimes we misunderstand one another.
Dipak	Where is he from?
Mahesh	He's from Manang. You once went to Manang too, didn't you?
Dipak	Yes, I went once. Over there they don't speak very much Nepali because the people have their own language.
Mahesh	But how did you like the place?
Dipak	I really liked Manang. You can see the Himalayas clearly from there. You can't hear anything except the sighing of the wind and the sound of running water. It's not like Thamel. It's a really beautiful and peaceful place.

🔊 Grammar

72 Feelings: the use of nouns with लाग्नु

In English, people actively experience physical or mental conditions such as hunger, thirst or happiness: I *feel* hungry, I *am* thirsty, I *was* happy. In Nepali, however, the relationship between the condition and the person who experiences it is reversed, and the condition (*hunger, thirst, happiness*) becomes an active agent which *affects* the person who experiences it. That person becomes the indirect object of the condition, and is therefore marked by the suffix -लाई, while the condition becomes the subject of the verb लाग्नु which can be translated in various ways according to context but here means *to affect/be felt*.

As with चाहिनु, *to be wanted*, if the person in the sentence is experiencing the condition at the time the sentence is uttered, the verb लाग्नु must be in the simple past tense, to show that the condition has *affected* that person or *been felt* by him/her. Thus, an English phrase such as *I feel hungry* becomes in Nepali translation *me+object-marker hunger affected*:

मलाई भोक लाग्यो ।   *I feel hungry.*

If the person in the sentence experienced the condition in the past, the verb लाग्नु should be in one of the various past tenses, including the simple past tense. However, if the simple past tense is used, the time needs to be mentioned to avoid ambiguity:

हिजो मलाई भोक लाग्यो ।   *I felt hungry yesterday.*

If the verb लाग्नु is in the habitual present tense, it implies a regular or habitual occurrence:

हरेक दिन पाँच बजेतिर मलाई भोक लाग्छ। *I feel hungry at about 5 o'clock every day.*

In all such sentences, despite the fact that they translate as *I feel, you are,* etc., the grammatical subject of the verb is the condition that is experienced, not the person who experiences it, and so the verb लाग्नु *to be felt* can take only third person singular endings (लाग्छ/लाग्दैन or लाग्यो/लागेन).

हिजो मैले धेरै चिउरा खाएँ र मलाई तिर्खा लाग्यो ।	*Yesterday I ate a lot of* chiurā *and I was thirsty.*
तपाईंसँग भेटेर मलाई खुशी लाग्यो ।	*I am very pleased to have met you.*
राति उसलाई जाडो लाग्यो ।केही दिनपछि उसलाई रुघा लाग्यो ।	*In the night he felt cold. A few days later he caught a cold.*
रामेकी आमा चैतमा खस्नुभयो र सबैजनालाई दुःख लाग्यो । *	*Rame's mother died in (the month of) Chait and everyone was sad.*
मलाई मध्यराततिर निद्रा लाग्यो ।	*I fell asleep around midnight.*

* खस्नु, literally *to fall*, is used as an honorific verb meaning *to die*. The non-honorific verb meaning *to die* is मर्नु.

In statements of general fact, the person or people affected need not always be mentioned:

पूस महिनामा जाडो लाग्छ ।	*In the month of Pus one feels cold.*
यहाँका बसहरूमा कहिले काहीं उकुस-मुकुस लाग्छ ।	*On the buses here one sometimes feels suffocated.*

Another meaning of लाग्नु is *to apply* in a more literal, physical sense:

मेरो कमिजमा हिलो लाग्यो ।	*My shirt became muddy.*
घरमा आगो लाग्यो ।	*The house caught fire.*

EXERCISE 38 Construct sentences that say that the following people felt, experienced or contracted the following things:

Example: म   *happiness* (खुशी)   =   मलाई खुशी लाग्यो ।

१   तपाई   *thirst* (तिर्खा)
२   दिदी   *hunger* (भोक)
३   रामेकी बहिनी   *sadness* (दुःख)
४   मेरो दाइ   *diarrhoea* (दिसा)
५   बुवा   *tiredness* (थकाइ)
६   तिमी   *coldness* (जाडो)
७   हामी   *a headcold* (रुघा)
८   म   *a cough* (खोकी)
९   केटी   *embarrassment* (लाज)
१०   छोरा   *sleep* (निद्रा)
११   वहाँ   *fear* (डर)
१२   रामे   *liquor* (रक्सी)

73 *How do you like Nepal?* using adjectives with लाग्नु

The verb लाग्नु occurs with adjectives with the basic sense of *to strike one as,* or *to seem,* and the person affected by the verb takes the postposition -लाई. The question कस्तो लाग्यो? means *what did you think of it?, how did you like it?* or *how did you find it?* with reference to a particular point in time:

(तपाईलाई) नेपाल कस्तो लाग्यो ?	*How did you like Nepal?*
नेपाल मलाई धेरै राम्रो लाग्यो ।	*I liked Nepal very much.*
अँग्रेजी भाषा कस्तो लाग्यो ?	*How did you find the English language?*
मलाई असाध्य गाह्रो लाग्यो ।	*I found it very difficult indeed.*
अनि जापानी भाषा कस्तो लाग्यो ?	*And how did you find Japanese?*
त्यो भाषा झन् गाह्रो लाग्यो ।	*I found that language even harder.*

The question कस्तो लाग्छ? with the verb लाग्नु in the habitual present tense means *what do you think of it?* or *how do you like it?* in more general terms. Contrast the following pairs:

हिजो रातिको खाना कस्तो लाग्यो ?	*How did you find the food last night?*
नेपाली खाना कस्तो लाग्छ ?	*What do you think of Nepali food?*
त्यो उपन्यास कस्तो लाग्यो ?	*How did you like that novel?*
नेपाली साहित्य तपाईलाई कस्तो लाग्छ ?	*How do you find Nepali literature?*

EXERCISE 39 Construct sentences that say that the people in the left-hand column did **not** find the things in the central column to be as described in the right-hand column.

Example

तपाई	this food	good-tasting = तपाईलाई यो खाना मीठो लागेन ।
१ म	that song	sweet-sounding (मीठो)
२ रामेकी आमा	his village	strange (अनौठो)
३ उनीहरू	Japanese	difficult
४ बुवा	India	nice
५ मेरो भाइ	Nepali	easy

74 More passive verbs

Every transitive verb in Nepali can, at least in theory, produce a passive 'i-stem' counterpart:

Examples of active and passive verbs

बोल्नु	to speak	बोलिनु	to be spoken
देख्नु	to see	देखिनु	to be seen
सुन्नु	to hear	सुनिनु	to be heard
बुझ्नु	to understand	बुझिनु	to be understood
भन्नु	to say	भनिनु	to be said
खानु	to eat	खाइनु	to be eaten

There are also a few intransitive verbs that can do the same:

पुग्नु	to arrive	पुगिनु	to be reached

जापानमा नेपाली भाषा बुझिंदैन ।	*In Japan the Nepali language is not understood.*
भनिन्छ एउटा भूत यहाँ हरेक रात आउँछ ।	*It is said (that) a ghost comes here every night.*
नेपाल सँसारको एकमात्र हिन्दू राज्य हो ।त्यस कारणले यहाँ गाईको मासु खाईदैन ।	*Nepal is the world's only Hindu kingdom. For that reason, beef is not eaten here.*

Often the passive form of the verb is used instead of the active form to indicate that something is or is not possible: सुनिन्छ *can be heard, is audible,* देखिन्छ *can be seen, is visible:*

मेरो स्वर त्यहाँबाट सुनिन्छ कि सुनिदैन ?	*Can you or can you not hear my voice from there?*
नगरकोटबाट सगरमाथा राम्रोसँग देखिन्छ ।	*From Nagarkot, Everest is easily visible.*
अब हाम्रो गाउँ एक घण्टाभित्र पुगिन्छ ।	*Now our village can be reached within one hour.*

75   *Similar to:* जस्तो

जस्तो is a member of the group of words that also includes यस्तो *like this,* उस्तो or त्यस्तो *like that,* and कस्तो *like what ? / how?* It is used in two slightly different ways:

■ जस्तो can be used as a postposition to mean *similar to* or *like:*

मजस्तो मान्छे ।	*A person like me.*
तपाईंको छोरा मेरो भाइजस्तो छ ।	*Your son is like my younger brother.*
तपाईंहरूको भाषा नेपालीजस्तो सुनिन्छ ।	*Your language sounds like Nepali.*

■ The following phrases can also be appended to a statement to make it less categorical:

... जस्तो छ ।	*... it seems*
... जस्तो मलाई लाग्छ ।	*... it seems to me*
... जस्तो मलाई लाग्यो ।	*... it seemed to me*
आज पानी पर्दैन जस्तो छ ।	*It looks like it won't rain today.*
ऊ आज आउँछ जस्तो मलाई लाग्दैन ।	*It doesn't seem to me that he will come today.*
नेपाल एउटा भूस्वर्ग हो जस्तो मलाई लाग्यो ।	*It seemed to me that Nepal was a heaven on earth.*

76   Making adjectives into adverbs

Adjectives (words that describe nouns) can be made into adverbs (words that describe the actions of a verb) in a variety of ways. Some have the postposition -सँग added to them:

छिटो	*quick*	छिटोसँग	*quickly*
ढिलो	*slow*	ढिलोसँग	*slowly*
सजिलो	*easy*	सजिलोसँग	*easily*
राम्रो	*good*	राम्रोसँग	*well*

Some adjectives can also be made into adverbs simply by emphasising them:

| छिटो | *quick* | छिटै | *quickly* |

Others can be made into adverbs by adding the postposition -ले to them:

| गाह्रो | *difficult* | गाह्रोले | *with difficulty* |
| मुश्किल | *difficult* | मुश्किलले | *with difficulty* |

The two sets of adverbs in the following box are derived from the set of adjectives to their left:

Adjective		*Adverb*		
यस्तो	*like this*	यसरी or	यसो	*in this manner*
त्यस्तो or उस्तो	*like that*	त्यसरी or उसरी	त्यसो or उसो	*in that manner*
जस्तो	*similar to*	जसरी or	जसो	*similarly*
कस्तो	*like what?*	कसरी or	कसो	*how?*

The ubiquitous adjective राम्रो can also take the adverbial form राम्ररी.

त्यो काम मुश्किलले गरियो ।	*That work was done with difficulty.*
यो अक्षर यसरी लेख्नुहोस् ।	*Write this letter like this.*
त्यो मान्छे जर्मन हो तर नेपाली राम्ररी बोल्छ ।	*That man is German but he speaks Nepali well.*

EXERCISE 40   Insert -लाई or -ले in the gaps in the following sentences:

१   म _____ तिर्खा लागेन ।
२   मेरो भाइ _____ एउटा किताब किन्यो ।
३   उस _____ मेरो घर राम्रो लाग्यो ।
४   मेरी आमा_____ थकाइ लाग्यो ।
५   हामीहरू _____ गीत गायौं ।
६   उस _____ दाहिने हात _____ भात खायो ।
७   वहाँ _____ चार बजेतिर सधैं निद्रा लाग्छ ।
८   तपाई _____ पोखरा कस्तो लाग्यो ?
९   म _____ रक्सी लागेन ।
१० हामी _____ धेरै रक्सी खायौं ।

EXERCISE 41   Translate into Nepali:

1   The Himalayas can be seen from my window.
2   The Magar language is spoken around Pokhara.
3   Your (High) voice cannot be heard from here.
4. Your (Middle) village will not be reached in an hour.
5   It is said (that) there is a witch (**boksī**) in that house.
6   In Tibet the Nepali language is sometimes understood.
7   Please walk slowly (High). We'll reach the village easily now.
8   I am very happy to have met your (High) son. He seemed like a very
    clever (**calāk**) boy to me.

12 | WHERE HAS HE GONE?
ऊ कता गएको छ ?

In this unit you will learn how to:

■ use the completed tenses
■ state the time of day
■ report what others have said
■ use verb forms to specify causes

21 A late start

The Paudel family have overslept, and to make matters worse Father has lost his watch and they do not know what time it is.

लक्ष्मी   बा, बा, अहिले कति बज्यो ?

बा   थाहा छैन छोरी । शायद आठ बजेको होला ।भाइ उठेको छैन ?

लक्ष्मी   उठेको छैन बा ।अझ पनि आफ्नै कोठामा छ ।

बा   उसलाई उठाऊ अब ।पहिला तिमी छिटो तल गएर पसलको भित्ते-घडी हेरेर आऊ त ।

लक्ष्मी   हवस् ।पहिला म घडी हेरेर आउँछु अनि त्यसपछि मात्र भाइलाई उठाउँछु ।

बा   उमा, मेरो घडी कता पऱ्यो ? तिमीले देख्यौ ?

आमा   खै, कुन्नि मैले त देखिनँ ।तपाईले हिजो कुन कोट लाउनुभयो ? ऊ त्यो कालो कोट, होइन ?त्यसको भित्री खल्तीमा छाम्नुहोस् त ।त्यहाँ छ कि ?

लक्ष्मी   बा ! बा ! आठ बजेको होइन, पौनें नौ बजेको छ ।

बा   अहो आज साह्रै ढिलो भयो । तिम्रो भाइ उठेको छैन अहिलेसम्म ? खोइ चिया बनाएनौ तिमीहरूले ?

लक्ष्मी   पानी भरखर उम्लेको छ ।अब म तुरुन्तै बनाउँछु ।

आमा   लक्ष्मी, ए लक्ष्मी ! धोबी आएन अहिलेसम्म ?

लक्ष्मी   आएको छैन, आमा ।तपाईले उसलाई मेरो नयाँ सारी दिनुभएन ?

आमा   दिएको छैन छोरी, तिम्रो भाइको स्कूलको लुगा मात्रै दिएँ ।

लक्ष्मी   ठीकै छ नि ।आज आइतवार हो ।भाइको स्कूल छुट्टी छँदै छ ।भरेसम्म लुगा ल्याउँछ नि ।ल, चिया तयार भयो, आउनुहोस् ।बा पनि आउनुहोस् ।

आमा   ल, ल, बाबुछोरी चिया खानुहोस् । म भाइलाई पनि उठाएर ल्याउँछु ।

बा *father, dad*	लाउनु *to wear*
अहिले *now*	भित्री *inner*
बज्नु *to ring, strike*	खल्ती *pocket*
शायद *perhaps*	छाम्नु *to feel with the hand*
होला *it might be* (see **Grammar 92** on होला)	पौने *a quarter to*
अझ पनि *still, even now*	खोइ *well; I don't know*
उठाउनु *to rouse, lift up*	उम्लनु *to come to the boil*
पहिला *first* (adverb)	तुरुन्तै *immediately*
तल *down, below*	धोबी *laundryman*
भित्ते-घडी *wall clock*	सारी *sari; woman's dress*
खै *well; I don't know*	लुगा *clothes*
कुन्नि *who knows? search me!*	भरे *this evening*
कोट *coat*	बाबुछोरी *father and daughter*

Lakshmi Father, Father, what time is it now?

Father I don't know, daughter. Perhaps it's 8 o'clock. Is your brother not up yet?

Lakshmi No he's not. He is still in his own room.

Father Get him up now. But first go quickly downstairs, look at the wall clock in the shop and come back.

Lakshmi Very well. First I'll look at the clock, and only after that I'll get brother up.

Father Uma, where's my watch got to? Have you seen it?

Mother Well I don't know, I haven't seen it. Which coat did you wear yesterday? It was that black coat over there, wasn't it? Feel inside its inner pocket, then. Is it there?

Lakshmi Father, father! It's not 8 o'clock, it's a quarter to nine!

Father Oho, we're really late today. Hasn't your brother got up yet? And haven't you made any tea?

Lakshmi The water has only just boiled. Now I'll make it right away.

Mother Lakshmi, oh Lakshmi! Hasn't the washerman come yet?

Lakshmi No he hasn't, mother. You haven't given him my new sari?

Mother No I haven't, daughter, I only gave him your brother's school clothes.

Lakshmi Then that's all right, you know. Today is Sunday. It's brother's school holiday. He'll bring the clothes by this evening, you know. There, the tea's ready, please come. Father please come too.

Mother There, there, father and daughter drink your tea. I'll get brother up and bring him too.

🗂 Grammar

77 The completed present tense

This tense describes an event or action that happened in the past but still has some bearing on the present because nothing has happened since to supersede or negate it. It is the equivalent of the English *he has come, she has seen, they have done,* but in Nepali the English *has* is replaced by the Nepali for *is* or *are* (छ, छन्, छौं etc.)

The tense consists of two words. Technically, the first word is called the 'perfect participle', because it describes an action that has been 'perfected' or 'completed'. We shall see later that this participle can be used on its own and in other tenses too. It is formed very simply by adding the ending -एको **-eko** to the past tense base of the verb or, in the case of the High forms, by adding -भएको **-bhaeko** to the dictionary form of the verb. The -एको participle describes the condition of its subject in terms of something it has done or has been in the past.

High forms			*All other forms*				
गर्नु + भएको	=	गर्नुभएको	गर्-	+	एको	=	गरेको *done*
बस्नु + भएको	=	बस्नुभएको	बस्-	+	एको	=	बसेको *seated*
बिर्सनु + भएको	=	बिर्सनुभएको	बिर्स्-	+	एको	=	बिर्सेको *forgotten*
आउनु + भएको	=	आउनुभएको	आ-	+	एको	=	आएको *come*
जानु + भएको	=	जानुभएको	ग-	+	एको	=	गएको *gone*
रुनु + भएको	=	रुनुभएको	रो-	+	एको	=	रोएको *cried*
हुनु + भएको	=	हुनुभएको	भ-	+	एको	=	भएको *been*

The second word in the completed present tense is the appropriate form of the verb छ, according to the number and gender of the subject of the verb. If the verb is transitive, the subject must take -ले because grammatically this is a past tense:

मैले गरेको छु ।	*I have done.*
तिमी सुतेको छैनौ ।	*You are not asleep.*
उसले किनेको छ ।	*He has bought.*
हामीले बिर्सेका छौं ।	*We have forgotten.*
उनीहरू गएका छैनन् ।	*They have not gone.*

The -एको participle can take feminine and plural endings, just as adjectives do. If the subject of the verb is feminine, the ending should be -एकी **-ekī**:

बहिनी स्कूल गएकी छे ।   *Younger sister has gone to school.*

If the subject is plural the ending should change to -एका **-ekā:**

केटाहरूले नमस्ते भनेका छन् ।   *The boys have said hello.*

These rules are observed consistently in written Nepali, but less consistently in the spoken language. As always, the High forms are the same regardless of the number and gender of the subject.

Although the completed present tense generally refers to an action that was completed in the past, certain verbs must be translated into the continuous present in English. These verbs should be thought of as verbs that indicate a specific limited action (for instance, बस्नु *to sit down* and सुत्नु *to go to bed* or *to fall asleep*), or that refer to the *beginning* of an action:

ऊ मेचमा बसेको छ ।   *He is sitting on a chair (he has sat down on a chair).*

पानी परेको छ ।   *It is raining (it has begun to rain).*

मेरो टाउको दुखेको छ ।   *My head is hurting (my head has begun to hurt).*

पानी उम्लेको छ ।   *The water is boiling (the water has come to the boil).*

ऊ माथिको कोठामा सुतेको छ ।   *He is sleeping (he has gone to bed/fallen asleep) in the upstairs room.*

The completed present tense is often used to give negative answers to questions that have been posed in the simple past tense, because the simple past (as explained earlier) does sometimes mean much the same as the completed present:

Q को आयो ?   *Who has come?*
A कोही आएको छैन ।   *No one has come.*

In everyday speech, the -एको **-eko** ending is often dropped in the negative, and if the base ends in **-a** or **-ā** the vowel is lengthened:

कोही आ'छैन ।   *No one has come.*
म गा'छैन ।   *I have not gone.*

EXERCISE 42   Translate into Nepali:

1   Elder brother has gone to Darjeeling.
2   Sister-in-law has stayed in Kathmandu.

3   Has anyone come to your (High) house? Your (Middle) younger
    brother has come, but apart from him nobody has come.
4   The water hasn't boiled yet.
5   I have given your clothes to the washerman.
6   He (Low) has bought five new books.

EXERCISE 43   Answer the following questions with (a) a simple past
affirmative and (b) a completed present negative:

Example
   कान्छाले भाँडा माझ्यो ?   (a) अँ, माझ्यो । (*Yes he has*).
   (*Has Kānchā scrubbed the pots?*)   (b) अहँ, माझेको छैन । (*No he   hasn't*).

१   दाइ दार्जीलिङ्ग जानुभयो ?
२   भाउज्यू काठ्माडौँ आउनुभयो ?
३   तपाईंको घरमा त्यो मान्छे आयो ?
४   तिमीले भात खायौ ?

78   Stating the time of day using बज्यो

बज्यो is the simple past tense of the verb बज्नु, *to ring* or *to strike*. Literally,
बज्यो means *it struck* or *it rang*, and its subject is a number: *three rang, half
past four rang*, etc. The verb remains singular (that is, it ends in -यो in the
affirmative) in all instances.

Although it is grammatically in the past tense, बज्यो is used to ask or tell
the present time. The negative form is usually बजेको छैन.

अहिले चार बज्यो ?   *Is it 4 o'clock now?*
अँ, चार बज्यो ।   *Yes, it is 4 o'clock .*

or

अहँ, चार बजेको छैन ।   *No, it is not 4 o'clock .*

It is very important to distinguish between the verb ... बज्यो ... **bajyo**, *it is...
o'clock now*, and the adverb ... बजे ... **baje**, *at... o'clock*:

तपाई कति बजे घर जानुहुन्छ ?   *At what time do you go home?*
म साढे पाँच बजे जान्छु ।   *I go at half past 5.*
अहिले सवा पाँच बज्यो, होइन ?   *It's a quarter past 5 now, isn't it?*
हो, म पन्ध्र मिनेटपछि जान्छु ।   *Yes, I'll go in ('after') 15 minutes.*

Stating times that include minutes past or minutes to the hour (other than half and quarter hours) involves the use of two different forms of the verb बज्नु *to ring:* these are the **-era** participle बजेर and the infinitive form बज्न plus the postposition -लाई:

पाँच बजेर बीस मिनेट ।   *Twenty minutes past 5.*
पाँच बज्नलाई बीस मिनेट ।   *Twenty minutes to 5.*

EXERCISE 44   Answer the following questions about the clockfaces below:

घडी न॰ १ मा कति बज्यो ?

घडी न॰ २ मा कति बज्यो ?

घडी न॰ ३ मा कति बज्यो ?

घडी न॰ १ मा साढे दस बज्यो ? कति बज्यो त ?

घडी न॰ २ बाह्र बज्यो ? कति बज्यो त ?

i.   **ii.**

iii.

22 Which countries have you visited?

Surya Prakash has come to visit Om Bahadur and his son Dhan Bahadur, and the conversation has turned to the subject of foreign travel. Dhan Bahadur relates an unfortunate experience he once had in London.

सूर्य प्रकाश   तपाई विदेशमा कहाँ कहाँ घुम्नुभएको छ ?

ओम बहादुर   म भारतमा घुमेको छु र बर्मामा पनि । तपाई नि ?

सूर्य प्रकाश   पोहोर सालसम्म म भारतसम्म मात्रै घुमेको थिएँ तर गएको पूस महिनामा म बेलायत गएँ । तपाई यूरोप जानुभएको छैन ?

ओम बहादुर   यूरोप त म गएको छैन । मेरो जेठो छोरा धन बहादुर दुई वर्ष अघि लण्डन पुगेको थियो कामको सिलसिलामा । ऊबाहेक हाम्रो परिवारको कोही पनि यूरोप गएको छैन ।

सूर्य प्रकाश   तपाईको छोरालाई लण्डन मन पऱ्यो त ?

ओम बहादुर   साहै रमाइलो छ रे । अस्ति मात्रै म अलिपछि दोस्रो पटक बेलायत जान्छु भनेर भन्दै थियो । लण्डनका रमाइला अनुभवहरू बिर्सेको छैन उसले । तर लण्डन बसेको बेलामा उसलाई एउटा नरमाइलो घटना पनि भयो रे ।

सूर्य प्रकाश   के भयो त ?

ओम बहादुर   ए धने, यता आएर सूर्य प्रकाशजीलाई आफ्नो कथा सुनाऊ न !

धन बहादुर   हवस् त बुवा । एक दिन मेरो काम साँझतिर सिद्धिएको थियो । मेरो डेरा अफिसबाट टाढा भएकोले र पानी परेकोले म बस चढेर त्यसैमा घर गएँ । बस हिँडेको बेलासम्म खाली सीट नपाएकोले म अर्को मान्छेको छेउमा बसें । बीचबाटोमा छेउमा बसेको मान्छे उठेर गयो र त्यसको अलि बेरपछि बस कण्डक्टर आएर मसँग टिकटको पैसा माग्यो ।

सूर्य प्रकाश   अँ, अनि के भयो ?

धन बहादुर   छेउमा बसेको मानिसले मेरो झोलाबाट वालेट निकालेर भागेको थियो तर मैले केही पनि थाहा पाएको थिइनँ ।

सूर्य प्रकाश   अनि त्यसपछि के भयो ?

धन बहादुर   कण्डक्टर साहै असल मानिस थियो । उसले अबदेखि आफ्नो पैसा सुरक्षित ठाउँमा राख्नुहोस् भनेर मलाई सल्लाह दियो ।

सूर्य प्रकाश   पैसाबाहेक अरू थोक त हराएको थिएन ?

धन बहादुर   थिएन । पैसा मात्रै हरायो ।

ओम बहादुर   अनि पैसा यसरी हराएर तिमीले एउटा उपयोगी पाठ सिक्यौ, होइन त ?

धन बहादुर   हजुर ! सिकें ।

विदेश *abroad*	कण्डक्टर *conductor*
घुम्नु *to travel*	टिकट *ticket*
बर्मा *Burma*	माग्नु *to ask for*
पोहोर साल *last year*	झोला *bag*
गएको *last, previous*	वालेट *wallet*
पूस *Pūs* (the name of a month)	निकाल्नु *to extract, take out*
यूरोप *Europe*	भाग्नु *to run away*
सिलसिला *course, process*	असल *of good character, honest*
अनुभव *experience*	सुरक्षित *secure*
घटना *incident*	सल्लाह *advice*
धने the familiar form of the son's name	थोक *thing, item*
कथा *story*	हराउनु *to be lost*
बेला *time, occasion*	उपयोगी *useful*
सीट *seat*	पाठ *lesson*
-को छेउमा *beside*	सिक्नु *to learn*

Surya Prakash To which places have you travelled abroad?

Om Bahadur I have travelled in India and in Burma too. What about you?

Surya Prakash Up until last year I had travelled only as far as India, but last Pūs I went to England. Have you not visited Europe?

Om Bahadur Europe is somewhere I haven't visited. My eldest son Dhan Bahadur got to London two years ago in the course of his work. Apart from him, no-one in our family has visited Europe.

Surya Prakash Did your son like London then?

Om Bahadur He says it's very pleasant. Just the other day he was saying that after a little while he will go to London a second time. He hasn't forgotten the enjoyable experiences of London. But when he stayed in London one unpleasant incident apparently also occurred.

Surya Prakash What happened?

Om Bahadur Oh Dhane, come here and tell Surya Prakash your story, won't you?

Dhan Bahadur Certainly, father. One day my work had finished around dusk. Because my lodgings were far from the office and because it was raining, I boarded a bus and went home in that. Because I couldn't find an empty seat before the bus set off, I sat down beside another man. On the way, the man who was sitting beside me got up and left, and a little while later the bus conductor came and asked me for the money for the ticket.

Surya Prakash   Yes, and then what happened?

Dhan Bahadur   The man who was sitting beside me had taken the wallet out of my bag and run away, but I had not known at all.

Surya Prakash   And what happened after that?

Dhan Bahadur   The conductor was a very good man. He advised me, saying that I should from now on keep my money in a secure place.

Surya Prakash   Apart from the money, no other thing was lost?

Dhan Bahadur   No. Only the money was lost.

Om Bahadur   And, having lost money like this, you learned a useful lesson, didn't you?

Dhan Bahadur   Yes, I did!

Grammar

79 The completed past tense

The -एको participle is used with the appropriate form of the verb थियो (*was, were*) to describe an action that occurred in the past and does not necessarily tell us anything about the present. The technical name for this tense is the 'pluperfect'. Often, the sense is that the action or event described has been superseded or negated by some other action or event. This tense can usually be translated by using the English word *had,* but in Nepali the tense is used whenever the speaker feels that there is a certain remoteness between the event that is described and the present time. The following examples illustrate the contrast in meaning between the 'completed present' tense that takes छ and the 'completed past' tense that takes थियो:

म घर फर्केको छु ।	*I have returned home (and that is where I am now).*
म घर फर्केको थिएँ।	*I had returned home (but I am not necessarily there any more).*
उसकी दिदीले बिहा गरेकी छैनन् ।	*His elder sister has not married (she is currently unmarried).*

उसकी दिदीले बिहा गरेकी थिइनन् ।	*His elder sister had not married (but this is not to say that she has not married since).*
मेरो छोराले यो किताब पढेको छैन ।	*My son has not read this book (and still hasn't read it).*
मेरो छोराले यो किताब पढेको थिएन ।	*My son had not read this book (but he might have read it by now).*
पानी परेको छ ।	*It is raining (it has begun to rain).*
पानी परेको थियो ।	*It was raining (it had begun to rain).*
मेरो टाउको दुखेको छ ।	*My head is hurting (my head has begun to hurt).*
मेरो टाउको दुखेको थियो ।	*My head was hurting (my head had begun to hurt).*

EXERCISE 45 Translate into Nepali:

1 My father had never been abroad.
2 In 1978 I went ('had gone') to Nepal for the first time.
3 They (Middle) were sitting in the bus station (**bas bisaunī**) but the bus had not come.
4 It was raining but Rame had not brought his umbrella.
5 His (Low) head was hurting but he had not taken any medicine.
6 They (Middle) had come from Ilām but they had not brought any tea.

80 Reporting speech using भनेर

In English, when one reports what someone else has said, the usual construction is 's/he said that' following which one summarises what was said: 'she said that she was going out'. In Nepali, however, speech is usually reported by quoting the actual words that a person has uttered: 'she said "I am going out".' If a woman has told you that she will come to visit your mother tomorrow, in Nepali you would report her words verbatim to your mother: 'the woman said "I will come to visit your mother tomorrow".'

The natural place for a Nepali verb is at the end of a Nepali sentence, and so the Nepali for *said* or *asked* or *told* usually comes after the words that are being quoted. In addition, the word for *said* or *asked* or *told* is usually preceded by the -एर **-era** participle of the verb भन्नु *to say,* (i.e. भनेर, but occasionally भनी) which serves the purpose of marking the end of the quotation. Speech marks are not usually used when reported speech is written down. The basic structure of a sentence that reports what someone has said is:

quoted person + -ले — verbatim quote — भनेर — said / told / asked, etc.

उसले तिम्रो नाम के हो भनेर मलाई सोध्यो । *He asked me what my name was.*

उसले टोपी लगाऊ भनेर केटालाई अह्रायो । *He ordered the boy to put his hat on.*

तिम्रो साथीले म आउँछु तर आमा आउनुहुन्न *Your friend has said that he will*
भनेर भनेको छ । *come but his mother will not.*

If the person whose words are being quoted was making an enquiry of any kind, the quotation will end with the interrogative word कि to show that it was a question:

उसले आज तिमी बाहिर गयौ कि भनेर *He asked me whether I had been*
मसँग सोध्यो । *out today.*

मेरो गाइडले तपाईलाई थकाइ लाग्यो *My guide asked whether*
कि भनी सोध्यो । *I was tired.*

EXERCISE 46 Report that the person in column A said the thing in column B to the person or persons in column C:

	A	**B**	**C**
1	my younger brother	it won't rain today	said to father
2	that tall man	are you English?	asked me
3	mother	is your friend hungry?	asked my sister
4	the teacher	close your books	told the children
5	father	don't go out tomorrow	advised us

81 *Because it is, because it was*: the -एको **participle with** -ले

The -एको **-eko** participle is used in combination with the word कारण (*cause, reason*) plus -ले (the subject-marking suffix introduced in **Grammar 59**) to show that the action of a verb is the cause of something else:

हिजो पानी परेको कारणले मैले एउटा *Because it was raining yesterday I*
छाता किनें । *bought an umbrella.*
टाउको दुखेको कारणले म दिनभरि घरै बसें । *Because I had a headache I stayed*
 home all day.

The word कारण is very often dropped from this construction, leaving only the -एको participle plus -ले :

अमेरिकामा नेपाली साथी नभएकोले कृष्णलाई विरह लाग्यो ।	*Because he had no Nepali friend in America, Krishna felt lonely.*
तातो चिया खानुभएकोले वहाँको जिब्रो पोल्यो ।	*Because he drank hot tea, his tongue got burned.*

EXERCISE 47 Combine the pairs of sentences to produce a single sentence, along the following lines:

Example: खाना चिसो छ । त्यसैले मैले खाइनँ । = खाना चिसो भएकोले मैले खाइनँ ।

१   तपाईले धेरै पिरो खाना खानुभयो । त्यसैले तपाईलाई दिसा लाग्यो ।
२   वहाँको पेट दुख्यो । त्यसैले वहाँ स्कूल जानुभएन ।
३   बाहिर गर्मी छ । त्यसैले हामी बाहिर जाँदैनौँ ।
४   उसँग कलम छैन । त्यसैले उसले चिठी लेखेन ।
५   उनको श्रीमान बिरामी हुनुभयो । त्यसैले उनलाई दुःख लाग्यो ।

82   Using the -एको participle as an adjective

In English, sentences containing constructions such as 'the man who... ' or 'the house where... ' are very common, but in Nepali such constructions are rare. Instead, a phrase such as 'the man who came yesterday' becomes in Nepali 'the yesterday-came man' and 'the house where Ram lives' becomes 'the Ram-lived house':

		Literally:
हिजो आएको मान्छे	*the man who came yesterday*	yesterday-came man
राम बसेको घर	*the house where Ram lives*	Ram-lived house
तिमीले भनेका कुराहरू	*the things you said*	by-you-said things
पोहोर साल परेको पानी	*the rain that fell last year*	last-year-fallen rain
हामीहरू सुतेको बेला	*the time we went to bed*	we-slept time
गएको सम्बिवार	*last Monday*	gone Monday

In these phrases, the -एको participle behaves like an adjective, and its **-o** ending must change according to the number and gender of the nouns it describes:

हिजो आएको लोग्ने-मान्छे	the man who came yesterday
हिजो आएकी केटी	the girl who came yesterday
हिजो आएका केटाहरू	the boys who came yesterday

देवकोटाले लेखेको चिठी कुनचाहिं हो ?	Which is the letter that Devkota wrote?
तपाईंलाई भेटेको दिन अस्ति जस्तो लाग्छ ।	The day I met you seems like just the other day.
पढे-लेखेका मान्छेहरू यस्ता किताबहरू पढ्दैनन् ।	Educated people do not read books like this.

83 Ordinal numbers

The ordinal numbers (*first, second, third*, etc.) function as adjectives, just as they do in English. With five exceptions, they are all formed by adding the suffix -ौं to the number in question. Thus:

चार	four	चारौं	fourth
पाँच	five	पाँचौं	fifth
बीस	20	बीसौं	20th
तेत्तीस	33	तेत्तीसौं	33rd

The following numbers have special forms:

एक	one	पहिलो	first
दुई	two	दोस्रो	second
तीन	three	तेस्रो	third
छ	six	छैटौं	sixth
नौ	nine	नवौं	ninth

| यो महाराजाधिराजको आठौं नेपाल-भ्रमण हो । | This is His Majesty's eighth tour of Nepal. |
| असारको पहिलो दिनमा हाम्रो गाउँमा पहिरो गएको थियो । | On the first day of Asar there had been a landslide in our village. |

पहिलो, *first*, can also be used as an adverb to mean *before* or *previously*, by changing its ending from -o to -ā:

| तपाई पहिला पनि नेपाल आउनुभयो ? | Have you visited Nepal previously as well? No, this is the first time for me. |
| होइन, यो मेरो लागि पहिलो पटक हो । | |

When it is added to certain large numbers, the suffix - ौं modifies their meanings in a rather different way:

सय	hundred	सयौं	hundreds of
हजार	thousand	हजारौं	thousands of
लाख	hundred thousand	लाखौं	hundreds of thousands of ('lakhs of')
करोड	ten million	करोडौं	tens of millions of ('crores of')

दोस्रो विश्व-युद्धमा लाखौं मान्छेहरू मरे ।
तीमध्य हजारौं नेपाली नागरिकहरू
पनि थिए ।

Hundreds of thousands of people died in the Second World War. There were thousands of Nepali citizens among them too.

EXERCISE 48 Translate into Nepali:

1 The guests who came yesterday are all English.
2 It's raining outside. Take that umbrella you (Middle) bought in the bazaar last week.
3 The month when you (Middle) arrived in Nepal is Baisākh.
4 This is the tenth time that I have visited Nepal.
5 The house that you (High, plural) stayed in is very old.
6 Last Friday I had not received the letter you (High) wrote.
7 He (Low) is not the man who came from India.
8 This is not the present you (Middle) gave to mother.

13 DEAR RAJU...
प्रिय राजु...

In this unit you will learn how to:

■ say how long ago something happened
■ talk about seeing or hearing actions performed by others
■ discuss intentions and the meanings of words
■ use dates

23 An exchange of letters*

*This text is adapted from a passage in TW Clark's *Introduction to Nepali*, first published in 1963.

काठ्माडौँ
२०४५ / ६ / ६

प्रिय मित्र राजु

भोलिदेखि म स्कूल जाँदिन । आज स्कूलमा मेरो अन्तिम दिन थियो । ढोकानेर उभिएर मैले मभन्दा साना उमेरका केटाहरूले गट्टा खेलेको हेरें । कस्तो रमाइलो ! एउटा मास्टरले मलाई देखेर अबेर भयो किन घर नगएको भनेर सोध्नुभयो । मैले मुख फर्काएँ किनभने मेरा आँखाबाट आँसु बगेको थियो ।

बिस्तारै ढोकासम्म पुगें । ढोकाबाहिर एउटा गाइने उभिएको थियो । मैले बाल्यकालमा धेरै चोटि उसले गाएको र सारङ्गी बजाएको सुनेको थिएँ । मैले उसको हातमा अलिकति पैसा राखेर यतिका दिनसम्म स्कूलमा किन नआएको भनेर सोधें । म बिरामी भएँ, हैजा लागेर झण्डै मरेको हजुर भनेर भन्यो ।

बाले मलाई घरभित्र पसेको देख्नुभयो । किन यस्तो ढिलो भएको भनेर सोध्नुभयो । मैले जवाफ दिइनँ तर वहाँले बुझ्नुभएको जस्तो थियो ।

तपाईको चिठी नपाएको धेरै भयो । अब चाँडै लेख्नुहोला । तपाई र तपाईका प्रियजनलाई प्रेम र शुभकामना ।

तपाईको मित्र, कुमार

दार्जीलिङ्ग
२५ फेब्रेरी १९८६

प्रिय मित्र कुमार

तिमीले काठमाडौँबाट पठाएको चिठी पाएर खुशी लाग्यो । गएको महिनादेखि नै अब जवाफ लेख्छु लेख्छु भनेको तर हरेक दिन कुनै न कुनै काम परेकोले लेखिनँ । यति ढिलो गरेकोमा मलाई माफी देऊ ।

तिमीले लेखेको स्कूलको अन्तिम दिनको बयान मर्मस्पर्शी थियो । मैले एकजना सम्पादक साथीलाई सुनाएँ । उनको नाम कुमार भण्डारी हो । उनले ज्यादै मन पराए । अलि लामो बयान लेखेर मलाई पठाऊ भनेका छन् । मनमा लागेको जे कुरा पनि लेख्नू भनेका छन् । कुमार भण्डारी तिम्रो दाइले चिनेका मान्छे हुन् क्यारे, होइन ? तर तिम्रो दाइसँग नभेटेको धेरै महिना भयो रे । उनी सिक्किमबाट बसाइँ सरेर आएका हुन् ।

आमालाई मेरो नमस्कार सुनाऊ । चिठी नलेखेकोमा म वहाँसँग क्षमा माग्छु । वहाँको दर्शन नपाएको पनि धेरै वर्ष भयो । कति वर्ष भयो सम्झना छैन ।

तिम्रो हितैषी, राजु

प्रिय *dear*	पस्नु *to enter*
मित्र *friend*	बुझ्नु *to understand*
-नेर *near to*	प्रियजन *loved ones*
उभिनु *to stand upright*	प्रेम *love*
गट्टा *a game played with pebbles*	शुभकामना *good wish(es)*
मास्टर *schoolmaster*	फेब्रेरी *February*
मुख *face*	पठाउनु *to send*
फर्काउनु *to turn*	जवाफ *reply*
आँसु *tear(s)*	लेख्नु *to write*
बग्नु *to flow*	माफी *forgiveness*
गाइने a member of a caste of itinerant village singers or minstrels	बयान *account, description*
	मन पराउनु *to like*
बाल्यकाल *childhood*	चिन्नु *to know (a person)*
चोटि *time, turn*	क्यारे *I think*
सारङ्गी *fiddle, Nepali violin*	क्षमा *forgiveness*
गाउनु *to sing*	दर्शन पाउनु *to get to see someone* (ultra-polite)
बजाउनु *to play music*	
बिरामी *ill*	सम्झना *memory*
हैजा *cholera*	
झण्डै *almost*	
मर्नु *to die*	

Kathmandu, 2045/9/9

Dear friend Raju,

From tomorrow I will not go to school. Today was my last day at school. I stood near the gate and watched boys younger than me playing with pebbles. What fun! A master saw me and asked me why I hadn't gone home, it was late. I turned my face away because tears were flowing from my eyes.

Slowly I reached the gate. A Gaine was standing outside the gate. In my childhood I had heard him singing and playing the fiddle many times. I put a little money in his hand and asked him why he hadn't been to the school for so many days. He said that he had been ill, that he had caught cholera and nearly died.

Father saw me enter the house. He asked me why I was so late. I did not answer him, but Father seemed to understand.

It's been a long time since I received a letter from you. Now please write soon. Love and good wishes to you and your loved ones.

Your friend, Kumar.

Darjeeling, 25 February 1989

Dear friend Kumar,

I was happy when I received the letter you sent from Kathmandu. Since last month I have been intending to write but I didn't write because every day some job or other came my way. Forgive me for being so late.

The description you wrote of your last day at school was very touching. I read it out to an editor friend. His name is Kumar Bhandari. He liked it very much. He says you should write a slightly longer account and send it to him. He says you should write whatever you like. I think Kumar Bhandari is someone your brother knows, is that not so? But he says he hasn't met your brother for many months. He has moved here from Sikkim.

Please convey my greetings to your mother. I ask her forgiveness for not having written a letter. It is many years since I have seen her. I cannot remember how many years it is.

Your well-wisher, Raju.

🔟 Grammar

84 Using the -एको participle as a verb

The -एको participle is used on its own, without any auxiliary verb, to form an abbreviated completed present tense. In this case, the negative is formed by adding the prefix न-:

ऊ कहिले आएको ?	*When did he come?*
हिजो आएको ।	*He came yesterday.*
तिमीहरू अघि किन नआएको ?	*Why didn't you come before?*
खै, कुन्नि किन नआएको हजुर !	*Well, who knows why we didn't come sir!*
के गरेको तिमीले ?	*What have you done?*
आफ्नै काम गरेको ।	*Just my own work.*

85 *How long is it since... ?*

The -एको participle is used to express the idea of time having elapsed since something happened. For example, if you wish to ask someone how long they have been in Nepal you can phrase the question 'you Nepal come how much time happened':

तिमी नेपाल आएको कति दिन भयो ?	*How many days has it been since you came to Nepal?*

The word दिन *day(s)* is optional here. It can be left out, or have another word for a period of time (e.g. हप्ता *week*, महिना *month*, or वर्ष *year*) substituted for it. A person who has *not* visited Nepal for a long time might be asked the question

तिमी नेपाल नगएको कति वर्ष भयो ?	*How many years is it that you have not gone to Nepal? (i.e. since you last went to Nepal?)*
मासु नखाएको दुई महिना भयो ।	*It's two months since I ate meat.*
हिन्दी फिलिम नहेरेको धेरै भएको छ ।	*It's been a long time since I watched a Hindi film.*

86 Seeing or hearing another person's actions

The -एको participle is used to describe what someone is doing when another person sees or hears them. The sentences on the left-hand side below say that someone saw or heard someone else. The sentences on the right amplify them by noting what the person who is seen or heard was doing at the time.

In such sentences, the -एको participle translates as *going, singing, playing, speaking* etc. and in the word order it must follow the person who is being seen or heard. If the person who is seen or heard is performing a transitive verb, then s/he must take the suffix -ले

अस्ति मैले तिमीलाई देखें ।
I saw you two days ago.

अस्ति मैले तिमीलाई स्कूल गएको देखें ।
I saw you going to school two days ago.

बुवाले मलाई सुन्नुभयो ।
Father heard me.

बुवाले मैले गीत गाएको सुन्नुभयो ।
Father heard me singing a song.

आमाले बच्चाहरूलाई हेर्नुभयो ।
Mother watched the children.

आमाले बच्चाहरूले गट्टा खेलेको हेर्नुभयो ।
Mother watched the children playing pebbles.

EXERCISE 49   Translate into Nepali:

1   She (Middle) saw him (Low) playing cards yesterday.
2   I heard her (Middle) singing that song last month.
3   He (Low) saw him (High) coming home three days ago.
4   I saw you (Middle) smoking a cigarette last Wednesday.
5   He (High) heard her (Middle) speaking Hindi last week.
6   They (Middle) saw you (Middle) going to school the day before yesterday.

87   The -एको **participle with** हो **or** होइन

The -एको participle is also used in combination with the appropriate form of the verb हो to form a completed present tense which identifies and emphasises the subject of the verb (this is less common than the combinations with छ and थियो):

त्यो काम उसले गरेको हो ।
ऊ मेरी प्रेमिका हो, बिहा गरेको होइन ।

That job is the one he did.
She is my girlfriend, we are not married.

The -एको participle is also used with हो or होइन to form a completed present tense which emphasises the fact that something is or is not the truth:

मैले माछा किनेको होइन ।
उनीहरू मन्दिर गएका होइनन् ।

It is not fish that I bought.
It is not true that they went to the temple.

88 Thoughts and intentions using भनेर and भनेको

The primary meaning of the verb भन्नु is *to say* or *to tell,* but it also has the important secondary meaning of *to think/to remember.* You might find it helpful to think of the -एर participle of भन्नु, (i.e., भनेर) as meaning *saying to oneself* in the following sentences:

भरे घरमा पाहुनाहरू आउँदै छन् भनेर म बजारतिर लागें ।	*Remembering ('saying (to myself)') that guests were coming to my home in the evening, I headed for the market.*
जिरीबाट खुम्बु टाढा छ भनेर उनीहरू चामल, दाल, नून र चिया बोकेर हिंडे ।	*They set out carrying rice, dāl, salt and tea, remembering ('saying (to themselves)') that Khumbu is far from Jirī.*
भाँडामा कोदो बाँकि छ कि भनेर उसले भित्र हेर्यो ।	*Wondering ('saying (to himself)') if there was any millet left in the pot, he looked inside.*

The -एको participle of भन्नु followed by त or तर, (i.e. भनेको त... or भनेको तर...) means *I intended to but...* It follows a statement of what the speaker intended to do:

आज बिहान बजार जान्छु भनेको त पैसा नै भएन ।	*This morning I thought I'd go to the market, but I didn't even have any money.*
चिठी लेख्छु भनेको त बत्ती नै गयो ।	*I thought I'd write a letter, but there was a power cut.*

89 *What does this word mean?*

Another use of the -एको participle of भन्नु is to state or ask the meaning of a word.

अँग्रेजीमा 'किताब' भनेको के हो ? अँग्रेजीमा 'किताब' भनेको book हो ।	*What is the meaning of the word 'किताब' in English? In English 'किताब' means 'book'.*
नेपालीमा 'book' भनेको के हो ? नेपालीमा 'book' भनेको किताब हो ।	*What is the meaning of the word 'book' in Nepali? In Nepali, 'book' means 'किताब'.*

A second way of asking the meaning of a word involves the use of the word अर्थ, *meaning:*

हिमालयको अर्थ हिउँको घर हो ।   *The meaning of **himālaya** is 'home of snow'.*

पुस्तकालयको अर्थ पुस्तकहरूको घर हो ।पुस्तक   *The meaning of **pustakālaya** is*
भनेको किताब हो ।   *'home of books'. **pustak** means 'book'.*

EXERCISE 50   Fill in the gaps in the following sentences:

१   अँग्रेजीमा पुल भनेको _____ हो ।
२   अँग्रेजीमा ओरालो भनेको _____ हो ।
३   अँग्रेजीमा हैजा भनेको _____ हो ।
४   नेपालीमा letter भनेको _____ हो ।
५   नेपालीमा face भनेको _____ अथवा _____ हो ।
६   नेपालीमा month भनेको _____ हो ।

90   The Nepali year

In Nepal, most people use the traditional Bikram calendar, the विक्रम संवत, instead of the Western or Gregorian calendar. The Bikram year begins on the first day of the spring month of बैसाख, which falls sometime around the middle of April (on April 19 in 1998). The months are solar rather than lunar, so the correspondence between Western and Bikram dates is slightly different from year to year.

The Bikram calendrical era runs 56 years ahead of the Western calendar from January 1 to the first day of बैसाख, and 57 years ahead from the first day of बैसाख until December 31. Thus, January 1998 begins in the middle of the month of पूस and ends in the middle of the following month of माघ in the Bikram year of 2054, while September 1998 begins in the middle of the month of भदौ and ends in the middle of असोज in the Bikram year of 2055.

Bikram Sambat dates may be expressed in full:

२०५४ साल कात्तिक २२ गते शुक्रवार   *Friday, the 22nd day of Kāttik, year 2054 (= 7 November, 1997)*

or in an abbreviated form:

२०५४ असार ३१ गते   *31st day of Asār, 2054 (= 15 July, 1997)*

The word गते means *day of the solar month*. Thus, if you want to know the date in the Bikram year it is common to ask

आज कुन गते हो ?	*What's the date today?*
आज एक्काईस गते हो ।	*It's the 21st today.*

The Bikram Sambat is used less commonly among Nepali-speakers outside Nepal itself. In Nepali-speaking communities in North-east India and Bhutan, the Western calendar is more generally used, and in this case the word गते is replaced by the word तारीख, *day of a month in the Western calendar:*

१९९३ मा मेरी कान्छी छोरीको जन्म भयो ।कुन महिनामा ? जून महिनाको तेईस तारीखमा ।	*My youngest daughter was born in 1993. In which month? On the 23rd of the month of June.*

The word साल is used to refer to particular years, instead of the other word for *year,* वर्ष, which is used for periods of time (तीन वर्ष *three years,* एक सय वर्ष *one hundred years*). Nepali-speakers often omit the दुई हजार *two thousand* when mentioning a particular year, just as English speakers might talk about what happened in '97, rather than '1997'. So, instead of saying that something happened in दुई हजार सात साल *the year 2007*, they will often simply refer to that year as सात साल *the year seven*.

तपाई कुन सालमा पहिलो पटक नेपाल आउनुभयो ?	*In which year did you first come to Nepal?*
म चार वर्ष अघि, एकाउन्न सालमा आएँ ।	*I came four years ago, in the year 51.*

The months of the Hindu year have classical Sanskrit names which take slightly different colloquial forms in each of the languages of South Asia. The classical names are used on formal or official documents, the colloquial names in everyday speech and also often in writing.

The months of the Nepali year

	Classical name	Colloquial name	
१	वैशाख	बैसाख	mid-April to mid-May
२	ज्येष्ठ	जेठ	mid-May to mid-June
३	आषाढ	असार	mid-June to mid-July
४	श्रावण	साउन	mid-July to mid-August
५	भाद्र	भदौ	mid-August to mid-September
६	आश्विन	असोज	mid-September to mid-October
७	कार्त्तिक	कात्तिक	mid-October to mid-November
८	मार्गशीर्ष	मङ्सीर	mid-November to mid-December
९	पौष	पूस	mid-December to mid-January
१०	माघ	माघ	mid-January to mid-February
११	फाल्गुण	फागुन	mid-February to mid-March
१२	चैत्र	चैत	mid-March to mid-April

EXERCISE 51   Translate the following dates into Nepali:

1 Thursday 10th January 1921.
2 Tuesday 10th Chaitra 2016.
3 Sunday 26th November 1956
4 Friday 1st Phalgun 2042.

EXERCISE 52

पढेर बुझ्नुहोस् ।

सुरेन्द्रको दाइ जापान गएको दुई वर्ष भयो । गएको साल दाइले नेपाल फर्केर सुरेन्द्रलाई एउटा राम्रो क्यामेरा दिनुभयो । दुई हप्ता अघि एउटा राम्रो रेडियो पनि पठाउनुभयो । दाइले दिएका क्यामेरा र रेडियो दुवै जापानमा बनेका हुन् । त्यस कारणले राम्रा र बलिया छन् । एक हप्ता अघि दार्जीलिङ्बाट आउनुभएको काकाले पनि सुरेन्द्रलाई एउटा क्यामेरा दिनुभयो । तर काकाले दिएको क्यामेरा दाइले दिएको क्यामेरा जस्तो राम्रो र बलियो देखिएन । सुरेन्द्रलाई दुइटा क्यामेरा चाहिंदैन । उसलाई एउटा क्यामेरा मात्रै चाहिन्छ । गएको सोमवार काका दार्जीलिङ्ग फर्कनुभयो । र आज बिहान सुरेन्द्रले काकाले दिएको क्यामेरा एउटा साथीलाई बेच्यो । उसले ठूलो नाफा गरेको छ तर उसकी आमा यो कुरा थाहा पाएर रिसाउनुभएको छ । आमा भन्दै हुनुहुन्छ 'केही दिनपछि तेरो काका फेरि आउनुहुन्छ नि । अनि तँ वहाँलाई के भन्छस् ? 'तपाईंले दिनुभएको क्यामेरा मैले बेचें' भनेर भन्छस् ? तरुन्तै साथीकहाँ गएर बेचेको क्यामेरा फिर्ता ले र साथीलाई पैसा फिर्ता दे । नातेदारले दिएको कोसेली बेच्नु अपराध हुन्छ, बुझिस् ? ।

प्रश्नहरू

१ सुरेन्द्रको दाइ जापान गएको कति वर्ष भयो ?

२ सुरेन्द्रको दाइले जापानबाट के पठाउनुभयो ?

३ दाइले दिएका क्यामेरा र रेडियो किन बलिया र राम्रा छन् ?

४ सुरेन्द्रको काका कहाँबाट आउनुभएको थियो ?

५ सुरेन्द्रलाई कतिवटा क्यामेरा चाहिन्छ ?

६ आमा सुरेन्द्रसँग किन रिसाउनुभयो ?

14 IF IT RAINS...
पानी पर्‍यो भने...

In this unit you will learn how to:

■ construct conditional sentences
■ express doubt
■ make suggestions
■ discuss whether something is enough

24 Out trekking

Subhas is leading a group of foreign visitors on a trek from Pokhara to Jomsom. They have just arrived at a lodge after a long wet first day. As they eat their evening meal, served by Dilmaya, Subhas discusses the route for the next day with Bekh Bahadur, the lodgekeeper.

दिलमाया तपाईहरू यतातिर बसेर भात खानुहोस् है त ! यति भातले पुग्छ कि पुग्दैन ?

सुभास यति भातले मलाई शायद पुग्दैन होला दिदी । अरू पनि छ कि ?

दिलमाया पुगेन भने केही छैन । अरू थुप्रै छ ।

बेख बहादुर भोलि तपाईहरू कतातिर लाग्ने नि ?

सुभास गण्डकी पुल झरेर जोमसोमतिर जाने । बाटो ओरालो छ, होइन ? भोलि मौसम सफा भयो भने हामीहरू साँझतिर तातोपानी पुग्छौं होला । तर आज जस्तो भोलि पनि पानी पर्‍यो भने अलि गाह्रो होला । बाटो चिप्लो हुन्छ, बिस्तारै बिस्तारै हिंडेर तातोपानी साँझसम्म पुगिंदैन होला । साँझसम्म तातोपानी पुगिएन भने राति कहाँ बास बस्ने त ?

बेख बहादुर तातोपानीभन्दा तल अर्को एउटा सानो गाउँ छ । बाटोमा ढिलो भयो भने त्यहाँ बास बस्नुहोस् न । गाउँको नाम त बिर्सें । तर त्यहाँबाट तातोपानी माथितिर पर्छ, बाटो अलि उकालो पनि छ । तपाईहरू त्यहीं बस्नुभयो भने बेस होला । ए दिलमाया, भात खोइ त !

दिलमाया अरू केही लिनुहुन्छ कि ?

सुभास भात अलिकति थप्ने ।

दिलमाया लौ, लिनुहोस् । तरकारी पनि थप्ने ?

सुभास हवस्, तरकारी पनि थप्नुहोस् । अलिकति दाल छ कि ?

दिलमाया दाल त सकियो । साथीहरूलाई भात पुग्यो ?

सुभास पुग्यो होला । विदेशीहरूले त त्यति धेरै भात खाँदैनन् ।

दिलमाया हातले पनि खाँदैनन्, होइन ?

सुभास हो, उनीहरूलाई अलि अप्ठ्यारो हुन्छ ।

बेख बहादुर भोलि तपाईहरू घोडेपानी भएर जाँदै हुनुहुन्छ, होइन ?

सुभास अर्को बाटै छैन । अरू कसरी जाने त ?

बेख बहादुर यहाँबाट घोडेपानी जाने बाटो र घान्द्रुङ जाने बाटो एउटै हो । तर पल्लो गाउँदेखि बाटो छुट्टिन्छ । तलको बाटोचाहिं घोडापानी जाने बाटो हो, माथिकोचाहिं घान्द्रुङ जाने बाटो हो । भोलि ठूलो पानी पर्‍यो भने घान्द्रुङ बाटोबाट जानुहोस्, अलि सजिलो होला ।

सुभास त्यो बाटोबाट धवलागिरी देखिंदैन होला । घोडेपानीबाट राम्रोसँग देखिन्छ रे । हिमाल हेर्ने यिनीहरूको कस्तो रहर हुन्छ, हगि ?

बेख बहादुर त्यो त हो तर ठूलो पानी परेको बेलामा कतैबाट केही पनि देखिंदैन । आउने हप्ता तपाईहरू त्यही बाटोबाट फर्कनुहुन्छ, होइन त ? भोलि पानी परेन भने मात्र घोडेपानी जानुहोस् ।

सुभास ल त, धन्यवाद । अब त सुत्ने बेला भयो । है त ? भोलि भेटौंला ।

भात *cooked rice, food, meal*	बास बस्नु *to stay for a night*
पुग्नु (1) *to be enough*	-भन्दा तल *below, lower down than*
शायद *perhaps*	बेस *best, better*
थुप्रै *heaps*	थप्नु *to add, supplement, top up*
गण्डकी *the Gandaki river*	सकिनु *to be finished*
पुल *bridge*	घोडेपानी *Ghorepani* (a village)
झर्नु *to descend*	घान्दुङ्ग *Ghandrung* (a village)
जोमसोम *Jomsom* (a village)	पल्लो *next, further*
मौसम *weather*	छुट्टिनु *to divide, bifurcate*
सफा *clear*	धवलागिरि *Dhaulagiri* (a mountain)
तातोपानी *Tatopani* (a village)	रहर *desire*
पुग्नु (2) *to reach, arrive*	हगि ? *isn't that so?*
	भेटौँला *we will meet* (probable future tense: see **Grammar 96**)

Dilmaya	Please sit over here and eat. Will this much rice be enough or not?
Subhas	This much rice might not be enough for me, sister. Is there any more?
Dilmaya	If it's not enough it doesn't matter. There's heaps more.
Bekh Bahadur	Where are you heading tomorrow, eh?
Subhas	We're going down to the Gandaki bridge and then towards Jomsom. The path is downhill, isn't it? If the weather is clear tomorrow we'll probably reach Tatopani around dusk. But if it also rains tomorrow like it did today it will be rather difficult. The path will be slippery, and walking slowly we probably won't reach Tatopani by dusk. If we don't reach Tatopani by dusk, where shall we lodge for the night?
Bekh Bahadur	Below Tatopani there is another small village. If you are slow on the way stay there. I've forgotten the name of the village, though. But from there Tatopani is higher up, the path is rather steep too. If you stay there that will be better. Oh Dilmaya, where's the rice?
Dilmaya	Will you have something more?
Subhas	A little more rice, please.
Dilmaya	There you are. Shall I put vegetables too?
Subhas	Sure, please put vegetables too. Is there a little bit of **dāl** too?

Dilmaya	I'm afraid the **dāl**'s finished. Have your friends had enough rice?
Subhas	I expect they've had enough. Foreigners don't eat such a lot of rice.
Dilmaya	They don't eat with their hands either, do they?
Subhas	Yes, it's a bit difficult for them.
Bekh Bahadur	Tomorrow you're going via Ghorepani, aren't you?
Subhas	There's no other way. How else can we go?
Bekh Bahadur	From here, the path to Ghorepani and the path to Ghandrung are one and the same. But from the next village the path divides. The lower path is the path going to Ghorepani, the higher one is the path going to Ghandrung. If it rains heavily tomorrow, go by the Ghandrung path, it will be a bit easier.
Subhas	You probably can't see Dhaulagiri from that path. I gather that you can get a good view of it from Ghorepani. How they long to see the Himalayas, right?
Bekh Bahadur	That's true, but when it rains heavily nothing can be seen from anywhere. Next week you will come back by that path, won't you? Only go to Ghorepani if it doesn't rain tomorrow.
Subhas	Right then, thank you. Now it's time for bed. OK? We'll meet tomorrow.

Grammar

91   Real conditional sentences

A real conditional sentence is the equivalent of a sentence in English that begins with *if,* and talks about events that might happen or situations that might exist in the future. It is called a 'real' conditional sentence because it always refers to what will be or what might be, and therefore what it describes is *possible*: *if it doesn't rain I will go out.* There is another kind of conditional sentence that talks about what might have been, but was not, and is therefore *impossible* or *unreal*: *if it hadn't rained I wouldn't have gone out.* This second kind of conditional sentence is introduced in **Grammar 130**.

To form a real conditional sentence in Nepali, you take two sentences and link them together with the word भने. भने is a participle of the verb भन्नु *to say* that is not easily translated when it is used in this way, because it simply marks the end of the 'if' clause of the sentence. The closest English parallel is found in an informal expression such as *say / suppose it doesn't rain...* The 'if' clause of the sentence usually comes before the main clause. When it is referring to some possibility in the future, its verb must be in the *simple past* tense. The 'if' clause of a conditional sentence can begin with यदि *if*, and in fact it often does, but यदि *if* is not essential. भने is essential in such sentences whether यदि is used or not.

To construct a Nepali sentence that means *if it doesn't rain I will go out*, begin with the simple past tense of *to rain* as the 'if' clause, then add भने to show that the 'if' clause has ended, and then state that you will go out:

(यदि) पानी परेन	भने	म बाहिर जान्छु ।
(If) it didn't rain	(marks end of 'if' clause)	*I will go out.*
(condition)		(consequence)

= पानी परेन भने म बाहिर जान्छु ।   *If it doesn't rain I will go out.*

यदि तिमी आएनौ भने म एक्लै जान्छु।   *If you don't come I will go alone.*

यदि आमा रुनुभयो भने दिदी पनि रुन्छिन् ।   *If mother cries elder sister will cry too.*

यदि दालमा खुर्सानी राख्नुभएन भने मीठो हुँदैन ।   *If you don't put any chilli in the dāl it won't taste good.*

The second half of a real conditional sentence can also take the form of a request or a command, instead of a prediction:

यदि तपाईलाई थकाई लाग्यो भने मेरो कोठामा सुत्नुहोस् ।   *If you feel tired, please lie down in my room.*

यदि बजारमा लसुन पाइएन भने अदुवा मात्रै किन्नू, बुझ्यौ ?   *If garlic is not available in the market, just buy ginger, do you understand?*

✔ **EXERCISE 53**   Translate into Nepali:

1 If you are tired, please rest.
2 If you are thirsty, please drink this water.
3 If our guests are hungry I will go to the market and buy fruit and vegetables.
4 If you (Middle) do not come tomorrow, mother will stay at home and cry.

5 If I do not come to the office by 5 o'clock, please meet me at the temple.

6 If father does not send me a letter this week I will phone him at home.

92 Using होला to mean *perhaps, might be*

होला is the *probable future* tense of the verb हुनु *to be,* and means *it (probably) will be.* It can be added to the end of statements, regardless of their tense, to qualify them and make them less categorical.

For instance, shopkeeper A is asked whether there is any rice in his shop, and he is sure that there isn't, so he answers categorically:

Q साहूजी, चामल छ ?   *Any rice, shopkeeper?*
A छैन !   *No!*

But shopkeeper B is less certain; he thinks there probably isn't any, but feels he had better check:

Q साहूजी, चामल छ ?   *Any rice, shopkeeper?*
B छैन होला ।   *Probably not...*

आज पानी पर्दैन होला ।   *It probably won't rain today.*
आज गिरीश घरै छ ? थाहा छैन, घरै छ होला । *Is Girish at home? I don't know, he probably is at home.*
बजारमा मासु पाइँदैन होला ।   *You probably won't get any meat in the market.*

The probable future tense is introduced in full in **Grammar 96**.

93 The -ने -ne participle as an adjective

This participle is simply the dictionary form of a verb with its ending changed from -नु -**nu** to -ने -**ne**:

dictionary form		-**ne** participle	
जानु	*to go* (verb)	जाने	*going* (adjective)
खानु	*to eat* (verb)	खाने	*eating* (adjective)
गर्नु	*to do* (verb)	गर्ने	*doing* (adjective)

The first use of the -ने -**ne** participle is to describe nouns:

पोखरा जाने बाटो   *the road to Pokhara ('Pokhara going road')*
खाने कुरा   *things to eat ('eating things')*
आउने हप्ता   *next week ('coming week')*

सुत्ने कोठा	bedroom ('sleeping room')
काम गर्ने मान्छे	a working man
नेपाली बोल्ने मानिस	a Nepali-speaking person

It is important to distinguish between the -ने participle and the -एको participle, because both are used to describe nouns. However, the -एको participle always refers to actions or situations that are in the past as compared with the main verb of the sentence, while the -ने participle refers to situations that are either coterminous or in the future as compared with the main verb:

हामी नेपाल बसेको बेलामा ।	When we lived in Nepal.
हामी नेपाल बस्ने बेलामा ।	When we live in Nepal.
सगरमाथा चढेको मान्छे ।	A person who has climbed Everest.
सगरमाथा चढ्ने मान्छे ।	A person who does/will climb Everest.
प्रवचन दिएको मान्छे ।	The person who gave the lecture.
प्रवचन दिने मान्छे ।	The person who gives lectures / will give a lecture.

The negative is formed simply by adding the prefix न- to the verb:

नपाइने	unavailable
नखाने	not eating
नबिर्सिने	unforgettable

रक्सी नखाने मान्छेलाई किन रक्सी दिएको तिमीले ?	Why have you given raksī to a person who does not drink?
अँग्रेजी नबुझ्ने केटालाई अँग्रेजीमा किन गाली गर्छौ ?	Why do you tell off a boy who does not understand English in English?
नेपालमा नपाइने फलफूल अमेरिकामा जताततै पाइन्छ ।	Fruits that are not available in Nepal can be found everywhere in America.
आज बादल लागेकोले सगरमाथा देख्ने कुरै छैन ।	Because it is cloudy today there's no chance of seeing Everest.

94 Using the -ने participle to talk about future actions

The second use of the -ने participle is as a kind of grammatical shortcut to talk about plans and intentions for the near future. It is used frequently in informal conversation, and people who speak Nepali as a second language (both Nepalis and foreigners) find it so convenient (because the verb ending is the same no matter who the subject of the verb is) that they sometimes use it excessively:

तपाईंहरू भोलि जाने ?	*Are you leaving tomorrow?*
होइन, भोलि बस्ने, पर्सि जाने ।	*No, we're staying tomorrow and leaving the day after tomorrow.*
तपाई चिया खाने कि कफी खाने ?	*Will you drink tea or coffee?*
म चिया खाने ।	*I'll drink tea.*
चियामा चिनी राख्ने ?	*Shall I put sugar in the tea?*
चिनी नराख्ने, दूध मात्रै राख्ने ।	*Don't put sugar, just put milk.*
अब जाने, होइन ?	*We're off now, aren't we?*
हो, अबेर भयो, अब अलिपछि जाने ।	*Yes, it's late, we'll leave in a little while now.*

These usages are acceptable, but it is more polite to use the variable verb endings, especially when talking to someone you are addressing as तपाई.

95 The verb पुग्नु *to arrive, suffice*

This verb has two different uses. In the first, it is used to mean *to reach/arrive* at a destination, and in this context it is intransitive (that is, the subject never needs to take -ले):

यो विमान साढे तीन बजे दिल्ली पुग्छ ।	*This flight reaches Delhi at half past 3.*

Although it is an intransitive verb, पुग्नु also has a passive 'i-stem' version, which is पुगिनु *to be reached*:

मेरो गाउँ टाढै छ ।साँझसम्म पनि पुगिंदैन होला ।	*My village is quite a long way away. We probably won't reach it even by nightfall.*

When the subject of the verb *to arrive* is *coming towards* the speaker, rather than going away from him/her, then the compound verb आइपुग्नु (consisting of the 'i-stem' of आउनु + पुग्नु) is commonly used:

ल, हेर त, वाराणसीको विमान आइपुग्यो ।	*There, look, the Varanasi flight has arrived.*

The second use of पुग्नु is to mean *to suffice/be enough*, and in these contexts the verb is transitive (i.e. its subject must take -ले in past tenses, and will most often take -ले in the habitual present tense too). The person for whom the commodity mentioned suffices or has sufficed must take the object-marking suffix -लाई. For instance, if you wish to say that five rupees will be enough money for you, the sentence will be constructed as follows:

मलाई	पाँच रुपियाँले	पुग्छ ।
for me	*five rupees* + -ले	*suffices.*

EXERCISE 54   Write Nepali sentences stating that the amounts or commodities in the right-hand column were or were not enough for the people in the left-hand column:

1. the tourists who came yesterday	food	✓
2. the Sherpa who helped us	ten rupees	✗
3. the woman who cooked the food	a kilo of ghee	✗

EXERCISE 55   Write Nepali sentences stating that the amounts or commodities in the right-hand column might or might not be enough for the people in the left-hand column:

1. the tourists who are coming tomorrow	food	✗
2. the Sherpa who is going to help us	ten rupees	✓
3. the woman who cooks the food	a kilo of ghee	✓

15 | I'LL GO NEXT YEAR
म आउने साल जाउँला

In this unit you will learn how to:

■ use the probable future tense
■ talk about how much time and/or money it takes to do something

25 Going home for Dasain

Saroj and Krishna both live and work in London, but as the great annual festival of Dasain approaches they begin to wonder whether they might go home to Nepal to celebrate it.

सरोज यो साल तपाई दसैंको लागि घर जानुहुन्छ ?

कृष्ण अहिलेसम्म निश्चय गरेको छैन।तपाई नि ?

सरोज पैसा पाइयो भने जाउँला ।तर पैसा मात्रै होइन, छुट्टी पनि चाहिन्छ नि ।

कृष्ण एक हप्ताको छुट्टी त पाइएला नि ।त्यो समस्या नहोला ।मेरो लागि मुख्य समस्या पैसा नै हो ।आजकाल नेपाल पुग्न कति पैसा लाग्छ ?

सरोज हवाई जहाजबाट जानुभयो भने पाँच सय पाउण्ड लाग्छ, होइन ?

कृष्ण हो, पाँच सय जति लाग्ला ।अनि हवाई जहाजबाट जानुभएन भने पनि कसरी जानुहुन्छ त ? लण्डनबाट बस अथवा रेल काठ्माडौं जान्छ त ?

सरोज केही टूरिष्ट बसहरू त जान्छन् ।तर बसमा नेपाल पुग्न कम्तिमा दुई हप्ता लाग्ला ।

कृष्ण अनि हामीलाई साहूजीले चार हप्ताको छुट्टी देला र ? मेरो विचारमा दिंदैन !

सरोज दिंदैन ! हवाई जहाजबाट जानु बाहेक अर्को उपाय छैन ।

कृष्ण दसैंको बेलामा तपाईको घरमा को को होलान् त ?

सरोज बुवा र आमा हुनुहुन्छ ।कान्छा र साहिंला भाइहरू पनि हुन्छन् ।अरू नातेदारहरू पनि आउलान् ।भगवानको कृपा भयो भने म पनि पुगुँला ।

कृष्ण अनि दिदी नि ?

सरोज तीन वर्ष अघि दिदीको बिहा भयो । अहिलेसम्म उनी हरेक साल भाइ टीकाको लागि माइत आएकी छिन् । यो साल पनि आउलिन् ।

कृष्ण माहिँला भाइचाहिं आउँदैन ?

सरोज माहिँलो भाइ शायद आउँदैन होला यस पालि । ऊ दुई महिनादेखि अरबमा काम गर्दै छ । यो साल छुट्टी लिएन भने शायद अर्को साल पाइएला रे । तर यो साल आउने कुरै छैन रे । एक वर्षपछि अलि सजिलो होला उसलाई ।

कृष्ण अरबमा नेपालीहरूको जिन्दगी कस्तो हुन्छ ? भाइले लेखेको होला नि ?

सरोज गाह्रो होला, तर तपाई हेर्नुहोला । दुई-चार वर्षभित्र ऊ दस लाख कमाएर फर्किन्छ । अनि पोखरा गएर उसले महल जस्तो घर बनाउला र त्यसैमा बसेर हामी धूमधामसित दसैं मनाऔंला । अनि हामी हेरौंला, कसको जिन्दगी गाह्रो छ भनेर !

दसैं *(the festival of) Dasain*	कृपा *kindness*
निश्चय गर्नु *to decide*	टीका *anointing*
मुख्य *main*	माइत *a married woman's parents'*
पाउण्ड *pound*	*home; her natal home*
जति *as much as*	अरब *Arabia*
कम्तिमा *at least*	कमाउनु *to earn*
जानु बाहेक *except for / apart from going*	फर्किनु *to return*
उपाय *means*	महल *palace*
नातेदार *relative*	धूमधाम *pomp and splendour*
भगवान *God*	मनाउनु *to celebrate*

Saroj   Will you go home for Dasain this year?

Krishna   I haven't decided yet. What about you?

Saroj   If I get the money I'll go. But it's not just the money, I need time off too, you know.

Krishna   You'll probably get one week's leave, you know. That won't be a problem. For me the main problem is money. How much does it cost to get to Nepal these days?

Saroj   If you go by air it costs £500, doesn't it?

Krishna   Yes, it probably costs about 500. And if you don't go by air how else will you go? Does a bus or a train go to Kathmandu from London?

Saroj   Some tourist buses do go. But to get to Nepal by bus will probably take at least two weeks.

Krishna   And will the boss give us four weeks' leave, indeed?*[1] I think he won't!

Saroj   He won't! There is no alternative to going by plane.

Krishna	But who will be at your house at Dasain?
Saroj	Father and Mother will be there. Youngest and third eldest brother will also be there. Other relatives will probably come too. If God is kind I'll also get there.
Krishna	And what about your elder sister?
Saroj	Three years ago my sister got married. So far she has come to the natal home every year for Bhai Tika.*² She'll probably come this year.
Krishna	Won't your second eldest brother come?
Saroj	My second eldest brother might not come this time. He's been working in Arabia for two months. He says that if he doesn't take leave this year he'll probably get it next year. But this year he says there's no question of coming. After a year it will be a bit easier for him.
Krishna	What is life like for Nepalis in Arabia? Your brother must have written?
Saroj	It's probably hard, but you watch! Within a few years he will earn a million and come back. Then he'll go to Pokhara and build a house like a palace, and we'll stay in it and celebrate Dasain with pomp and splendour. Then we'll look to see whose life is hard!

*¹ The addition of र makes a question rhetorical: the person asking knows that the answer is 'no'.

*² भाइ टीका is a day of the Dasain festival when sisters anoint their brothers.

🔊 Grammar

96 The probable future tense

Nepali has several different ways of expressing the future tense, and the main difference between them lies in their degree of certainty.

The habitual present and continuous present tenses can be used to refer to the future, just as they can in English:

| भोलि मेरो भाइ भारत जान्छ । | *Tomorrow my brother goes to India.* |
| भोलि मेरो भाइ भारत जाँदै छ । | *Tomorrow my brother is going to India.* |

Of course, both of these sentences would be in the present tense if the word भोलि were removed from them. The probable future tense, however, is used exclusively to refer to the future, and it contains within it a measure of uncertainty:

भोलि मेरो भाइ भारत जाला ।   *Tomorrow my brother will*
                                     (probably) go to India.

In the affirmative, the probable future tense consists of a verb base plus an ending; the endings are as follows:

Probable future tense: verb endings	
म	-उँला
हामी, हामीहरू	-औँला
तैँ	-लास्
तिमी, तिमीहरू	-औला
ऊ, यो, त्यो (m.)	-ला
ऊ, यो, त्यो (f.)	-ली
उनी, यिनी, तिनी (m.)	-लान्
उनी, यिनी, तिनी (f.)	-लिन्
यी, ती, उनीहरू etc.	-लान्

Probable future tense: verb bases

The formation of the verb bases for the probable future tense has five rules:

1) The endings are added to the bases of C-verbs in a regular manner (म गर्ँला *I will do,* तैँ गर्लास् *you will do,* तिमी गरौला *you will do,* etc.)
2) If the base of a V-verb ends in **-ā**, the endings are added in a regular manner (म खाउँला *I will eat,* ऊ खाला *he will eat,* उनी खालान् *he will eat,* etc.).
3) The V-verbs दिनु *to give,* लिनु *to take,* and हुनु *to be* are irregular:
   a) दिनु employs the base दि- in first person forms (म दिउँला *I will give,* हामी दिऔँला *we will give*) and दे- in all others (ऊ देला *he will give,* उनीहरू देलान् *they will give,* etc.)
   b) लिनु employs the base लि- in first person forms (म लिउँला *I will take,* हामी लिऔँला *we will take*) and ले- in all others (ऊ लेला *he will take,* उनीहरू लेलान् *they will take,* etc.)

c) हुनु employs the base हो- in all forms except the first person singular; thus म हुँला *I will be*, but उनी होलिन् *she will be*.

4) Verbs other than दिनु and लिनु whose bases end in **-i** (principally the passive 'i-stem' verbs) take an intervening **-e-** between base and ending, e.g. बिर्सिएला *it will be forgotten*, पाइएला *it will be obtained*, etc.

5) The base of a VV-verb is usually the normal present tense base (आउ- from आउनु, पिउ- from पिउनु etc.) But for the first person forms the second vowel is dropped. Thus: म आउँला *I will come*, हामी आओंला *we will come*, but ऊ आउला *he will come*, उनीहरू आउलान् *they will come*, etc.

Probable future tense

	हुनु *to be*	जानु *to go*	गर्नु *to do*	आउनु *to come*	दिनु *to give*
म	हुँला	जाउँला	गर्ला	आउँला	दिउँला
हामीहरू	होओंला	जाओंला	गरौंला	आओंला	दिओंला
तँ	होलास्	जालास्	गर्लास्	आउलास्	देलास्
तिमी, तिमीहरू	होओला	जाओला	गरौला	आओला	देओला
ऊ (m.)	होला	जाला	गर्ला	आउला	देला
ऊ (f.)	होली	जाली	गर्ली	आउली	देली
उनी (m.)	होलान्	जालान्	गर्लान्	आउलान्	देलान्
उनी (f.)	होलिन्	जालिन्	गर्लिन्	आउलिन्	देलिन्
यी, ती, उनीहरू	होलान्	जालान्	गर्लान्	आउलान्	देलान्

Formally, Nepali grammar contains negative forms of these verbs in which their endings change to -ओइन, -ओइनस्, -ओइनौ, etc. but these are encountered very rarely indeed and there is very little purpose in the foreign learner memorising them. Generally, the future negative is formed either by adding the prefix न- to the forms listed above, or by using the habitual present tense in the negative and adding होला *perhaps* to the end of the statement. The meaning varies slightly, according to which form is used:

म जाउँला ।	*I'll probably go.*
म नजाउँला ।	*I'll probably not go* (with the sense that the person who is being spoken to would prefer the person who is speaking not to go).
म जाँदिन होला ।	*I probably won't go.*
ऊ एउटा सिपाही होला ।	*He may be a soldier.*
ऊ सिपाही नहोला ।	*He may not be a soldier.*
ऊ सिपाही हुँदैन होला ।	*He probably won't be a soldier.*

Because of the slightly doubtful tone of this future tense, it *has* to be used in sentences that refer to the future and begin with the word शायद, *perhaps:*

आज जाँदिन । शायद भोलि-पर्सि जाउँला ।   *I won't go today. Perhaps I'll go*
   tomorrow or the day after.

The following proverb uses the probable future tense of the verb भर्नु *to fill:*

तैं रानी मै रानी को भर्ला कुवाँको पानी ?   *(If) you're a queen and I'm a*
   queen, who will fill water from
   the well ?

The High form of the probable future tense consists of the dictionary form of the verb + होला . It is therefore identical to the Super-Polite imperative (see **Grammar 44**) and in fact the two meanings do converge:

बेलायतबाट मलाई चिठी लेख्नुहोला ।   *Please write me a letter*
   from England.
बेलायतबाट मलाई चिठी लेख्नुहोला कि ?   *Will you write me a letter*
   from England?

97   The infinitive + लाग्नु: *What does it cost to... ?,*
How long does it take to... ?

The verb लाग्नु is used to mean:

■ *to cost* when it is combined with a sum of money:

कति पैसा लाग्छ ?   *How much does it cost?*
बीस रुपियाँ लाग्छ ।   *It costs 20 rupees.*

■ *to take* when it is combined with a quantity of time:

कति समय लाग्छ ?   *How much time does it take?*
तीन घण्टा लाग्छ ।   *It takes three hours.*

Note: there is no Nepali equivalent of the English 'it' in these sentences; and, although the subject of the verb लाग्नु may be plural (e.g. *three hours*), the verb behaves as if it is singular; hence तीन घण्टा लाग्छ, not तीन घण्टा लाग्छन्.

These sentences may be extended by prefacing them with a verb, which must appear in its infinitive form. This is very simply the dictionary form minus its final **-u**:

Dictionary form	Infinitive		
जानु	जान	**jāna**	*to go*
आउनु	आउन	**āuna**	*to come*
पुग्नु	पुग्न	**pugna**	*to reach*

Both forms of the verb (-नु and -न) can be translated as *to go, to come* and so on, and there is very little difference in their meaning. However, only the form ending in -न may be used in this kind of sentence:

गोरखा जान कति पैसा लाग्छ ?	*How much does it cost to go to Gorkha?*
गोरखा पुग्न तीन घण्टा लाग्छ ।	*It takes three hours to reach Gorkha.*
गोरखा जान र आउन पूरा एक दिन लाग्छ ।	*It takes a whole day to go to Gorkha and come (back).*

If the sentence involves nouns or pronouns (e.g. *how long does it take you...*, or *how much does it cost them...*) then these must take the postposition -लाई:

पोखराबाट मुक्तिनाथ पुग्न उनीहरूलाई एक हप्ता लाग्यो ।	*It took them a week to reach Muktinath from Pokhara.*
जुम्लाबाट हुम्ला पुग्न हामीलाई एक हप्ता लाग्दैन होला, तीन-चार दिन मात्रै लाग्ला ।	*It probably won't take us a week to reach Humla from Jumla, it will probably only take us three or four days.*

EXERCISE 56 Put the following sentences into the probable future tense, substituting the word भोलि for हिजो in each:

१ हिजो मौसम साह्रै राम्रो थियो ।
२ हिजो दिल्लीबाट काठमाडौं पुग्न दुई घण्टा जति लाग्यो ।
३ हिजो नानीहरूले खेतमा फुटबल खेले । उनीहरूको लुगामा हिलो लाग्यो ।
४ हिजो सीताले घर राम्रोसँग सफा गरिन् ।
५ हिजो दिदीले भात पकाइनन्, दाइले पकाए ।
६ हिजो घरमा पाहुनाहरू भएको कारणले उनीहरू स्कूल आएनन् ।

98 Words for *approximately*

Nepali has various words that can be used to mean *about* or *approximately*:

-तिर	*about* (with expressions of time only)
करीब	*approximately, roughly*
जति	*about as much as*
झण्डै	*almost, virtually*

The postposition -तिर (see **Grammar 47**) is used with expressions of time to mean *at roughly such-and-such a time:*

दस बजेतिर आउनुहोस् ।
Please come at about 10 o'clock.

छिटो हिंड्यौँ भने हामी साँझतिर पुगौँला ।
If we walk quickly we will arrive at around dusk.

The word करीब is used before an expression of quantity to mean *about* or *approximately:*

एक महिनाको लागि हामीलाई करीब दुई किलो नून चाहिन्छ होला ।
We will probably need about two kilos of salt for a month.

यहाँबाट मेरो घर पुग्न करीब दस मिनेट लाग्छ ।
It takes about ten minutes to reach my house from here.

The word जति is used after an expression of quantity or time to mean *as much as* or *as many as:*

यस गाउँका बाह्रजना जति मानिसहरू दोस्रो विश्व-युद्धमा मरे ।
As many as 12 people from this village died in the Second World War.

झण्डै has the sense of *almost* or *very nearly:*

यी व्यापारीहरूलाई ल्हासा पुग्न झण्डै एक हप्ता लाग्यो ।
It took these traders almost a week to reach Lhasa.

EXERCISE 57   Translate into Nepali:

It costs £500 to go to Nepal by air from London, and it takes 15 hours to reach Kathmandu. I always buy an interesting book at the airport! When I went to Nepal last year I bought a very fat novel and it took me about ten hours to read it. I will probably go to Nepal again next year, and I might buy two novels this time. In Nepal, I went to Bhadrapur. If you go to Bhadrapur by bus from Kathmandu it's quite cheap but it takes a whole day to arrive there. There were a lot of people on the bus going to Bhadrapur and the road leading to Bhadrapur was very bad. I didn't buy a book for that journey, because I was going with one or two Nepali friends. If you go to Bhadrapur by plane it costs a lot of money but it doesn't take much time. A plane going to Bhadrapur leaves the capital every morning at 10 o'clock. If I go to Bhadrapur again next year, I will probably go by plane.

16 | WHAT SHOULD I DO?
के गर्नुपर्छ ?

In this unit you will learn how to:

■ use expressions meaning *should, ought, must* and *had to*

26 Arriving at Tribhuvan International Airport

Harish has returned to Nepal after an absence of 20 years. He finds the airport completely unrecognisable, and he enlists the help of Nirmal, an airport attendant, to see him through the various formalities.

हरिश   नमस्ते !
निर्मल   नमस्ते हजुर । तपाई लण्डनबाट आउनुभएको हो ?

हरिश	हजुर, भरखरै आइपुगेको आर॰ ए॰ को विमानमा ।सुन्नुहोस् न, मलाई नेपाल नआएको धेरै वर्ष भयो । पहिले विमानस्थल गौचर मात्रै थियो । भन्नुहोस् न, कता जानुपर्छ, के के गर्नुपर्छ ?
निर्मल	ठीक छ, म तपाईंको लागि सबै कुरा मिलाउँछु ।तपाईंलाई भिसा चाहियो? त्यसो हो भने तपाईंलाई ऊ त्यो लाइनमा उभिनुपर्छ ।
हरिश	म त नेपाली नागरिक हुँ नि । भिसा लिनुपर्दैन !
निर्मल	ए, माफ गर्नुहोस् है ।ऊ, सामान आइपुग्यो ।अब सामान टिप्नुपऱ्यो ।
हरिश	मेरो सामान त अहिलेसम्म निस्केको छैन ।यहाँ धेरै बेरसम्म कुर्नुपर्छ कि के हो ?
निर्मल	पर्दैन होला ।धेरै जसो पाँच मिनेट पनि लाग्दैन ।
	(पाँच मिनेटपछि)
हरिश	अझ पनि आएको छैन ।बीचबाटोमै हरायो कि के हो ?
निर्मल	चिन्ता गर्नुपर्दैन ।म भित्र गएर तपाईंको सामान निकाल्छु ।तर तपाईंले मलाई दस रुपियाँ दिनुपर्छ ।
हरिश	दस रुपियाँ ? मसँग नेपाली पैसा छैन ।पैसा साट्नुपऱ्यो ।
निर्मल	ऊ त्यहाँ बैंक छ ।त्यहीं गएर साट्नुहोस् ।
	(पाँच मिनेटपछि)
निर्मल	भयो ? हेर्नुहोस्, तपाईंको सामान आइपुग्यो ।अब तपाईंलाई सामान लिएर भन्सारतिर जानुपऱ्यो ।
	(भन्सारमा)
हरिश	नमस्कार, नमस्कार ।
भन्सार अधिकृत	पासपोर्ट देखाउनुहोस् त ।आज कहाँबाट आउनुभएको ?
हरिश	लण्डनबाट ।झोला खोल्नुपर्छ ?
भन्सार अधिकृत	खोल्नुपर्छ ।हामीले भित्र हेर्नुपर्छ एक चोटि ।तपाईंले आफै प्याक गरेको हो ?
हरिश	हो, मैले आफै प्याक गरेको ।लुगा-फाटाबाहेक यसमा अरू खास त केही छैन ।
भन्सार अधिकृत	त्यस्तै होला, तर हामीले हेर्नैपर्छ, के गर्ने ? ल, ठीक छ ।भयो ।
निर्मल	आउनुहोस् हजुर म तपाईंको लागि ट्याक्सी बोलाउँछु ।सामान पनि दिनुहोस्, तपाई त थाक्नुभयो होला, म बोक्छु ।
हरिश	पर्दैन, गह्रुँगो छैन ।
निर्मल	तपाई कहाँसम्म जाने ? होटेलको रिजर्वेशन भयो ?
हरिश	पर्दैन ।दाइको घर छ नक्सालमा ।
निर्मल	लौ त ।यहाँबाट नक्साल पुग्न ट्याक्सीमा एक सय रुपियाँ जति लाग्छ ।अनि तपाईंले मलाई पनि एक सय दिनुपऱ्यो ।धन्यवाद ।फेरि भेटौंला है ।

आर॰ ए॰ *R.A.* (Royal Nepal Air Corporation)	अधिकृत *official*
गौचर *cow pasture*	पासपोर्ट *passport*
भिसा *visa*	खोल्नु *to open*
लाइन *queue, line*	आफै *self, oneself*
नागरिक *citizen*	प्याक गर्नु *to pack*
सामान *luggage*	लुगा-फाटा *clothes and such like*
टिप्नु *to pick up*	खास *special, particular*
कुर्नु *to wait*	थाक्नु *to be tired*
अझ पनि *still*	बोक्नु *to carry*
चिन्ता गर्नु *to worry*	गह्रौंगो *heavy*
साट्नु *to exchange*	रिजर्वेशन *reservation*
भन्सार *Customs*	नक्साल *Naxal* (a district of Kathmandu)

Harish Hello!

Nirmal Hello sir. Have you come from London?

Harish Yes, on the R.A. flight that has just arrived. Listen, I have not visited Nepal for many years. Before, the airport was just a cow pasture. Tell me, where should I go, what things do I have to do?

Nirmal OK, I'll organise everything for you. Do you need a visa? If so, you have to stand in that queue over there.

Harish But I'm a Nepali citizen, you know. I don't need to get a visa.

Nirmal Oh, please forgive me. Look, the luggage has arrived. Now you must pick up your luggage.

Harish But my luggage hasn't come out yet. Does one have to wait a long time here, or what?

Nirmal Probably not. It usually doesn't even take five minutes.
After five minutes:

Harish It still hasn't come. Has it been lost on the way or something?

Nirmal No need to worry. I'll go inside and get your luggage out. But you must give me ten rupees.

Harish Ten rupees? I haven't any Nepali money. I must exchange some money.

Nirmal There's a bank over there. Go there and exchange it.
After five minutes:

Nirmal Done? Look, your luggage has arrived. Now you must take the luggage and go towards Customs.
At Customs…

Harish Hello, hello.

Customs official	Show me your passport then. Where have you come from today?
Harish	From London. Should I open my bag?
Customs official	Yes. We have to take a look inside. Did you pack it yourself?
Harish	Yes, I packed it myself. There's nothing special in it apart from clothes and such like.
Customs official	That's probably how it is, but we have to look, what to do? There, that's OK. It's done.
Nirmal	Come sir, I'll call a taxi for you. Give me your luggage too, you must be tired, I'll carry it.
Harish	There's no need, it's not heavy.
Nirmal	How far are you going? Have you made a hotel reservation?
Harish	No need. There's my brother's house in Naksal.
Nirmal	That's that then. To get from here to Naksal by taxi costs about 100 rupees. And you must give me 100 too. Thank you. See you again!

Grammar

99 *Must, should, don't have to*

The combination of the dictionary form of a verb with third person singular forms of the verb पर्नु *to fall* (पर्छ and पर्दैन in the present tense, and पर्‍यो and परेन in the past) is used to express meanings such as *must, need to, should, have to,* and *ought to.* The two words are joined together when written:

हुनुपर्छ	*must be / should be / has to be / ought to be*
बोल्नुपर्छ	*must speak / should speak / has to speak / ought to speak*
गर्नुपर्छ	*must do / should do / has to do / ought to do*

If the sentence mentions a person upon whom this need or obligation 'falls', s/he must be marked in the sentence – with the postposition -लाई if the verb is intransitive:

तिमीहरूलाई भोलि आउनुपर्दैन ।   *You do not have to come tomorrow.*

– or with -ले if the verb is transitive:

केटा-केटीहरूले साँचो बोल्नुपर्छ ।   *Boys and girls should speak the truth.*

The affirmative construction is commonly used to prescribe correct behaviour in general terms:

विद्यार्थीहरूले गुरुलाई आदर गर्नुपर्छ ।

Students should respect their teacher.

सबैले ईश्वरलाई मान्नुपर्छ ।
लोग्नेले स्वास्नीलाई माया गर्नुपर्छ ।

Everyone should believe in God.
A husband should love his wife.

स्वस्थ भइर बाँच्न पाउनु एक मानव अधिकार हो,
यो अधिकार हरेक महिलाले पाउनु पर्छ ।

मेरी श्रीमती गर्भवती भएको बेलामा उनको स्याहार पुग्यो कि पुगेन भनेर मैले विचार पुर्‍याउनु पर्छ । मलाई थाहा छ, हामीकहाँ गर्भवतीको खाना र पोषणमा त्यति ध्यान दिने चलन छैन । गर्भको बच्चालाई

स्वस्थ जन्माउने कुरामा परिवारका सदस्यहरूको निकै ठूलो हात हुन्छ । छोरीलाई थोरै महत्व दिने र छोरी जन्मंदा राम्रो हेरचाह नगर्ने पनि चलन छ । यसो गर्दा छोरीलाई सानैदेखि कमजोरीको 'हीन' भावना आउँछ र

पछि सम्म पनि समाजमा अघि बढन गाह्रो हुन्छ ।
हामी पुरूष जातिले समाज र परिवार बाटै यस्तो 'हीन' भावना हटाएर समाजमा महिला प्रति राम्रो धारणा ल्याउन सक्छौं ।

महिला प्रति हामी पुरूष जातिले व्यवहार बदल्नु पर्छ,
हामी बदलियौं भने यसबाट परिवारका सबैलाई फाइदा हुन्छ ।

CHILDREN FIRST!
unicef 50

A UNICEF advertisement in Nepali. The main heading translates 'To be able to live healthily is a human right, every woman should get this right'.

The meaning of the negative construction with पर्दैन is not exactly the opposite of this. Rather than saying that it is wrong to do something, it simply states that there is no need to do it:

उनीहरूलाई म भन्छु, तपाईंले भन्नुपर्दैन ।
मसँग दुइटा कलम छ, तपाईंले किन्नुपर्दैन ।

I will tell them, you do not need to.
I have two pens, you do not need to buy (one).

सुन्दरी केटीले गहना लाउनुपर्दैन ।

A pretty girl does not need to wear jewellery.

The word पर्दैन is commonly used on its own, without being attached to a verb, to mean *no need* or *don't bother*:

म तपाईको लागि पानी लिएर आउँछु है ? पर्दैन, *I'll bring some water for you, OK?*
हामीसँग दुई बोतल पानी छ ।   *No need, we have two bottles of*
                                       water.

If a need or obligation to *be* something or somewhere 'falls' upon an inanimate noun, that noun takes neither ले nor लाई:

तपाईको खल्तीमा पैसा त हुनैपर्छ ।   *There simply must be money in*
                                       your pocket.

✔ **EXERCISE 58** Change the following statements of fact into statements of general obligation.

Example

ऊ हरेक दिन अफिस जान्छ ।   = उसलाई हरेक दिन अफिस जानुपर्छ ।
He goes to the office every day. *He has to go to the office every day.*
ऊ हरेक दिन अफिस जाँदैन   = उसलाई हरेक दिन अफिस जानुपर्दैन
He doesn't go to the office   *He doesn't have to go to the office*
every day.   *every day.*

१ हामी ईश्वरलाई पूजा गर्छौं ।
२ मेरो भाइ हरेक दिन दाल भात खान्छ ।
३ आज बिदा हो, हामीहरू अफिसमा जाँदैनौं ।
४ उनीहरू हामीलाई त्यो कथा सुनाउँदैनन् ।
५ सीताले घर सफा गर्दिन ।त्यो काम एउटा नोकरले गर्छ ।
६ आज म भात पकाउँदिन ।मेरो श्रीमानले पकाउनुहुन्छ ।

100 *Must, had to*

The obvious meaning of a verb followed by the simple past tense of पर्नु *to fall* (पर्‍यो or परेन) is an obligation in the past:

हिजो घरमा तरकारी नभएर मलाई बजार   *Yesterday there were no vegetables*
जानुपर्‍यो ।   *in the house and I had to go to the*
                                       market.
अस्ति अफिस बन्द थियो, त्यस कारण मलाई *The day before yesterday the*
शहर जानुपरेन ।   *office was shut, so I did not have*
                                       to go to town.
हिजो शहरमा मलाई यता-उता धेरै   *Yesterday I had to run here and*
ठाउँ दौड्नुपर्‍यो ।   *there to many places in town.*

However, the same construction is used when the speaker is talking about the immediate present, because he considers the obligation that presses upon him as he speaks to have 'fallen' in the past tense. Because the obligation has already 'fallen', the speaker expresses his intention to carry out the action without further delay:

नानीको लुगामा हिलो लाग्यो, अब धुनुपर्‍यो । *Mud has got on to the child's clothing, now I must wash it.*

ल, गुरुजी आउनुभयो ।अब किताब खोलेर   *Look, teacher has arrived. Now we*
पढ्नुपर्‍यो ।   *must open (our) books and read.*

रेष्टुराँ पाँच मिनेटपछि बन्द हुन्छ ।अब पैसा   *The restaurant will close in five*
तिर्नुपर्‍यो ।   *minutes. Now I must pay the bill.*

EXERCISE 59 Change the following statements of fact into statements of past or immediate need:

Example   अब म जान्छु । = अब मलाई जानुपर्‍यो ।
हिजो म गइनँ ।= हिजो मलाई जानुपरेन ।

१ अब बुवा पशुपतिनाथको मन्दिर जानुहुन्छ ।
२ अब तिमी अलिकति भात खान्छौ ।
३ अब म चाँडै सुत्छु ।
४ हिजो मैले धेरै काम गरिनँ ।
५ हिजो किसानहरू खेतमा गएनन् ।
६ हिजो आमा बजार जानुभएन ।

101 The verbs मिल्नु and मिलाउनु

The verb मिल्नु is very versatile, and can mean *to come together, match, fit, get along,* etc. It is best explained through examples:

त्यो रँग यो रँगसँग पटक्कै मिल्दैन ।   *That colour really doesn't match with this colour.*

ताल्चामा यो साँचो मिलेको छैन ।   *This key hasn't fitted the lock.*
उनीहरूको कुरा मिल्यो ।   *They came to an agreement.*
यस वाक्यमा त्यो शब्द अलि मिल्दैन ।   *In this sentence that word is a little unsuitable.*

मेरो छोरा आफ्ना साथीहरूसँग राम्रोसँग मिल्छ । *My son gets along well with his friends.*

The verb मिलाउनु is the causative of मिल्नु. That is, it causes a coming together, a matching, etc. and translates into English as *to arrange, assemble, adjust, bring together, sort out:*

त्यो त अलि महँगो भयो, साहूजी ।दाम   *That's a little expensive, shopkeeper.*
मिलाएर दिनुहोस् ।   *Please adjust the price for me.*

भोलि कति बजे भेट्ने ? समय मिलाउनुपर्‍यो । *What time shall we meet tomorrow?*
                                          We must arrange a time.

एक छिन पर्खनुहोस् है । कपाल मिलाउनुपर्‍यो । *Wait a moment, won't you. I have*
                                            to tidy my hair.

अब तपाईंहरूको कुरा मिल्यो । हात   *Now you are in agreement. Please*
  मिलाउनुहोस् ।   *shake hands.*

17 | YOU'RE NOT ALLOWED IN

भित्र जान हुँदैन

In this unit you will learn how to:

■ how to ask and state what is right and what is wrong
■ how to ask and state what one is allowed to do
■ identify some basic facts about religion in Nepal

27 Americans at Pashupati temple

Jim has been living in Nepal for three months, and he is showing some American friends who have come to visit him the sights of the Kathmandu Valley. He wonders if he might take them into Pashupati temple. The policeman at the entrance explains why he cannot.

जिम हामी मन्दिरभित्र जान हुन्छ ?

प्रहरी तपाईंहरू कुन देशबाट आउनुभएको ?

जिम हामीहरू अमेरिकाबाट आएको ।

प्रहरी हो र ? कति राम्रो नेपाली बोल्नुहुन्छ तपाई । तपाईंले नेपाली भाषा कहाँ सिक्नुभयो ?

जिम वहीं अमेरिकामा अलिकति सिकें ।अहिले नेपाल बसेको तीन महिना भयो । २०४
हामी मन्दिरभित्र...

प्रहरी अहो, अमेरिकामा पनि नेपाली भाषा सिक्न पाइन्छ ? मलाई थाहा थिएन । नेपाली सिकाउने मानिसहरू छन् ?

जिम प्रशस्त छन् । भन्नुहोस् न, हामी मन्दिरभित्र पस्न हुन्छ कि हुन्न ?

प्रहरी तपाई हिन्दू धर्मावलम्बी हुनुहुन्छ ?

जिम धर्मावलम्बी भनेको के हो ? मैले बुझिनँ ।

प्रहरी भनाइको मतलब, तपाई हिन्दू हुनुहुन्छ ?

जिम अहँ, म हिन्दू होइन । हामीहरू हिन्दू नभएको कारणले तपाई हामीलाई भित्र पस्न दिनुहुन्न ?

प्रहरी अलि मिल्दैन । यो पशुपतिनाथको मन्दिर नेपालको सबैभन्दा प्राचीन तीर्थस्थल हो । त्यो तपाईलाई थाहा हुनुपर्छ । त्यसैले यहाँ विशेष नियमहरू लाग्छन् । पुजारीहरूले हिन्दूहरूलाई मात्र भित्र पस्न दिन्छन् । अनि हिन्दू भएर पनि कसैले छालाबाट बनेको कुनै कुरा लाउन हुँदैन ।

जिम केही छैन । हामी हिन्दू नभएकोले भित्र पस्ने कुरै छैन जस्तो छ । तर मन्दिरको आँगन हेर्न पाइन्छ कि ?

प्रहरी बाग्मती खोलाभन्दा पर ऊ त्यो रूखैं रूखले ढाकेको थुम्को छ नि । त्यसलाई मृगस्थली भन्छन् । तपाईहरू बाग्मती खोला ऊ त्यो पुरानो पुलबाट तर्नुहोस् । पुलबाट राजराजेश्वरी घाट देखिन्छ । त्यहाँ काठ्माडौंका हिन्दूहरूले आफ्ना मृतहरू जलाउँछन् । त्यसको फोटो खिंच्न हुँदैन । साह्रै अनुचित हुन्छ ।

जिम बुझें । तर मृगस्थलीमा के छ ? रूखहरू मात्रै ?

प्रहरी होइन, मृगस्थलीमा पुराना शिवालयहरू धेरै छन् । बाँदरहरू पनि थुप्रै छन् । त्यहाँ घाममा बसेर पशुपतिनाथको मन्दिरको साह्रै राम्रो दृश्य हेर्न पाइन्छ ।

जिम त्यहाँबाट मन्दिरको फोटो खिंच्न हुन्छ ?

प्रहरी हुन्छ, एकदमै ठीक छ । तर बाँदरहरूसँग होश गर्नुहोस् । बाँदरहरूलाई फलफूल दिन हुँदैन ।

वहीं *there; in that very place*	-भन्दा पर *the other side of*
सिकाउनु *to teach*	ढाक्नु *to be covered*
धर्मावलम्बी *a follower of a religion*	थुम्को *hillock*
भनाइ *utterance, something said*	तर्नु *to cross*
मतलब *meaning*	मृत *dead person*
प्राचीन *ancient*	जलाउनु *to burn, cremate*
तीर्थस्थल *place of pilgrimage*	फोटो खिंच्नु *to take a photograph*
विशेष *special*	अनुचित *improper*
नियम *rule*	शिवालय *Shiva temple*
छाला *leather*	दृश्य *view*
बन्नु *to be made*	होश गर्नु *to be careful*
आँगन *courtyard, compound*	दुःख *trouble*
बाग्मती खोला *the Bagmati river*	

दुःख दिन्छन् ।

Jim   Is it all right for us to go into the temple?

Policeman   Which country have you come from?

Jim   We have come from America.

Policeman   Is that so? What good Nepali you speak! Where did you learn the Nepali language?

Jim   Right there in America I learned a little. Now I have lived in Nepal for three months. Can we...

Policeman   Aho, can you learn Nepali language in America too? I didn't know. Are there people who teach Nepali?

Jim   There are plenty. Tell me, is it or isn't it all right for us to enter the temple?

Policeman   Are you a follower of Hinduism?

Jim   What does **dharmāvalambī** mean? I didn't understand.

Policeman   What I mean is, are you a Hindu?

Jim   No, I am not a Hindu. Will you not allow us into the temple because we are not Hindus?

Policeman   It's a bit inappropriate. This temple of Pashupatinath is Nepal's most ancient pilgrimage place. That you should know. So special rules apply here. The priests only allow Hindus to enter. And even if they are Hindus, no-one is supposed to wear anything made from leather.

Jim   It doesn't matter. It seems that because we are not Hindus there is no question of going inside. But can one get to look at the temple courtyard?

Policeman   On the far side of the Bagmati river over there, the hillock covered by trees, right? They call that Mrigasthali. Cross the Bagmati river by that old bridge over there. From the bridge you can see Rajarajeshwari Ghat.[*] There, Kathmandu's Hindus burn their dead. It is not right to take a photo of that. It is extremely improper.

Jim   I've understood. But what is there at Mrigasthali? Just trees?

Policeman   No, at Mrigasthali there are many Shiva shrines. There are lots of monkeys too. You can sit in the sun there and look at a very fine view of Pashupatinath temple.

Jim   Is it all right to take a photo of the temple from there?

Policeman   Yes, that's absolutely fine. But be careful with the monkeys. You shouldn't give the monkeys any fruit. They'll give you trouble.

* A ghāṭ is a stepped platform leading down to a river. Ghāṭs are often used for the performance of religious devotions and as cremation sites.

☷ Grammar

102 *Is it all right to... ?* Using the infinitive with हुन्छ / हुँदैन

The combination of the infinitive of a verb + हुन्छ / हुँदैन expresses meanings such as *should / should not, is / is not permitted, is / is not advisable, is / is not all right*. Often, no subject is mentioned in these sentences, which are often general statements about what is and what is not correct behaviour: in such cases it can be understood to mean *one should...* or *one should not...*

मन्दिरमा जुत्ता लाउन हुँदैन ।	*One should not wear shoes in a temple.**
हिन्दू धर्म अनुसार गाई काट्न हुँदैन ।	*According to Hindu religion, it is wrong to kill a cow.*
इस्लामी धर्म अनुसार सुँगूरको मासु खान हुँदैन ।	*According to Islamic religion, it is wrong to eat pork.*

* The soles of the feet or shoes are unclean, and shoes should be removed before entering the interiors of houses, temples, etc. It is also insulting to sit with one's legs crossed in such a way that the sole of one's shoe is in front of another person's face. Similarly, care should be taken not to let one's feet pass above any part of a Nepali person's body, nor should one touch another person on the crown of the head.

The alternative negative form of हुनु (हुन्न instead of हुँदैन) is also frequently used in these contexts. The subject of a verb in a sentence of this type must take -ले if the verb is transitive:

तिमीले पिरो धेरै खान हुन्न, अलिकति खान त हुन्छ ।	*You should not eat too much spicy (food), but it's OK to eat a little.*

103 *They don't allow you to...*

Nepali uses the verb दिनु *to give* to mean *to let* or *to allow*. The subject of दिनु will usually take -ले in all tenses, to make it absolutely clear who the subject is. When one of the first person pronouns (म or हामी) is the subject, however, it is unlikely to take -ले except in past tenses. The structure of such a sentence is typically:

Allower + -ले   Person allowed+ -लाई   Infinitive   दिनु (*to allow*)

मैले घरमा उसलाई चुरोट खान दिइनँ ।	*I did not allow him to smoke a cigarette in the house.*
प्रहरीले तिमीलाई मन्दिरमा जुत्ता लाउन दिँदैन होला ।	*The policeman probably won't allow you to wear shoes in the temple.*
बत्ती किन बन्द गर्‍यौ तिमीले ? बत्ती खोलेर मलाई अखबार पढ्न देऊ न ।	*Why have you switched off the light? Switch it on and let me read the newspaper, won't you!* [*]
यहाँभन्दा माथि जान दिँदैनन् । पहिरो जाने खतरा छ ।	*(They) don't let you go higher than this. There is a danger of landslides.*

[*] The Nepali equivalent of *to switch on* is खोल्नु *to open*, while *to switch off* is बन्द गर्नु, *to shut*.

EXERCISE 60 Create five sentences along the following lines:

allower	allowee	place/ time	verb	allow?
I	people	in my house	smoke	x

=   म मान्छेहरूलाई मेरो घरमा चुरोट खान दिन्नँ ।

	allower	allowee	place/ time	verb	allow?
1	mother	my friends	in our house	drink alcohol	✗
2	they	us	into the temple	go	✓
3	elder brother	children	in the morning	watch TV	✓
4	father	us	in the evening	go out	✗
5	you (High)	tourists	in the temple	wear shoes	✓ ?

104   भएर *being* and भएर पनि *despite being*

भएर, the -एर participle of हुनु , is commonly used to point out the cause of something, in much the same way that the -एको participle is used in combination with -ले to create a part of a sentence beginning with *because*. When भएर is used, however, the cause is stated less emphatically:

नेवार भएर उनीहरू नेपाली मात्रै होइन नेपाल भाषा पनि बोल्छन् ।	*Being Newars, they speak not only Nepali but Nepal Bhasha too.* [*]
मेरी हजुरआमा बूढी भएर घरबाट धेरै कम निस्कनुहुन्छ ।	*Being old, my grandmother very seldom comes out of the house.*

[*] The official name for the Newari language is नेपाल भाषा. The Kathmandu Valley, where it is the indigenous language, was known as नेपाल until the present century.

The English translation of each of the above sentences could equally begin *because they are Newars...* and *because she is old...*

The addition of पनि (*even, also*) to भएर makes the sentence mean that although what is stated is indeed the case, other things are not as might be expected:

नेवार भएर पनि उनीहरू नेपाली मात्रै
बोल्छन् ।

Despite being Newars, they speak only Nepali.

बूढी भएर पनि मेरी हजुरआमा हरेक
दिन मन्दिर जानुहुन्छ ।

Despite being old, my grandmother goes to the temple every day.

105   Religion in Nepal

Religion is an integral part of traditional life in Nepal, which is the only country in the world with Hinduism as its official religion. The concept of धर्म (*righteousness, duty, morality, religion*) pervades many activities, and religious concepts have played an important role in the shaping of society. Most Nepali-speaking people are Hindus, though there are many Buddhist Newars and Buddhism is also prevalent among the people of the high mountain regions. Islam is represented in most Tarai towns, and there is a Muslim community in Kathmandu. The Christian community is very small.

For Hindus, religion consists in the worship (पूजा) of special beings (*gods:* देव, देवता) at particular times (certain times of the day, holy days of the week or month, annual festivals, etc.), in particular holy places (at a family altar, at a temple, etc.). They share a belief in the principle of rebirth, the consequence of actions (कर्म), and the illusory nature of the material world (सँसार). The ultimate aim of religious practice is deliverance (मोक्ष) from the endless cycle of birth and rebirth, but most Hindus simply hope for a better rebirth through the accumulation of merit (पुण्य).

Buddhism and Hinduism are closely intertwined in the Kathmandu Valley towns, and sometimes it is difficult to decide whether a particular temple has a Buddhist or a Hindu dedication. For many Nepalis, the distinction is meaningless. However, Buddhism is a distinct religion which, unlike Hinduism, has a founder, the historical Buddha called Gautama, who is also given the title Shakyamuni. Buddhism shares many beliefs in common with Hinduism, but it has a different conception of the concept of deliverance, which is निर्वाण, the 'snuffing out' of desire. Unlike Hinduism, Buddhism is also practised by monastic communities. The religion has its own pantheon of deities. Of these, the Bodhisattvas (beings who have delayed their own attainment of निर्वाण and have vowed to work for the enlightenment of all sentient beings) are widely worshipped.

To state that a particular deity is worshipped at a particular place or time, use the verb phrase -को पूजा हुनु

यो मन्दिरमा महादेवको पूजा हुन्छ ।   *Mahādev is worshipped at this*
                                                                                          temple.

दसैंको ठूलो पर्वमा दुर्गा देवीको पूजा हुन्छ ।   *The goddess Durga is worshipped*
                                                                                          in the great festival of Dasain.

EXERCISE 61   Translate into Nepali:

A   Which god does this temple belong to? Is it all right to go inside?

B   This is the temple of Ganesh. Yes, it is all right for you to go inside, but you must take your shoes off.

A   Is this a very old temple?

B   Yes, it is very ancient. People come here every morning and do **pūjā** of Ganesh.

A   Why do they have to come here every morning?

B   They do not have to come, but it is good to come here every day. If you do **pūjā** of Ganesh every morning your day will be successful. That is a belief of ours.

A   What should I do now?

B   You have done **darśan** of the god, and that is good. Please give a little money for the temple.

A   I do not have very much money on me. But perhaps it will be all right to give ten rupees?

B   Yes, that is fine. Please come, it is late. Now we must go to Paśupati temple. It is not so far. If we walk there we can reach it in half an hour.

A   Which deity is worshipped at Paśupati temple?

B   Shivajī is worshipped there.

18 | I CAN LEARN NEPALI
म नेपाली सिक्न सक्छु

In this unit you will learn how to:

■ use the Nepali verbs that mean *can*
■ describe verbs
■ talk about learning and teaching
■ talk about wanting to do something

28 How many languages can you speak?

हर्षराज तपाई कतिवटा भाषा बोल्न सक्नुहुन्छ ?

तिलविक्रम म बाल्यकालदेखि नै लिम्बू भाषा बोल्छु । लिम्बू भाषा मेरो मातृभाषा नै हो । मेरो लागि लिम्बू भाषा आमाको दूध जस्तो हो ।

हर्षराज लिम्बू भाषा तपाईको मातृभाषा नै होला, तर तपाईको लागि नेपाली पनि दोस्रो मातृभाषा जस्तो छ, होइन ?

तिलविक्रम लिम्बू भाषा मैले आमाबाट सिकेको भाषा हो, तर सानो उमेरदेखि नै म नेपाली भाषा पनि बोल्छु । वास्तवमा मातृभाषा भनेको के हो ? आफुले जन्मदेखि बोलेको भाषा हो कि आमाबाट सिकेको भाषा हो ?

हर्षराज मेरो विचारमा तपाई मातृभाषा भन्ने शब्दलाई ती दुवै अर्थ दिन सक्नुहुन्छ ।तपाईकी आमा पनि नेपाली भाषा बोल्न सक्नुहुन्छ ?

तिलविक्रम वहाँलाई नेपाली बोल्न आउँदैन ।

हर्षराज पटक्कै आउँदैन ?

तिलविक्रम त्यसो त होइन, तर धेरै कम आउँछ वहाँलाई । बुवा त नेपालीमा काम चलाउन सक्नुहुन्छ ।हाम्रो गाउँका लोग्ने-मान्छेहरू गाउँभन्दा बाहिर व्यापारको लागि घुम्छन् अथवा काम गर्छन् तर स्वास्नी-मानिसहरू प्राय जसो गाउँभित्र नै बस्छन् । त्यसै कारणले उनीहरू लिम्बूबाहेक अन्य भाषाहरू सिक्न पाउँदैनन् ।अनि बूढा बूढीहरू धेरै जसो कुनै पनि भाषा लेख्न पढ्न सक्दैनन् ।

हर्षराज लिम्बू र नेपालीबाहेक तपाईलाई कुन कुन भाषाहरू बोल्न आउँछन् ?

तिलविक्रम म हिन्दी बुझ्न सक्छु र अलि अलि बोल्न पनि सक्छु ।नेपालीभाषीहरूलाई हिन्दी बुझ्न त्यति गाहो हुँदैन ।युवा-युवतीहरू सिनेमा घरमा हिन्दी फिलिमहरू हेर्छन् । आजकाल नेपालमा दूरदर्शन पनि हेर्न पाइन्छ । हिन्दी बुझ्न नसक्ने युवा-युवती अब बिरलै पाइन्छन् नेपालमा ।

हर्षराज त्यो त हो । अनि नयाँ पुस्ताका केटाकेटीहरू आफ्ना पुर्खाहरू जस्ता अपढ हुँदैनन्, होइन त ? उनीहरू स्कूलहरूमा नेपाली मात्रै होइन, अँग्रेजी पनि लेख्न पढ्न सिक्छन् ।

तिलविक्रम तर केटाकेटीहरू मात्रै होइन, अँग्रेजी भाषा बोल्न सक्ने केही बूढाहरू पनि छन् हाम्रो गाउँमा । उनीहरू धेरै जसो ब्रिटिश आर्मीको पिन्सेन खान्छन् । बोल्न मात्रै होइन, कोही-कोही बूढाहरू त अँग्रेजी भाषा पढ्न पनि सक्छन् । गजबको कुरा हो नि । एक समयमा मलाई पनि अँग्रेजी सिक्न मन लागेको थियो । तपाईंलाई कहिल्यै अँग्रेजी सिक्न मन लागेन ?

हर्षराज अँग्रेजी त म पढ्न सक्छु तर बोल्न सक्दिन ।अभ्यास गर्नै त मन लाग्छ तर अँग्रेजी जान्ने साथी छैन ।के गर्ने ?

भाषा *language*		अन्य *other*	
बोल्नु *to speak*		पाउनु *to get to, manage to*	
सक्नु *to be able to*		बूढा *old man*	
दूध *milk*		बूढी *old woman*	
मातृभाषा *mother tongue*		युवा-युवतीहरू *young men and women*	
वास्तव *reality*		दूरदर्शन the state-run Indian TV channel	
आफु *one's self*		बिरलै *rarely*	
जन्म *birth*		पुर्खा *ancestor*	
शब्द *word*		ब्रिटिश आमी *British Army*	
दुवै *both*		पिन्सेन खानु *to receive* ('consume') *a pension*	
काम चलाउनु *to get by, function*		गजब *surprise, amazement*	
पटक्कै *at all*		जान्नु *to know*	
प्राय जसो *usually, mostly*			

Harsharaj	How many languages can you speak?
Tilbikram	I speak the Limbu language ever since childhood. The Limbu language is my mother tongue, in fact. For me the Limbu language is like mother's milk.
Harsharaj	The Limbu language might well be your mother tongue, but for you Nepali too is like a second mother tongue, isn't it?
Tilbikram	The Limbu language is the language I learned from my mother, but I also speak Nepali from a young age. In reality, what does 'mother tongue' mean? Is it the language spoken from birth or the language learned from your mother?
Harsharaj	I think you can give both those meanings to the word 'mother tongue'. Can your mother speak Nepali too?
Tilbikram	She can't speak Nepali.
Harsharaj	Not at all?

Tilbikram	It's not quite like that, but she knows very little. Father can get by in Nepali. The men of our village travel for trade or they work outside the village, but the women generally stay right in the village. So they don't get to learn any languages other than Limbu. And the old men and women usually can't read or write any language.
Harsharaj	What languages can you speak except for Limbu and Nepali?
Tilbikram	I can understand Hindi and I can speak just a little as well. It's not so hard for Nepali-speakers to understand Hindi. The young men and women watch Hindi films at the cinema. Nowadays you can get to watch Doordarshan in Nepal as well. It's rare to find young people who cannot understand Hindi in Nepal today.
Harsharaj	That's true. And the children of the new generation are not illiterate like their ancestors, are they? In schools they learn to write and read not only Nepali but English too.
Tilbikram	But it's not just children, there are also some old men in our village who can speak English. Most of them receive British Army pensions. And there are some old men who can not only speak but can also read English. It's amazing, you know. At one time I wanted to learn English too. Did you never want to learn English?
Harsharaj	I can read English but I can't speak it. I'd like to practise it but I don't have a friend who knows English. What to do?

Grammar

106 *To be able to...*

Nepali has two verbs that mean *can*. They are each used in combination with the infinitive of a verb. सक्नु means *can* in a way that refers to the inherent or physical capability of its subject to perform the verb in question:

ऊ सगरमाथा चढ्न सक्छ ।	*He can climb (is capable of climbing) Everest.*
ऊ सगरमाथा चढ्न सक्दैन ।	*He cannot climb (is not capable of climbing) Everest.*

In sentences in past tenses, the subject will take -ले if the verb that it was able or unable to perform is transitive:

Present tense   *Past tense*

ऊ तपाईको कुरा बुझ्न सक्दैन ।   उसले तपाईको कुरा बुझ्न सकेन ।
He can't understand what you say.   *He couldn't understand what you said.*

म त्यो किताब पढ्नु सक्दिन ।   मैले त्यो किताब पढ्नु सकिनँ ।
I can't read that book.   *I couldn't read that book.*

When discussing a person's ability to speak a language, a common construction has it that the language *comes* to that person:

मलाई नेपाली अलि अलि आउँछ ।   *I know just a little Nepali.*
मलाई अँग्रेजी बोल्न आउँछ तर लेख्न आउँदैन ।   *I can speak English but I cannot write it.*

EXERCISE 62   Write nine short Nepali sentences stating that each of the persons on the left is able to perform each of the verbs on the right:

I	speak Nepali
she (Middle)	cook Nepali food
you (High)	understand this book

107 *To get to, manage to*

पाउनु means *can* in the sense of *getting the opportunity to/managing to*. It suggests that permission has been granted, or that circumstances are in some other way favourable. The difference in meaning between पाउनु and सक्नु is particularly marked in negative sentences:

लण्डनमा म नेपाली बोल्न पाउँदिन ।   *In London I can't (don't get the chance to) speak Nepali.*

नेपालमा मैले अँग्रेजी सिक्न पाइनँ ।   *In Nepal I couldn't (didn't get the chance to) learn English.*

उसले सगरमाथा चढ्न पाएन ।   *He could not (did not get a chance to) climb Everest.*

लण्डनमा तपाई गुन्द्रुक खान पाउनुहुन्न ।   *You won't be able to (won't get the chance to) eat gundruk in London.*

The passive form of पाउनु , i.e. पाइनु , can also be used impersonally to state that something is permitted, or that the opportunity exists to do something:

लण्डनमा नेपाली बोल्न पाईदैन ।	*In London one doesn't get to speak Nepali.*
जाडो मौसममा सगरमाथा चढ्न पाईदैन ।	*One cannot (get permission to) climb Everest during the cold weather.*
हेलाम्बुतिर गुन्दुक खान पाइन्छ ।	*One gets (the chance) to eat* gundruk *in the Helambu area.*

EXERCISE 63   Write nine short Nepali sentences stating that each of the persons on the left managed to perform each of the verbs on the right yesterday:

he (Low)	climb Everest
they (Middle)	make a phone call
you (Middle)	eat **gundruk**

108   Describing a verb

Nepali usually uses the infinitive of the verb (e.g. सिक्न *to learn, learning*) when that verb is being described with an adjective. If you wish to celebrate the ease with which you have mastered Nepali so far, you might like to declare:

नेपाली सिक्न सजिलो हुन्छ ।	*To learn Nepali is easy.*
उसको उच्चारण अलि अनौठो छ । त्यस कारणले उसको नेपाली बुझ्न गाह्रो छ ।	*His pronunciation is a little odd. So it is difficult to understand his Nepali.*
नातेदारबाट पैसा माग्न अप्ठ्यारो हुन्छ ।	*It is awkward to ask a relative for money.*

अप्ठ्यारो and गाह्रो can both be translated as *difficult*, but they have slightly different connotations. गाह्रो means *difficult* in the sense of something being hard or tough, while अप्ठ्यारो means that something is problematic, awkward or tricky.

109   *To learn to, teach to*

सिक्नु means *to learn*. It is used with both nouns and verbs; when combined with another verb in a phrase meaning *to learn to...* , the verb that is learned takes its infinitive form:

| म नेपाली भाषा सिक्दै छु । | *I am learning Nepali.* |
| म नेपाली भाषा पढ्न सिक्दै छु । | *I am learning to read Nepali.* |

म चिनियाँ भाषा सिक्दै थिएँ।	I was learning Chinese.
म चिनियाँ भाषा लेख्न सिक्दै थिएँ।	I was learning to write Chinese.
अब रामे गाडी हाँक्न सिक्दै छ ।	Now Rame is learning to drive a car.
मेरी छोरीले अहिलेसम्म साइकल चढ्न सिकेकी छैन ।	My daughter has not learned to ride a bicycle yet.

सिकाउनु is the causative of सिक्नु and it therefore means *to cause to learn* or *to teach*.

| गाउँको एउटा बूढाले मलाई यो गीत गाउन सिकाएको थियो । | An old man in the village taught me to sing this song. |
| वहाँ यी साना बच्चाहरूलाई अक्षर पढ्न सिकाउँदै हुनुहुन्छ । | She is teaching these small children to read the alphabet. |

A second verb that means *to teach* is पढाउनु, which is actually the causative of पढ्नु *to read, to study.* Therefore, पढाउनु is only used in more academic contexts, and only सिकाउनु is used in combination with the infinitive of a verb to mean *to teach to...*

तपाई यो स्कूलमा के पढाउनुहुन्छ ?	What do you teach at this school?
म गणित पढाउँछु यहाँ ।	I teach mathematics here.
आज तपाई बच्चाहरूलाई के गर्न सिकाउनुहुन्छ ?	What will you teach the children to do today?
आज म उनीहरूलाई हिसाब गर्न सिकाउँछु ।	Today I shall teach them to add up.

School subjects

इतिहास	*History*	विज्ञान	*Science*
गणित	*Mathematics*	अँग्रेजी	*English*
भूगोल	*Geography*	नेपाली	*Nepali*

---

110   *To want to...*

There are several ways of expressing a wish to do something. The first is to use the verb चाहनु *to want to* in combination with the infinitive form of a verb:

| गुरुजीले नानीहरूलाई एउटा कुरा भन्न चाहनुहुन्छ। | Guruji wants to tell the children something. |

नेपालमा तपाई आफ्नो परिवारको लागि कस्ता	*What sort of presents do you want*
उपहारहरू किन्न चाहनुहुन्छ ?	*to buy for your family in Nepal?*

The second way of expressing a wish to do something is to use the past tense of the verb phrase मन लाग्नु ,which is मन लाग्यो . This is perhaps a more typically Nepali way of expressing the same idea. मन लाग्यो means something like *mind struck* or *mind tended*. It is in the past tense because the person in question has in the very recent past conceived the wish to perform whatever the verb might be: the wish has just 'struck' him/her. In their simplest form, such sentences are structured as follows:

subject + लाई – infinitive verb – मन लाग्यो

मलाई रुन मन लाग्यो ।	*I want to cry.*
उसलाई घर जान मन लाग्यो ।	*He wants to go home.*

The negative form is मन लागेन:

तपाईलाई हामीकहाँ बस्न मन लागेन ?	*Don't you want to stay at our place?*
खै, तिमीलाई गीत गाउन किन मन लागेन ?	*Well, why don't you want to sing a song ?*

If the sentence is about a wish that was conceived in the past but is no longer entertained, मन लाग्नु must take the completed past tense:

मलाई अमेरिकाको कुनै यूनिवर्सिटीमा पढ्न मन लागेको थियो, तर सकिनँ ।	*I wanted to study in some American university, but I could not.*
मलाई नेपाल पुगेर तपाईको परिवारलाई फोन गर्न मन लागेको थियो, तर नम्बर फेला परेन ।	*I wanted to phone your family when I reached Nepal, but I could not find the number.*

111 Verbs meaning *to believe*

The English verb *to believe* translates into Nepali in several different ways, and the question of which verb to use depends very much on context. The three main verbs are:

(-लाई) मान्नु	*to accept, regard well, respect*
(-मा) विश्वास गर्नु	*to trust in, have faith in*
पत्याउनु	*to accept as a factual truth*
म तपाईको दाईलाई धेरै मान्छु ।	*I respect your elder brother a lot.*

म हिन्दू धर्मलाई पनि मान्छु, बौद्ध धर्मलाई पनि मान्छु ।

I believe in both Hinduism and Buddhism.

म उनीहरूको कुरामा विश्वास गर्दिन ।

I don't trust in what they say.

देवी-देवताहरूमा म धेरै विश्वास गर्छु ।

I believe strongly in the gods and goddesses.

उनीहरूले भनेको कुरा पत्याउन गाह्रो छ ।

It is difficult to believe what they say.

19 | AT THE DOCTOR'S
डाक्टरकहाँ

In this unit you will learn how to:

■ talk about purpose and beginning to do something
■ talk about remembering and forgetting

29 Kalyani visits the doctor

Jivan takes his daughter Kalyani to see Dr Shrestha because she has been complaining of sore eyes.

जीवन नमस्ते डाक्टर साहेब ।

डा॰ श्रेष्ठ नमस्ते । बस्नुहोस् । भन्नुहोस् त, के भयो ?

जीवन डाक्टर साहेबलाई मेरी छोरी बिरामी भएर देखाउन आएको । बिसन्चो भएको दुई-चार दिन भयो । आज बिहान टाउको दुखेको कुरा गर्न थाली । अनि त्यो सुनेपछि डाक्टरलाई देखाउनुपर्‍यो भनेर हामीहरू हतार हतार आयौं ।

डा॰ श्रेष्ठ ए, ठीक गर्नुभयो तपाईंले... नानी, तिम्रो नाम के हो त ?

कल्याणी कल्याणी, डाक्टर साहेब ।

डा॰ श्रेष्ठ अनि तिम्रो उमेर ?

कल्याणी सात वर्ष, डाक्टर साहेब ।

डा॰ श्रेष्ठ इनको टाउको आज मात्र दुख्न थालेको ? यसभन्दा अघि बिरामी थिइनन् ?

जीवन केही दिनदेखि आँखा दुखेको कुरा गर्दै थिई । हिजो हेरेर थाहा पाएँ दुवै आँखा रातो भएका थिए ।

डा॰ श्रेष्ठ भन त नानी, तिमीलाई कस्तो छ ?

कल्याणी आँखा दुख्यो डाक्टर साहेब ।

डा॰ श्रेष्ठ एक चोटि जिब्रो देखाऊ त । कुनचाहिं आँखा दुख्यो नि ?

कल्याणी दुवै आँखा दुख्छ डाक्टर साहेब ।

डा॰ श्रेष्ठ आँखा कहिले दुख्न थाल्यो ?

कल्याणी बुधवार स्कूल पुगेपछि दुख्न थाल्यो डाक्टर साहेब । म किताब पढ्न बसें अनि त्यही बेला मेरो आँखा दुख्न थाल्यो ।

डा॰ श्रेष्ठ टाउको पनि दुख्छ ?

कल्याणी आज बिहान दुखेको थियो, डाक्टर साहेब । अब त निको भयो ।

डा॰ श्रेष्ठ अनि पेट नि ?

कल्याणी दुख्दैन डाक्टर साहेब ।

डा॰ श्रेष्ठ तपाईकी छोरीको स्वास्थ्य धेरै जसो कस्तो हुन्छ ?

जीवन केही महिना अघि यसलाई दिसा लागेको थियो डाक्टर साहेब । दिसा लागेपछि हामीले जीवन-जल दियौं अनि चाँडै निको भयो । त्यसबाहेक केही त भएको छैन ।

डा॰ श्रेष्ठ घरमा तपाईहरू केमा भात पकाउनुहुन्छ ?

जीवन चूल्होमा डाक्टर साहेब ।

डा॰ श्रेष्ठ मट्टीतेलको चूल्हो ?

जीवन होइन, डाक्टर साहेब, हामी दाउरामा पकाउँछौं । हामी गरीब मान्छे, मट्टीतेल किन्न सकिंदैन ।

डा॰ श्रेष्ठ घरभित्रको धुवाँले इनका आँखालाई अलि बिगारेको हुन सक्छ । म तपाईलाई यसको औषधि दिन्छु । अनि केही दिनसम्म बिहान र बेलुका दिनको दुई पटक उमालेर सेलाएको पानीले सफा गर्न नबिर्सनू, है त ?

जीवन हवस् डाक्टर साहेब, धन्यवाद । औषधि किन्न कता जानुपर्छ ?

डा॰ श्रेष्ठ कुनै पनि औषधि पसलमा पाइन्छ । ल, बिस्तारै जानुहोस् । चार दिनभित्र निको भएन भने मलाई देखाउन फेरि आउनुहोस् ।

डा॰ *Dr*	जीवन-जल *life-water:* a diarrhoea remedy
बिरामी *ill*	चूल्हो *cooker, stove, cooking hearth*
बिसन्चो *unwell* (opposite of सन्चो)	दाउरा *firewood*
टाउको *head*	धुवाँ *smoke*
दुख्नु *to hurt*	बिगार्नु *to spoil, pollute, cause harm to*
थाल्नु *to start, begin*	उमाल्नु *to boil*
-पछि *after*	सेलाउनु *to cool*
नानी *child, little one*	औषधि *medicine*
जिब्रो *tongue*	किन्नु *to buy*
दिसा *diarrhoea*	फेरि *again*

Jivan Hello Doctor Saheb.

Dr Shrestha Hello. Sit down, Tell me then, what's happened?

Jivan My daughter's become ill and I have come to show her to Doctor Saheb. She's been unwell for several days. This morning she began to say that her head hurt. And when we heard that we thought we should show her to Doctor Saheb and we came in a hurry.

Dr Shrestha Oh, you did the right thing... Child, what is your name?

Kalyani	Kalyani, Doctor Saheb.
Dr Shrestha	And your age?
Kalyani	Seven years, Doctor Saheb.
Dr Shrestha	Did her head only begin to hurt today? She wasn't ill before this?
Jivan	For several days she was saying that her eyes hurt. Yesterday I looked and discovered that both eyes had become red.
Dr Shrestha	Tell me child, how are you?
Kalyani	My eyes hurt, Doctor Saheb.
Dr Shrestha	Just show me your tongue then. Which eye hurts?
Kalyani	Both eyes hurt, Doctor Saheb.
Dr Shrestha	When did your eyes begin to hurt?
Kalyani	My eyes began to hurt after I got to school on Wednesday, Doctor Saheb. I sat down to read a book and at that moment my eyes started to hurt.
Dr Shrestha	Does your head hurt too?
Kalyani	It was hurting this morning, Doctor Saheb. But now it's better.
Dr Shrestha	And what about your stomach?
Kalyani	It doesn't hurt, Doctor Saheb.
Dr Shrestha	How is your daughter's health usually?
Jivan	A few months ago she had diarrhoea, Doctor Saheb. When she got diarrhoea we gave her 'Jivan-Jal' and she got better quickly. Apart from that, nothing has happened.
Dr Shrestha	What do you cook your food on at home?
Jivan	On a cooker, Doctor Saheb.
Dr Shrestha	A kerosene cooker?
Jivan	No, Doctor Saheb, we cook on firewood. We are poor people, kerosene cannot be afforded.
Dr Shrestha	The smoke inside the house might have harmed her eyes a little. I will give you medicine for this. And for a few days do not forget to wash her eyes twice a day, morning and evening, with water that has been boiled and cooled, OK?
Jivan	Very well, Doctor Saheb, thank you. Where should I go to buy the medicine?
Dr Shrestha	You can get it in any medicine shop. There, take care. If she is not better within four days come to show (her to) me again.

⚙ Grammar

112 Expressing purpose

The infinitive of a verb can be used in combination with verbs such as जानु *to go*, आउनु *to come*, and also with other verbs, to express purpose. In these contexts, the infinitive of the verb means *in order to* do whatever the verb might be:

हेर्न जानु	*to go (in order) to watch*
लिन पठाउनु	*to send (in order) to get*
गर्न आउनु	*to come (in order) to do*
हामीहरू दाउरा काट्न वनतिर जाँदै छौं ।	*We are going to the forest to cut firewood.*
आज दिउँसो पल्लो गाउँको मान्छे हाम्रो गाई हेर्न आउँदै छ ।	*This afternoon a man from the next village is coming to look at our cow.*

Sometimes, the postposition -लाई is added to the infinitive of the verb to emphasise the sense of purpose. This is especially necessary in spoken Nepali, when purpose is often expressed outside the framework of a full sentence:

उनीहरू किन पोखरा जाँदै छन् ? सिनेमा हेर्नलाई ?	*Why are they going to Pokhara. To watch a film?*
तिमीहरू किन वनभित्र पसेको ? दाउरा काट्नलाई ?	*Why have you entered the forest? To cut firewood?*

Another context in which purpose is expressed is one in which you wish to say that some thing is needed in order for a particular verb to happen. In this case, the postposition -को लागि *for* is added to the infinitive of the verb:

फोटो खिंच्नको लागि के चाहिन्छ ? फोटो खिंच्नको लागि क्यामेरा चाहिन्छ ।	*What does one need to take a photograph? To take a photograph you need a camera.*
यो रेडियो बजाउनको लागि मैले एउटा ब्याटरी किन्नुपऱ्यो ।	*In order to play this radio I had to buy a battery.*

113 Beginning to do something

Nepali has four verbs that mean *to begin*. These are: शुरु हुनु, शुरु गर्नु, थाल्नु, and लाग्नु .

i) शुरु हुनु and शुरु गर्नु

शुरु is a noun meaning *beginning.* Thus, शुरुमा means *in the beginning.* शुरु हुनु is intransitive, while शुरु गर्नु is transitive; they have the sense of *to commence* and *to start* respectively. They are both used as the main verb of a sentence and cannot be combined with any other verb:

आजको कार्यक्रम कति बजे शुरु हुन्छ ?	*At what time does today's programme begin?*
काम साह्रै ढिलो भयो ।अब हामीले शुरु गर्नुपर्‍यो ।	*The work is very overdue. We must start now.*

ii) थाल्नु

थाल्नु and लाग्नु can both be used with the infinitive of a verb to indicate the beginning of an event or action. Although थाल्नु and लाग्नु both mean *to begin,* there are certain tenses and contexts in which one should be used instead of the other, and in some contexts there is some difference in meaning between the two verbs. Nepali-speakers use these two verbs rather more than English-speakers use the English verb *to begin.*

थाल्नु has the sense *to start to...* In the past tense, it means that the subject began to perform the verb with which थाल्नु is combined, but it does not imply that the verb is still being performed:

ऊ मन्दिर जान थाल्यो ।	*He started to go to the temple.*
मेरी बहिनी रुन थाली ।	*My younger sister started to cry.*

थाल्नु is transitive when it is used with transitive verbs, so the subject must take -ले in the past tense:

मैले अस्ति बुधवारदेखि अफिसमा काम गर्न थालें ।	*I started to work at the office from last Wednesday.*
बाले भरखरै अखबार पढ्न थाल्नुभएको थियो ।	*Father had just started to read the newspaper.*

थाल्नु is used in the present tense in situations where the subject makes a voluntary choice to perform the verb:

म आजै गर्न थाल्छु ।	*I shall start to do it today.*
भोलिदेखि ऊ अँग्रेजी सिक्न थाल्छ रे ।	*He says he will start to learn English from tomorrow.*

iii) लाग्नु

लाग्नु has the sense *to begin to...* It is very rarely used in the present tense, where it gives way to थाल्नु. In the past tense, it often means that the verb has begun to happen or be performed, but is still on-going. For instance, the sentences म घर जान लागें and म घर जान लागेको छु might be taken literally to mean *I began to go home* and *I have begun to go home* but in fact they can both mean *I am going home* or *I am on my way home*:

ए भाइ, तिमी कता जान लागेको ? *Hey, brother, where are you off to?*
म ठमेल जान लागेको । तिमी नि ? *I'm going to Thamel. What about you?*

म भोटाहिटी जान लागेको । *I'm on my way to Bhotahiti.*

Compare the translations of the following sentences, one of which uses लाग्नु and the other थाल्नु:

ऊ मन्दिर जान लागेको छ । *He is on his way to the temple / he is about to set out for the temple.*
ऊ मन्दिर जान थालेको छ । *He has started going to the temple.*

The first sentence means that he has *begun to go* to the temple, and is currently headed in that direction. The second sentence suggests that he was not previously in the habit of visiting the temple, but has *started to go* recently.

लाग्नु is more suited than थाल्नु to casual or involuntary actions or events. It never takes -ले, even in the past tense when the verb it is linked with is transitive.

Further examples of लाग्नु **and** थाल्नु

ए दीपक, तिमी के गर्न लाग्यौ ? *Hey Deepak, what are you doing?*
म भात खान लागेको, आमा ! *I'm eating rice, mother!*
पानी पर्न लाग्यो । अब छाता खोल्नुपर्‍यो । *It's started to rain. Now we must open the umbrella.*
कार्त्तिक महिनादेखि मौसम अलि चिसो *From the month of Karttik the*
हुन थाल्छ । *weather starts to be rather cold.*

114 After doing something

The postposition -पछि *after* is added to the past tense base of verbs, with the -e- vowel forming a junction between them, to mean:

खाएपछि *after eating*
गएपछि *after going*
भनेपछि *after saying*
उठेपछि *after getting up*
भएपछि *after being /becoming*

रातमा नराम्रो सपना देखेपछि ऊ फेरि निदाउन सकेन ।	*After he had a nightmare in the night, he could not sleep again.*[*]
बा-आमा मरेपछि साना बच्चाहरूलाई कसले हेर्छ ?	*After mother and father have died, who will look after the small children?*
झिसमिसे बिहानमा उठेर हातमुख धोएर दाँत माझ्नेपछि म बाहिर निस्कें ।	*I went out after I had got up in the pale early dawn, washed my hands and face, and brushed my teeth.*

[*] In Nepali, one 'sees' a dream or nightmare.

115 Remembering and forgetting

The verb बिर्सनु means *to forget:*

हामीलाई नबिर्सनुहोस् ! [*]	*Don't forget us!*
माफ गर्नुहोस् है, मैले तपाईंको नाम बिर्सें ।	*Please forgive me, I have forgotten your name.*
आज तिमी स्कूलबाट किन ढिलो आयौ ? बाटो बिर्सेर कि क्या हो ?	*Why did you come home late from school today? Did you forget the way or what?*

[*] Note also the expression माया नमार्नुहोस् ! literally, *don't kill affection,* which means 'don't forget me/us' or 'keep in touch'.

बिर्सनु is also combined with the infinitive of a verb to mean *to forget to...*

क्षमा गर्नुहोला, मैले तपाईंको ठेगाना टिप्न बिर्सें ।	*Please forgive me, I forgot to take a note of your address.*
बिहा गर्ने हतपतले उसले केटी माग्न बिर्स्यो ।	*Because of (his) hurry to get married he forgot to ask for a girl.*[*]

[*] A proverb which describes how in one's rush to get something done one can often forget some crucial ingredient.

If you wish to tell someone to remember to do something, you should tell them *not to forget* to do it, using बिर्सनु:

बेलायत फर्केपछि हामीलाई चिठी लेख्न नबिर्स है त !	*After you return to England, remember (don't forget) to write us a letter, OK?*
भरे बेलुका रेडियोमा समाचार सुन्न नबिर्सनुहोस् ।	*Please remember (don't forget) to listen to the news on the radio this evening.*

There are two verbs that mean *to remember* – याद हुनु and सम्झनु . These are used in slightly different ways.

याद is a noun meaning *memory* or *recollection*. One way of saying that you do or do not remember something is simply to state:

मलाई याद छ ।	*I remember* ('to me there is memory').
मलाई याद छैन ।	*I don't remember* ('to me there is not memory').

In practice, this construction is used most commonly in the negative to state that someone has no recollection of some fact or event from the past:

यो धेरै अघिको कुरा हो । तपाईंलाई याद छैन होला ।	*This is something that happened a long time ago. Perhaps you don't remember.*

In the constructions that use याद, the person who is or is not remembering is passive. S/he is not actively remembering or forgetting the matter in question. But the verb सम्झनु is used to mean *to remember/recall* in a more active sense. As explained above, it rarely occurs in the negative, because the verb बिर्सनु *to forget* fulfills that role.

बल्ल सम्झें । तपाईंले छ बजे आउनू भनेर भन्नुभएको थियो, होइन ?	*At last I've remembered. You said to come at 6 o'clock, didn't you?*
कहिले काहीं म आफ्नो बिहाको दिन सम्झेर हाँस्छु ।	*Sometimes I recall my wedding day and I smile.*

The causative of सम्झनु is सम्झाउनु, which literally means *to remind*. However, it is most commonly used to mean *to explain/counsel*:

मेरो छोरा बिहा गर्न मान्दैन । उसलाई अलि सम्झाउनुहोस् न ।	*My son refuses to marry. Just explain things to him, would you?*

116 Before doing something: postpositions beginning with -भन्दा

There is a set of two-word postpositions of which the first word is -भन्दा. Because -भन्दा is also used to make comparisons (see **Grammar 51**), these postpositions have at least a vaguely comparative sense to them. Three of them mean *before,* and can be used with nouns or verbs:

-भन्दा पहिले	*before, previous to, ago*
-भन्दा अघि	*before, previous to, ago*
-भन्दा अगाडि	*before, previous to, ago*

आजभन्दा दस वर्ष अघि यस टोलमा एउटा चियापसल पनि थिएन ।	*Ten years ago there wasn't even a teashop in this part of town.*
सन् १९६९ भन्दा पहिले कसैले चन्द्रमामा पाइला टेकेको थिएन ।	*Before 1969 no-one had set foot on the moon.*

These three postpositions are also used with verbs to mean *before*. In such constructions, -भन्दा must be added to the dictionary form of the verb:

मन्दिरभित्र पस्नुभन्दा पहिले जुत्ता खोल्न नबिर्सनुहोस् ।	*Please remember (don't forget) to take off your shoes before going into the temple.*
घर जानुभन्दा अगाडि म तपाईलाई यो कोसेली दिन चाहन्छु ।	*Before going home I want to give you this gift.*
सुत्नुभन्दा अघि तिमीहरूले हात खुट्टा किन नधोएको ?	*Why didn't you wash your hands and feet before going to bed?*

EXERCISE 64   Translate into Nepali:

My elder sister got married two weeks ago. Now she lives in Dhulikhel (**dhulikhel**). Dhulikel is about ten miles from Bhaktapur. Last Sunday we went there to meet her husband and her new family.

To get to Dhulikhel we had to take a taxi as far as Ratna Park. At Ratna Park we had to board a bus that was going to Panchkhal (**pā̃cakhāl**). Dhulikel is on the way to Panchkhal.

After we arrived at Ratna Park father had to go into a shop. He had forgotten to buy any presents (**upahār**). You have to give presents when you are visiting someone for the first time. Father had to go into three shops to buy cloth (**kapaḍā**), sweets (**miṭhāī**) and bangles (**curā**). Mother began to feel worried because it had begun to get rather late. We did not know that it takes only one hour to reach Dhulikhel. We did not know either that buses leave (**chuṭnu**) every hour.

After father had bought the gifts we began to search for the Dhulikhel bus. A man standing beside a new blue bus had begun to shout (**karāunu**) 'Panchkhal! Panchkhal!' Father went to the office to buy our tickets. Before father returned with the tickets I asked the driver (**cālak**) if the bus would also go to Dhulikhel. He said that it would. He also said that there was no question of not going to Dhulikhel because there is a good hotel there. Before the bus sets out from Dhulikhel for Panchkhal all the passengers (**yātruharū**) eat their morning meal there, he said. Suddenly it began to rain, so we all found a place to sit on the bus. After a few minutes our journey (**yātrā**) began.

20 | THE MAP OF NEPAL
नेपालको नक्सा

In this unit you will learn:

- about the geography of Nepal
- how to use **bhanne** to mean *called* and *that*
- how to discuss physical locations

Passage 30 The map of Nepal

[Mountain] 1	धवलगिरी
[Mountain] 2	अन्नपूर्ण
[Mountain] 3	सगरमाथा

[Town] 4	वीरगंज
[Town] 5	जनकपुर
[Town] 6	विराटनगर

[Town] 1	काठ्माडौं
[Town] 2	नेपालगंज
[Town] 3	पोखरा

[River] A	कर्णाली
[River] B	गण्डकी
[River] C	कोशी

नेपालको नक्सा हेर्नुहोस् । यसबाट तपाई नेपालको बारेमा धेरै कुरा थाहा पाउन सक्नुहुन्छ। यसलाई हेरेपछि नेपालको भोगौलिक स्थिति पनि बुझिन्छ ।

नेपालका दुइटा छिमेकी राष्ट्रहरू छन् । उत्तरमा भोट छ ।भोट चालीस वर्षदेखि चीनको एउटा प्रान्त भएको छ । दक्षिणमा भारतका उत्तर प्रदेश, बिहार, र पश्चिम बंगाल भन्ने प्रदेशहरू छन् । पूर्वतिर सिक्किम छ, अनि सिक्किमभन्दा पर भूटान पनि देखिन्छ यो नक्सामा ।तर भूटान चीन र भारतजस्तो नेपालको छिमेकी राष्ट्र होइन ।

तपाई दक्षिण नेपालको सिमानादेखि उत्तरतिर चढ्नुभयो भने तपाईले तीनवटा भोगौलिक
क्षेत्रहरू पार गर्नुपर्छ । दक्षिणमा तराई क्षेत्र छ । यसलाई नेपालीहरू मदेस पनि भन्छन् । तराईको
जमिन समतल छ अनि त्यहाँ उत्तर भारतको जस्तो गर्मी हुन्छ । पहिला पहिला यहाँ जंगल थियो
तर करीब दुई सय वर्ष अघि किसानहरू यहाँ खेतीपाती गर्न आए । उनीहरूले जङ्गल फाँडेर खेती
गर्न थाले । अहिले अलिकति जंगल मात्रै बाँकि छ । नेपालगंज, वीरगंज, जनकपुर र विराटनगर
तराईका शहरहरू हुन् । तराईमा नेपाली मात्रै होइन, मैथिली, भोजपुरी, अवधी, थारु र अन्य
भाषाहरू पनि बोलिन्छन् ।

तराई क्षेत्रभन्दा माथि पहाडी क्षेत्र छ । यहाँको जमिन प्राय जसो उकालो र ओरालो हुन्छ ।
किसानहरू बेंसीहरूमा धान रोप्न तल झर्छन्, पाखाहरूमा मकै रोप्न माथि चढ्छन् । उनीहरू
भैंसी, बाखा र अन्य पशुहरू पनि पाल्छन् । काठ्माडौंको ठूलो उपत्यका पहाडी क्षेत्रमा पर्छ । यो
नेपाल अधिराज्यको राजनैतिक र साँस्कृतिक केन्द्र हो । पहाडी क्षेत्रमा जन-संख्या ज्यादै बढेको
कारणले खेतीपातीको लागि जमिनको अभाव छ । त्यस कारणले पहाडका मानिसहरू हिजोआज
कामको खोजीमा विदेशिन लागेका छन् । नेपाली भाषाको जन्मस्थल सुदूर पश्चिम नेपालमा पर्छ,
तर मध्य र पूर्व नेपालमा नेवारी, गुरुङ्ग, मगर, लिम्बू, तामाङ्ग र राई जस्ता भोट-बर्मेली भाषाहरू
पनि बोलिन्छन् ।

पहाडी क्षेत्रभन्दा माथि हिमाली क्षेत्र छ । यहाँ सगरमाथा, मकालु, अन्नपूर्ण, धवलागिरी जस्ता
सँसारका सबैभन्दा अग्ला शिखरहरू पाइन्छन् । यहाँको जन-संख्या तराई र पहाडको जन-
संख्याको दाँजोमा सानो छ । यस क्षेत्रमा बस्ने मानिसहरूको भाषा भोटको भाषासँग मिल्छ ।
उनीहरू बौद्ध धर्म मान्छन् अनि उनीहरूको मुख्य व्यवसाय व्यापार हो ।

भोटको सिमानाबाट अनेकौं खोलाहरू निस्केर भारततिर बग्छन् । तीमध्ये कर्णाली, गण्डकी र
कोशी नदीहरू धेरै महत्त्वपूर्ण छन् । जाडोमा पानी कम पर्छ । त्यस कारणले यी खोलाहरू जाडोमा
साना हुन्छन् । तर वर्षातमा पानी परेपछि सबै खोला-नालाहरू बढ्छन् । त्यो खेतीपातीको लागि
साह्रै आवश्यक हुन्छ ।

नेपालमा बाटोहरू धेरै कम छन् भन्ने कुरा यो नक्सालाई हेरेर तपाई थाहा पाउन सक्नुहुन्छ । ती
बाटोहरूमा बस, ट्रक र गाडीहरू प्रशस्त चल्छन् । तर पनि आ-आफ्ना घर पुग्न धेरै जसो
नेपालीहरूलाई अझै पनि हिंड्नैपर्छ ।

नक्सा	*map*	पशु	*animal, livestock*
-को बारेमा	*about*	पाल्नु	*to rear*
भोगौलिक	*geographical*	उपत्यका	*valley*
स्थिति	*situation*	पर्नु	*to be located*
छिमेकी	*neighbour*	अधिराज्य	*kingdom*
राष्ट्र	*nation*	राजनैतिक	*political*
उत्तर	*north*	साँस्कृतिक	*cultural*
प्रान्त	*province*	केन्द्र	*centre*

प्रदेश *state*	जन-संख्या *population*
पूर्व *east*	बढ्नु *to increase, grow*
दक्षिण *south*	खोजी *search*
सिमाना *border*	विदेशिनु *to go abroad*
क्षेत्र *region*	जन्मस्थल *birthplace*
पार गर्नु *to cross, traverse*	सुदूर *remote, far*
जमीन *land*	पश्चिम *west*
समतल *level, flat*	मध्य *mid-*
गर्मी *heat*	भोट-बर्मेली *Tibeto-Burman*
पहिला पहिला *long ago*	शिखर *peak*
जंगल *jungle, uninhabited place*	-को दाँजोमा *compared to*
खेतीपाती *agriculture, farming*	व्यवसाय *occupation*
फाड्नु *to cut down*	अनेकौं *many*
खेती *agriculture, farming*	मध्ये *among*
बाँकि *remaining*	नदी *river*
पहाडी क्षेत्र *the hill region*	महत्त्वपूर्ण *important*
धान *growing rice, paddy*	जाडो *the cold season*
रोप्नु *to plant*	वर्षात *the rainy season*
झर्नु *to descend*	आवश्यक *necessary*
मकै *maize*	ट्रक *truck*
भैंसी *buffalo*	गाडी *car*
बाखा *goat*	तर पनि *none the less*

Look at the map of Nepal. From this you can discover many things about Nepal. After looking at this Nepal's geograpical situation can be understood.

Nepal has two neighbour nations. In the north is Tibet. Tibet has been a province of China for 40 years. In the south are the states of India called Uttar Pradesh, Bihar and West Bengal. To the east is Sikkim, and beyond Sikkim Bhutan is also seen on this map. But Bhutan is not a neighbour nation of Nepal as China and India (are).

If you climb from the border of southern Nepal towards the north you have to cross three geographical regions. In the south is the Tarai region. Nepalis also call this Mades. The land of the Tarai is flat and there there is heat like northern India's. Long ago there was jungle here but about 200 years ago farmers came here to do agriculture. They cut down the jungle and began to farm. Now there is only a little jungle left. Nepalganj, Birganj, Janakpur and Biratnagar are towns of the Tarai. In the Tarai not only Nepali but also Maithili, Bhojpuri, Awadhi, Tharu and other languages are spoken.

Above the Tarai region is the Hill region. Here the land is mostly uphill and downhill. The farmers go down to plant paddy rice in the valleys, and climb up to plant maize on the hillsides. They also rear buffaloes, goats and other animals. The large valley of Kathmandu is located in the Hill region. This is Nepal's political and cultural centre. Because the population has increased greatly in the Hill region there is a shortage of land for agriculture. For that reason the people of the hills have begun nowadays to go abroad in search of work. The birthplace of the Nepali language is in far west Nepal, but in middle and east Nepal Tibeto-Burman languages such as Newari, Gurung, Magar, Limbu, Tamang and Rai are also spoken.

Above the Hill region is the Himalayan region. Here one finds the world's highest peaks, such as Sagarmatha, Makalu, Annapurna, Dhaulagiri. The population here is small compared to the population of the Tarai and the Hills. The language of the people who live in this region is similar to the language of Tibet. They believe in Buddhism and their main occupation is trade.

Many rivers emerge from the Tibetan border and flow toward India. Among them, the Karnali, Gandaki and Koshi are very important. In the winter little rain falls. Therefore these rivers are small in the winter. But after rain falls in the rainy season all the rivers and streams grow. That is very necessary for agriculture.

You can discover that there are very few roads in Nepal by looking at this map. Many buses, trucks and cars run on those roads. None the less, most Nepalis still have to walk to reach their homes.

EXERCISE 65 Answer the following questions about the geography of Nepal:

१   नेपालीहरू तराई क्षेत्रलाई के भन्छन् ?

२   नेपाली भाषाबाहेक तराई क्षेत्रमा अरू कुन कुन भाषाहरू बोलिन्छन् ?

३   पहाडी क्षेत्रको जमीन प्राय जसो कस्तो हुन्छ ?

४   नेपाली भाषाबाहेक पहाडी क्षेत्रमा अरू कुन कुन भाषाहरू बोलिन्छन् ?

५   नेपालका नदीहरूमध्ये कुन कुनचाहिं महत्त्वपूर्ण छन् ?

६   घर पुग्नलाई धेरै जसो नेपालीहरूले के गर्नुपछ ?

⚙ Grammar

117 Using पर्नु with locations

The simplest way to state the location of something is to use the verb हुनु *to be*, which in the present tense must take its छ form. However, the verb पर्नु, literally *to fall*, is often used when the discussion of a location involves some sense of direction:

तपाईको गाउँ कतातिर पर्छ ?

> *Where (in which direction) is your village located?*

It is also used to locate places within countries, districts or zones, in which case it can be thought of as meaning *falls within:*

ललितपुर शहर बागमती अञ्चलमा पर्छ ।

> *The town of Lalitpur falls within the Bagmati zone.*

118 *Above, below, beyond*: more postpositions beginning with -भन्दा

A set of two-word postpositions, of which the first word is -भन्दा, deals with the physical locations of things, in terms of height, distance and so on:

-भन्दा माथि	*above*
-भन्दा तल	*below*
-भन्दा पर	*beyond, on the far side of*

हाम्रो गाउँभन्दा माथि बस्ती छैन ।गाउँभन्दा माथि वनै वन छ ।तर गाउँभन्दा तल त धेरै खेतहरू छन् ।गाउँभन्दा तलका खेतहरूमा हामी धान रोप्छौं ।

> *There are no settlements above our village. Above our village there is nothing but forest. But below the village there are many fields. We plant rice in the fields below our village.*

Of course, both माथि and तल are also used as adverbs to describe the up-and-down way in which much human movement must take place in the Himalayas:

मिरमिरे बिहानमा हामी गाई-बाख्रा चराउन माथि चढ्यौं ।साँझ पर्नुभन्दा अघि हामी तल गाउँतिर झर्यौं ।

> *In the pale early dawn we climbed up to graze the cows and goats. Before dusk fell we came down to the village.*

119 The use of भन्ने to mean *named*

भन्ने is the -ने participle of the verb भन्नु *to say*. It can often be translated as *called* or *named:*

पूर्व नेपालको इलाम भन्ने सानो शहर	*a small town called Ilam in east Nepal*
यती भन्ने अनौठो प्राणी	*a strange creature called the Yeti*
गीता खड्का भन्ने नयाँ विद्यार्थी	*a new student named Gita Khadka*

Note the word order of the phrases above. Instead of 'a new student named Gita Khadka', Nepali has *Gita-Khadka-named new student*.

120 The use of भन्ने to mean *that*

भन्ने is also used to link a question, a fact, etc. with its content:

कुनचाहिं होटेल सबभन्दा राम्रो होला भन्ने प्रश्न उठ्यो ।	*The question arose as to which hotel would be the best.*
तपाई नेपाल आउनुभएको थियो भन्ने मलाई थाहा थिएन ।	*I did not know that you had come to Nepal.*
तपाई चाँडै निको हुनुहुन्छ भन्ने म आशा गर्छु ।	*I hope that you will be well soon.*

It is perhaps useful to think of the sentences given above as containing a question or an item of knowledge that is described by भन्ने, *saying:*

the 'which hotel will be the best'-saying question
the 'you had come to Nepal'-saying knowledge
a 'you will be well soon'-saying hope

Nepali is rich in proverbs (उखान), which might also be quoted using भन्ने:

बालुवा निचोरेर तेल आउन्न भन्ने उखान ।	*The proverb that says that oil does not come from squeezing sand.*
इमान भनेको लाख हो, धन भनेको खाक हो भन्ने उखान ।	*The proverb that says that honour means a great deal (but) wealth means ashes.*
हीराको मोल कीराले जान्दैन भन्ने उखान ।	*The proverb that says that an insect doesn't know the value of diamonds.*

21 | I USED TO SMOKE
म चुरोट खान्थें

In this unit you will learn how to:

■ use the habitual past tense
■ use expressions meaning *while* and *as soon as*
■ talk about hopes and desires

31 Bad habits

An old man tells his grandson about how he decided to give up smoking.

नाति तपाई कुनै बेला चुरोट खानुहुन्थ्यो, हजुरबा ?

हजुरबा पहिला खान्थें, अब खाँदिन । करीब बीस वर्ष अघि मैले चुरोट खान छाडें ।

नाति तपाई धेरै चुरोट खानुहुन्थ्यो ?

हजुरबा अँ, थुप्रै खान्थें । बिहान उठ्नेबित्तिकै एउटा चुरोट झिकेर सल्काउन्थें । अनि चिया खान्थें । तर चिया खाँदाखेरि पनि चुरोट पनि खानुपर्थ्यो ।

नाति एक दिनमा तपाई कति किल्ली चुरोट खानुहुन्थ्यो, हजुरबा ?

हजुरबा खै, अहिले सम्झनै छैन ! हिंड्दाखेरि खान्थें, बस्दाखेरि खान्थें, खेतमा काम गर्दाखेरि खान्थें, भात खानुभन्दा अघि खान्थें, भात खाएपछि खान्थें । धेरै खान्थें !

नाति अनि सुत्दाखेरि नि ?

हजुरबा सुत्न गएपछि एक-दुई वटा खान्थें तर निदाएपछि चुरोट खान अलि अप्ठ्यारो हुन्छ, कान्छा । शायद सपनामा पनि खान्थें कि ? खै, थाहा छैन !

नाति अनि छाड्ने निधो कसरी गर्नुभयो ?

हजुरबा सानो उमेरदेखि नै तेरो बाले डाक्टर बन्ने आकाँक्षा राखेको थियो । उसले कलकत्ता विश्वविद्यालयमा ठाउँ पायो अनि पढ्न गयो । डाक्टर बन्न उसले धेरै वर्षसम्म पढ्नुपऱ्यो त्यहाँ, तर बल्ल-बल्ल डाक्टर भयो । घर फर्केपछि उसले मलाई बा किन चुरोट खानुहुन्छ भनेर गाली गर्न थाल्यो ।

नाति डाक्टर भएपछि त वहाँले भन्नैपऱ्यो नि, हजुरबा !

हजुरबा हो, चुरोट खाने बानी स्वास्थ्यलाई हानीकारक छ भनेर भन्थ्यो, बारम्बार । कुनै दिन छाड्नैपर्ला भन्थ्यो । अनि ऊ कलकत्ताबाट फर्केको केही दिनभित्र नै मलाई रुघा-खोकी लाग्यो । अनि फोक्सो दुख्न थाल्यो । त्यही बेला उसकी आमाले पनि मलाई गाली गर्न थाली तिमी किन चाँडै मर्न चाहन्छौ भनेर ।

नाति अनि चुरोट खान छाड्नुभएको, हो ?

हजुरबा हो, छाड्नैपर्‍यो नि । अनि चुरोट नखाएको दुई-चार हप्तापछि मलाई केही फाइदा भएको थाहा पाएँ ।

नाति कस्तो फाइदा?

हजुरबा रुचि बढ्यो । पहिला म भात अलि कम खान्थें किनभने भात खाँदाखेरि चुरोटको तलतल लाग्थ्यो । तर चुरोट छाडेको केही दिनभित्र त्यो पुरानो तलतल हरायो अनि मैले राम्ररी खान थालें ।

नाति तपाईं त रक्सी खानुहुन्न, हो ?

हजुरबा म रक्सी खाँदिन । कहिले पनि खाएको छैन । यस जिल्लाका गाउँहरूमा धेरै जसो बाहुनहरू बस्छन् नि । यहाँका मानिसहरूले केही वर्ष अघिसम्म पुराना परम्पराहरूको पालन गर्थे । रक्सी खाँदैनथे, मासु पनि खाँदैनथे, जिल्लाबाहिरका केटीहरू ल्याउँदैनथे, तर...

नाति तर तपाई जस्तो उनीहरूले पनि चुरोट खान्थे, होइन ?

हजुरबा अहँ, खाँदैनथे । म र एउटा पसलको साहूजी मात्रै खान्थ्यौं । हामीहरूबाहेक कसैले खाँदैनथ्यो । छिमेकीहरू मलाई बिग्रेको भन्थे !

कुनै *any, some*	हानीकारक *harmful*
चुरोट खानु *to smoke cigarettes*	चाहनु *to want to*
छाड्नु *to give up, quit*	फाइदा *benefit*
झिक्नु *to take out*	रुचि *appetite*
सल्काउनु *to set light to*	तलतल *craving*
-दाखेरि *while*	परम्परा *tradition*
सपना *dream*	पालन गर्नु *to maintain, foster*
निघो *decision*	जिल्ला *district*
आकाँक्षा *ambition*	ल्याउनु *to bring*
बानी *habit*	बिग्रनु *to go wrong, be corrupted*
स्वास्थ्य *health*	

Grandson	Did you smoke at any time, grandfather?
Grandfather	I used to smoke before, now I don't. I quit smoking about 20 years ago.
Grandson	Did you smoke a lot?
Grandfather	Yes, I smoked heaps. As soon as I got up in the morning I would get out a cigarette and light it. Then I would drink tea. But even while I was drinking the tea I had to smoke a cigarette as well.
Grandson	In one day how many cigarettes did you smoke, grandfather?
Grandfather	Well, I don't even remember now! I smoked while I was

walking, I smoked while I was sitting down, I smoked while I was working in the field, I smoked before meals, I smoked after meals. I smoked a lot!

Grandson And what about while you were sleeping?

Grandfather After I had gone to bed I would smoke one or two but after you have fallen asleep it's a bit difficult to smoke a cigarette, Kancha. Perhaps I smoked in my dreams? Well, I don't know!

Grandson And how did you decide to give up?

Grandfather Your father had had an ambition to become a doctor from a very young age. He got a place at Calcutta University and he went to study. To become a doctor he had to study for many years there, but in the end he became a doctor. After he came home he began to tell me off saying 'Why does Father smoke cigarettes?'

Grandson But after he became a doctor he had to say that, you know grandfather!

Grandfather Yes, he used to say again and again that the habit of smoking cigarettes is harmful to health. He used to say that I'd have to quit some day. And within a very few days after he returned from Calcutta I caught a cough and cold. And my lungs began to hurt. At that very time his mother also began to tell me off, saying 'Why do you want to die soon?'*

Grandson And you quit smoking, right?

Grandfather Yes, I had to quit, you know! And a few weeks after I quit I realised that I had had some benefit.

Grandson What sort of benefit?

Grandfather My appetite increased. Before, I used to eat rather little rice because while I was eating I would crave a cigarette. But within a few days of quitting cigarettes that old craving was lost and I began to eat well.

Grandson But you don't drink alcohol, right?

Grandfather I don't drink alcohol. I never have. It's mostly Brahmins who live in the villages of this district. Up until a few years ago the people here maintained old traditions. They didn't drink alcohol, they didn't eat meat either, they didn't bring girls from outside the district (as brides), but...

Grandson But like you they also smoked cigarettes, no?

Grandfather   No, they didn't. Only I and one shopkeeper smoked. Apart from us no-one smoked. The neighbours said I was corrupted!

* When quoting what someone actually said to them, Nepali-speakers will usually refer to themselves using the Low or Middle pronoun (तँ or तिमी).

🔊 Grammar

121   The habitual past tense

The habitual past tense is used to describe an event or action that happened repeatedly or as a matter of habit or custom in the past: *I used to eat, he used to drink, they used to smoke.*

Bases and endings

The habitual past tense of a verb in the affirmative is formed in a similar way to the habitual present tense, as set out in **Grammar 33**. The verb base is exactly the same as it is in the habitual present, but in the habitual past tense the ending is simply the थियो form of the verb हुनु *to be*, minus its '**i**' vowel:

Pronoun	*थियो form*		*Habitual past ending*
म	थिएँ	becomes	-थेँ
हामी, हामीहरू	थियौँ	becomes	-थ्यौँ
तँ	थिइस्	becomes	-थिस
तिमी, तिमीहरू	थियौ	becomes	-थ्यौ
ऊ (m.)	थियो	becomes	-थ्यो
ऊ (f.)	थिई	becomes	-थी
उनी (m.)	थिए	becomes	-थे
उनी (f.)	थिइन्	becomes	-थिन्
यी, ती, उनीहरू	थिए	becomes	-थे

Affirmative forms in गर्नु

	Habitual present		*Habitual past*	
म	गर्छु	*I do*	गर्थेँ	*I used to do*
हामी, हामीहरू	गर्छौं	*we do*	गर्थ्यौँ	*we used to do*
तँ	गर्छस्	*you do*	गर्थिस्	*you used to do*
तिमी, तिमीहरू	गर्छौ	*you do*	गर्थ्यौ	*you used to do*
ऊ (m)	गर्छ	*he does*	गर्थ्यो	*he used to do*
ऊ (f)	गर्छे	*she does*	गर्थी	*she used to do*
उनी (m)	गर्छन्	*he does*	गर्थे	*he used to do*
उनी (f)	गर्छिन्	*she does*	गर्थिन्	*she used to do*
यी, ती, उनीहरू	गर्छन्	*they do*	गर्थे	*they used to do*

The negative form of the habitual past tense is very simply the third
person singular negative form of the habitual present (गर्दैन, हुँदैन, आउँदैन
etc.) + the appropriate ending, taken from the list above. The one
exception to this rule is the form that is used with म *I*, which takes the
ending on to the first person form (that is, आउँदिन instead of आउँदैन).

Negative forms

		Habitual present		*Habitual past*
म	आउँदिन	*I do not come*	आउँदिनथें	*I used not to come*
हामी, हामीहरू	पकाउँदैनों	*we do not cook*	पकाउँदैनथ्यौं	*we used not to cook*
तैँ	खाँदैनस्	*you do not eat*	खाँदैनथिस्	*you used not to eat*
तिमी, तिमीहरू	सुत्दैनौ	*you don't sleep*	सुत्दैनथ्यौ	*you used not to sleep*
ऊ (m)	हुँदैन	*he is*	हुँदैनथ्यो	*he used not to be*
ऊ (f)	गर्दिन	*she does not*	गर्दैनथी	*she used not to do*
उनी (m)	जाँदैनन्	*they do not go*	जाँदैनथे	*they used not to go*
उनी (f)	रँदिनन्	*she does not cry*	रँदैनथिन्	*she used not to cry*
उनीहरू	दिंदैनन्	*they do not give*	दिंदैनथे	*they used not to give*

Alternative negative forms

The same endings may also be added to the alternative negative forms of
the habitual present (for which, see **Grammar 46**):

Habitual present		*Habitual past*	
म जान्नँ	*I do not go*	म जान्नथें	*I used not to go*
ऊ खान्न	*he does not eat*	ऊ खान्नथ्यो	*he used not to eat*
तिमी आउन्नौ	*you do not come*	तिमी आउन्नथ्यौ	*you used not to come*

High forms

The High forms of the habitual past tense are simply adapted forms of the
habitual present tense:

■ In the affirmative, the habitual present ending -हुन्छ becomes the
habitual past ending -हुन्थ्यो.

■ In the negative, the habitual present ending -हुन्न becomes the habitual
past ending -हुन्नथ्यो.

High forms

Habitual present		*Habitual past*	
तपाई हेर्नुहुन्छ	*you watch*	तपाई हेर्नुहुन्थ्यो	*you used to watch*
तपाई हेर्नुहुन्न	*you do not watch*	तपाई हेर्नुहुन्नथ्यो	*you used not to watch*
वहाँ आउनुहुन्छ	*s/he comes*	वहाँ आउनुहुन्थ्यो	*s/he used to come*
वहाँ आउनुहुन्न	*s/he does not come*	वहाँ आउनुहुन्नथ्यो	*s/he used not to come*

The habitual past tense may often be translated as *used to go, used to eat, used to watch, used to say* and so on. It cannot express an action or an event that has happened only once or is part of a discrete series, because this is the function of the simple past tense. For instance, ऊ काठ्माडौँ गयो means *he went to Kathmandu,* with the sense that this was a one-time action, whereas ऊ काठ्माडौँ जान्थ्यो means *he used to go to Kathmandu,* indicating that this was his regular routine at some time in the past.

The following sentences illustrate this difference further. Those on the left-hand side refer to a specific event or action, those on the right describe a regular habit or truth:

मैले साथीको घरमा भात खाएँ ।
I ate at a friend's house.

म साथीको घरमा भात खान्थें ।
I used to eat at a friend's house.

उसले गाउँ गएर रक्सी खायो ।
*He went to the village and
drank raksī.*

ऊ गाउँ गएर रक्सी खान्थ्यो ।
*He used to go the village and
drink raksī.*

Although the habitual past is obviously a past tense, the subject of a transitive verb need not take -ले in this tense unless it is being emphasised: this is the same rule that applies to the habitual present tense.

गर्मीमा घाँस काट्न चमेली कहाँ जान्थी ?
*Where used Chameli to go to
cut grass during the summer?*

पहिले हामीलाई बिजुली चाहिंदैनथ्यो, अहिले सधैं चाहिन्छ ।
*We didn't need electricity before,
now we need it all of the time.*

तीस वर्ष अघिसम्म तराई क्षेत्रमा धेरै मान्छेहरू औलोले मर्थे ।
*Up until 30 years ago many people
used to die of malaria in the
Tarai region.*

काठ्माडौँको वातावरण बिग्रेको छ । पहिला पहिला यहाँ साह्रै राम्रो हुन्थ्यो रे ।
*Kathmandu's environment has
been spoiled. Long ago it used to
be very good here, they say.*

✔ **EXERCISE 66** Change the following sentences into the habitual past tense:

१ यस गाउँका किसानहरू धान रोप्दैनन् । उनीहरू मकै रोप्छन् ।

२ भात खाएपछि हामीले हात-मुख धुनुपर्छ ।

३ चियापसलमा चिया पनि पाइन्छ, खाने कुरा पनि पाइन्छ ।

४ तिमी भारत गएर के काम गर्छौ ? म चौकिदारको काम गर्छु ।

५ दाइहरू जुम्लामा बस्नुहुन्न, दैलेखमा बस्नुहुन्छ ।

६ म हरेक हप्ता उसलाई एउटा लामो चिठी लेख्छु ।

122 Finishing, stopping, quitting

■ Nepali has a number of verbs that mean *to end, finish, be completed, stop,* that can be used only with nouns:

Intransitive		*Transitive*	
खतम हुनु	*to end*	खतम गर्नु	*to finish*
टुङ्गिनु	*to come to a end*	टुङ्ग्याउनु	*to bring to a end*
समाप्त हुनु	*to conclude*	समाप्त गर्नु	*to bring to a conclusion*
सिद्धिनु	*to be finished*	सिद्ध्याउनु	*to finish off*
रुक्नु	*to stop, cease moving*	रोक्नु	*to stop, prevent*
सकिनु	*to be finished*		

२००७ सालमा राणाहरूको शासन खतम भयो र नेपालमा प्रजातन्त्रको स्थापना भयो ।	*In the year 2007 the Ranas' regime ended and democracy was established in Nepal.*
आजको समाचार समाप्त भयो । तपाई रेडियो नेपाल सुन्दै हुनुहुन्छ ।	*That is the end of today's news. You are listening to Radio Nepal.*
यति शब्दहरू बोलेपछि प्रधान मन्त्रीको भाषण टुङ्गियो ।	*When he had spoken this many words, the Prime Minister's speech came to an end.*
भक्तपुर जाने बस त ठिमीमा रुक्दैन भाइ !	*But the Bhaktapur bus doesn't stop at Thimi, brother!*

■ The verb छाड्नु *to stop, leave off, quit,* is used with the infinitive of a verb to show that the subject has stopped performing that verb. In past tenses the subject of छाड्नु must take -ले if the verb is transitive.

आफ्नो स्वास्थ्य बिग्रिन थालेको देखेर बुवाले चुरोट खान छाड्नुभयो ।	*Seeing his health declining, Father gave up smoking cigarettes.*
आमालाई घरको काममा सघाउनुपरेकोले चमेली स्कूल जान छाडी ।	*Because she had to help Mother out at home, Chameli stopped going to school.*

छोरालाई औषधि खान छाड्न नदिनुहोस्   *Don't let your son stop taking the*
नत्र निको हुँदैन ।   *medicine, or else he won't get well.*

123   While doing, immediately after doing

Every complete Nepali sentence must contain a verb, whose normal place
is at the end of the sentence. This is the main verb of a sentence, and it
provides the sentence with a tense (past, present or future). Sentences may
contain other words which are derived from a verb but have no tense of
their own. So far we have met two of these:

    (i) the past tense base of a verb plus -एर (or -ई or -ईकन):

    (ii) the past tense base of a verb plus -एपछि :

Two new words of this type are introduced here.

a) Present tense verb base + -दाखेरि *while...*

The suffix -दाखेरि is added to the present tense base of a verb to mean that
the rest of the sentence happens/happened/ will happen at the same time
as that verb. It can often be translated as *while doing, while going, while
eating,* etc.

The ending is added to verb bases in exactly the same way as the -दै ending
is added to bases to form the continuous present tense (see **Grammar 64**):
it is added directly to the bases of C-verbs, but when a base ends in a
vowel that vowel must be nasalised:

Verb	Base		Suffix			
गर्नु	गर्		+ दाखेरि	=	गर्दाखेरि	*while doing*
बोल्नु	बोल्		+ दाखेरि	=	बोल्दाखेरि	*while speaking*
आउनु	आउ	+ँ	+ दाखेरि	=	आउँदाखेरि	*while coming*
जानु	जा	+ँ	+ दाखेरि	=	जाँदाखेरि	*while going*

भक्तपुर जाँदाखेरि म तिम्रो दाइसँग भेटुँला ।   *On my way to Bhaktapur I'll*
                                              (probably) meet your elder
                                              brother.

बच्चाहरू बारीमा खेल्दाखेरि घरभित्र   *While the children are playing in*
शान्ति हुन्छ ।   *the field there is peace in the*
                                              house.

भात खाँदाखेरि गफ गर्न हुँदैन ।   *It is not good to talk while eating.*

This suffix can be added to the हुँ- base of the verb *to be*, and also to its छ
form; there is a slight difference in meaning between the two:

हुँदाखेरि   *while becoming / being (in a defining sense)*
छँदाखेरि   *while being (in a describing or locating sense)*

मानिसहरू बूढो हुँदाखेरि धर्म मान्न थाल्छन् । *When people are becoming old*
                                                    they begin to believe in religion.

त्यो केटा सानो छँदाखेरि उसको बा मर्नुभयो । *When that boy was small his father*
                                                    died.

The -दाखेरि suffix is often shortened to -दा, with no change in meaning:

भक्तपुर जाँदा...   *While going to Bhaktapur...*
मानिसहरू बूढो हुँदा...   *When people are becoming old...*

b) The -ने participle + -बित्तिकै *as soon as*

This suffix is added to the -ने participle of a verb to mean that something else
happened immediately after it. If the verb is transitive, its subject must take -ले.

मैले भात खानुहोस् भन्नेबित्तिकै   *As soon as I said 'please eat',*
सबैजनाले खपाखप खान थाले ।   *everyone began to eat voraciously.*

सिपाहीले खुकुरी टिप्नेबित्तिकै सबैजना भागे । *As soon as the soldier picked up*
                                                    the kukri, everyone ran away.

मदनलाई देख्नेबित्तिकै मुनालाई उसको माया *As soon as she saw Madan, Muna*
लाग्यो ।   *fell in love with him.*[*]

[*] Muna and Madan are the eponymous hero and heroine of a narrative
poem by Lakshmi Prasad Devkota (1905–59), first published in the 1930s,
which is the most popular book ever written in Nepali.

124 Will have to, used to have to

Combinations of पर्छ / पर्दैन and पर्‍यो / परेन with the dictionary form of a verb
to mean *must, should, have to* and *had to* are introduced in **Grammar 99**
and **100**. It is of course sometimes necessary to talk about what someone
used to have to do in the past or what someone might have to do in the
future. In such cases पर्नु takes the habitual past tense forms पर्थ्यो / पर्दैनथ्यो
and the probable future tense form पर्ला respectively:

ब्रिटिश आर्मीमा हुँदाखेरि मैले चक्कु, काँटा र   *While I was a soldier in the British*
चम्चाले खाना खानुपर्थ्यो । तिमीले पनि   *Army, I used to have to eat with*
भर्तिमा गएपछि त्यसरी नै खानुपर्ला ।   *a knife, fork and spoon. After you*
                                                    have enlisted you will probably
                                                    have to eat in exactly the same way.

यहाँ बिजुली आउनुभन्दा अगाडि
दिदी-बहिनीहरूलाई पानी लिन
खोलासम्म झर्नुपर्थ्यो ।

*Before the electricity (supply)
came here, the young women used
to have to go down to the river to
fetch water.*

125 Wishing, hoping and deciding

In English, you say that someone wishes, hopes or decides *to do*
something. In Nepali, desires, hopes or decisions to do something are
often expressed passively, using the expression मन लाग्नु, or actively by
using the verb चाहनु *to want to* (**Grammar 110**). However, there is one
other way of expressing these ideas in Nepali, and this uses the -ने
participle of a verb to describe the wish, hope, etc.:

जाने इच्छा गर्नु	*to wish to go* ('to do a going wish')
हेर्ने रहर हुनु	*to have a desire to see* ('a seeing desire')
लेख्ने निधो गर्नु	*to decide to write* ('to do a writing decision')
बस्ने विचार गर्नु	*to consider staying* ('to do a staying thought')
पाउने आशा गर्नु	*to hope to get* ('to do a getting hope')
बन्ने आकाँक्षा राख्नु	*to have an ambition to become* ('a becoming ambition')

हाम्रो घरमा बस्दाखेरि उनीहरूले बिहा गर्ने
निधो गरेका थिए ।

*While they were living in our
house they decided to get married.*

सानै उमेरदेखि नै मैले काठमाडौं जाने इच्छा
गरेको थिएँ, आखिर म जान पाएँ ।

*Right from a young age I wanted
to go to Kathmandu, eventually I
managed to go.*

म केही दिनभित्र उसको चिठी पाउने आशा
गर्दै छु ।

*I am hoping to receive a letter
from him within a few days.*

Note also the construction with -पर्ने:

पढ्नुपर्ने किताब
भेट्नुपर्ने मान्छे

a book one should read
a person one should meet

अँग्रेजी सिक्न मन लाग्यो भने तपाईंले पढ्नुपर्ने
किताब यही हो ।

*If you want to learn English this is
the book you should read.*

तपाईंलाई मुस्ताङ जान अनुमति चाहियो भने
भेट्नुपर्ने मान्छे लोबसाङ नामग्याल हुन् ।

*If you need permission to go to
Mustang, the man you should meet
is Lobsang Namgyal.*

EXERCISE 67   Translate into Nepali:

I used to live with my mother and father in a small town called Panauti.
Panauti is in the south-east corner of the Kathmandu Valley. I used to
study in a small school there. As soon as my age reached 11 years I had
to quit that small school. From that time on I had to study in a big school
in a town called Bhaktapur. I used to have to take a bus every morning at
seven o' clock. Many of my friends used to go on that bus too. While we
were returning in the evening we used to sing songs and when we reached
Paunati we were very happy.

Below my house there was a big river. In the summer months we used to
swim in the river as soon as we got home. Sometimes my school clothes
were all wet and Mother used to be angry. She would have to wash them
as soon as I came home and it was difficult to dry (**sukāunu**) them. But
because Saturday was a holiday she used to let me swim on Fridays.

While I was studying in the big school at Bhaktapur I decided to become
a teacher when I was big. Because I hoped to become a teacher I studied
well. As soon as I left that school I went to Tribhuvan University and
nowadays I live in Kathmandu. After a few days I will have to give my
final exams (**parikṣā**). I am still hoping to become a teacher. If I am
successful in my exams I will have to seek (**khojnu**) a job (**jāgir**).

22 | SHALL I MAKE TEA?
म चिया पकाऊँ ?

In this unit you will learn how to:
- ■ use the subjunctive forms of verbs
- ■ use compound verbs with दिनु
- ■ talk about trying and searching

32 Cancelling the tea party

Like many middle-class urban Nepali housewives, Parvati has an older woman to help her with her chores. On this particular Wednesday the weather is against them.

जाई आज के काम छ ? पहिले चिया पकाऊँ ?

पार्वती हुन्छ दिदी, पकाउनुहोस् न । चिया खाएर म तपाईलाई भनुँला ।

जाई चियामा चिनी र दूध राखिदिऊँ ?

पार्वती एक चम्चा चिनी र अलिकति दूध राखिदिनुहोस् ।

जाई चिनी कता पर्‍यो ?

पार्वती दराजभित्र खोज्नुहोस् । त्यहाँ हुनुपर्छ ।

जाई हवस्... । ल, चिया कहाँ राखूँ ? टेबुलमा राखिदिऊँ ?

पार्वती टेबुल डढ्ला कि ? ऊ त्यो कपडामाथि राखिदिनुहोस् ।

जाई हवस् । आज के के गर्नुपर्छ ? म थाहा पाऊँ न ?

पार्वती आज दिउँसो श्रीमान अफिसका साथीहरू लिएर आउँदै हुनुहन्छ ।

जाई उनीहरू बेलुकासम्म बस्ने कि ? म भरे भात पकाइदिऊँ ?

पार्वती आज बुधवार भएकोले भान्से आउँदैन । त्यस कारण भात पकाउनु नपरोस् भनेर मैले चिया-सियाको लागि मात्रै निम्त्याउनू भनेको छु वहाँलाई । वहाँ सम्झनुहुन्छ कि बिर्सनुहुन्छ म भन्न सक्किन । तपाईलाई थाहै छ न दिदी, लोग्ने-मान्छेको जात !

जाई हेरौं न । बिर्सनुहुन्न क्यारे । कतिजना आउँदै छन् ?

पार्वती मैले उनीहरूको लागि बगैँचामा दुइटा टेबुल राखेको छु । पछि तपाई आठवटा मेचहरू मिलाइदिनुहोस् । आज पानी नपरोस् । घरभित्र आठजना अटाउने ठाउँ नै छैन !

जाई हवस् त । एक छिनपछि बजार जानुपर्ला, बिस्कुट-सिस्कुट किन्नलाई, होइन ?

पार्वती हो, जानुपर्छ । मलाई पनि उता जानुपर्छ दिउँसो । सँगै जाऔं ।

जाई हवस् । अब म घर सफा गर्न थाल्छु ।

पार्वती हुन्छ । एक पटक चर्पी र नुहाउने कोठामा पनि हेर्नुहोस् । भरसक पाहुनाहरूलाई असुविधा नहोओस् न । म भान्सा-कोठामा हुन्छु ।

जाई सुत्ने कोठा पनि मिलाइदिऊँ ?

पार्वती पर्दैन दिदी । सबै अलपत्र छ । म पछि आफै मिलाउँला ।

जाई आमै ! पानी आयो ! सर्वनाश भयो !

पार्वती धन्दा नमान्नुहोस् । म अफिसमा फोन गरेर एक पटक सम्झाउन खोज्छु । अब उनीहरू आऊन् कि नआऊन् हामीलाई त घरभित्रै बस्नुपर्‍यो नि ।

पहिले *first*	चर्पी *lavatory*
चम्चा *spoon*	नुहाउने कोठा *bathroom*
दराज *drawer*	भरसक *as much as possible*
खोज्नु *to search, look for*	असुविधा *inconvenience*
डढ्नु *to burn, scorch*	भान्सा-कोठा *kitchen*
चिया-सिया *tea and snacks*	सुत्ने कोठा *bedroom*
निम्त्याउनु *to invite*	अलपत्र *untidy*
जात *species, type*	आमै! *mother!* (an exclamation of alarm)
बगैँचा *garden*	सर्बनाश *disaster*
अटाउनु *to fit, be accommodated*	धन्दा मान्नु *to worry*
बिस्कुट-सिस्कुट *biscuits and such like*	

Jai	What work is there today? Shall I make tea first?
Parvati	OK sister, please do make some. I'll tell you while we drink tea.
Jai	Should I put sugar and milk in the tea?
Parvati	Please put one spoonful of sugar and a little milk.
Jai	Where has the sugar got to?
Parvati	Search in the drawer. It should be there.
Jai	Very well... Now, where shall I put the tea? Shall I put it on the table?
Parvati	Might the table be marked? Put it on that cloth over there.
Jai	Very well. What things do we have to do today? May I know?
Parvati	This afternoon my husband is bringing some office friends.
Jai	Will they stay until the evening? Shall I cook rice this evening?
Parvati	Because it's Wednesday today the cook won't come. For that reason, so that we wouldn't have to cook food, I have told him to invite them only for tea and snacks.[*] Whether he will remember or forget I cannot say. You know, don't you sister, what men are like!
Jai	Well, let's see. Perhaps he won't forget. How many are coming?
Parvati	I have put two tables for them in the garden. Later, please arrange eight chairs. I hope it won't rain today. There really isn't room in the house for eight people!
Jai	Certainly. In a moment I'll have to go to the market to buy biscuits and such like, no?
Parvati	Yes, you will. I have to go that way too this afternoon. Let's go together.

Jai	Of course. Now I'll start cleaning the house.
Parvati	Fine. Take a look in the lavatory and the bathroom too. As far as possible let there be no inconvenience for the guests. I'll be in the kitchen.
Jai	Shall I tidy the bedroom too?
Parvati	It's not necessary sister. Everything's untidy. I'll tidy it myself later.
Jai	Oh mother! It's raining. It's a disaster!
Parvati	Don't worry. I'll phone the office and try to explain. Now, whether they come or they don't, we have to sit inside the house.

* चिया-सिया *tea* and *snacks*. It is possible to add a meaningless rhyming word to certain words to mean *and things associated with it.*

🗣 Grammar

126 *May I?* Verbs in the subjunctive

The subjunctive form of a Nepali verb is used in three contexts:

A Nepali AIDS warning

(i) to ask whether or suggest that you might do something:
may I come in? let's wash these clothes!

(ii) to express a wish that something might happen: *may the weather be good today! may you all be successful in your examination!*

(iii) in phrases along the lines of *whether it does or it doesn't.*

Nepali grammar provides subjunctive forms of the verb for all possible subjects, but in practice you rarely need to know more than the four that are set out below.

Subject	*ending*	गर्नु	हुनु	आउनु	दिनु
म	-ũ	गरूँ	होऊँ	आऊँ	दिऊँ
ऊ, त्यो, यो	-os	गरोस्	होओस्	आओस्	देओस्
हामी	-aũ	गरौं	होऔं	आऔं	दिऔं
उनीहरू	-ūn	गरून्	होऊन्	आऔन्	दिऊन

With म *I* and हामी*we*, the subjunctive is very similar to the probable future tense minus its -ला ending (see **Grammar 96**), except that हुनु *to be* keeps the base हो- in every instance, even with म *I*.

म तपाईलाई एउटा गुनासो सुनाऊँ? तपाई रिसाउनुहुन्न ?	*May I tell you of a complaint? You won't be angry?*
ऊ ठीक समयमा आइपुगोस् ।	*He'd better arrive on time.*
नेपाली साहित्य फलोस् फुलोस् !	*May Nepali literature fruit and bloom!*
बाहुनको बाबुले न च्याउ खाओस् न च्याउको स्वाद पाओस् ।	*A Brahman's boy shall neither eat a mushroom nor know its taste.**

*A proverb. Certain Brahmans follow a strict dietary code, and avoid garlic, onions, mushrooms and many other foods.

EXERCISE 68   Finish the following sentences with a subjunctive verb:

१   तपाईको छोरा चाँडै निको (*be*).
२   भोलि हामीहरू फिलिम हेर्न पोखरा (*go*)?
३   हामीहरू तपाईकी आमालाई के (*say*)?
४   तपाईको जिन्दगी सुखी (*be*).
५   आजको बस ढिलो (*not be*).
६   म तपाईकहाँ कति बजे (*come*)?

An environmental message from Kathmandu Municipal Council.

127   Doing something for another person: compound verbs with दिनु

Any transitive verb may be combined with the verb दिनु *to give*, producing what is called a 'compound verb', when the action of the verb is being referred away from the person who performs the action. Often this means that the verb is being performed for someone else's benefit, or on someone else's behalf. In this context, the verb in question must take its 'i-stem', in which a short **i** vowel is attached to its past tense base:

verb	base	i-stem	compound verb	
गर्नु	गर-	गरि	गरिदिनु	to do for someone else
भन्नु	भन-	भनि	भनिदिनु	to inform
लेख्नु	लेख-	लेखि	लेखिदिनु	to write for

Because the meaning of a compound verb focuses very much on its positive aspect, it rarely occurs in the negative.

डाक्टर साहेबले हाम्रो लागि औषधि लेखिदिनुभयो ।	*The doctor wrote out a prescription for us.*
चिठी चाँडै पठाइदिनुहुन्छ कि ?	*Will you send the letter immediately?*
अलि पर्खनुपर्ला ।थाहा पाउनेबित्तिकै म तपाईंलाई भनिदिन्छु ।	*You might have to wait a while. As soon as I find out I will tell you.*

128 Trying and seeking

The verb खोज्नु has two meanings:

■ खोज्नु means *to search for* when it is associated with a noun or pronoun:

घरको साँचो कता पर्‍यो ? दिनभरि खोजेर पनि भेट्टाउन सकिनँ ।	*Where has the house key got to? Despite searching all day I could not find it.*
म उनीहरूको घर खोज्दै थिएँ ।त्यो बेला उनीहरू पनि त्यहाँ टुप्लुक्क आइपुगे ।	*I was looking for their house. Then they suddenly arrived there too.*

■ खोज्नु means *to try to* when it is associated with the infinitive of a verb:

मैले बारम्बार सरकारी जागिर पाउन खोजें तर म हरेक पटक असफल भएँ ।	*I tried again and again to get a government job, but I was unsuccessful every time.*
मैले तपाईंलाई फोन गर्न खोजें तर लाइन एकदम बिजी थियो ।	*I tried to phone you but the line was really busy.*

An alternative to खोज्नु is the verb कोशिश गर्नु, which can be used in combination with the infinitive of a verb in much the same way as खोज्नु, or on its own:

मैले भोटिया भाषा पनि सिक्न कोशिश त गरेको थिएँ, तर पढ्ने फुर्सद नभएको कारणले असफल भएँ ।	*I did try to learn Tibetan, but I failed because I didn't have the time to study.*
हामीलाई भोलि आउन अलि अप्ठ्यारो होला, तर कोशिश गरौंला ।	*It might be a bit difficult for us to come tomorrow, but we will try.*

23 | IF HE'D TAKEN THE MEDICINE

उसले औषधि खाएको भए

In this unit you will learn how to:

■ say that things have already happened
■ construct unreal conditional sentences
■ convey the sense that something has just been realised

33 A death in the neighbourhood

One of Sita's neighbours has died. She tells Manju how it happened.

मंजु हिजो मैले तपाईलाई अस्पताल जान लागेको देखेको थिएँ, हो ? बिरामी हुनुहुन्छ कि के हो ?

सीता होइन, म छिमेकको एउटा चिनेको मान्छेसँग भेट्न गएको थिएँ । अस्ति उसको छोरासँग बजारमा भेट्दा उसले बालाई कमलपित्त भएर अस्पताल जानुभएको छ भन्यो ।

मंजु ए, सिकिस्त बिरामी भएको रहेछ तपाईको छिमेकी ? अहिले कस्तो छ रे ?

सीता अस्पताल पुग्नेबित्तिकै मैले उसलाई जाँच्ने डाक्टरसँग सोधें । तर बिचरा दुई घण्टा अघि नै मरिसकेको रहेछ ।

मंजु ए । तपाई अस्ति जानुभएको भए भेट हुन्थ्यो, हगि ?

सीता हो नि, तर के गर्ने र ? ऊ त्यति छिट्टै मर्छ भन्ने कुरा मैले कल्पना पनि गरेको थिइनँ । त्यस्तो थाहा भएको भए त म चाँडै जान्थेँ नि । यस्तो उमेरमा नमरेको भए हुन्थ्यो । उसको आत्माले शान्ति पाओस् भन्नुपर्‍यो, अरू के भन्ने र ?

मंजु मान्छे त्यति बूढो होइन, क्यारे ?

सीता बूढो भएको भए त त्यति दुःखको कुरा पनि हुँदैनथ्यो नि । तर मान्छे पैंतीस वर्षको मात्रै रहेछ ! डाक्टरको भनाइ अनुसार रक्सी धेरै खान्थ्यो रे । रक्सी नखाइकन औषधि खाएको भए त यसरी अकालै मर्ने नै थिएन नि ।

मंजु दाह-सँस्कार भइसकेको छ ?

सीता आज बिहानै पशुपतिमा भइसक्यो नि । कति चाँडै भएछ ! अफिसमा काम नभएको भए मेरो श्रीमान् जानुहुन्थ्यो । तर मिलेन । भरे बेलुका उसकी स्वास्नीलाई भेट्न जानुपर्ला ।

मंजु छोराछोरी कत्रो रहेछन् नि ?

सीता छोराको बिहा भइसक्यो क्यारे । छोरी पनि तरुनी भइसकेको छ । अब बिचरा त्यो आइमाईले एक्लै छोरीको बिहाको कुरा मिलाउनुपर्‍यो ।

मंजु तर सन्तान नभएको भए उसलाई झन् गाह्रो हुन्थ्यो नि । छोरा ठूलो भइसकेको रहेछ नि, केही छैन, उसले आमालाई सघाइदिन्छ ।

चिन्नु *to know, be acquainted with*	शान्ति *peace*
कमलपित्त *jaundice*	दुःख *sorrow*
सिकिस्त *gravely, seriously (ill)*	अनुसार *according to*
रहनु *to remain, be*	अकालै *early, untimely*
जाँच्नु *to examine*	दाह-संस्कार *cremation rite*
भेट *meeting*	कत्रो *how big?*
कल्पना गर्नु *to imagine*	तरुनी *young woman*
हुन्थ्यो *it would have been all right*	सन्तान *offspring*
आत्मा *soul*	सघाउनु *to help*

Manju   I saw you going to the hospital yesterday, did I? Are you ill, or what is it?

Sita   No, I went to see a man I know from the neighbourhood. The other day when I met his son in the market he said his father had contracted jaundice and had gone to hospital.

Manju   Oh is he seriously ill, your neighbour? How do they say he is now?

Sita   As soon as I reached the hospital I asked the doctor who examined him. But the poor man had already died just two hours earlier.

Manju   Oh. If you had gone two days ago you'd have seen him, no?

Sita   That's right, but what to do, indeed? I had never even imagined that he would die quickly like that. If I'd known that I'd have gone right away. It would have been better if he hadn't died at such an age. We must say 'may his soul find peace', what else can we say, after all?

Manju   So the man wasn't so old, eh?

Sita   If he'd been old then it wouldn't have been such a sad affair either, you know. But the man is only 35 years old! According to the doctor, he used to drink a lot. If he had taken his medicine and hadn't drunk alcohol he wouldn't have died such an untimely death, you know.

Manju   Has the funeral ceremony taken place?

Sita   It took place at Pashupati early this morning. How quickly it has happened! If there hadn't been work at the office my husband would have gone. But it wasn't convenient. This evening I'll have to go and see his wife.[*]

Manju How big are the children?

Sita I think the son's already married. The daughter's a young woman already too. Now, poor thing, that woman has to arrange her daughter's marriage alone.

Manju But if she didn't have children it would be even harder for her, you know. The son's grown up already you know, it doesn't matter, he will help his mother.

* Among Nepali Hindus, it is unusual for a woman to attend a funeral.

📖 Grammar

129 Already done: compound verbs with सक्नु

The verb सक्नु has been encountered before, in combination with the infinitive of a verb, where it means *can/be able*. However, the same verb has the second meaning of *to finish/be completed*. Its i-stem form सकिनु can therefore be used interchangeably with the verb सिद्धिनु to mean *to finish*:

आजको काम सकियो ।	*Today's work is finished.*
हिजोको पाठ अझै पनि सिद्धिएको छैन ।	*Yesterday's lesson is still not finished.*

The i-stem form of any verb (see **Grammar 69**), whether transitive or intransitive, may also be combined with सक्नु to emphasise that its action has already been completed. The compound verb consists of the i-stem of the verb + सक्नु, written as a single word:

मैले पढिसकें ।	*I have already read.*
तिमी आइसकेको थियौ ।	*You had already come.*
ऊ सुतिसकेको छ ।	*He is already asleep.*
वहाँ मरिसक्नुभयो ।	*He has already died.*

Because it serves to emphasise that something is over and done with when it is the second part of a compound verb, the verb सक्नु almost always takes a past tense in this context – usually this is the simple past or the completed past. For the same reason, it is rarely used in the negative. The completed present tense is also sometimes used, but often its meaning (*has already...*) is conveyed by the shorter simple past tense.

In Nepali, compound verbs with सक्नु are used much more commonly than the English translation *already* might suggest. In a context where an

English-speaker might say *it's become dark* or *he has left*, a Nepali-speaker will often say अँध्यारो भइसक्यो *it's already become dark* and ऊ गइसक्यो *he's already left*.

मेरो त बिहा भइसक्यो नि । मेरो लागि दुलही खोज्नुपर्दैन ।	*But I am already married, you know. You don't need to seek for a bride for me.*
आज म मन्त्रालय दुई पटक गइसकें । अब तेस्रो पटक जानु नपरोस् !	*I've already been to the ministry twice today. Let me not have to go a third time now!*
त्यो उपन्यास त मैले धेरै अघि पढिसकें । कुनै उपन्यास एक पटक पढिसकेपछि दोस्रो पटक पढ्न मनै लाग्दैन ।	*I read that novel a long time ago. After I have read any novel once I really don't wish to read it a second time.*

130 Unreal conditional sentences

Unreal conditional sentences state that if something *had been* the case in the past something else *would have* happened: *if it had rained I wouldn't have gone out; if it hadn't rained I would have gone out.* Such sentences are 'unreal' because anyone who utters, hears, reads or writes them knows that in fact the reality turned out differently.

The 'if' clause must end with a combination of the -एको participle of whichever verb is involved, followed by the short -**e** participle of the verb हुनु *to be*, i.e. -एको भए. If the verb is negative it takes the prefix न-.

Real condition	**Unreal condition**
पानी पर्‍यो भने...	पानी परेको भए...
If it rains...	*If it had rained...*
ऊ आउन भने...	ऊ नआएको भए...
If he doesn't come...	*If he hadn't come...*

In general, the form -एको भए is used no matter who or what the subject is, regardless of number, gender, or level of politeness. But occasionally, if the subject is felt to deserve especial deference or politeness, the High form consisting of the dictionary form + भएको भए is used instead:

तपाई जानुभयो भने...	तपाई जानुभएको भए...
If you go...	*If you had gone...*
तपाई जानुभएन भने...	तपाई नजानुभएको भए...
If you don't go...	*If you hadn't gone...*

The second part of an unreal conditional sentence usually ends with a verb that is exactly the same as the habitual past tense. However, the meaning of this tense when it is the conclusion of an unreal conditional sentence is very different:

त्यो रेष्टुराँमा हामीहरू गुन्द्रुक खान्थ्यौं ।	*We <u>used to eat</u> gundruk in that restaurant.*
त्यो रेष्टुराँमा गएको भए हामीहरू गुन्द्रुक खान्थ्यौं ।	*If we had gone into that restaurant we <u>would have eaten</u> gundruk.*

In fact, the final verb of an unreal conditional sentence is actually a shortened form of a tense that consists of the -ने participle + थियो. The second of the two sentences above could read as follows:

हामी त्यो रेष्टुराँमा गएको भए हामी गुन्द्रुक खाने थियौं ।	*If we had gone into that restaurant over there we <u>would have eaten</u> gundruk.*

This tense is also used on its own to talk about intentions in the past – usually intentions that were not fulfilled:

म सगरमाथा चढ्ने थिएँ ।	*I was going to climb / would have climbed Everest.*

This sentence does not make it clear whether the speaker actually got on to the mountain or not. When the same phrase becomes the second half of an unreal conditional sentence, however, it becomes clear that he did not:

हिउँ नपरेको भए म सगरमाथा चढ्ने थिएँ ।	*If it had not snowed I would have climbed Everest.*

The meaning remains exactly the same when the shorter form of the verb (the habitual past) is used instead:

हिउँ नपरेको भए म सगरमाथा चढ्थें ।	*If it had not snowed I'd have climbed Everest.*
मसँग पैसा भएको भए म परिवारको लागि कोसेलीहरू किन्थें ।	*If I'd had any money on me I'd have bought presents for the family.*
तपाईंले त्यो कुरा अँग्रेजीमा भन्नुभएको भए उसले बुझ्थ्यो ।	*If you had said that thing in English he would have understood.*
घाम लागेको भए बच्चाहरू बाहिर खेल्थे ।	*If the sun had shone the children would have played outside.*

बासी भात नखाएको भए तिम्रो पेट दुख्दैनथ्यो । *If you hadn't eaten stale rice your stomach wouldn't be hurting.*

EXERCISE 69 Match up the beginnings and ends below to create five unreal conditional sentences. Translate the five sentences into English.

१ मलाई भोक लागेको भए...　　　... त्यो मान्छे अकालै मर्दैनथ्यो ।
२ पानी नपरेको भए...　　　　　... हाम्रो घरमा बिजुली हुँदैनथ्यो ।
३ पहाडमा खोलाहरू नभएको भए...　... बेलुका झन रमाइलो हुन्थ्यो ।
४ बेलामा औषधि खाएको भए...　　... उनीहरू भात खान आउँथे ।
५ साथीले गीत गाएको भए...　　　... म खपाखप भात खान्थें ।

131　The short completed present tense

The completed present tense is explained in **Grammar 77**. In everyday spoken Nepali, this tense may take a shortened form, partly because it is rather longwinded. After all, why use five syllables to say 'I've done' in Nepali when you need only use three? The short forms of the completed present tense are also used to imply that something happened suddenly or unexpectedly.

The short form of the completed present tense is simply the full form minus the final -को of the -एको participle that is the first word of the pair. The two words of the full form become a single word in the short form:

Full form	**Short form**
म गएको छु	म गएछु
उनीहरू आएका छन्	उनीहरू आएछन्
तपाईंले गर्नुभएको छ	तपाईंले गर्नुभएछ

132　Realisation: using रहेछ at the end of sentences

रहेछ is the short form of रहेको छ, the completed present tense of the verb रहनु *to remain/continue to be.* रहेछ can be thought of as an add-on word similar to होला (**Grammar 92**), although there is a difference in that रहेछ must take the place of another verb, and cannot simply be appended to any statement. रहेछ or its negative form रहेनछ may be used instead of छ, छैन, हो or होइन at the end of a sentence to indicate that the speaker has just realised what s/he is saying. It has no real equivalent in English, unless it be the exclamation mark, or the old-fashioned exclamation 'why!' with which an observation can begin in English.

Simple statements	Realisations
तपाईको घर राम्रो छ ।	तपाईको घर राम्रो रहेछ !
Your house is nice.	*Why, your house is nice!*
उसको हातमा बन्दूक छ ।	उसको हातमा बन्दूक रहेछ !
There is a gun in his hand.	*Hey, he's got a gun in his hand!*
तपाईको छोरा अग्लो भइसक्यो ।	तपाईको छोरा अग्लो भइसकेको रहेछ !
Your son has become tall.	*Why, your son has become tall!*
मेरो खल्तीमा पैसा छैन ।	मेरो खल्तीमा पैसा रहेनछ !
There is no money in my pocket.	*Why, there's no money in my pocket!*

133 The verb चिन्नु *to know/recognise*

This verb is used exclusively with human nouns as indirect objects. In the
habitual present tense it means *to recognise* while in past tenses it means
to be acquainted with.

तपाई त्यस मान्छेलाई चिन्नुहुन्छ ? अहँ,   *Do you recognise that person? No,*
चिन्दिन । वहाँ को हुनुहुन्छ ?   *I don't. Who is he?*

त्यहाँ कोही चिनेको मान्छे भएको भए   *If there had been anyone there that*
म उसैलाई भन्थें ।   *I knew, I'd have told him/her.*

खबरदार, मैले तिमीलाई राम्रोसँग चिनेको छु ! *Beware, I know you very well!*

EXERCISE 70   Translate into Nepali:

Today some people we know are coming to our house for dinner at
6 o'clock. I return home from the university at 4 o'clock, but the house is
empty! And I look in my bag to see if the key is there and the bag is empty
too! Where might it have gone? I search in every place but I cannot find
the key.

The cook should have come at half past 3 but he has not come yet. Perhaps
he has already come to the house and then gone to the market. If he had
stayed in the house until 4 o'clock this problem would not have occurred.
Should I break a window to get in ? Or shall I go back to the university
and search for the key in my office? I don't know, what shall I do?

Oh, now the cook has arrived and he has the key in his hand! If I had broken
(फोड्नु *to break*) a window my husband would have really told me off!

It is already a quarter past 4. He opens the door for me. Shall I phone my
husband and tell him to come home soon? No, there's probably no need.
The cook has already bought all the food and now he will cook it for us.

24 | IF THAT'S HOW IT IS...
त्यसो भए...

In this unit you will learn:

- some verses of a Nepali folksong
- how to intensify the action of a verb
- the longer continuous tenses
- the short real conditional sentence

34 Two porters and a folksong

Mahila works as a porter in the hills. On his way home one day he meets another porter, and they agree to keep each other's company along the way.

भरिया ए भाइ, आज कतातिर ?

माहिंला आज घरतिर जाने ।

भरिया कहाँ हो घर ?

माहिंला त्रिसुली नदीपारि, फेदी गाउँ ।

भरिया आज कहाँबाट हिंडेको ?

माहिंला आज नुवाकोटबाट बिहानै हिंडेको ।

भरिया एक्लै हिंड्दाखेरि अलि डर हुन्छ नि । साथी छैन ?

माहिंला साथी-भाइहरूसँग हिंडेको थिएँ उनीहरू त धादिङ्गतिर गएछन् । उनीहरूको बाटो उता पर्‍यो, मेरो बाटो यता पर्‍यो । के गर्ने ?

भरिया ल, त्यसो भए तपाईंको र मेरो बाटो यहाँदेखि एउटै भयो । यहाँबाट सँगै जाऔं ।

माहिंला हुन्छ, रमाइलो हुन्छ । तपाईंको भारी ठूलो रहेछ । के छ त्यसमा ?

भरिया यसमा नून, तेल र कपडा छ । देउरालीको एउटा साहूको भारी हो यो ।

माहिंला मलाई थकाइ लाग्यो । कस्तो चर्को घाम लागेको, हगि ? ऊ त्यो पीपलको बोटमुनि एक छिन थकाइ मारौं न ।

भरिया हुन्छ, बसौं । कस्तो तिर्खा लाग्यो ! यतातिर पानी पाइन्छ कि ?

माहिंला हेर्नुहोस्, ऊ त्यहाँ तलबाट एउटा केटा आइरहेको छ । घर नजिकै होला उसको । म सोध्छु, है... ए कान्छा, तिम्रो घर कहाँ हो ?

केटा यहीनेर छ, दाइ । किन र ?

माहिंला त्यसो भए एक लोटा पानी ल्याउन सक्छौ ? चर्को घाम लागेको छ, हामीलाई तिर्खा लाग्यो ।

केटा भइहाल्छ नि दाइ, म लिएर आउँछु ।

(पाँच मिनेटपछि)

केटा ल, पानी लिनुहोस् । ए तपाईंको साथी त सुतिहाल्नुभएछ ।

माहिंला ल, उसलाई उठाउन एउटा गीत गाउनुपर्‍यो । तिमीलाई गीत गाउन आउँछ ?

केटा आउँछ दाइ । गाऊँ त ? ल, सुन्नुहोस् है त ।
रेसम फिरिरि, रेसम फिरिरि
उडेर जाऊँ कि डाँडामा भन्ज्याङ्ग, रेसम फिरिरि
कुखुरालाई कुटीमा कुटी, बिरालोलाई सुरी
तिम्रो हाम्रो माया प्रीति दोबाटोमा कुरी
रेसम फिरिरि, रेसम फिरिरि
उडेर जाऊँ कि डाँडामा भन्ज्याङ्ग, रेसम फिरिरि

एकनाले बन्दुक दुईनाले बन्दुक मृगलाई ताकेको
मृगलाई मैले ताकेको होइन मायालाई डाकेको
रेसम फिरिरि, रेसम फिरिरि
उडेर जाऊँ कि डाँडामा भन्ज्याङ्ग, रेसम फिरिरि

माहिंला ए यो भाइले पानी ल्याइदिएको छ । मैले त खाएँ । तिमी सुतिरहेको थियौ । खाने हो ?

-पारि *on the far side of*	कुखुरा *chicken*
डर *fear*	बिरालो *cat*
चर्को *hot, sharp*	माया *love, affection*
थकाइ मार्नु *to rest ('to kill weariness')*	प्रीति *love, affection*
यहीं *right here*	दोबाटो *crossroads*
-नेर *near*	एकनाले *single-barrelled*
लोटा *jug, steel cup*	बन्दुक *gun*
रेसम *silk (handkerchief)*	दईनाले *double-barrelled*
फिरिरि *rippling (in the breeze)*	मृग *deer*
उड्नु *to fly*	ताक्नु *to aim*
डाँडा *hill, ridge*	डाक्नु *to call, invite*
भन्ज्याङ्ग *pass*	

Porter	Oh brother, where are you going today?
Mahila	I'm going home today.
Porter	Where's home?
Mahila	The other side of the Trisuli river, Phedi village.
Porter	Where did you start from today?
Mahila	Early this morning I set out from Nuwakot.
Porter	It's a bit frightening when you walk alone, you know. Have you no companions?
Mahila	I set out with some friends, but they have gone to Dhading. Their path was in that direction, mine in this. What to do?
Porter	Well, if that's how it is your path and mine are the same from here. Let's go together from here.
Mahila	OK, it will be pleasant. Your load is big. What is in it?
Porter	There's salt, oil and cloth in this. This is a load for a businessman in Deurali.
Mahila	I'm tired. How hot the sun is, don't you think? Let's rest beneath that pipal tree for a moment.
Porter	Yes, let's sit down. How thirsty I am! Can we get some water somewhere here?

Mahila	Look, there's a boy coming from lower down. His house will be nearby. I'll ask... Hey Kancha, where's your house?
Boy	It's just near here. Why do you ask?
Mahila	If that's so, can you bring a jug of water? The sun is hot, we are thirsty.
Boy	No problem brother, I'll bring it.
	After five minutes:
Boy	Here, take the water. Oh, your friend has gone to sleep.
Mahila	Right, we'll have to sing a song to wake him up. Can you sing?
Boy	Yes I can, brother. Shall I sing then? Right, listen to me.[1]

Silk (handkerchief) rippling (in the breeze), Silk (handkerchief) rippling (in the breeze), [2]
Shall I go flying (over the) hills and passes? Silk (handkerchief) rippling (in the breeze).
(Saying) 'kuti kuti' to a chicken, (saying) 'suri' to a cat
Your love and my love, waiting at the crossroads.
Silk (handkerchief) rippling...
One-barrelled gun, two-barrelled gun, aiming at a deer,
It's not a deer that I am aiming at, it's love that I am calling.
Silk (handkerchief) rippling...

| Mahila | Oh, this brother has brought some water. *I* have drunk some. You were sleeping. Will you drink? |

[1] The boy sings a few verses of one of the most famous Nepali folksongs, रेसम फिरिरि. Like many folksongs, रेसम फिरिरि contains a lot of wordplay that is difficult to translate.

[2] It is an old tradition for young men and women to exchange handkerchiefs as love tokens.

🔊 Grammar

134 Compound verbs with हाल्नु

When used on its own, the verb हाल्नु means *to insert, put in*. It may be compared to the verb राख्नु *to place upon, keep*. In fact, राख्नु is felt by some Nepali-speakers to be a more polite way of saying *to put in*, so that one will hear some speakers saying म चियामा चिनी हालिदिऊँ ? *shall I put sugar in the tea?* and others saying म चियामा चिनी राखिदिऊँ ?

When it is combined with the i-stem of a verb to form a compound verb, however, हाल्नु simply reinforces and underlines the sense of that verb without changing its essential meaning.

ऊ गयो	he went	ऊ गइहाल्यो	he's gone away
भयो	it's happened	भइहाल्यो	it's over and done with
तपाईले देख्नुभयो	you saw	तपाईले देखिहाल्नुभयो	you have surely seen

ऊ धेरै दिन बसेन । तीन दिनपछि त
गइहाल्यो नि ।

तपाईले देखिहाल्नुभयो यहाँ दिन दिनै
बत्ती जान्छ ।

तीनवटा उदाहरण भएपछि त भइहाल्यो नि ।

He didn't stay long. After three
days he was gone, you know.

You have seen very well that there
is a power cut here every day

After three examples it's over and
done, you know.

135 Continuous tenses using रहनु

When used on its own, the verb रहनु means *to remain, continue*. It is
frequently combined with the i-stem of a verb to form a compound verb
that emphasises the continuous nature of an action. The -एको participle of
such a compound verb is used to form a continuous tense:

अब हेर्नुहोस् नगर पालिकालाई आज म यो
सुझाव लेखिरहेको छु । यस्तै सुझाव
पोहोर साल पनि यही बेला लेखिरहेको थिएँ ।
तर कसैल पनि ध्यान
दिइरहेका छैनन् ।

*Look now, today I am writing this
suggestion for the municipality.
Last year too I was writing the
same kind of suggestion at exactly
this time. But no-one is giving this
matter any attention.*

म एउटा नेपाली भाषाको पाठच पुस्तक लेख्न
सोचिरहेको थिएँ । साथीहरू नलेख
भनिरहेका थिए । तर लेख्न शुरु गरिहालें ।
अहिलेसम्म पनि लेखिरहेको छु ।

*I was thinking of writing a textbook
of the Nepali language. (My)
friends were telling me not to
write (it). Even so I began to write.
I am still writing it now.*

Because of the greater length of these verbs, they are used instead of the
other continuous tenses (गर्दै छ, गर्दै थियो etc.) when there is a need to stress
the continuous nature of an activity.

EXERCISE 71 Convert the tense of the following sentences from an
habitual tense to a continuous tense with रहनु:

Examples

म अफिसमा काम गर्छु ।   म अफिसमा काम गरिरहेको छु ।
म अफिसमा काम गर्थे ।   म अफिसमा काम गरिरहेको थिएँ ।

१ उनीहरू जाँड-रक्सी धेरै पिउँथे ।
२ गोपाल राम्रा राम्रा गीत गाउँथ्यो ।

३ मेरो भाइ टाढाको एउटा स्कूलमा जान्छ ।

४ खैरेनीबाट काठ्माडौंमा धेरै तरकारी आउँछ ।

५ म यहाँबाट कीर्तिपुरसम्म हिंडेर जान्थें ।

136 Short real conditional sentences

The **-e** participle consists of a verb's past tense base + the vowel **e** or (another way of looking at it) the -एको participle minus its -को.

Grammar 91 explained how to construct a real conditional sentence by using the simple past tense of a verb followed by भने for the 'if' clause, and a present or future tense (or an imperative) for the 'then' clause. A second, quicker way of expressing the same meaning replaces the verb of the 'if' clause with the short **-e** participle of the verb, and leaves out the word भने. For example, compare the long and short versions of the sentences *if it rains I won't go out* and *if it doesn't rain I will probably go out*:

Long version	Short version
पानी पर्‍यो भने म बाहिर जाँदिन ।	पानी परे म बाहिर जाँदिन ।
पानी परेन भने म बाहिर जाउँला ।	पानी नपरे म बाहिर जाउँला ।

Often, the **-e** participle will be followed by त, *though, but,* to underline the conditional nature of the sentence.

अलिकति भात भए पुग्छ ।	*A little rice will be enough* ('if there is a little rice it will suffice').
भोक लागे त भात खाऊ न भाइ ।	*If you're hungry just eat, younger brother,*
पैसा नभए त बिल कसरी तिर्ने ?	*But if there is no money how will we pay the bill?*
अँग्रेजी बोले पनि हुन्छ, नेपाली बोले पनि हुन्छ ।	*It is OK if you speak English, and it's OK if you speak Nepali too.*

EXERCISE 72   Create one short real conditional sentence from each pair of sentences below:

Example
पानी पर्दैन । म बाहिर जाउँला । = पानी नपरे म बाहिर जाउँला ।

१ भोक लाग्दैन । म खाजा नखाउँला ।

२ थकाइ लाग्यो । म आराम गरूँला ।

३ काठ्माडौं छाडेर जान मन लाग्दैन । काठ्माडौंमै बसूँला ।

४ नेपाली सिक्न गाह्रो लाग्यो । हिन्दी सिक्न पनि गाह्रो लाग्यो । जापानी सिकूँला ।

५ गुन्द्रुक मीठो लागेन र आलु-तामा पनि मीठो लागेन । कालो दाल खाउँला ।

EXERCISE 73   Translate into Nepali:

I went with elder brother to the airport yesterday. Some guests were coming from Delhi to stay with us. Early in the morning we had phoned the RNAC office and a woman had said that the Delhi flight would arrive at 3 o'clock in the afternoon. 'If that's the case then we must set out from home at 2.30', said elder brother.

As soon as we arrived at the airport elder brother asked an official (कर्मचारी) about the flight. The official told him that it had left Delhi only recently because the weather had been very bad. 'In that case how long will we have to wait here?', elder brother asked. 'It is flying (उड्नु) towards Nepal now', the official said, 'it will arrive within one hour'.

'The aeroplane is late and we will have to wait here', elder brother said. 'But mother and father are waiting at home', I told him, 'They do not know that the plane is coming late.'

'You go and phone them', elder brother said. 'Tell them that we will come straight home after the plane arrives.'

APPENDICES

Cardinal numbers

०	शून्य								
१	एक	११	एघार	२१	एक्काइस	३१	एकतीस	४१	एकचालीस
२	दुई	१२	बाह्र	२२	बाईस	३२	बत्तीस	४२	बयालीस
३	तीन	१३	तेह्र	२३	तेईस	३३	तेत्तीस	४३	त्रिचालीस
४	चार	१४	चौध	२४	चौबीस	३४	चौंतीस	४४	चवालीस
५	पाँच	१५	पन्ध्र	२५	पच्चीस	३५	पैंतीस	४५	पैंतालीस
६	छ	१६	सोह्र	२६	छब्बीस	३६	छत्तीस	४६	छयालीस
७	सात	१७	सत्र	२७	सत्ताईस	३७	सैंतीस	४७	सतचालीस
८	आठ	१८	अठार	२८	अट्ठाइस	३८	अठ्तीस	४८	अठचालीस
९	नौ	१९	उन्नाईस	२९	उन्तीस	३९	उनन्चालीस	४९	उनन्चास
१०	दस	२०	बीस	३०	तीस	४०	चालीस	५०	पचास

५१	एकाउन्न	६१	एकसट्ठी	७१	एकहत्तर	८१	एकासी	९१	एकानब्बे
५२	बाउन्न	६२	बैंसट्ठी	७२	बहत्तर	८२	बयासी	९२	बयानब्बे
५३	त्रिपन्न	६३	त्रिसट्ठी	७३	त्रिहत्तर	८३	त्रियासी	९३	त्रियानब्बे
५४	चउन्न	६४	चौंसट्ठी	७४	चौहत्तर	८४	चौरासी	९४	चौरानब्बे
५५	पचपन्न	६५	पैंसट्ठी	७५	पचहत्तर	८५	पचासी	९५	पञ्चानब्बे
५६	छपन्न	६६	छैंसट्ठी	७६	छहत्तर	८६	छयासी	९६	छयानब्बे
५७	सन्ताउन्न	६७	सतसट्ठी	७७	सतहत्तर	८७	सतासी	९७	सन्तानब्बे
५८	अन्ठाउन्न	६८	अठसट्ठी	७८	अठहत्तर	८८	अठासी	९८	अन्ठानब्बे
५९	उनन्साठी	६९	उनहत्तर	७९	उनासी	८९	उनानब्बे	९९	उनान्सय
६०	साठी	७०	सत्तरी	८०	असी	९०	नब्बे	१००	सय

Above 100, the numbers proceed as they do in English, but omitting the English 'and':

१०१	एक सय एक
२६२	दुई सय बैंसठ्ठी
१०००	एक हजार or हजार
१४२३	एक हजार चार सय तेईस
२५१०८	पच्चीस हजार एक सय आठ
१०००००	एक लाख
११६४३३	एक लाख तेह्र हजार चार सय तेत्तीस
३१०००००	सैंतीस लाख
१०००००००	एक करोड

If commas are used to split up large numbers, the placing of the commas reflects the system of हजार, लाख, and करोड, rather than thousands and millions. For example, the number 31,350,226 will appear as:

३,१३,५०,२२६ तीन करोड तेह्र लाख पचास हजार दुई सय छब्बीस

Kinship terms

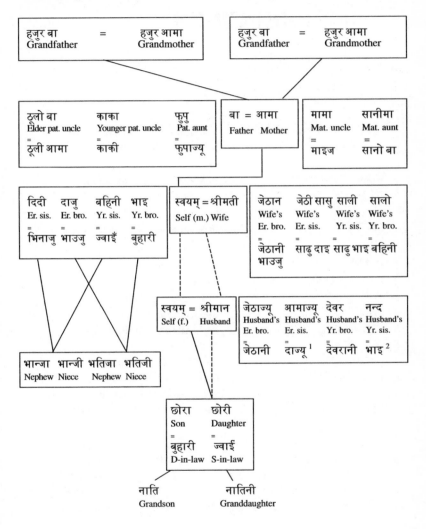

[1] more formally, आमाज्यू दाज्यू
[2] more formally, नन्दे भाइ

KEY TO
EXERCISES

1

1 होइन, म बिमल कुमार होइन । hoina, ma Bimal Kumār hoina.
2 हो, म विद्यार्थी हुँ । ho, ma vidyārthī hū̃.
or
होइन, म विद्याथी होइन । hoina, ma vidyārthī hoina.
3 हो, म नेपाली हुँ । ho, ma nepālī hū̃.
or
होइन, म नेपाली होइन । hoina, ma nepālī hoina.

2

1 म अँग्रेज हुँ । ma ãgrej hū̃.
2 हामी विद्यार्थी हौं । hāmī vidyārthī haũ.
3 तिमी हिन्दुस्तानी हौ । timī hindustānī hau.
4 तिमीहरू किसान हौ । timīharū kisān hau.
5 तपाई शिक्षक हुनुहुन्छ । tapāī̃ sikṣak hunuhuncha.
6 ऊ शिक्षक हो । ū śikṣak ho.
7 उनी धनी मान्छे हुन् । unī dhanī mānche hun.
8 ती मान्छेहरू प्रहरी हुन् । tī māncheharū praharī hun.
9 वहाँ नेपाली हुनुहुन्छ । vahā̃ nepālī hunuhuncha.
10 यहाँहरू भारतीय हुनुहुन्छ । yahā̃harū bhāratīya hunuhuncha.

3

1 ... होइन । ... hoina.   6 ... होइन । ... hoina.
2 ... होइनौं । ... hoinaũ.   7 ... होइनन् । ... hoinan.
3 ... होइनौ । ... hoinau.   8 ... होइनन् । ... hoinan.
4 ... होइनौ । ... hoinau.   9 ... हुनुहुन्न । ... hunuhunna.
5 ... हुनुहुन्न । ... hunuhunna.   10 ... हुनुहुन्न । ... hunuhunna.

4

1 राम्रो किसान rāmro kisān   6 धनी किसानहरू dhanī kisānharū
2 ठूलो किताब ṭhūlo kitāb   7 राम्रा किताबहरू rāmrā kitābharū
3 धनी केटी dhanī keṭī   8 साना केटीहरू sānā keṭīharū
4 नयाँ केटा nayā̃ keṭā   9 गरीब केटाहरू garīb keṭāharū
5 नयाँ राम्रो राजा rāmro rājā   10 धनी राजाहरू dhanī rājāharū

5

१	हो, काठ्माडौँ ठूलो छ ।	ho, kāṭhmāḍaū ṭhūlo cha.
२	होइन, भक्तपुर गाउँ होइन, शहर हो ।	hoina, bhaktapur gaū hoina, śahar ho.
३	हो, काठ्माडौँ राम्रै छ ।	ho, kāṭhmāḍaū rāmrai cha.
४	हो, काठ्माडौँ ठूलो शहर हो ।	ho, kāṭhmāḍaū ṭhūlo śahar ho.
५	हो, भक्तपुर पुरानो छ ।	ho, bhaktapur purāno cha.
६	होइन, भक्तपुर नयाँ शहर होइन, पुरानो शहर हो ।	hoina, bhaktapur nayā̃ śahar hoina, purāno śahar ho.

6

१ भाइ स्कूलमा छ ।
bhāi skūlmā cha.

२ दाजु दार्जीलिङ्गमा हुनुहुन्छ ।
dāju dārjīliṅgmā hunuhuncha.

३ दिदी महेन्द्र महाविद्यालयमा हुनुहुन्छ ।
didī mahendra mahāvidyālaymā hunuhuncha.

४ भोलि आमा र बुवा घरमा हुनुहुन्छ ।
bholi āmā ra buvā gharmā hunuhuncha.

५ परिवारमा दाजु-भाइ र दिदी-बहिनीहरू धेरै छन् ।
parivārmā dāju-bhāi ra didī-bahinīharū dherai chan.

7

१	... छैन ।	... chaina.
२	... हुनुहुन्न ।	... hunuhunna.
३	... हुनुहुन्न ।	... hunuhunna.
४	... हुनुहुन्न ।	... hunuhunna.
५	... छैनन् ।	... chainan.

8

१ प्रहरी थाना नजिक छैन, अलि टाढा छ ।
praharī thāna najik chaina, ali ṭāḍhā cha.

२ हो, हुलाक घर अलि टाढा छ ।
ho, hulāk ghar ali ṭāḍhā cha.

३ लजबाट बजार तीन किलोमीटर टाढा छ ।
lajbāṭa bajār tīn kilomīṭar ṭāḍhā cha.

४ बजारमा प्रहरी थाना, पसलहरू, हुलाक घर र बैंक छ ।
bajārmā praharī thānā, pasalharū, hulāk ghar ra baĩk cha.

५ प्रहरी थाना बजारमा छ ।
praharī thānā bajārmā cha.

६ सरस्वती मन्दिर बजारबाट तीन किलोमीटर टाढा छ ।
sarasvatī mandir bajārbāṭa tīn kilomīṭar ṭāḍhā cha.

9

नेपाली कक्षामा:
१ दसजना विद्यार्थीहरू छन् ।
२ पाँचजना अँग्रेजहरू छन् ।
३ दुईजना जर्मनहरू छन् ।
अँग्रेजी कक्षामा:
४ उन्नाइसजना विद्यार्थीहरू छन् ।
५ नौजना केटाहरू छन् ।
६ दसजना केटीहरू छन् ।

nepālī kakṣāmā:
  dasjanā vidyārthīharū chan.
  pā̃cjanā āgrejharū chan.
  duījanā jarmanharū chan.
āgrejī kakṣāmā:
  unnāisjanā vidyārthīharū chan.
  naujanā keṭāharū chan.
  dasjanā keṭīharū chan.

10

१ मसँग दस रुपियाँ र एक बट्टा चुरोट छ ।
masā̃ga das rupiyā̃ ra ek baṭṭā curoṭ cha.

२ हामीहरू तीन हप्तादेखि नेपालमा छौं ।
hāmīharū tīn haptādekhi nepālmā chaũ.

३ हुलाक घरमा दसजना लोग्ने-मान्छे, तीनजना आइमाई र पाँचजना केटा छन् ।
hulāk gharmā dasjanā logne-mānche, tīnjanā āimaī ra pā̃cjanā keṭā chan.

४ तपाईंसँग कति पैसा छ ?
tapāī̃saga kati paisā cha?

५ त्यो भारतीय मान्छेसँग पैसा छैन, तर नेपाली केटासँग दस रुपियाँ छ ।
tyo bhāratīya mānchesaga paisā chaina, tara nepālī keṭāsāga das rupiyā̃ cha.

६ धनी किसानसँग दस पाथी चामल र दस किलो आलु छ ।
dhanī kisānsāga das pāthī cāmal ra das kilo ālu cha.

७ हरेक टेबुलमा दुई कप चिया छ ।
harek ṭebulmā duī kap ciyā cha.

८ शिक्षकसँग किताब छैन र विद्यार्थीहरूसँग कलम छैन ।
śikṣaksāga kitāb chaina ra vidyārthīharūsāga kalam chaina.

11

भाइ शिक्षक हो ।	bhāi śikṣak ho.	भाइ घरमा छ ।	bhāi gharmā cha.
दिदी शिक्षक हुन् ।	didī śikṣak hun.	दिदी घरमा छिन् ।	didī gharmā chin.
भाइहरू शिक्षक हुन् ।	bhāiharū śikṣak hun.	भाइहरू घरमा छन् ।	bhāiharū gharmā chan.
दाज्यू शिक्षक हुनुहुन्छ ।	dājyū śikṣak hunuhuncha.	दाज्यू घरमा हुनुहुन्छ ।	dājyū gharmā hunuhuncha.
आमा शिक्षक हुनुहुन्छ ।	āmā śikṣak hunuhuncha.	आमा घरमा हुनुहुन्छ ।	āmā gharmā hunuhuncha.
म शिक्षक हुँ ।	ma śikṣak hũ.	म घरमा छु ।	ma gharmā chu.

12

1 एक हप्ता **ek haptā**
2 दुईजना मान्छे **duījanā mānche**
3 तीनवटा किताब **tīnvaṭā kitāb**
4 चारजना केटा **cārjanā keṭā**
5 पाँच रुपियाँ **pā̃c rupiyā̃**
6 छवटा मेच **chavaṭā mec**
7 सातजना आइमाई **sātjanā āimāī**
8 आठवटा कक्षा **āṭhvaṭā kakṣā**
9 नौ किलो **nau kilo**
10 दसजना विदेशी **dasjanā videśī**
11 दुई किलो **duī kilo**
12 साढे सात किलो **sāḍhe sāt kilo**
13 तीन पाथी **tīn pāthī**
14 अढाई माना **aḍhāī mānā**
15 तीन रुपियाँ पचहत्तर पैसा **tīn rupiyā̃ pacahattar paisā**
16 साढे नौ रुपियाँ **sāḍhe nau rupiyā̃**

13

१ रतनजीको आफ्नो मोटर छैन ।
Ratanjīko āphno moṭar chaina.
२ रातो मोटर रतनको होइन । रतनको साथीको हो ।
rāto moṭar Ratanko hoina. Ratanko sāthīko ho.
३ सुबीरको आफ्नो मोटर छैन ।
Subīrko āphno moṭar chaina.
४ सुबीरको दाज्यूको एउटा मोटर छ ।
Subīrko dājyūko euṭā moṭar cha.

14

१ धन बहादुरकी श्रीमतीका दुईजना दिदी छन् ।
Dhan Bahādurkī śrīmatīkā duījanā didī chan.
२ मेरो बुवा-आमा छैन ।
mero buva-āmā chaina.
३ मेरी आमाका चारजना नाति-नातिनी छन् ।
merī āmākā cārjanā nāti-nātinī chan.
४ उनीहरूको छोराछोरी छैन ।
unīharūko chorāchorī chaina.
५ वहाँका नौवटा गाई छन् ।
vahā̃kā nauvaṭā gāī chan.

६ हाम्रा पाँचवटा मोटा भैंसी छन् ।

  hāmrā pā̃cvaṭā moṭā bhaĩsī chan.

15

१ तिमी मेरो छोराको साथी हौ, होइन ? तिम्रो नाम गौतम हो ?

  timī mero chorāko sāthī hau, hoina? timro nām Gautam ho?

२ तिम्रो साथीको बुवाको नाम गणेश मान हो ? थाहा छ कि छैन ?

  timro sāthīko buvāko nām Gaṇeś Mān ho? thāhā cha ki chaina?

३ वहाँको नाम लक्ष्मी नाथ हो । त्यो मलाई थाहा छ ।

  vahā̃ko nām Lakṣmī Nāth ho. tyo malāī thāhā cha.

४ मेरो घर यहाँबाट टाढा छैन । तिम्रो घर कहाँ छ ?

  mero ghar yahā̃bāṭa ṭāḍhā chaina. timro ghar kahā̃ cha?

५ तपाईको बुवा बैंकमा हुनुहुन्छ । तपाईकी आमालाई थाहा छ ?

  tapāī̃ko buvā baĩkmā hunuhuncha. tapāī̃kī āmālāī thāhā cha?

६ उनीहरूका गाई हाम्रो खेतमा छन् । उनीहरूलाई थाहा छैन ?

  unīharūkā gāī hāmro khetmā chan. unīharūlāī thāhā chaina?

७ हाम्रो थर पोखरेल हो । हामी बाहुन हौं ।

  hāmro thar pokharel ho. hāmī bāhun haũ.

८ यो तिम्रो घडी होइन । मेरी आमाको हो ।

  yo timro ghaḍī hoina. merī āmāko ho.

16

मेरो नाम... हो । मेरो घर... मा छ । मेरो परिवारमा हामी... जना हौं:... ... ... र ... ।

  mero nām... ho. mero ghar... mā cha. mero parivārmā hāmī... janā
  haũ:... ... ... ra...

मेरी दिदीको नाम... हो । वहाँ... मा हुनुहुन्छ ।

  merī didīko nām... ho. vahā̃... mā hunuhuncha.

मेरी दिदीको श्रीमानको नाम... हो ।

  merī didīko śrīmānko nām... ho.

17

१ सूर्यका एकजना छोरा र एकजना छोरी छन् ।

  sūryakā ekjanā chorā ra ekjanā chorī chan.

२ प्रीतिको विचारमा सूर्यकी छोरी छ ।

  Prītiko vicārmā Sūryakī chorī cha.

३ सूर्यको छोराको नाम गिरीश हो ।

  Sūryako chorāko nām Girīś ho.

४ किताबमा गिरीशको नाम छ ।

  kitābmā Girīśko nām cha.

18

१ त्यस केटाका दुइटा घर छन् ।

tyas keṭākā duiṭā ghar chan.

२ यस ठूलो गाउँको एउटा चियापसल मात्रै छ ।

yas ṭhūlo gāū̃ko euṭā ciyāpasal mātrai cha.

३ उसका आठजना छोरी छन् ।

uskā āṭhjanā chorī chan.

४ उनका चारजना छोरा छन् ।

unkā cārjanā chorā chan.

५ यस मान्छेका धेरै साथीहरू छन् ।

yas mānchekā dherai sāthīharū chan.

६ कसको साथी छैन ?

kasko sāthī chaina?

19

१ आज हामी बजार जाँदैनौँ । घरमा एक रुपियाँ पनि छैन ।

२ राजु के काम गर्छ ? ऊ नेपाल राष्ट्र बैंकमा काम गर्छ । उसको दाजु पनि त्यहाँ काम गर्छ ।

३ तपाईं कहाँ बस्नुहुन्छ ? हिजोआज म काठ्माडौँमा बस्छु ।

४ तपाईंको भाइ ट्याक्सीबाट अफिस जान्छ ? होइन, ऊ बसबाट जान्छ ।

५ दार्जिलिङ्का मान्छेहरू धेरै जसो राम्रो नेपाली बोल्छन् ।

20

१ म हरेक दिन काठ्माडौँ जान्छु ।

२ उनीहरू धेरै जसो पोखरामा बस्छन् ।

३ तिमी सधैँ बुवाको पसलमा नेपाली बोल्छौ ।

४ हामीहरू हिजोआज रामको अफिसमा काम गर्छौँ ।

५ ऊ कहिल्यै पनि स्कूलमा अँग्रेजी बोल्दैन ।

६ त्यो मान्छे एक हप्तापछि लण्डन जान्छ ।

21

१ तपाईं सात बजे घरमा भात खानुहुन्छ ।

२ त्यो मान्छे बेलुका होटेलमा चिया खान्छ ।

३ वहाँहरू बिहिवार मकहाँ (मेरो घर) आउनुहुन्छ ।

४ यिनीहरू हप्ताको दुई पटक मन्दिर जान्छन् ।

५ यो केटी शनिवार साथीकहाँ (साथीको घरमा) सुत्छे ।

22

१ म दिउँसो दुई बजेदेखि छ बजेसम्म घरमा हुँदिन ।

२ तपाईं बुधवारदेखि शुक्रवारसम्म बिराटनगरमा हुनुहुन्न ।

३ उनीहरू मङ्गलवारदेखि बिहिवारसम्म काम गर्दैनन् ।

४ तिमी आठ बजेदेखि साढे दस बजेसम्म बाहिर जाँदैनौ ।

५ यिनीहरू दिउँसो एक बजेदेखि दुई बजेसम्म पढ्दैनन् ।

23

१ ए, त्यो मेचमा नबस, यो मेचमा बस ।

२ काठ्माडौंमा नेपाली बोल, अँग्रेजी नबोल ।

३ ठूलो रातो किताब पढ, अखबार नपढ ।

४ केटालाई एउटा स्याऊ देऊ, सुन्तला नदेऊ ।

५ छ बजे नआउनुहोस्, आठ बजेतिर आउनुहोस् ।

६ मलाई भन्नुहोस् तर उसलाई नभन्नुहोस् ।

७ यो कप लिनुहोस् र त्यो कप उसलाई दिनुहोस् ।

८ नेपाल जानुहोस् । त्यहाँ नेपाली बोल्नुहोस् ।

24

१ ती आइमाईहरू बिहिवार कहिल्यै पनि बजारमा आउँदैनन् । कहिले आउँछन् त ? उनीहरू धेरै जसो मङ्गलवार आउँछन् ।

२ विदेशीहरू काठ्माडौंबाट लुक्लासम्म हवाई जहाजमा जान्छन् । नेपालीहरू धेरै जसो बसबाट जिरीसम्म जान्छन् । जिरीबाट उनीहरू लुक्लासम्म हिंड्छन् ।

३ ती लोग्ने-मान्छेहरू कति बजे खेतमा जान्छन् ? उनीहरू आठ बजेतिर जान्छन् अनि तीन घण्टापछि फर्किन्छन् ।

४ म भोलिसम्म मात्रै नेपालमा बस्छु । भोलि बिहान साढे दस बजे म दिल्ली जान्छु । त्यसपछि म लण्डन जान्छु ।

५ राति आठ बजेपछि सबै पसल बन्द हुन्छन् । म तपाईको लागि अहिले बजार जान्नँ । म भोलि बिहान जान्छु, हुन्छ ?

६ तिमी मेरो लागि के काम गर्छौ ? म तपाईको लागि बजार जान्छु, हुन्छ ?

७ मेरी बहिनी कहिल्यै पनि परिवारको लागि खाना पकाउँदिन । कहिले काहीं दिदी पकाउनुहुन्छ, कहिले काहीं आमा पकाउनुहुन्छ ।

८ ऊ हरेक दिन स्कूल जान्छे, ऊ पनि जान्छ । तर उनीहरूको भाइ जाँदैन ।

25

१ लण्डन काठ्माडौंभन्दा ठूलो छ ।

२ अमेरिकनहरू धेरै जसो अँग्रेजहरूभन्दा धनी हुन्छन् ।

३ काठ्माडौं बेलायतबाट दिल्लीभन्दा टाढा छ ।

४ काठ्माडौं नेपालको सबभन्दा ठूलो शहर हो ।

५ सँसारको सबभन्दा गरीब देश कुन हो ?

६ नेपाली भाषाभन्दा सजिलो भाषा छैन ।

26

१ हजुरबालाई नीलो रँग मन पर्छ ।

२ मेरा दिदीहरूलाई कालो रँग मन पर्दैन ।

३ तपाईलाई हरियो रँग मन पर्छ ।

४ उसका भाइहरूलाई पहेँलो रँग मन पर्दैन ।

५ उनीहरूलाई प्याजी रँग मन पर्छ ।

27

१ तपाईहरू साँखुमा बस्नुहुन्छ ।

२ किनभने भोलि धेरै किनमेल छ अनि तपाई बालाई मदत गर्नुहुन्छ ।

३ मा कहिल्यै पनि काठमाडौं जानुहुन्न ।

४ घरमा मा घरको काम गर्नुहुन्छ र भात पकाउनुहुन्छ ।

५ बेलुका तपाईकी कान्छी बहिनी धारा जान्छे ।

६ किनभने उनीहरू इनारको पानी खान्छन् ।

28

१ झ्याल खोल्नुहोस् , यस कोठामा धेरै गर्मी भयो ।

२ हिजो बिहान बच्चाहरू सबै यहाँ थिए । तर आज कोही पनि स्कूल आएन ।

३ अस्ति बुधवार ठूलो पानी पऱ्यो । मसँग छाता थिएन अनि म भिजें ।

४ हजुरबाका दुईजना छोरा थिए । एकजनाको नाम संजु थियो, र एकजनाको नाम निरोज थियो । संजु धेरै धनी हुनुभयो तर निरोज धेरै गरीब हुनुहुन्थ्यो ।

५ त्यो देशका मानिसहरू धेरै गरीब थिए अनि उनीहरूका घरहरूमा केही पनि थिएन ।

६ हिजो धेरै मानिसहरू पशुपतिनाथको मन्दिर गए, किनभने हिजो पूर्णिमा थियो ।

29

१ हिजो तपाईले चिया खानुभएन ?

२ हिजो मैले एउटा किताब किनें ।

३ हिजो हामीहरूले मासु खाएनौं ।

४ हिजो उनीहरूले भात खाएनन् । उनीहरूको घरमा चामल थिएन ।

५ हिजो तिमीले रेडियो किन सुनेनौ ? हिजो अम्बर गुरुङ्गले गीत गाउनुभयो ।

६ हिजो आमा उठ्नुभएन । वहाँ बिरामी हुनुहुन्थ्यो ।

30

१ अस्ति शनिवार थियो ।

२ अस्ति ठूलो पानी पऱ्यो ।

३ उसले एउटा किताब पढ्यो ।

४ हिजो आइतबार थियो ।

५ हिजो राम अफिस गयो ।

६ हिजो रामकी आमा मन्दिर जानुभयो ।

७ राम र माया साढे छ बजेसम्म सुते ।

31

१ म नेपाल गएर तपाईलाई चिठी लेख्छु ।

२ म विचार गरेर तपाईलाई भन्छु ।

३ उनीहरू किताब किनेर तपाईकहाँ आउँछन् ।

४ यो केटी स्कूल गएर अँग्रेजी सिक्छे ।

५ म अफिस गएर तपाईलाई फोन गर्छु ।

६ वहाँ झापा गएर मेरो दाइको घरमा बस्नुभयो ।

32

१ तिमी घर गएर काम गर ।
२ तपाई रेडियो सुनेर घर जानुहोस् ।
३ तिमी चुरोट लिएर आऊ ।
४ तपाई यो किताब पढेर मलाई दिनुहोस् ।
५ तिमी लण्डन पुगेर मकहाँ आऊ ।
६ तपाई झापा गएर मेरो दाइको घरमा बस्नुहोस् ।

33

१ तपाई अखबार पढ्दै हुनुहुन्छ ?
२ भाइ किताब पढ्दै छ ।
३ म बाहिर जाँदै छु ।
४ उनीहरू नेपाली भाषा बोल्दै छन् ।
५ अब ऊ त्यही कलमले चिठी लेख्दै छ ।

34

१ बुवा अखबार पढ्दै हुनुहुन्थ्यो ।
२ तिमी त्यो किताब पढ्दै थियौ ?
३ म जापानी भाषा सिक्दै थिएँ ।
४ उनीहरू टी॰ भी॰ हेर्दै थिए ।
५ बुवा बारीमा के गर्दै हुनुहुन्थ्यो ?

35

उनका छोराहरूले भात नखाईकन चिठी लेखे ।
मेरी आमाले भात नखाईकन चिठी लेख्नुभयो ।
तिमीले भात नखाईकन चिठी लेख्यौ ।
रामेले भात नखाईकन चिठी लेख्यो ।
रामेकी दिदीले भात नखाईकन चिठी लेखिन् ।
मैले भात नखाईकन चिठी लेखें ।
उनका छोराहरू भात नखाईकन मन्दिर गए ।
मेरी आमा भात नखाईकन मन्दिर जानुभयो ।
तिमी भात नखाईकन मन्दिर गयौ ।
रामे भात नखाईकन मन्दिर गयो ।
रामेकी दिदी भात नखाईकन मन्दिर गइन् ।
म भात नखाईकन मन्दिर गएँ ।

36

१ पाइन्छ । दिल बहादुरको पसलमा तरकारी पाइन्छ ।
२ रातो आलुको दाम किलोको आठ रुपियाँ हो ।
३ सेतो आलुको दाम किलोको छ रुपियाँ हो ।
४ पाईंदैन । दिल बहादुरको पसलमा मासु पाईंदैन ।

५ मासु खिचापोखरीमा पाइन्छ ।
६ अञ्जलीलाई खुर्सानी चाहिंदैन ।

37

मान्छेहरूलाई पानी चाहिन्छ ।
मान्छेहरूलाई हावा चाहिन्छ ।
मान्छेहरूलाई घाँसपात चाहिंदैन ।
मान्छेहरूलाई शिक्षा चाहिन्छ ।
मान्छेहरूलाई बिजुली चाहिन्छ ।
भैंसीहरूलाई पानी चाहिन्छ ।
भैंसीहरूलाई हावा चाहिन्छ ।
भैंसीहरूलाई घाँसपात चाहिन्छ ।
भैंसीहरूलाई शिक्षा चाहिंदैन ।
भैंसीहरूलाई बिजुली चाहिंदैन ।

38

१ तपाईंलाई तिर्खा लाग्यो ।
२ दिदीलाई भोक लाग्यो ।
३ रामेकी बहिनीलाई दुःख लाग्यो ।
४ मेरो दाइलाई दिसा लाग्यो ।
५ बुवालाई थकाइ लाग्यो ।
६ तिमीलाई जाडो लाग्यो ।
७ हामीलाई रुघा लाग्यो ।
८ रामेलाई रक्सी लाग्यो ।
९ वहाँलाई डर लाग्यो
१० छोरालाई निद्रा लाग्यो ।
११ केटीलाई लाज लाग्यो ।
१२ मलाई खोकी लाग्यो ।

39

१ मलाई त्यो गीत मीठो लागेन ।
२ रामेकी आमालाई उसको गाउँ अनौठो लागेन ।
३ उनीहरूलाई जापानी भाषा गाह्रो लागेन ।
४ बुवालाई भारत राम्रो लागेन ।
५ मेरो भाइलाई नेपाली भाषा सजिलो लागेन ।

40

१ मलाई तिर्खा लागेन ।
२ मेरो भाइले एउटा किताब किन्यो ।
३ उसलाई मेरो घर राम्रो लाग्यो।
४ मेरी आमालाई थकाइ लाग्यो ।

५ हामीहरूले गीत गायौं ।

६ उसले दाहिने हातले भात खायो ।

७ वहाँलाई चार बजेतिर सधैं निद्रा लाग्छ ।

८ तपाईलाई पोखरा कस्तो लाग्यो ?

९ मलाई रक्सी लागेन ।

१० हामीले धेरै रक्सी खायौं ।

41

१ मेरो झ्यालबाट हिमालय देखिन्छ ।

२ मगर भाषा पोखरातिर बोलिन्छ ।

३ तपाईको स्वर यहाँ सुनिँदैन ।

४ तिम्रो गाउँ एक घण्टामा पुगिँदैन ।

५ भनिन्छ त्यो घरमा बोक्सी छ ।

६ भोटमा नेपाली भाषा कहिले काहीं बुझिन्छ ।

७ बिस्तारै हिंड्नुहोस् है । अब गाउँ सजिलै पुगिन्छ ।

८ तपाईको छोरासँग भेटेर मलाई खुशी लाग्यो । मलाई धेरै चलाक केटा जस्तो लाग्यो ।

42

१ दाजु दार्जीलिङ्ग जानुभएको छ ।

२ भाउज्यू काठ्माडौंमा बस्नुभएको छ ।

३ तपाईको घरमा कोही आयो ? तिम्रो भाइ आएको छ, तर ऊबाहेक कोही आएको छैन ।

४ पानी अहिलेसम्म उम्लेको छैन ।

५ मैले तिम्रो लुगा धोबीलाई दिएको छु ।

६ उसले पाँचवटा नयाँ किताब किनेको छ ।

43

१ अँ, जानुभयो । अहँ, जानुभएको छैन ।

२ अँ, आउनुभयो । अहँ, आउनुभएको छैन ।

३ अँ, आयो । अहँ, आएको छैन ।

४ अँ, खाएँ । अहँ, खाएको छैन ।

44

घडी न॰ १ मा एघार बज्यो ।

घडी न॰ २ मा साढे तीन बज्यो ।

घडी न॰ ३ मा पौने आठ बज्यो ।

घडी न॰ १ मा साढे दस बजेको छैन । एघार बजेको छ ।

घडी न॰ २ बाह्र बजेको छैन । साढे तीन बजेको छ ।

45

१ मेरो बुवा कहिल्यै पनि विदेश जानुभएको थिएन ।

२ १६७८ मा म पहिलो पटक नेपाल गएको थिएँ ।

३ उनीहरू बस बिसौनीमा बसेका थिए तर बस आएको थिएन ।

४ पानी परेको थियो तर रामेले छाता ल्याएको थिएन ।
५ उसको टाउको दुखेको थियो तर उसले औषधि खाएको थिएन ।
६ उनीहरू इलामबाट आएका थिए तर उनीहरूले चिया ल्याएका थिएनन् ।

46

१ मेरो भाइले आज पानी पर्दैन भनेर बुवालाई भन्यो ।
२ त्यो अग्लो मान्छेले तिमी अँग्रेज हो कि भनेर मलाई सोध्यो ।
३ आमाले तिम्रो साथीलाई भोक लाग्यो कि भनेर मेरी दिदीसँग सोध्यो ।
४ शिक्षकले किताबहरू बन्द गर भनेर बच्चाहरूलाई अह्लाउनुभयो ।
५ बुवाले भोलि बाहिर नजाऊ भनेर हामीलाई सल्लाह दिनुभयो ।

47

१ (तपाईंले) धेरै पिरो खाना खानुभएकोले तपाईंलाई दिसा लाग्यो ।
२ (वहाँको) पेट दुखेकोले वहाँ स्कूल जानुभएन ।
३ (बाहिर) गर्मी भएकोले हामी बाहिर जाँदैनौं ।
४ (ऊसँग) कलम नभएकोले उसले चिठी लेखेन ।
५ (उनको) श्रीमान बिरामी हुनुभएकोले उनलाई दुख लाग्यो ।

48

१ हिजो आएका पाहुनाहरू सबै अँग्रेज हुन् ।
२ बाहिर पानी परेको छ । तिमीले गएको हप्ता बजारमा किनेको छाता लिएर जाऊ ।
३ तिमी नेपाल पुगेको महिना बैसाख हो ।
४ म नेपाल आएको यो दसौं पटक हो ।
५ तपाईंहरू बस्नुभएको घर धेरै पुरानो छ ।
६ अस्ति शुक्रवार मैले तपाईंले लेख्नुभएको चिठी पाएको थिइनँ ।
७ ऊ भारतबाट आएको मान्छे (त) होइन ।
८ यो तिमीले आमालाई दिएको उपहार होइन ।

49

१ हिजो उनले उसले ताश खेलेको देखिन् ।
२ गएको महिना मैले उनले त्यो गीत गाएको सुनें ।
३ तीन दिन अघि उसले वहाँलाई घर आएको देख्यो ।
४ अस्ति बुधवार मैले तिमीले चुरोट खाएको देखें ।
५ गएको हप्ता वहाँले उनले हिन्दी बोलेको सुन्नुभयो ।
६ अस्ति उनीहरूले तिमीलाई स्कूल गएको देखे ।

50

१ अँग्रेजीमा पुल भनेको *bridge* हो ।
२ अँग्रेजीमा ओरालो भनेको *downhill* हो ।
३ अँग्रेजीमा हैजा भनेको *cholera* हो ।
४ नेपालीमा *letter* भनेको चिठी अथवा अक्षर हो ।

५ नेपालीमा *face* भनेको मुख अथवा अनुहार हो ।

६ नेपालीमा *month* भनेको महिना हो ।

51

१ बिहिवार, १० जनवरी १९२१

२ २०१६ साल चैत्र १० गते, मङ्गलवार

३ आइतवार, २६ नोवेम्बर १९५६

४ २०४२ साल फाल्गुण १ गते, शुक्रवार

52

१ सुरेन्द्रको दाइ जापान गएको दुई वर्ष भयो ।

२ सुरेन्द्रको दाइले जापानबाट एउटा राम्रो रेडियो पठाउनुभयो ।

३ दाइले दिएका क्यामेरा र रेडियो दुवै जापानमा बनेका हुन् ।त्यसै कारण बलिया र राम्रा छन् ।

४ सुरेन्द्रको काका दार्जीलिङ्गाट आउनुभएको थियो ।

५ सुरेन्द्रलाई एउटा क्यामेरा मात्रै चाहिन्छ ।

६ किनभने सुरेन्द्रले काकाले दिएको क्यामेरा एउटा साथीलाई बेचेको छ ।

53

१ यदि (तपाईलाई) थकाइ लाग्यो भने आराम गर्नुहोस् ।

२ यदि (तपाईलाई) तिर्खा लाग्यो भने यो पानी खानुहोस् ।

३ यदि हाम्रा पाहुनाहरूलाई भोक लाग्यो भने म बजार गएर फलफुल र तरकारी किन्छु ।

४ यदि तिमी भोलि आएनौ भने आमा घरै बसेर रुन्हुन्छ ।

५ यदि म पाँच बजेसम्म अफिसमा आइनँ भने मलाई मन्दिरमा भेट्नुहोस् ।

६ यदि यो हप्ता बुवाले मलाई चिठी पठाउनुभएन भने म वहाँलाई घरमा फोन गर्छु ।

54

१ हिजो आएका पर्यटकहरूलाई खानाले पुगेन ।

२ हामीलाई मदत गरेको शेर्पालाई खानाले पुग्यो ।

३ खाना पकाएकी आइमाईलाई दस रुपियाँले पुगेन ।

55

१ भोलि आउने पर्यटकहरूलाई खानाले पुग्दैन होला ।

२ हामीलाई मदत गर्ने शेर्पालाई दस रुपियाँले पुग्छ होला ।

३ खाना पकाउने आइमाईलाई एक किलो घिउले पुग्छ होला ।

56

१ भोलि मौसम साह्रै राम्रो होला ।

२ भोलि दिल्लीबाट काठमाडौं पुग्न दुई घण्टा जति लाग्ला ।

३ भोलि नानीहरू खेतमा फुटबल खेल्लान् ।उनीहरूको लुगामा हिलो लाग्ला ।

४ भोलि सीताले घर राम्रोसँग सफा गर्लिन् ।

५ भोलि दिदीले भात नपकाउलिन् दाइले पकाउलान् ।

६ भोलि घरमा पाहुनाहरू भएको कारणले उनीहरू स्कूल नआउलान् ।

57

लण्डनबाट नेपाल जान पाँच सय पाउण्ड लाग्छ र काठ्माडौं पुग्न पन्ध्र घण्टा लाग्छ । म विमानस्थलमा सधैं एउटा चाखलाग्दो किताब किन्छु । पोहोर साल नेपाल गएको बेलामा मैले एउटा मोटो उपन्यास किनें अनि त्यो पढ्न मलाई करीब दस घण्टा लाग्यो । म आउने साल फेरि नेपाल जान्छु होला अनि यस पालि चाहिं दुइटा उपन्यास किन्छु होला । नेपालमा म भद्रपुर गएँ । काठ्माडौंबाट बसमा जानुभयो भने एकदम सस्तो हुन्छ तर त्यहाँ पुग्न पूरै एक दिन लाग्छ । भद्रपुर जाने बसमा धेरै मान्छेहरू थिए अनि भद्रपुर जाने बाटो साह्रै खराब थियो । मैले त्यो यात्राको लागि कुनै किताब किन्निनँ किनभने म एक-दुईजना नेपाली साथीहरूसँग गएको थिएँ । तपाई भद्रपुर हवाई जहाजबाट जानुभयो भने धेरै पैसा लाग्छ तर समय धेरै लाग्दैन । भद्रपुर जाने हवाई जहाज हरेक बिहान दस बजे राजधानी छोड्छ । म अर्को साल फेरि भद्रपुर गएँ भने हवाई जहाजबाटै जान्छु होला ।

58

१ हामीले ईश्वरलाई पूजा गर्नुपर्छ ।
२ मेरो भाइले हरेक दिन दाल भात खानुपर्छ ।
३ आज बिदा हो, हामीहरूलाई अफिसमा जानुपर्दैन ।
४ उनीहरूले हामीलाई त्यो कथा सुनाउनुपर्दैन ।
५ सीताले घर सफा गर्नुपर्दैन । त्यो काम एउटा नोकरले गर्नुपर्छ ।
६ आज मैले भात पकाउनुपर्दैन । मेरो श्रीमानले पकाउनुपर्छ ।

59

१ अब बुवालाई पशुपतिनाथको मन्दिर जानुपर्‍यो ।
२ अब तिमीले अलिकति भात खानुपर्‍यो ।
३ अब मलाई चाँडै सुत्नुपर्‍यो ।
४ हिजो मैले धेरै काम गर्नुपरेन ।
५ हिजो किसानहरूलाई खेतमा जानुपरेन ।
६ हिजो आमालाई बजार जानुपरेन ।

60

१ आमाले मेरा साथीहरूलाई हाम्रो घरमा रक्सी खान दिनुहुन्न ।
२ उनीहरूले हामीलाई मन्दिरभित्र जान दिन्छन् ।
३ दाजुले बच्चाहरूलाई बिहान टी० भी० हेर्न दिनुहुन्छ ।
४ बुवाले हामीलाई बेलुका बाहिर जान दिनुहुन्न ।
५ तपाई पर्यटकहरूलाई मन्दिरमा जुत्ता लाउन दिनुहुन्छ ?

61

(A) यो कुन देवताको मन्दिर हो ? भित्र जान हुन्छ ?
(B) यो गणेशको मन्दिर हो । भित्र जान हुन्छ तर जुत्ता खोल्नुपर्छ ।
(A) यो धेरै पुरानो मन्दिर हो ?
(B) हो, धेरै पुरानो हो । मान्छेहरू हरेक दिन बिहान आएर गणेशको पूजा गर्छन् ।
(A) उनीहरूलाई हरेक बिहान किन आउनुपर्छ ?
(B) आउनैपर्दैन तर हरेक दिन यहाँ आउनु राम्रो हो । तपाईले हरेक दिन गणेशको पूजा

गर्नुभयो भने तपाईंको दिन सफल हुन्छ । त्यो हाम्रो एउटा विश्वास हो ।
(A) अब मैले के गर्नुपर्छ त ?
(B) तपाईंले भगवानको दर्शन गर्नुभयो, राम्रो भयो । मन्दिरको लागि अलिकति पैसा दिनुहोस् ।
(A) मसँग त्यति पैसा छैन । तर दस रुपियाँ दिन हुन्छ होला ?
(B) हुन्छ, ठीक छ । ल, आउनुहोस्, ढिलो भयो । अब हामीलाई पशुपतिको मन्दिर जानुपर्छ । त्यति टाढा छैन । हिंडेर आधा घण्टामा पुगिन्छ ।
(A) पशुपतिको मन्दिरमा कुन देवताको पूजा हुन्छ ?
(B) त्यहाँ शिवजीको पूजा हुन्छ ।

62

१ म नेपाली बोल्न सक्छु ।
२ म नेपाली खाना पकाउन सक्छु ।
३ म यो किताब बुझ्न सक्छु ।
४ उनी नेपाली बोल्न सक्छिन् ।
५ उनी नेपाली खाना पकाउन सक्छिन् ।
६ उनी यो किताब बुझ्न सक्छिन् ।
७ तपाईं नेपाली बोल्न सक्नुहुन्छ ।
८ तपाईं नेपाली खाना पकाउन सक्नुहुन्छ ।
९ तपाईं यो किताब बुझ्न सक्नुहुन्छ ।

63

१. उसले हिजो सगरमाथा चढ्न पायो ।
२. उसले हिजो फोन गर्न पायो ।
३. उसले हिजो गुन्द्रुक खान पायो ।
४. उनीहरूले हिजो सगरमाथा चढ्न पाए ।
५. उनीहरूले हिजो फोन गर्न पाए ।
६. उनीहरूले हिजो गुन्द्रुक खान पाए ।
७. तिमीले हिजो सगरमाथा चढ्न पायौ ।
८. तिमीले हिजो फोन गर्न पायौ ।
९. तिमीले हिजो गुन्द्रुक खान पायौ ।

64

दुई हप्ता अघि मेरी दिदीको बिहा भयो । अहिले वहाँ धुलिखेलमा बस्नुहुन्छ । धुलिखेल भक्तपुरबाट झण्डै दस माइल टाढा छ । अस्ति आइतवार हामीहरू भिनाज्यू र दिदीको नयाँ परिवारलाई भेट्न गएका थियौं । धुलिखेल जान (लाई) हामीहरूले रत्न पार्कसम्म ट्याक्सी लिनुपर्‍यो । रत्न पार्कमा पाँचखाल जाने बस चढ्नुपर्‍यो । धुलिखेल पाँचखाल जाने बाटोमा पर्छ । रत्न पार्क पुगेपछि बुवालाई एउटा पसलमा जानुपर्‍यो । वहाँले उपहार किन्न बिर्सनुभएको थियो । पहिलो पटक कसैको घरमा जाँदा (-खेरि) उपहार दिनुपर्छ । बुवालाई लुगा, मिठाई र चुरा किन्न तीनवटा पसलमा जानुपर्‍यो । अलि ढिलो हुन लागेकोले आमालाई अलि चिन्ता लाग्न थाल्यो । धुलिखेल पुग्न एक घण्टा मात्रै लाग्छ

भन्ने कुरा हामीलाई थाहा थिएन । बसहरू एक एक घण्टामा छुट्छन् भन्ने कुरा पनि हामीलाई थाहा थिएन । बुवाले उपहारहरू किन्नुभएपछि हामीहरूले धुलिखेल जाने बस खोज्न थाल्यौं । एउटा नयाँ नीलो बसको छेउमा उभिएको मान्छे पाँचखाल पाँचखाल भनेर कराउन थालेको थियो । बुवा हाम्रो टिकट किन्न अफिसमा जानुभयो । बुवा टिकट लिएर फर्किनुभन्दा पहिला नै यो बस धुलिखेल जाने हो कि भनेर मैले चालकलाई सोधें । जाने हो भनेर उसले भन्यो । धुलिखेल नजाने कुरै छैन किनभने त्यहाँ राम्रो होटेल छ भनेर उसले भन्यो । धुलिखेलबाट पाँचखालको लागि बस जानुभन्दा पहिला नै सबै यात्रुहरू बिहानको खाना त्यहीं खान्छन् भनेर भन्यो । अकस्मात पानी पर्न थाल्यो अनि हामीले बसभित्र बस्ने ठाउँ पायौं । केही मिनेटपछि हाम्रो यात्रा सुरु भयो ।

65

१ नेपालीहरू तराई क्षेत्रलाई मदेस भन्छन् ।

२ नेपाली भाषाबाहेक तराई क्षेत्रमा मैथिली, भोजपुरी, अवधी, थारु र अन्य भाषाहरू बोलिन्छन् ।

३ पहाडी क्षेत्रको जमीन प्राय जसो उकालो र ओरालो हुन्छ ।

४ नेपाली भाषाबाहेक पहाडी क्षेत्रमा नेवारी, गुरुङ्ग, मगर, लिम्बू, तामाङ्ग र राई जस्ता भोट- बर्मेली भाषाहरू बोलिन्छन् ।

५ नेपालका नदीहरूमध्ये कर्णाली, गण्डकी र कोशी महत्त्वपूर्ण छन् ।

६ घर पुग्नलाई धेरै जसो नेपालीहरूले हिंड्नैपर्छ ।

66

१ यस गाउँका किसानहरू धान रोप्दैनथे । उनीहरू मकै रोप्थे ।

२ भात खाएपछि हामीले हात-मुख धुनुपर्थ्यो ।

३ चियापसलमा चिया पनि पाइन्थ्यो, खाने कुरा पनि पाइन्थ्यो ।

४ तिमी भारत गएर के काम गर्थ्यौ ? म चौकिदारको काम गर्थें ।

५ दाइहरू जुम्लामा बस्नुहुन्थ्यो, दैलेखमा बस्नुहुन्थ्यो ।

६ म हरेक हप्ता उसलाई एउटा लामो चिठी लेख्थें ।

67

म पनौती भन्ने एउटा सानो शहरमा मेरो बुवा-आमासँग बस्थें । पनौती काठ्माडौं उपत्यकाको दक्षिण-पूर्व कुनामा पर्छ । म त्यहाँको एउटा सानो स्कूलमा पढ्थें । म एघार वर्ष पुग्नेबित्तिकै मैले त्यो सानो स्कूल छाड्नुपर्‍यो । त्यो बेलादेखि मैले भक्तपुर भन्ने शहरको एउटा ठूलो स्कूलमा पढ्नुपर्‍यो । मैले हरेक बिहान सात बजे बस लिनुपर्थ्यो । मेरा धेरै जसो साथीहरू त्यही बसबाट जान्थे । साँझमा फर्किंदाखेरि हामीहरू गीत गाउँथ्यौं अनि पनौती आइपुगेपछि धेरै खुशी हुन्थ्यौं । मेरो घरभन्दा तल एउटा ठूलो नदी थियो । गर्मीको महिनामा घर पुग्नेबित्तिकै हामी त्यो नदीमा पौडी खेल्न जान्थ्यौं । कहिले काहीं मेरा स्कूलका लुगाहरू भिज्थे अनि आमा रिसाउनुहुन्थ्यो । म घर आउनेबित्तिकै वहाँले ती लुगा धुनुपर्थ्यो अनि सुकाउन गाह्रो हुन्थ्यो । तर शनिवार बिदा भएको कारणले आमा मलाई शुक्रवार पौडी खेल्न दिनुहुन्थ्यो । भक्तपुरको ठूलो स्कूलमा पढ्दाखेरि मैले ठूलो

भएपछि शिक्षक बन्ने निधो गरें । शिक्षक बन्ने आशाले मैले राम्ररी पढें । स्कूल छाड्नेबित्तिकै म त्रिभुवन विश्वविद्यालयमा पढ्न गएँ अनि हिजोआज म काठ्माडौंमा बस्छु । केही दिनपछि मैले मेरो अन्तिम परिक्षा दिनुपर्छ । अझै पनि मेरो शिक्षक बन्ने आशा छ । परिक्षामा सफल भएँ भने एउटा जागिर खोज्नुपर्ला ।

68

१ तपाईंको छोरा चाँडै निको होस् ।
२ भोलि हामीहरू फिलिम हेर्न पोखरा जाऔं ?
३ हामीहरू तपाईंकी आमालाई के भनौं ?
४ तपाईंको जिन्दगी सुखी होस् ।
५ आजको बस ढिलो नहोस् ।
६ म तपाईंकहाँ कति बजे आऊँ ?

69

१ मलाई भोक लागेको भए म खपाखप भात खान्थें ।
२ पानी नपरेको भए उनीहरू भात खान आउँथे ।
३ पहाडमा खोलाहरू नभएको भए हाम्रो घरमा बिजुली हुँदैनथ्यो ।
४ बेलामा औषधि खाएको भए त्यो मान्छे अकालै मर्दैनथ्यो ।
५ साथीले गीत गाएको भए बेलुका झन रमाइलो हुन्थ्यो ।

1 If I had been hungry I would have eaten voraciously.
2 If it had not rained they would have come for a meal.
3 If there were no streams in the hills there would not be electricity in our house.
4 If he had taken the medicine on time that man would not have died young.
5 If a friend had sung a song the evening would have been even more enjoyable.

70

आज केही चिनेका मान्छेहरू हाम्रो घरमा साँझ छ बजेतिर खाना खान आउँदै छन् । म चार बजे विश्वविद्यालयबाट घर फर्किन्छु त घर रित्तै रहेछ ! अनि झोलामा साँचो छ कि भनेर हेर्छु त झोला पनि रित्तै रहेछ । साँचो कहाँ गयो होला त ? म सबै ठाउँमा खोज्छु तर पाउँदिन । भान्से साढे तीन बजे आउनुपर्थ्यो तर अहिलेसम्म आएको छैन । शायद घरमा त आइसकेको होला तर पसलतिर गयो होला । घरमा चार बजेसम्म बसेको भए त यो समस्या आउने थिएन । झ्याल फोडेर भित्र जाऊँ कि ? विश्वविद्यालयमा फर्केर अफिसमा गएर साँचो खोजूँ कि ? खै, के गरूँ ? ल भान्से पनि आइपुगेछ । साँचो उसको हातमा रहेछ । मैले झ्याल फोडेको भए मेरो श्रीमानले मलाई गाली गर्नुहुन्थ्यो । सवा चार बजिसकेछ । ऊ मेरो लागि ढोका खोलिदिन्छ । श्रीमानलाई फोन गरेर अलिक छिटो घर आउनुहोस् भनूँ कि ? खै, के गरूँ ? पर्दैन होला । भान्सेले सबै कुरा किनेर ल्याएको छ अनि हामीलाई खाना पकाइदिन्छ ।

71

१ उनीहरू जाँड-रक्सी धेरै पिइरहेका थिए ।

२ गोपाल राम्रा राम्रा गीत गाइरहेका थियो ।

३ मेरो भाइ टाढाको एउटा स्कूलमा गइरहेको छ ।

४ खैरेनीबाट काठ्माडौंमा धेरै तरकारी आइरहेको छ ।

५ म यहाँबाट कीर्तिपुरसम्म हिँडेर गइरहेको थिएँ ।

72

१ भोक नलागे म खाजा नखाउँला ।

२ थकाइ लागे म आराम गरूँला ।

३ काठ्माडौं छाडेर जान मन नलागे काठ्माडौंमै बसुँला ।

४ नेपाली सिक्न गाह्रो लागे र हिन्दी सिक्न पनि गाह्रो लागे जापानी सिकुँला ।

५ गुन्द्रुक मीठो नलागे र आलु-तामा पनि मीठो नलागे कालो दाल खाउँला ।

73

म हिजो दाइसँग विमानस्थल गएँ । दिल्लीबाट हामीकहाँ बस्न केही पाहुनाहरू आइरहेका थिए । बिहानै हामीहरूले आर॰ एन॰ ए॰ सी॰ अफिसमा फोन गरेका थियौं अनि एउटी आइमाईले दिल्लीबाट विमान दिउँसो तीन बजे आइपुग्छ भनेर भनेकी थिइन् । त्यसो भए हामीलाई ठीक साढे दुई बजे घर छोड्नुपर्छ भनेर दाइले भन्नुभयो । विमानस्थलमा पुग्नेबित्तिकै दाइले विमानको बारेमा त्यहाँको कर्मचारीसँग सोध्नुभयो । मौसम खराब भएकोले विमान भरखरै मात्रै दिल्लीबाट उड्यो भनेर कर्मचारीले दाइलाई भन्यो । त्यसो भए हामीहरूलाई कति बेरसम्म पर्खनुपर्ला भनेर दाइले सोध्नुभयो । अब नेपालतिर उडिरहेको छ एक घण्टाभित्र आइपुग्छ भनेर कर्मचारीले भने । हवाई जहाज ढिलो भयो र हामीलाई यहाँ पर्खनैपर्ला भनेर दाइले भन्नुभयो । तर बुवा-आमा घरमा पर्खिरहनुभएको छ भनेर मैले भनें, हवाई जहाज ढिलो भएको कुरा वहाँहरूलाई थाहा छैन नि । तिमी गएर वहाँहरूलाई फोन गर भनेर दाइले भन्नुभयो । हामीहरू हवाई जहाज आइपुगेपछि घर सीधै आउँछौं भनेर भनिदेऊ ।

NEPALI–ENGLISH GLOSSARY

Words marked * are transitive verbs.

अ

अँ	yes
अँग्रेज	English
अँग्रेजी	English language
अँध्यारो	dark, darkness
अकालै	untimely
अक्षर	letter of alphabet
अखबार	newspaper
अग्लो	tall, high
अघि	ago, before
अचार	pickle
अझ पनि	yet, still
अञ्चल	administrative zone
अटाउनु	to fit into a space
अढाई	two and a half
अथवा	or
अदुवा	ginger
अधिकृत	official
अधिराज्य	kingdom
अनि	and, then
अनिकाल	famine
अनुचित	inappropriate
अनुभव	experience
अनुमति	permission
अनुसार	according to
अनुहार	face
अनौठो	strange, odd
अन्तिम	final, last
अपढ	illiterate
अपराध	crime, offence
अप्ठ्यारो	difficult, awkward
अफिस	office
अब	now, from now
अबेर	late, lateness
अभाव	lack, absence
अभ्यास गर्नु *	to practise
अमेरिकन	American
अम्बा	guava
अम्रीकन	American
अरब	Arabia; the Middle East
अरू	other, more
अर्को	another, next
अर्थ	meaning
अलपत्र	untidy
अलि	quite, rather
अलिक	slightly
अलिकति	a small amount of
अलिपछि	after a little while
अवधी	Awadhi (language)
अवश्य	certainly
असफल	unsuccessful
असल	of good character
असाध्य	extremely, very
असार (आषाढ)	third month of the Nepali year
असुविधा	inconvenience
असोज (आश्विन)	sixth month of the Nepali year

अस्ति	the day before yesterday; last week	**इ**	
		इच्छा	wish, desire
अस्पताल	hospital	इतिहास	history
अहँ	no	इनार	well
अहिले	now	इमान	honour
अहिलेसम्म	yet	इस्लामी	Islamic
अह्राउनु *	to order, command		
		ई	
आ		ईश्वर	the Lord; God
आँखा	eye		
आँगन	courtyard	**उ**	
आँप	mango	उकालो	uphill; steep
आँसु	tear, tears	उकुस-मुकुस	feeling of suffocation
आइतवार	Sunday	उखान	proverb
आइपुग्नु	to arrive	उचाइ	height
आइमाई	woman	उच्चारण	pronunciation
आउनु	to come	उठ्नु	to get up
आकाँक्षा	ambition	उड्नु	to fly
आकाश	sky	उता	there, over there
आखिर	in the end, after all	उत्तर	north
आगो	fire	उदाहरण	example
आज	today	उनी	s/he (Middle)
आजकाल	nowadays	उनीहरू	they (Middle)
आठ	eight	उपत्यका	valley
आठौं	eighth	उपन्यास	novel
आत्मा	soul	उपयोगी	useful
आदर गर्नु *	to respect	उपहार	gift
आधा	half	उपाय	means
आफु	oneself	उभिनु	to be standing up
आफै	oneself (emphasised)	उमाल्नु *	to boil
आफ्नो	one's own	उमेर	age
आमा	mother	उम्लनु	to come to the boil
आराम, आरामै	in good health	उसरी	in that manner
आराम गर्नु *	to rest	उसो	in that manner
आलु	potato	उहाँ	see वहाँ
आलु-तामा	potatoes and bamboo shoots	**ऊ**	
		ऊ	s/he (Low)
आवश्यक	necessary	**ए**	
आशा	hope	ए	hey, oh

एउटा	one, a
एक	one
एकदम	absolutely
एकनाले	single-barrelled
एकमात्र	one and only
एक्लै	alone

ओ

ओढ्ने	quilt
ओत	shelter from rain
ओरालो	downhill; steep

ओ

औंला	finger, toe
औलो	malaria
औषधि	medicine

क

कक्षा	class
कण्डक्टर	conductor
कता	where? to where?
कता-न-कता	somewhere or other
कति	how many? how much?
कतिजना	how many people?
कतिवटा	how many things?
कतै	anywhere
कत्रो	how big?
कथा	story
कप	cup
कपडा	cloth
कपाल	hair (of the head)
कफी	coffee
कम	rarely, less, few
कमलपित्त	jaundice
कमिज	shirt
कम्तिमा	at least
कम्मर	waist
कराउनु	to shout, make a loud noise
करीब	approximately

करोड	ten million
कलकल	sound of running water
कलम	pen
कलिलो	young, tender
कलेज	college
कल्पना गर्नु *	to imagine
कविता	poem, poetry
कसको	whose?
कसरी	in what manner? how?
कसो?	in what manner? how?
कस्तो	like what? how?
कहाँ?	where?
-कहाँ	at the home of
कहिले?	when?
कहिले काहीं	sometimes
कहिल्यै पनि	ever
कहीं	somewhere
काँक्रो	cucumber
काँटा	fork
काँध	shoulder
काउली	cauliflower
काका	younger paternal uncle
कागत	paper
कागती	lime
काट्नु *	to cut, to kill
कार्तिक (कार्त्तिक)	seventh month of the Nepali year
कान	ear
कान्छी	youngest girl
कान्छो	youngest boy
काम	work
काम गर्नु *	to work
कारण	reason
कार्यक्रम	programme
कालो	black

काहिंलो	fourth eldest	-को दाँजोमा	compared with
कि	or	कोदो	millet
किताब	book	-को लागि	for
किन	why?	कोशिश गर्नु *	to try
किनभने	because	कोस	approximately two miles
किनमेल	shopping		
किन्नु *	to buy	कोसेली	gift
किलो	kilogramme	क्यामेरा	camera
किलोमिटर	kilometre	क्यारे	I guess, I suppose
किल्ली	stick	क्षमा	forgiveness
किसान	farmer	क्षमा गर्नु *	to forgive
किसिम	type, kind	क्षेत्र	area, region
कीरा	insect, worm		
कुखुरा	chicken		
कुन	which?		
कुनचाहिं	which one?		
कुन्नि	I don't know		
कुरसी	chair		
कुरा	thing, matter, talk		
कुरा गर्नु *	to talk, converse		
कुरुवा	a measure of weight equal to two **mānās**		

ख

खतम गर्नु *	to stop
कुर्कुच्चा	heel	खतम हुनु	to end
कुर्नु	to wait for	खतरा	danger
कुवाँ	well	खपाखप खानु *	to gobble up
कुहिनो	elbow	खबर	news
कृपा	kindness, favour	खबर गर्नु *	to inform
के	what?	खबरदार	beware!
केन्द्र	centre	खराब	bad
केटा	boy	खल्ती	pocket
केटी	girl	खसाल्नु *	to drop, post (a letter)
केरा	banana		
केही	some, something	खसी	gelded goat
केही-न-केही	something or other	खस्नु	to fall; die
को	who?	खाइनु	to be eaten
कोट	coat	खाक	ash
कोठा	room	खाजा	snack, light meal
		खाना	food
		खानु *	to eat, drink, consume
		खाने कुरा	food
		खाली	empty, only
		खास	special, particular
		खिंच्नु *	to pull, take a photograph
		खुकरी	kukri knife

खुट्टा	leg, foot	गाग्री	water pitcher
खुर्सानी	chilli pepper	गाडी	car, wheeled vehicle
खुल्नु	to open	गाली गर्नु *	to tell off
खुवाउनु *	to feed	गाह्रो	difficult, hard
खुशी	happy, happiness	गीत	song
खूब	very, thoroughly	गुनासो	complaint
खेत	irrigable field	गुन्दुक	a traditional dish
खेती	farming, agriculture		made from dried
खेतीपाती	farming, agriculture		vegetables
खेल	game	गुरु	guru, teacher
खेल्नु *	to play	गुरुङ	Gurung (an
खै	well! what about?		ethnic group)
खैरो	brown	गोजी	pocket
खोइ	well! what about?	गोलभेंडा	tomato
खोकी	cough	गौचर	cow pasture
खोजी	search		
खोज्नु *	to seek; try to	**घ**	
खोला	river, stream	घटना	incident, event
खोला-नाला	rivers and streams	घडी	watch, clock
खोल्नु *	to open	घण्टा	hour, bell
		घर	house, home
ग		घरपति	landlord
गजब	wonder, amazement	घाँटी	thoat, neck
गट्टा खेल्नु *	to play a game	घाट	steps beside river
	with pebbles	घाँस	grass
गणित	mathematics	घाम	sunshine
गते	day of a month	घिउ	ghee (clarified butter)
	in the Bikram	घुँडा	knee
	calendar	घुमाउरो	indirect
गफ गर्नु *	to chat, converse	घुम्नु	to turn, travel
गरीब	poor		
गर्नु *	to do	**च**	
गर्मी	heat	चकु	knife
गहना	jewellery	चढ्नु	to climb, mount
गह्रुँगो	heavy	चना	chickpea
गाइड	guide	चन्द्रमा	moon
गाइने	minstrel	चम्चा	spoon
गाउँ	village	चराउनु *	to take to graze
गाउनु *	to sing	चर्को	hot, loud

चर्पी	lavatory
चलाउनु *	to cause to move, drive
चल्नु	to move, go, function
चाँडै	quickly, immediately, early
चाँदी	silver
चानचुन	small change
चामल	uncooked rice
चार	four
चारौं	fourth
चाहनु *	to want to
चाहिनु	to be wanted, needed
चिउँडो	chin
चिउरा	parched beaten rice
चिठी	letter
चिनापर्ची	acquaintance
चिनियाँ	Chinese
चिनी	sugar
चिन्ता गर्नु *	to worry
चिन्नु *	to recognise, be acquainted with
चिप्लो	slippery
चिया	tea
चियापसल	teashop
चिया-सिया	tea and snacks
चिसो	cold, damp
चीन	China
चुरोट	cigarette
चूल्हो	stove, hearth
चैत (चैत्र)	twelfth month of the Nepali year
चोखो	pure, unsullied
चोटि	turn, time
चौकिदार	watchman, guard
चौथाई	one quarter
च्याउ	mushroom

छ

छक्क पर्नु	to be surprised
छर्लङ्ग	clearly
छाड्नु *	to leave, quit
छाता	umbrella
छाती	breast, chest
छाम्नु *	to feel with the hand
छायाँ	shade from the sun
छाला	skin
छिमेक	neighbourhood
छिमेकी	neighbour
छिटै	quickly
छिटो	quick, fast
छिन	moment
छुट्टिनु	to split, bifurcate
छुट्टी	time off work
छेउ	side
छैटौं	sixth
छोटो	short, brief
छोरा	son
छोराछोरी	sons and daughters
छोरी	daughter

ज

जंगल	jungle; uninhabited land
जटिल	complicated, difficult
जताततै	everywhere
जति	approximately, as much as
जन-संख्या	population
जन्म	birth
जन्मनु	to be born
जन्मस्थल	birthplace
जमीन	land
जम्मा	all together, in total
जम्मा हुनु	to gather, assemble
जर्मन	German
जलाउनु *	to burn

जवाफ	reply, answer
जसरी	in a similar manner to
जसो	in a similar manner to
जस्तो	similar to
जाँच	examination
जाँच्नु *	to examine
जाँड-रक्सी	alcoholic drink
जागिर	salaried job
जाडो	cold, coldness
जात	species, type, caste
जानिनु	to be known
जानु	to go
जान्नु *	to know
जिन्दगी	life
जिब्रो	tongue
जिल्ला	district
-जी	honorific suffix added to names
जीवन	life
जीवन-जल	diarrhoea remedy
जुत्ता	shoe, shoes
जूठो	impure, sullied, polluted
जे	that which
जेठ (ज्येष्ठ)	second month of the Nepali year
जेठो	eldest, elder
जोई	wife
जोर	pair
ज्यादा	more
-ज्यू	honorific suffix added to names

झ

झण्डै	almost
झन्	even more
झर्नु	to descend
झिक्नु *	to take out, extract
झिसमिसे	very early morning
झोला	bag
झ्याल	window

ट

टाउको	head
टाढा	distant, far
टिकट	ticket, postage stamp
टिप्नु *	to pick up
टी॰भी॰	TV
टुङ्गिनु	to come to an end
टुङ्च्याउनु *	to bring to an end
टुप्लुक्क	suddenly, out of nowhere
टूरिष्ट	tourist
टेक्नु *	to stand, set down, rest upon
टेबुल	table
टोक्नु *	to bite
टोपी	hat
टोल	town quarter
ट्याक्सी	taxi
ट्रक	truck

ठ

ठट्टा गर्नु *	to joke
ठाउँ	place
ठीक	fine, OK
ठूलो	big
ठेगाना	address

ड

डढ्नु	to scorch, burn
डर	fear
डलर	dollar
डाँडा	hill ridge
डाँफे	monal pheasant
डाक्टर	doctor

डाक्नु *	to summon, call for
डेढ	one and a half
डेरा	rented accommodation

ढ

ढिलो	slow, late, slack
ढोका	door, gate
ढोल	drum

त

तैँ	you (Low)
त	but, though, however
तपाई	you (High)
तयार	ready
तयार गर्नु *	to prepare
तर	but
तरकारी	vegetables
तराई	the Tarai region
तरुनी	young woman
तर्नु	to cross
तल	below, downwards
तलतल	craving
तथा	and
ताक्नु *	to take aim
तातो	hot
तामाङ्ग	Tamang (an ethnic group)
तारीख	day of a month in the Western calendar
ताल्चा	door lock
ताश	cards
तिनी	s/he (Middle)
तिमी	you (Middle)
तिम्रो	your
-तिर	towards, near, at about
तिर्खा	thirst

तिर्नु *	to pay
ती	they, those
तीन	three
तीर्थस्थल	place of pilgrimage
तुरुन्त, तुरुन्तै	immediately
तेरो	your
तेल	oil, fuel
तेस्रो	third
त्यति	that much
त्यसरी	in that manner
त्यसो	in that manner
त्यस्तो	like that
त्यहाँ	there
त्यही	that very
त्यो	that

थ

थकाइ	tiredness
थप्नु *	to add, refill
थर	family name
थाक्नु	to become tired
थारु	Tharu (an ethnic group)
थाल्नु *	to begin, start to
थाहा	knowledge, information
थाहा पाउनु *	to find out
थियो	was
थुप्रै	lots of, heaps of
थोक	thing, matter

द

दक्षिण	south
दरबार	palace
दराज	drawer
दर्जा	class
दर्शन	sight, vision
दशक	decade
दस	ten
दसैँ	Dasain festival

दसौं	tenth
दही	yoghurt
दाँत	tooth
दाइ	elder brother
दाउरा	firewood
दाजु	elder brother
दाज्यू	elder brother
दाढी	beard
दाम	price
दाल	lentils
दालभात	lentils and rice
दाह-सँस्कार	funeral ceremony
दाहिने	right
दिउँसो	afternoon, daytime
दिदी	elder sister
दिन	day
दिनभरि	all day
दिनु *	to give
दिसा	diarrhoea
दुइटा	two (with non-human nouns)
दुई	two
दुईनाले	double-barrelled
दुःख	sadness, pain, trouble
दुःखी	sad, suffering
दुख्नु	to hurt
दुब्लो	thin
दुलहा	bridegroom
दुलही	bride
दुबै	both
दूध	milk
दूरदर्शन	Indian television service
दृश्य	view
देखाउनु *	to show
-देखि	from, since
देखिनु	to be seen, be visible

देख्नु *	to see
देब्रे	left
देवर	husband's younger brother
देवता	god, deity
देवी	goddess
देश	country
दोबाटो	crossroads
दोस्रो	second
दौड्नु	to run
-द्वारा	by

ध

धनी	rich
धन्दा मान्नु *	to worry
धन्यवाद	thank you
धर्म	religion, righteousness
धर्मावलम्बी	religious adherent
धान	growing rice
धारा	spring, watersource
धुनु *	to wash
धुम्रपान	smoking
धुवाँ	smoke
धूमधाम	pomp, splendour
धेरै	very, many
धेरै जसो	usually, mostly
धोबी	washerman
ध्यान दिनु *	to pay attention
ध्वनी	sound

न

न	negative particle
नंग	fingernail
नक्सा	map
नगर पालिका	municipality, town council
नजिक	close, nearby
नत्र	otherwise

नदी	river	नेपालीभाषी	Nepali-speaker
नमस्कार	word of greeting	-नेर	near to
नमस्ते	word of greeting	नेवार	Newar (an
नयाँ	new		ethnic group)
नरमाइलो	unpleasant	नोकर	servant
नराम्रो	bad	नोट	note
नवौं	ninth	नौ	nine
नाक	nose	नौनी	butter
नागरिक	citizen	न्यानो	warm
नाति	grandson		
नातिनी	granddaughter	**प**	
नातेदार	relative	पकाउनु *	to cook
नानी	small child	पक्का	ripe, firm, proper
नाफा गर्नु *	to make a profit	पछि	after, later
नाम	name	-पछि	after
नि	you know;	पटक	turn, time
	what about?	पटक्कै	not even a little
निकाल्नु *	to take out, extract	पठाउनु *	to send
निको	well, healthy	पढाउनु *	to teach
निक्कै	very, extremely	पढे-लेखेको	educated
निचोर्नु *	to press, squeeze	पढ्नु *	to read, study
निदाउनु	to fall asleep	पण्डित	Pandit; a traditional
निद्रा	sleep, sleepiness		scholar
निधो गर्नु *	to decide	पता लगाउनु *	to find out
निबुवा	lemon	पत्याउनु *	to believe
निम्तो	invitation	पत्रिका	magazine
निम्त्याउनु *	to invite	पनि	also, even
नियम	rule	पप सँगीत	pop music
निराश	without hope	पर	beyond, on the
निर्वाण	Nirvana		other side of
निश्चय गर्नु *	to decide	परम्परा	tradition
निस्कनु	to emerge, come out	परिवार	family
नीलो	blue	पर्खनु	to wait
नुहाउनु	to bathe	पर्नु	to fall
नुहाउने कोठा	bathroom	पर्यटक	tourist
नून	salt	पर्व	festival
नेपाल भाषा	Newari (language)	पर्सि	the day after
नेपाली	Nepali		tomorrow
		पल्लो	next, further

पल्ट	turn, time	पाल्नु *	to rear, keep
पल्टनु	to lie down		(livestock)
पशु	animal	पासपोर्ट	passport
पश्चिम	west	पाहुना	guest
पसल	shop	पिउनु *	to drink
पस्नु	to enter	पिकनिक	picnic
पहाड	hill	पिठचूँ	back
पहाडी	of the hill region	पिन्सन	pension
पहिरो	landslide	पिरो	spicy
पहिला	previously, before, ago	पीपल	pipal tree
पहिलो	first	पीर गर्नु *	to worry, be troubled
पहेंलो	yellow	पुग-न-पुग	almost
पाँच	five	पुगिनु	to be reached
पाँचौं	fifth	पुग्नु *	to be enough,
पाइनु	to be acquired,		suffice
	be available	पुग्नु	to arrive
पाइलट	pilot	पुजारी	priest
पाइला	footstep, footprint	पुण्य	religious merit
पाइला टेक्नु *	to take a step	पुरानो	old
पाउण्ड	pound	पुर्खा	ancestor
पाउनु *	to get, acquire,	पुल	bridge
	be able to,	पुस्तक	book
	manage to	पुस्तकालय	library
पाकिस्तानी	Pakistani	पुस्ता	generation
पाक्नु	to ripen, be cooked	पूजा गर्नु *	to worship
पाखा	hillside	पूरा	whole
पाखुरा	upper arm	पूर्णिमा	full-moon day
पाठ	lesson	पूर्व	east
पाठ गर्नु *	to recite	पूस (पौष)	ninth month of
पाठच पुस्तक	textbook		the Nepali year
पाथी	measure of quantity	पेट	stomach
	or volume equal to	पैसा	money; one hundredth
	eight **mānās**		of one rupee
पानी	water, rain	पोई	husband
पार गर्नु *	to cross	पोल्नु *	to burn
-पारि	on the far side of	पोहोर	last year
पालन गर्नु *	to maintain, foster	पौडी खेल्नु *	to swim
पाला	heyday, turn, time	पौने	less one quarter

प्याक गर्नु *	to pack	फिलिम	film
प्याज	onion	फुकाल्नु *	to untie, take off
प्याजी	purple	फुटबल	football
प्रगति	progress	फुर्सद	spare time
प्रजातन्त्र	democracy	फुल	egg
प्रदेश	state	फुल पार्नु *	to lay an egg
प्रधान मन्त्री	prime minister	फुल्नु	to flower, bloom
प्रवचन	lecture, speech	फूल	flower
प्रशस्त	plentiful	फूलकोपी	cauliflower
प्रश्न	question	फेला पर्नु	to be found
प्रहरी	police, police officer	फोक्सो	lung
प्रहरी थाना	police station	फोटो	photograph
प्राचीन	ancient	फोन गर्नु *	to make a phone call
प्रान्त	province	फोहोर	dirty
प्राय जसो	mostly, usually		
प्रारम्भ हुनु	to commence	**ब**	
प्रिय	dear		
प्रियजन	dear people	बगर	riverbank
प्रीति	love	बगैंचा	garden
प्रेम	love	बग्नु	to flow
प्रेमिका	girlfriend	बच्चा	child
		बजाउनु *	to play a musical instrument
फ		बजार	bazaar, marketplace
		बजे	at... o'clock
फरक	difference	बज्यै	grandmother
फर्कनु	to return	बट्टा	packet
फर्काउनु *	to cause to return	बढी	more
फर्किनु	to return	बढ्नु	to increase, advance
फर्सी	pumpkin		
फलफुल	fruit	बत्ती	lamp, light, electricity
फल्नु	to flower		
फाइदा	benefit	बनाउनु *	to make, mend
फागुन (फाल्गुण)	eleventh month of the Nepali year	बन्द	shut
		बन्द गर्नु *	to shut
फाड्नु *	to smash, break open	बन्द हुनु	to be closed
		बन्दा कोपी	cabbage
फिरिरि	rippling	बन्दोबस्त	arrangements
फिर्ता दिनु *	to give back	बन्दूक	gun
फिर्ता लिनु *	to take back		

बन्नु	to become	बिचरा	unfortunate
बयान	account, description	बिजी	busy
बर्मा	Burma	बिजुली	electricity
बलियो	strong	बिताउनु *	to spend (time)
बल्ल	eventually, at last	बिदा	holiday, time off
बल्ल बल्ल	eventually, at last		work, leave
बस	bus	बियर	beer
बस चढ्नु	to board a bus	बिरलै	rarely, seldom
बसाइँ सर्नु	to move home	बिरामी	sick, ill
बस्ती	settlement, village	बिरालो	cat
बस्नु	to reside, sit	बिसन्चो	unwell
	down, stay	बिर्सनु *	to forget
बहिनी	younger sister	बिसिंनु	to be forgotten
बाँकि	left over,	बिस्कुट	biscuit
	remaining	बिस्तारै	slowly, carefully
बाँदर	monkey	बिहा	wedding, marriage
बा	father	बिहा गर्नु *	to marry
बाखा	goat	बिहान	morning
बाघ	tiger	बिहिवार	Thursday
बाजि	turn, time	बीच	between
बाजे	grandfather	बीचबाटोमा	on the way, en route
-बाट	from, by	बुझिनु	to be understood
बाटो	road, path, way	बुइनु *	to understand
बाठो	clever, smart	बुधवार	Wednesday
बादल	cloud	बुवा	father
बाबु	little boy	बूढा	old man, husband
बारम्बार	repeatedly	बूढी	old woman, wife
बारी	dry field	बूढी औंला	thumb
बालुवा	sand	बुढो	old, aged
बाल्यकाल	childhood	बेंसी	valley floor
बास	lodging	बेच्नु *	to sell
बास बस्नु	to lodge for a night	बेर	time
बासी	stale	बेला	time, occasion
बाहिर	outside	बेलायत	Britain, England
बाहुन	Brahmin	बेलुका	evening
बाहेक	except for, apart from	बेस	better, good
बिगार्नु *	to spoil	बैंक	bank
बिग्रनु	to be spoiled,	बैसाख (वैसाख)	first month of
	go to the bad		the Nepali year

बोकाउनु *	to cause to carry
बोक्नु *	to carry
बोट	tree
बोतल	bottle
बोलाउनु *	to call, invite
बोलिनु	to be spoken
बोल्नु *	to speak
बौद्ध	Buddhist
ब्याटरी	battery

भ

भगवान	God
भटमास	soybean
भट्टी पसल	inn
भदौ (भाद्र)	fifth month of the Nepali year
भनाइ	statement, utterance
भनिनु	to be said, be called
भन्ज्याङ्ग	pass, col
-भन्दा	than
-भन्दा अगाडि	before, in front of
-भन्दा अघि	before
-भन्दा तल	below
-भन्दा पर	beyond
-भन्दा पहिले	before
-भन्दा माथि	above
भन्नु *	to say, tell
भन्सार	Customs
भरखर, भरखरै	recently, just now
भरसक	as far as possible
-भरि	throughout, filling
भरिया	porter
भरे बेलुका	this evening
भर्ति	recruitment, enrolment
भर्नु *	to fill
भाँडा	pot, vessel
भाइ	younger brother

भाइ टीका	a special day on which women and girls anoint their brothers
भाउज्यू	elder brother's wife
भाग	share, portion
भाग्नु	to run away, escape
भात	cooked rice; a meal
भान्सा-कोठा	kitchen
भान्से	cook
भारत	India
भारतीय	Indian
भारी	load
भाषा	language
भाषण	speech, lecture
भिज्नु	to become wet
भित्ता	interior wall
भित्ते-घडी	wall clock
भित्र	within, inside
भिर्नु *	to strap on
भिसा	visa
भीड	crowd
भुई	ground
भूगोल	geography
भूटान	Bhutan
भूत	ghost
भूस्वर्ग	heaven on earth
भेक	area, district
भेट	meeting, encounter
भेट्नु	to meet
भेट्टाउनु *	to find, locate
भोक	hunger
भोको	hungry
भोगौलिक	geographical
भोजपुरी	Bhojpuri (language)
भोट	Tibet
भोट-बर्मेली	Tibeto-Burman

भोटिया	*Tibetan*	माघ	*tenth month of*
भोलि	*tomorrow*		*the Nepali year*
भ्रमण	*tour*	माछा	*fish*
		माइन्नु *	*to scrub, scour*
म		मातृभाषा	*mother tongue*
म	*I*	मात्र, मात्रै	*only*
मकै	*maize, corn*	माथि	*above, up*
मङ्गलवार	*Tuesday*	माना	*a measure: 0.7*
मङ्सीर (मार्गशीर्ष)	*eighth month of*		*litres or 20 ounces*
	the Nepali year	मानिस	*person*
मट्टीतेल	*kerosene*	मान्छे	*person*
मतलब	*meaning*	मान्नु *	*to agree, accept,*
मदत गर्नु *	*to help*		*believe*
मदेस	*Tarai (region)*	माफ गर्नु *	*to forgive*
मध्यरात	*midnight*	माफी दिनु *	*to forgive*
मध्य	*mid-*	माया	*love, affection*
मध्यान्न	*midday*	माया गर्नु *	*to love*
-मध्ये	*among*	माया मार्नु *	*to forget a friend*
मन	*heart, mind*	मासु	*meat*
मन पराउनु *	*to like*	मास्टर	*schoolmaster*
मन पर्नु	*to be liked*	माहिंलो	*second eldest*
मन लाग्नु	*to want to*	मिटर	*metre*
मनाउनु *	*to celebrate*	मिठाई	*sweets*
मन्त्रालय	*ministry*	मित्र	*friend*
मन्त्री	*minister*	मिनेट	*minute*
मन्दिर	*temple*	मिरमिरे	*very early in the*
मर्नु	*to die*		*morning*
मर्मस्पर्शी	*touching, moving*	मिलाउनु *	*to arrange,*
महंगो	*expensive*		*assemble,*
महत्त्वपूर्ण	*important*		*adjust, bring*
महल	*palace*		*together, sort out*
महाराजाधिराज	*His Majesty the King*	मिल्नु	*to come together,*
महाविद्यालय	*college*		*match, fit, get along*
महिना	*month*	मीठो	*good-tasting*
-मा	*in*	मुख	*face, mouth*
मा	*mother*	मुख्य	*main, principal*
माइत	*woman's natal home*	मुटु	*heart*
माइल	*mile*	मुठा	*bunch*
माग्नु *	*to ask for*		

मुरी	measure of weight or quantity equal to 20 **pāthīs**
मुश्किल	difficult, difficulty
मूर्ख	fool
मूला	radish
मूसा	mouse
मृग	deer
मृत	dead, deceased person
मेच	chair
मेरो	my, mine
मैथिली	Maithili (language)
मैलो	dirty
मोक्ष	salvation, deliverance
मोटर	motorcar
मोटो	fat
मोल	value, price
मोहर, मोहोर	a half-rupee
मौसम	weather

य

यता	here, in this direction
यति	this much
यती	Yeti
यसपालि	this time
यसरी	in this manner
यसो	in this manner
यस्तो	like this
यहाँ	here
यहीं	right here
यातायात	transport
यात्री	traveller, pilgrim
याद	memory
यिनी	s/he (Middle)
यी	they, these
युवती	young woman
युवा	young man

यूरोप	Europe
यो	this
योजना	plan

र

र	and
रँग	colour
रक्सी	liquor
रगत	blood
रमाइलो	pleasant, enjoyable
रमाइलो गर्नु *	to enjoy oneself
रहर	strong desire
राई	Rai (ethnic group)
राख्नु *	to put, keep
राङ्गो	a male buffalo
राजधानी	capital
राजनैतिक	political
राजमार्ग	national highway
राजा	king
राज्य	kingdom
राणा	Rana
राति	at night
रातो	red
रानी	queen
रामतोरियाँ	okra
राम्रो	good, nice
रायो	mustard
राष्ट्र	nation
राष्ट्रपति	president
राहदानी	passport
रिक्शा	rickshaw
रिजर्वेशन	reservation
रिन	debt
रिसाउनु	to be angry
रुक्नु	to stop
रुघा	head cold
रुघा-खोकी	cold and cough
रुचि	appetite
रुनु	to cry

रुपियाँ	rupee	लानु *	to take away
रूख	tree	लामो	long
रूमाल	handkerchief	लिनु *	to take
रे	particle indicating that the information imparted by the speaker comes from another source	लिम्बू	Limbu (ethnic group)
		लुगा	clothing, clothes
		लुगा-फाटा	clothes
		-ले	by, because of, due to
रेडियो	radio		
रेल	train	लेख्नु *	to write
रेष्टुराँ	restaurant	लोग्ने	husband
रेसम	silk	लोग्ने-मान्छे	man
रोक्नु *	to stop	लोटा	metal water pot
रोटी	bread	लौ	there! you see!
रोपाइँ	the planting of a crop	ल्याउनु *	to bring
रोप्नु *	to plant		

ल

व

ल	there!	वन	forest
लखतरान	exhausted	वर्ष	year
लगाउनु *	to put on	वर्षात	monsoon rain
लज	lodge	वहाँ	s/he (High)
लसून	garlic	वहीं	right there
लाइन	line, queue	वाक्य	sentence
-लाई	to, for, at	वातावरण	atmosphere, environment
लाउनु *	to wear		
लाख	one hundred thousand	वार	day of the week
		वालेट	wallet
लाखौं	hundreds of thousands	वास्तवमा	really, actually
		विचार	opinion
लाग्नु	to be felt, affect, seem, apply, begin, cost, take time, be imposed, head for, set in	विचार गर्नु *	to consider, think about
		विज्ञान	science
		विदेश	abroad, a foreign country
		विदेशिनु	to go abroad
		विदेशी	foreign, foreigner
लाज	embarrassment, shame	विद्यार्थी	student
		विद्यालय	school
लाटो	stupid	विभाग	department

विमान	flight
विमानस्थल	airport
विरह	loneliness
विशेष	special, particular
विश्व-युद्ध	world war
विश्वविद्यालय	university
विश्वास गर्नु *	to believe, trust
व्यवसाय	occupation
व्यवहार	behaviour
व्याकरण	grammar
व्यापार	trade
व्यापारी	trader

श

शताब्दी	century
शनिवार	Saturday
शब्द	word
शरीर	body
शहर	city, town
शाकाहारी	vegetarian
शान्त	peaceful
शान्ति	peace
शायद	perhaps
शासन	rule, regime
शिक्षक	teacher
शिक्षा	education
शिखर	mountain peak
शिवरात्री	Shivarati festival
शिवालय	Shiva temple
शील्ड	shield
शुक्रवार	Friday
शुभकामना	good wishes
शुभनाम	given name
शुरु गर्नु *	to start
शुरु हुनु	to begin
शेर्पा	Sherpa (ethnic group)
श्रीमती	wife
श्रीमान	husband

स

-सँग	with
सँग-सँगै	together
सँगीत	music
संरक्षण	conservation
संवत	calendrical era
सँसार	world
सकिनु	to finish
सक्नु	to be able to
सगरमाथा	Mount Everest
सघाउनु *	to help, to assist
सजिलो	easy
सडक	street, road
सधैँ	always
सन्चो	in good health
सन्तान	offspring
सपना	dream
सफल	successful
सफा	clean
सफा गर्नु *	to clean
सब	all
समतल	level, flat
समस्या	problem
समाचार	news
समाचार पत्र	newspaper
समाप्त	finished
सम्झना	memory
सम्झनु *	to remember
सम्झाउनु *	to remind, counsel
सम्पादक	editor
सम्भावना	possibility
-सम्म	up to, as far as, until
सम्मान	honour, respect
सय	hundred
सरकार	government
सरकारी	governmental

सरस्वती	Saraswati (goddess)	सिकाउनु *	to teach
सर्वनाश	disaster	सिकिस्त	gravely
सल्काउनु *	to set light to	सिक्किम	Sikkim
सल्लाह	advice	सिक्नु *	to learn
सवा	plus one quarter	-सित	with
ससुराली	wife's parents' home	सिद्धिनु	to end
सस्तो	cheap	सिद्ध्याउनु *	to finish
सस्तोमा	cheaply	सिनेमा-घर	cinema
सहयोग गर्नु *	to help	सिपाही	soldier
साँचो	true	सिमसिमे पानी	light rain
साँचो	key	सिमाना	border
साँझ	dusk	सिमी	bean
साँस्कृतिक	cultural	सिलसिला	series, sequence
साइकल	bicycle	सीट	seat
साउन (श्रावण)	fourth month of	सीधै	directly, straight
	the Nepali year	सुँगुर	pig
साग	greens	सुँघ्नु *	to sniff, smell
साट्नु *	to exchange (money)	सुईं-सुईं	the sound of the wind
साढे	plus one half	सुका	a quarter rupee
सात	seven	सुखी	happy
सातौं	seventh	सुझाव	suggestion
साथी	friend, companion	सुत्नु	to sleep; lie down
सानो	small	सुत्ले कोठा	bedroom
साबुन	soap	सुदूर	remote, very distant
सामान	luggage	सुनाउनु *	to relate, tell
सारङ्गी	Nepali violin	सुन्दर	beautiful
सारी	sari; a woman's dress	सुन्दरी	beautiful (woman)
साल	year	सुनिनु	to be heard,
साली	wife's younger		be audible
	sister	सुन्तला	orange
साहिंलो	third eldest	सुन्नु *	to hear, listen
साहित्य	literature	सुरक्षित	secure, protected
साहू	merchant; business	सुविधा	convenience
	proprietor	सेतो	white
साहेब	term used to	सेलाउनु	to cool down
	address a	सोच्नु *	to think
	professional	सोध्नु *	to ask
साह्रै	extremely	सोफा	sofa

Nepali	English
सोमवार	Monday
स्कूल	school
स्थापना	establishment
स्थिति	situation, circumstances
स्नान गर्नु *	to bathe
स्याउ	apple
स्वर	voice
स्वर्ग	heaven
स्वस्थ	healthy
स्वाद	taste, flavour
स्वादिलो	tasty
स्वास्थ्य	health
स्वास्नी	wife
स्वास्नी-मानिस	woman

ह

Nepali	English
हगि	right?, isn't that so?
हजार	thousand
हजारौं	thousands of
हजुर	sir, yes
हजुर?	pardon?
हजुरआमा	grandmother
हजुरबा	grandfather
हडताल	strike
हतपत	hurry
हतार	hurry
हप्ता	week
हराउनु	to be lost
हरियो	green
हरेक	every
हवाई जहाज	aeroplane
हाँक्नु *	to drive (a vehicle)
हाँस्नु	to smile, laugh
हाकिम	boss
हाड	bone
हात	hand, arm
हातमुख	hands and face
हानीकारक	harmful
हामी, हामीहरू	we
हाम्रो	our, ours
हालखबर	news
हावा	wind, air
हिउँ	snow
हिजो	yesterday
हिंडेर जानु	to go on foot
हिंड्नु	to walk, set out
हितैषी	well-wisher
हिन्दी	Hindi
हिन्दीभाषी	Hindi-speaker
हिन्दुस्तानी	Indian
हिन्दू	Hindu
हिमाल	the Himalayas
हिमाली	Himalayan
हिलो	mud
हिसाब गर्नु *	to add up
हीरा	diamond
हुलाक घर	post office
हुनु	to be
हेर्नु *	to look
होचो	short-statured
होटेल	hotel
होश गर्नु *	to be careful
है	do you hear?, OK?
हैजा	cholera

ENGLISH–NEPALI GLOSSARY

about (time)	-तिर	**-tira**	bank	बैंक	**baīk**
about (quantity)	करीब	**karīb**	become	बन्नु	**bannu**
abroad	विदेश	**videś**	before	-भन्दा अघि	**-bhandā**
acquire	पाउनु	**pāunu**			**aghi**
advice	सल्लाह	**sallāh**	begin	शुरु गर्नु,	**śuru garnu,**
advise	सल्लाह दिनु	**sallāh dinu**		शुरु हुनु	**śuru hunu**
after	-पछि	**-pachi**		लाग्नु, थाल्नु	**lāgnu,**
afternoon	दिउँसो	**diũso**			**thālnu**
age	उमेर	**umer**	belief	विश्वास	**viśvās**
ago	अघि, पहिले	**aghi, pahile**	below	तल	**tala**
airport	विमानस्थल	**vimānsthal**	big	ठूलो	**ṭhūlo**
alcohol	रक्सी	**raksī**	black	कालो	**kālo**
all	सब, सबै	**sab, sabai**	blue	नीलो	**nīlo**
allow	दिनु	**dinu**	board (vb)	चढ्नु	**caḍhnu**
always	सधैं	**sadhaĩ**	boil (vb)	उम्लनु	**umlanu**
angry, to be	रिसाउनु	**risāunu**	book	किताब	**kitāb**
anyone	कोही	**kohī**	born, to be	जन्मनु	**janmanu**
apple	स्याउ	**syāu**	boy	केटा	**keṭā**
arrive	पुग्नु, आइपुग्नु	**pugnu,**	Brahmin	बाहुन	**bāhun**
		āipugnu	break	फोड्नु	**phoḍnu**
ask	सोध्नु	**sodhnu**	bridge	पुल	**pul**
at home	घरै, घरमा	**gharai,**	bring	ल्याउनु	**lyāunu**
		gharmā	brother, elder	दाइ	**dāi**
			brother, younger	भाइ	**bhāi**
bad	खराब, नराम्रो	**kharāb,**	buffalo	भैंसी	**bhaĩsī**
		narāmro	bus	बस	**bas**
bag	झोला	**jholā**	bus station	बस बिसौनी	**bas bisaunī**
bangle	चूरा	**cūra**	buy	किन्नु	**kinnu**

English	Nepali	Roman
capital	राजधानी	rājdhānī
cards	ताश	tāś
central	मध्य	madhya
chair	मेच	mec
cheap	सस्तो	sasto
children	बच्चाहरू	baccāharū
Chinese	चिनियाँ	ciniyā̃
cholera	हैजा	haijā
cigarette	चुरोट	curoṭ
city	शहर	śahar
class	कक्षा	kakṣā
clean	सफा	saphā
clever	चलाक	calāk
climb (vb)	चढ्नु	caḍhnu
close	बन्द गर्नु	banda garnu
cloth	कपडा	kapaḍā
clothes	लुगा	lugā
cold	चिसो	ciso
coldness	जाडो	jāḍo
colour	रँग	rãg
come	आउनु	āunu
cook (n)	भान्से	bhānse
cook (vb)	पकाउनु	pakāunu
corner	कुना	kunā
cough	खोकी	khokī
country	देश	deś
cow	गाई	gaī
cry	रुनु	runu
cup	कप	kap
daughter	छोरी	chorī
day	दिन	din
day before yesterday	अस्ति	asti
decide	निधो गर्नु	nidho garnu
deity	देवता	devatā
Delhi	दिल्ली	dillī
diarrhoea	दिसा	disā
difficult	गाह्रो, अप्ठ्यारो	gāhro, apṭhyāro
dirty	मैलो	mailo
distant	टाढा	ṭāḍhā
door	ढोका	ḍhokā
downhill	ओरालो	orālo
drink	खानु, पिउनु	khānu, piunu
driver	ड्राइभर	ḍrāibhar
dry (vb)	सुकाउनु	sukāunu
each	हरेक	harek
easily	सजिलोसँग	sajilosãga
east	पूर्व	pūrva
easy	सजिलो	sajilo
eat	खानु	khānu
embarrassment	लाज	lāj
empty	रित्तो	ritto
English	अँग्रेज	ãgrej
evening	बेलुका	belukā
Everest	सगरमाथा	sagarmāthā
exam	जाँच	jā̃c
expensive	महंगो	mahãgo
eye	आँखा	ā̃khā
face	मुख, अनुहार	mukh, anuhār
family	परिवार	parivār
family name	थर	thar
farmer	किसान	kisān

English	Nepali	Transliteration	English	Nepali	Transliteration
fat	मोटो	**moṭo**	half	आधा	**ādhā**
father	बुवा, बा	**buvā, bā**	happiness	खुशी	**khuśī**
fear	डर	**ḍar**	he (High)	वहाँ	**vahā̃**
field	खेत, बारी	**khet, bārī**	he (Low)	ऊ	**ū**
find	पाउनु	**pāunu**	he (Middle)	उनी	**unī**
finish	सिद्धचाउनु	**siddhyāunu**	head	टाउको	**ṭāuko**
first	पहिलो	**pahilo**	head cold	रुघा	**rughā**
flight	विमान	**vimān**	heard, to be	सुनिनु	**suninu**
food	खाना, भात	**khānā,**	heat	गर्मी	**garmī**
		bhāt	help	मदत गर्नु	**madat**
foreigner	विदेशी	**videśī**			**garnu**
forget	बिर्सनु	**birsanu**	here	यहाँ	**yahā̃**
Friday	शुक्रवार	**śukravār**	Himalaya	हिमालय	**himālaya**
friend	साथी	**sāthī**	holiday	बिदा, छुट्टी	**bidā, chuṭṭī**
from	-देखि, -बाट	**-dekhi,**	home	घर	**ghar**
		-bāṭa	hope	आशा	**āśā**
fruit	फलफूल	**phalphūl**	hot	गर्म, तातो	**garm, tāto**
			hotel	होटेल	**hoṭel**
Ganesh	गणेश	**gaṇeś**	hour	घण्टा	**ghaṇṭā**
German	जर्मन	**jarman**	house	घर	**ghar**
get	पाउनु	**pāunu**	how much?	कति ?	**kati?**
ghee	घिउ	**ghiu**	how, like what?	कस्तो ?	**kasto**
gift	उपहार,	**upahār,**	how, in what		
	कोसेली	**koselī**	manner?	कसरी ?	**kasarī**
girl	केटी	**keṭī**	hunger	भोक	**bhok**
give	दिनु	**dinu**	hurt	दुख्नु	**dukhnu**
go	जानु	**jānu**	husband	श्रीमान, लोग्ने	**śrīmān,**
god	देवता	**devatā**			**logne**
good	राम्रो	**rāmro**			
granddaughter	नातिनी	**nātinī**	I	म	**ma**
grandfather	हजुरबा	**hajurbā**	in	-मा	**-mā**
grandmother	हजुरआमा	**hajurāmā**	India	भारत	**bhārat**
grandson	नाति	**nāti**	Indian	भारतीय	**bhāratīya**
green	हरियो	**hariyo**	inside	-भित्र	**-bhitra**
guest	पाहुना	**pāhunā**	interesting	चाखलाग्दो	**cākhlāgdo**

English	Nepali	Roman	English	Nepali	Roman
Japanese	जापानी	**jāpānī**	morning	बिहान	**bihāna**
job	जागिर	**jāgir**	mother	आमा, मा	**āmā, mā**
journey	यात्रा	**yātrā**	motorcar	मोटर	**moṭar**
			my	मेरो	**mero**
Kathmandu	काठ्माडौं	**kāṭhmāḍaũ**			
key	साँचो	**sãco**	name	नाम	**nām**
kilogramme	किलो	**kilo**	nearby	नजिक	**najik**
king	राजा	**rājā**	never	कहिल्यै पनि	**kahilyai**
knowledge	थाहा	**thāhā**			**pani**
			new	नयाँ	**nayã**
language	भाषा	**bhāṣā**	newspaper	अखबार	**akhbār**
last (previous			next day	भोलिपल्ट	**bholipalṭa**
week)	अस्ति	**asti**	nice	राम्रो	**rāmro**
last (year)	पोहोर	**pohor**	night	राति	**rāti**
last (final)	अन्तिम	**antim**	north	उत्तर	**uttar**
late	ढिलो	**ḍhilo**	novel	उपन्यास	**upanyās**
lateness	अबेर	**aber**	now	अहिले, अब	**ahile, aba**
letter	चिठी	**ciṭhī**	nowadays	हिजोआज	**hijoāja**
liquor	रक्सी	**raksī**			
live	बस्नु	**basnu**	o'clock	बजे	**baje**
lodge	लज	**laj**	office	अफिस	**aphis**
London	लण्डन	**laṇḍan**	official	अधिकारी	**adhikārī**
lose	हराउनु	**harāunu**	old	पुरानो	**purāno**
			open (adj)	खुला	**khulā**
man	लोग्ने-मान्छे	**logne-**	open (vb)	खोल्नु	**kholnu**
		mānche	opinion	विचार	**vicār**
many	धेरै	**dherai**	orange	सुन्तला	**suntalā**
market	बजार	**bajār**	order	अह्राउनु	**ahrāunu**
marry	बिहा गर्नु	**bihā garnu**	our	हाम्रो	**hāmro**
meat	मासु	**māsu**	outside	बाहिर	**bāhira**
meet	भेट्नु	**bheṭnu**	own	आफ्नो	**āphno**
mile	माइल	**māil**			
Monday	सोमवार	**somvār**	packet	बट्टा	**baṭṭā**
money	पैसा	**paisā**	passport	पासपोर्ट	**pāsport**
month	महिना	**mahinā**	pen	कलम	**kalam**

people	मान्छेहरू	**māncheharū**	river	खोला, नदी	**kholā, nadī**
person	मान्छे	**mānche**	road	बाटो	**bāṭo**
phone	फोन	**phon**	room	कोठा	**koṭhā**
pick up	उठाउनु	**uṭhāunu**	rupee	रुपियाँ	**rupiyā̃**
place	ठाउँ	**ṭhāū̃**			
plane	हवाई जहाज	**havāī jahāj**	sadness	दुःख	**duḥkh**
play	खेल्नु	**khelnu**	said, to be	भनिनु	**bhaninu**
Pokhara	पोखरा	**pokharā**	Saturday	शनिवार	**śanivār**
police	प्रहरी	**praharī**	say	भन्नु	**bhannu**
police station	प्रहरी थाना	**praharī thānā**	school	स्कूल	**skūl**
			search	खोज्नु	**khojnu**
poor	गरीब	**garīb**	see	देख्नु	**dekhnu**
post office	हुलाक घर	**hulāk ghar**	seen, to be	देखिनु	**dekhinu**
potato	आलु	**ālu**	send	पठाउनु	**paṭhāunu**
pound	पाउण्ड	**pāuṇḍ**	she (High)	वहाँ	**vahā̃**
present	उपहार,	**upahār,**	she (Low)	ऊ	**ū**
	कोसेली	**koselī**	she (Middle)	उनी	**unī**
problem	समस्या	**samasyā**	Shiva	शिव	**śiva**
purple	प्याजी	**pyājī**	shoes	जुत्ता	**juttā**
			shop	पसल	**pasal**
question	प्रश्न	**praśna**	since	-देखि	**-dekhi**
quit	छाड्नु	**chāḍnu**	sing	गाउनु	**gāunu**
quite	अलि	**ali**	sister, elder	दिदी	**didī**
			sister, younger	बहिनी	**bahinī**
rain	पानी	**pānī**	sister-in-law	भाउजु, बुहारी	**bhāuju,**
reached, to be	पुगिनु	**puginu**			**buhārī**
read	पढ्नु	**paḍhnu**	sleep	निद्रा	**nidrā**
receive	पाउनु	**pāunu**	sleep	सुत्नु	**sutnu**
recently	भरखर	**bharkhar**	slowly	बिस्तारै	**bistārai**
rest	आराम गर्नु	**ārām**	smoke	चुरोट खानु	**curoṭ**
		garnu			**khānu**
restaurant	रेष्टुराँ	**reṣṭurā̃**	soaked, to be	भिज्नु	**bhijnu**
return	फर्किनु	**pharkinu**	some (people)	कोही	**kohī**
rice (cooked)	भात	**bhāt**	some (thing)	केही	**kehī**
rice (uncooked)	चामल,	**cāmal**	somebody	कोही	**kohī**
rich	धनी	**dhanī**	sometimes	कहिले काहीं	**kahile kāhī̃**

son	छोरा	chorā	they	उनीहरू	unīharū
song	गीत	gīt	thirst	तिर्खा	tirkhā
south	दक्षिण	dakṣiṇ	this	यो	yo
speak	बोल्नु	bolnu	thousands	हजारौं	hajārau̐
spoken, to be	बोलिनु	bolinu	Thursday	बिहिवार	bihivār
stay	बस्नु	basnu	Tibet	भोट	bhoṭ
straight	सीधा	sīdhā	ticket	टिकट	ṭikaṭ
strange	अनौठो	anautho	time	बेला, समय	belā, samay
street	सडक	saḍak	tiredness	थकाइ	thakāi
student	विद्यार्थी	vidyārthī	today	आज	āja
student hostel	छात्रावास	chātrāvās	tomorrow	भोलि	bholi
study	पढ्नु	paḍhnu	tourist	पर्यटक	paryaṭak
successful	सफल	saphal	towards	-तिर	-tira
suddenly	अकस्मात	akasmāt	Tuesday	मङ्गलवार	maṅgalvār
summer	गर्मी	garmī	TV	टी॰भी॰	ṭī. bhī.
Sunday	आइतवार	āitavār	twice	दुई पटक	duī paṭak
sweet-sounding	मीठो	mīṭho			
sweets	मिठाई	miṭhāī	umbrella	छाता	chātā
swim	पौडी खेल्नु	pauḍī	understand	बुझ्नु	bujhnu
		khelnu	understood, to be	बुझिनु	bujhinu
			university	विश्वविद्यालय	viśvavid-
table	टेबुल	ṭebul			yālaya
take	लिनु	linu	until	-सम्म	-samma
take off	फुकाल्नु	phukālnu	up to	-सम्म	-samma
tall	अग्लो	aglo	uphill	उकालो	ukālo
tasty	मीठो	mīṭho	usually	धेरै जसो	dherai jaso
taxi	ट्याक्सी	ṭyāksī			
tea	चिया	ciyā	valley	उपत्यका	upatyakā
teacher	शिक्षक	śikṣak	vegetables	तरकारी	tarkārī
tell	भन्नु	bhannu	very	धेरै	dherai
tell off	गाली गर्नु	gālī garnu	village	गाउँ	gāu̐
temple	मन्दिर	mandir	violin	सारङ्गी	sāraṅgī
tenth	दसौं	dasau̐	visit	जानु	jānu
that	त्यो	tyo	voice	स्वर	svar
there	त्यहाँ	tyahā̐	wait	पर्खनु	parkhanu

wash	धुनु	**dhunu**	wife	श्रीमती,	**śrīmatī,**
washerman	धोबी	**dhobī**		स्वास्नी	**svāsnī**
watch	घडी	**ghaḍī**	window	झ्याल	**jhyāl**
water	पानी	**pānī**	witch	बोक्सी	**boksī**
we	हामी	**hāmī**	woman	आइमाई	**āimaī**
wear	लाउनु	**lāunu**	work	काम	**kām**
weather	मौसम	**mausam**	work	काम गर्नु	**kām garnu**
Wednesday	बुधवार	**budhvār**	worry	चिन्ता गर्नु	**cintā garnu**
week	हप्ता	**haptā**	worship	पूजा	**pūjā**
well	राम्ररी	**rāmrarī**	write	लेख्नु	**lekhnu**
west	पश्चिम	**paścim**			
wet	भिजेको	**bhijeko**	year	साल, वर्ष	**sāl, varṣa**
what?	के ?	**ke?**	yellow	पहेँलो	**pahēlo**
when?	कहिले ?	**kahile?**	yesterday	हिजो	**hijo**
where?	कहाँ ?	**kahā̃?**	yet	अहिलेसम्म	**ahilesamma**
white	सेतो	**seto**	you (High)	तपाई	**tapāī̃**
whole	पूरा, पूरै	**pūrā, pūrai**	you (Low)	तैं	**tã**
whose?	कसको	**kasko?**	you (Middle)	तिमी	**timī**